TIDELOG®

2024

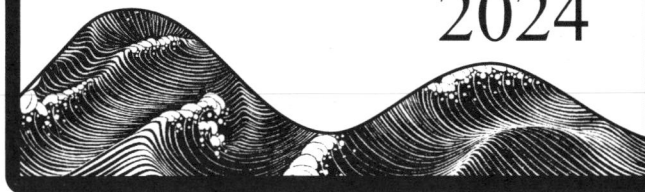

SOUTHERN CALIFORNIA

Daily Tide Graphics
based on predictions by

National Ocean Service
U.S. Department of Commerce
National Oceanic & Atmospheric Administration

Astronomical Data
Courtesy of the United States Naval Observatory

Illustrated by
M. C. Escher
"Second Day of Creation"
© *2023 The M. C. Escher Company - Baarn Holland*
All rights reserved.

Pacific Publishers, LLC
P.O. Box 2813
Tybee Island, GA 31328
912.472.4373
www.tidelog.com

TIDELOG 2024
GRAPHIC ALMANAC FOR SOUTHERN CALIFORNIA

Including Los Angeles, San Diego, and the Gulf of California

Tidelog brings the numbers to life!

TIDES: Daily graphics are based on official National Oceanic & Atmospheric Administration (NOAA) predictions for Los Angeles, with times and heights for Los Angeles and San Diego. Tide tables for Port San Luis as well as NOAA's historical corrections for other locations, are in the back of the Tidelog.

Tide height is relative to the NOAA chart datum for mean lower low water (MLLW) represented by the x-axis of the daily graphic. Also indicated is mean higher high water (MHHW) shown as a horizontal white line at 5.49 feet illustrating the Great Diurnal Range, which is the difference in height between MHHW and MLLW.

CURRENTS: Time and strength of maximum currents and times of slack water are shown daily at San Diego Bay Entrance. Maximum current times are indicated by a "∧" while slack water intervals are indicated by a "⊣ ⊢" at the points between ebbs and floods.

NOAA's historical corrections for other locations, are in the back of the Tidelog.

HOW TIDELOG BRINGS THE NUMBERS TO LIFE: the daily graphic below shows the tides, currents and astronomical movements to give you a visual picture for each day's conditions... at a glance!

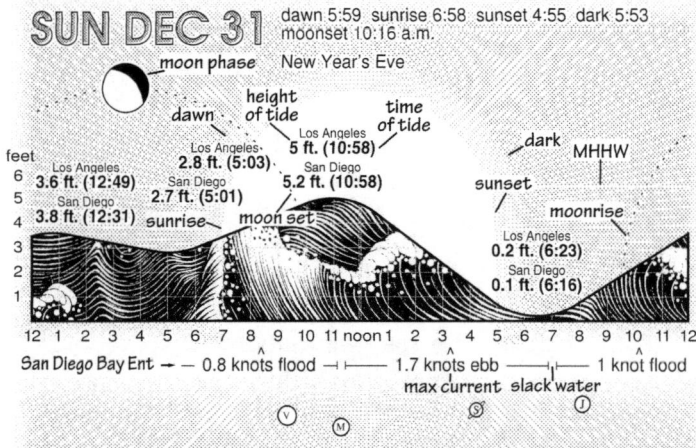

SUN DEC 31   dawn 5:59   sunrise 6:58   sunset 4:55   dark 5:53
moonset 10:16 a.m.

moon phase   New Year's Eve

height of tide   time of tide

dawn

Los Angeles 2.8 ft. (5:03)   Los Angeles 5 ft. (10:58)

San Diego 2.7 ft. (5:01)   San Diego 5.2 ft. (10:58)

dark   MHHW

sunset   moonrise

feet
Los Angeles 3.6 ft. (12:49)
6
5 San Diego 3.8 ft. (12:31)
4
3
2
1

sunrise   moon set

Los Angeles 0.2 ft. (6:23)
San Diego 0.1 ft. (6:16)

12 1 2 3 4 5 6 7 8 9 10 11 noon 1 2 3 4 5 6 7 8 9 10 11 12

San Diego Bay Ent → — 0.8 knots flood ⊣ ⊢— 1.7 knots ebb ——⊣⊢— 1 knot flood

max current   slack water

Moon: The principal determinant of the tides is treated in detail, showing the interplay of the tides with the moon's phase, distance (apogee, perigee), and declination (north, south or over the equator).

The moon is shown in its current phase each day at the time it is highest. The dotted arcs indicate moonrise and moonset, and show which night times will have moonlight and which will be dark.

For an explanation of terminology and a brief outline of the forces which influence the tides and currents, see the next-to-last page of the Tidelog.

Sunrise & Sunset, Dawn & Dusk: Shown by the skyshading. The lighter band near the sun indicates the duration of nautical twilight, which determines "dawn" and "dark." Actual times are given daily.

Daylight Saving Time: All information in Tidelog is adjusted for Daylight Saving Time beginning on the second Sunday of March and ending on the first Sunday of November.

NOAA Predictions: Assume normal weather with normal seasonal variations. You must adjust the predictions for particular conditions. Heavy rainfall, low barometric pressure and strong onshore winds increase tides, while the opposite will decrease them.

We have made every effort to ensure that Tidelog's graphics faithfully depict NOAA predictions, but we cannot guarantee accuracy.

Planets: The five planets visible to the naked eye are shown at zenith, sized according to brightness as shown below:

ⓥVenus   ⓜMars   ⓢSaturn   ⓙJupiter   ⓜ Mercury

The planets move slowly, so they are shown only once a week in the panel after the Sunday daily graphic. Generally, a planet crossing overhead before noon is visible in the east before sunrise (Venus and Mars on the facing page); a planet which is overhead after noon is seen in the west after sunset (Saturn and Jupiter on the facing page); and a planet overhead near midnight may be seen all night. A planet whose zenith is within 45 minutes of the sun's is usually too close to the sun for observation, and is not shown until it is again visible (Mercury in this instance).

Meteor Showers, Eclipses: Noted when appropriate.

MON JAN 1

dawn 5:59 sunrise 6:58 sunset 4:55 dark 5:54
moonset 10:42 a.m. moonrise 10:23 p.m.

New Year's Day

[handwritten notes: Surf thrm couple toobs / couple tims / Ryke finire explanation]

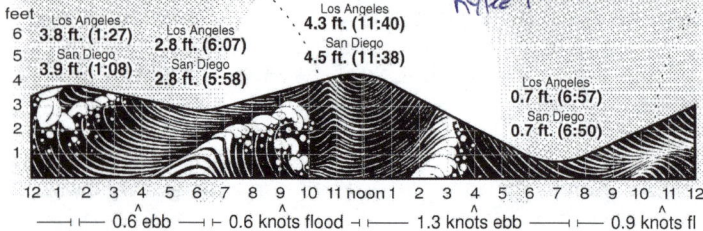

feet

Los Angeles
3.8 ft. (1:27)
San Diego
3.9 ft. (1:08)

Los Angeles
2.8 ft. (6:07)
San Diego
2.8 ft. (5:58)

Los Angeles
4.3 ft. (11:40)
San Diego
4.5 ft. (11:38)

Los Angeles
0.7 ft. (6:57)
San Diego
0.7 ft. (6:50)

12 1 2 3 4 5 6 7 8 9 10 11 noon 1 2 3 4 5 6 7 8 9 10 11 12

⊢— 0.6 ebb —⊢ ⊢ 0.6 knots flood ⊣ ⊢—— 1.3 knots ebb ——⊢ ⊢— 0.9 knots fl

TUE JAN 2

dawn 5:59 sunrise 6:58 sunset 4:56 dark 5:55
moonset 11:06 a.m. moonrise 11:18 p.m.

Earth at Perihelion 4:39 p.m.

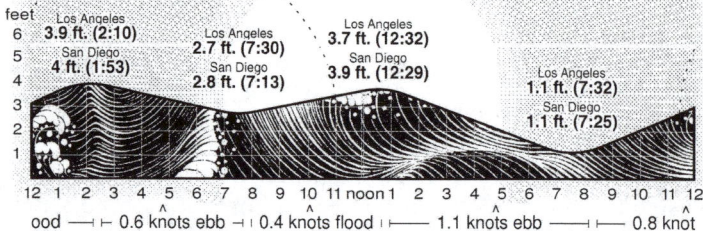

feet

Los Angeles
3.9 ft. (2:10)
San Diego
4 ft. (1:53)

Los Angeles
2.7 ft. (7:30)
San Diego
2.8 ft. (7:13)

Los Angeles
3.7 ft. (12:32)
San Diego
3.9 ft. (12:29)

Los Angeles
1.1 ft. (7:32)
San Diego
1.1 ft. (7:25)

12 1 2 3 4 5 6 7 8 9 10 11 noon 1 2 3 4 5 6 7 8 9 10 11 12

ood —⊢ ⊢ 0.6 knots ebb ⊣ ⊢ 0.4 knots flood ⊢—— 1.1 knots ebb ——⊢ ⊢— 0.8 knot

WED JAN 3

dawn 6:00 sunrise 6:58 sunset 4:57 dark 5:55
moonset 11:29 a.m.

Quadrantids Peak

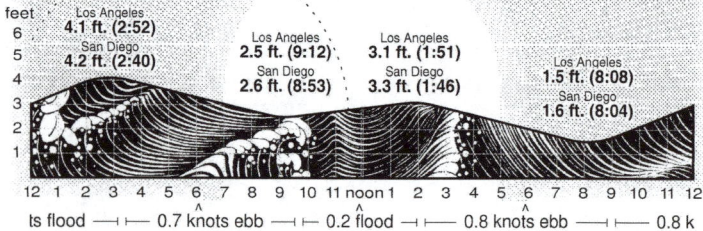

feet

Los Angeles
4.1 ft. (2:52)
San Diego
4.2 ft. (2:40)

Los Angeles
2.5 ft. (9:12)
San Diego
2.6 ft. (8:53)

Los Angeles
3.1 ft. (1:51)
San Diego
3.3 ft. (1:46)

Los Angeles
1.5 ft. (8:08)
San Diego
1.6 ft. (8:04)

12 1 2 3 4 5 6 7 8 9 10 11 noon 1 2 3 4 5 6 7 8 9 10 11 12

ts flood —⊢ ⊢ 0.7 knots ebb —⊢ ⊢ 0.2 flood ⊢ ⊢—— 0.8 knots ebb ——⊢ ⊢— 0.8 k

THU JAN 4

dawn 6:00 sunrise 6:58 sunset 4:58 dark 5:56
moonrise 12:14 a.m. moonset 11:54 a.m.

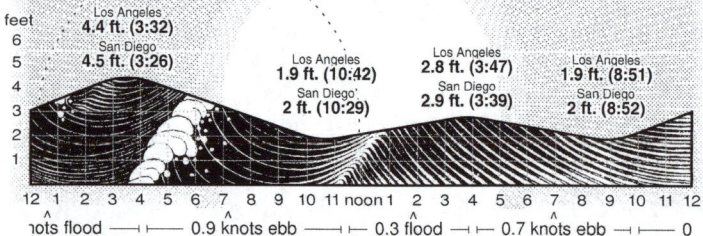

feet

Los Angeles
4.4 ft. (3:32)
San Diego
4.5 ft. (3:26)

Los Angeles
1.9 ft. (10:42)
San Diego
2 ft. (10:29)

Los Angeles
2.8 ft. (3:47)
San Diego
2.9 ft. (3:39)

Los Angeles
1.9 ft. (8:51)
San Diego
2 ft. (8:52)

12 1 2 3 4 5 6 7 8 9 10 11 noon 1 2 3 4 5 6 7 8 9 10 11 12

nots flood —⊢ ⊢ 0.9 knots ebb ——⊢ ⊢ 0.3 flood ⊢ ⊢— 0.7 knots ebb —⊢ ⊢— 0

FRI JAN 5
dawn 6:00 sunrise 6:58 sunset 4:59 dark 5:57
moonrise 1:11 a.m. moonset 12:20 p.m.

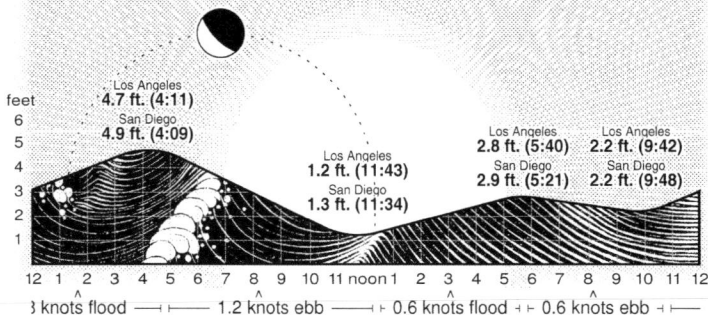

feet
6
5
4
3
2
1

Los Angeles
4.7 ft. (4:11)
San Diego
4.9 ft. (4:09)

Los Angeles
1.2 ft. (11:43)
San Diego
1.3 ft. (11:34)

Los Angeles
2.8 ft. (5:40)
San Diego
2.9 ft. (5:21)

Los Angeles
2.2 ft. (9:42)
San Diego
2.2 ft. (9:48)

12 1 2 3 4 5 6 7 8 9 10 11 noon 1 2 3 4 5 6 7 8 9 10 11 12

3 knots flood —⊢— 1.2 knots ebb —⊢⊦ 0.6 knots flood ⊣⊦ 0.6 knots ebb ⊣—

SAT JAN 6
dawn 6:00 sunrise 6:58 sunset 4:59 dark 5:58
moonrise 2:12 a.m. moonset 12:51 p.m.

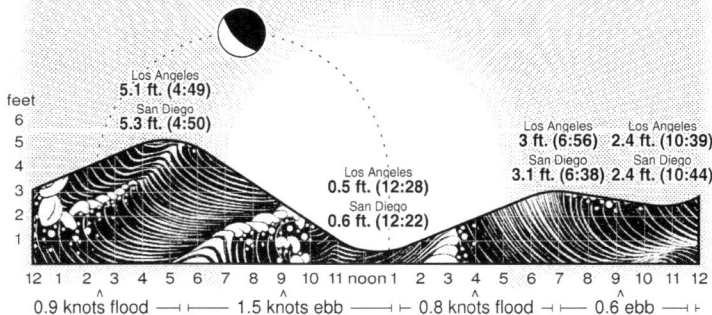

feet
6
5
4
3
2
1

Los Angeles
5.1 ft. (4:49)
San Diego
5.3 ft. (4:50)

Los Angeles
0.5 ft. (12:28)
San Diego
0.6 ft. (12:22)

Los Angeles
3 ft. (6:56)
San Diego
3.1 ft. (6:38)

Los Angeles
2.4 ft. (10:39)
San Diego
2.4 ft. (10:44)

12 1 2 3 4 5 6 7 8 9 10 11 noon 1 2 3 4 5 6 7 8 9 10 11 12

0.9 knots flood —⊢— 1.5 knots ebb ——⊢⊦ 0.8 knots flood ⊣⊦ 0.6 ebb —⊢

SUN JAN 7
dawn 6:00 sunrise 6:58 sunset 5:00 dark 5:58
moonrise 3:16 a.m. moonset 1:27 p.m.

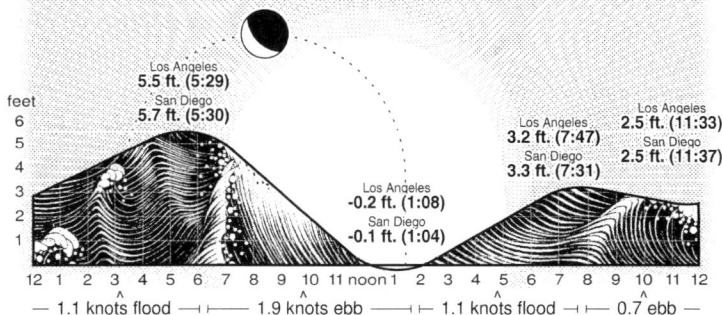

feet
6
5
4
3
2
1

Los Angeles
5.5 ft. (5:29)
San Diego
5.7 ft. (5:30)

Los Angeles
-0.2 ft. (1:08)
San Diego
-0.1 ft. (1:04)

Los Angeles
3.2 ft. (7:47)
San Diego
3.3 ft. (7:31)

Los Angeles
2.5 ft. (11:33)
San Diego
2.5 ft. (11:37)

12 1 2 3 4 5 6 7 8 9 10 11 noon 1 2 3 4 5 6 7 8 9 10 11 12

— 1.1 knots flood —⊣⊢— 1.9 knots ebb ——⊢⊦ 1.1 knots flood ⊣⊢ 0.7 ebb —

Quadrantids Meteor Shower The Quadrantids radiate from the constellation Bootes. The shower is active between Jan 1st to the 5th with its peak on Jan 3rd. The shower can produce up to 40 meteors per hour. Bootes will rise above the eastern horizon by 1:00 a.m. and the early setting Moon will provide a dark sky for viewing the Quadrantids.
Perihelion occurs on Jan 2nd at 7:39 p.m. when the Earth is at its closest to the Sun. Perihelion occurs each year roughly 2 weeks after the winter solstice.

MON JAN 8

dawn 6:00 sunrise 6:58 sunset 5:01 dark 5:59
moonrise 4:22 a.m. moonset 2:12 p.m.

Antares .8 degees S of Moon

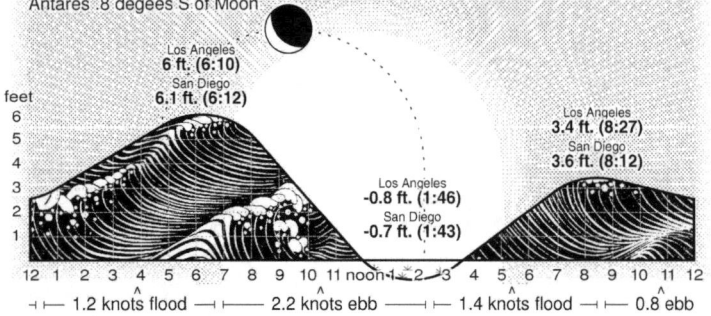

Los Angeles
6 ft. (6:10)
San Diego
6.1 ft. (6:12)

Los Angeles
3.4 ft. (8:27)
San Diego
3.6 ft. (8:12)

feet

Los Angeles
-0.8 ft. (1:46)
San Diego
-0.7 ft. (1:43)

12 1 2 3 4 5 6 7 8 9 10 11 noon 1 2 3 4 5 6 7 8 9 10 11 12

⊢ 1.2 knots flood ⊣ ⊢ 2.2 knots ebb ⊣ ⊢ 1.4 knots flood ⊣ ⊢ 0.8 ebb

TUE JAN 9

dawn 6:00 sunrise 6:58 sunset 5:02 dark 6:00
moonrise 5:30 a.m. moonset 3:07 p.m.

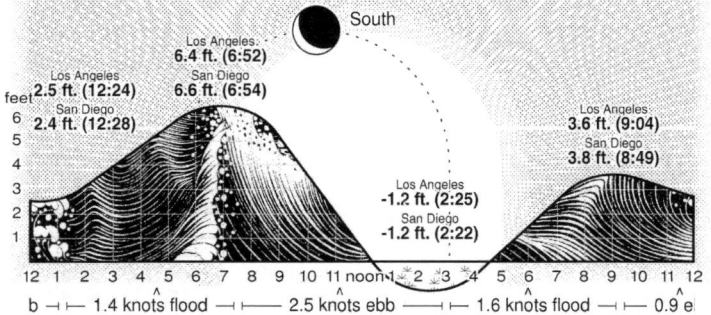

South

Los Angeles
6.4 ft. (6:52)
San Diego
6.6 ft. (6:54)

Los Angeles
2.5 ft. (12:24)
San Diego
2.4 ft. (12:28)

Los Angeles
3.6 ft. (9:04)
San Diego
3.8 ft. (8:49)

feet

Los Angeles
-1.2 ft. (2:25)
San Diego
-1.2 ft. (2:22)

12 1 2 3 4 5 6 7 8 9 10 11 noon 1 2 3 4 5 6 7 8 9 10 11 12

b ⊣ ⊢ 1.4 knots flood ⊣ ⊢ 2.5 knots ebb ⊣ ⊢ 1.6 knots flood ⊣ ⊢ 0.9 e

WED JAN 10

dawn 6:00 sunrise 6:58 sunset 5:03 dark 6:01
moonrise 6:34 a.m. moonset 4:11 p.m.

Mars 4 degrees N of Moon

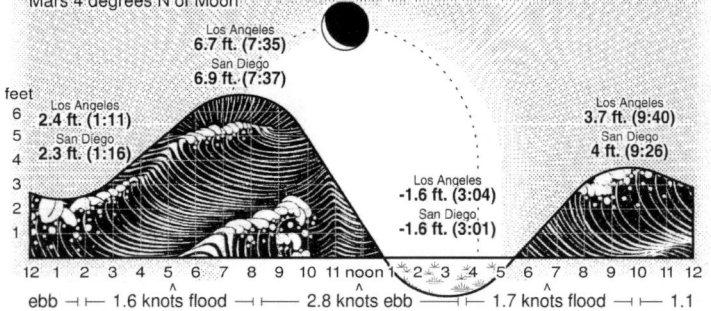

Los Angeles
6.7 ft. (7:35)
San Diego
6.9 ft. (7:37)

Los Angeles
2.4 ft. (1:11)
San Diego
2.3 ft. (1:16)

Los Angeles
3.7 ft. (9:40)
San Diego
4 ft. (9:26)

feet

Los Angeles
-1.6 ft. (3:04)
San Diego
-1.6 ft. (3:01)

12 1 2 3 4 5 6 7 8 9 10 11 noon 1 2 3 4 5 6 7 8 9 10 11 12

ebb ⊣ ⊢ 1.6 knots flood ⊣ ⊢ 2.8 knots ebb ⊣ ⊢ 1.7 knots flood ⊣ ⊢ 1.1

THU JAN 11

dawn 6:00 sunrise 6:58 sunset 5:04 dark 6:02
moonrise 7:31 a.m. moonset 5:23 p.m.

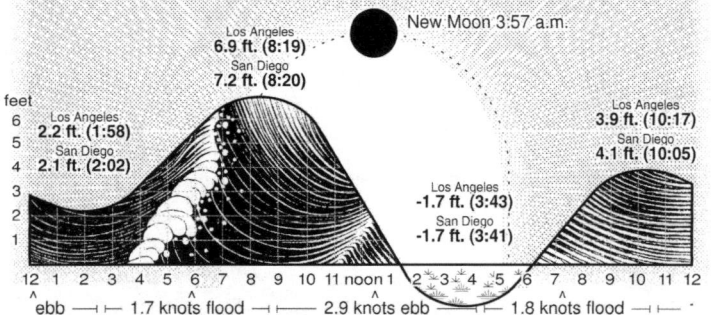

New Moon 3:57 a.m.

Los Angeles
6.9 ft. (8:19)
San Diego
7.2 ft. (8:20)

Los Angeles
2.2 ft. (1:58)
San Diego
2.1 ft. (2:02)

Los Angeles
3.9 ft. (10:17)
San Diego
4.1 ft. (10:05)

feet

Los Angeles
-1.7 ft. (3:43)
San Diego
-1.7 ft. (3:41)

12 1 2 3 4 5 6 7 8 9 10 11 noon 1 2 3 4 5 6 7 8 9 10 11 12

ebb ⊣ ⊢ 1.7 knots flood ⊣ ⊢ 2.9 knots ebb ⊣ ⊢ 1.8 knots flood ⊣ ⊢

FRI JAN 12

dawn 6:00 sunrise 6:58 sunset 5:05 dark 6:03
moonrise 8:20 a.m. moonset 6:39 p.m.

Mercury western elongation

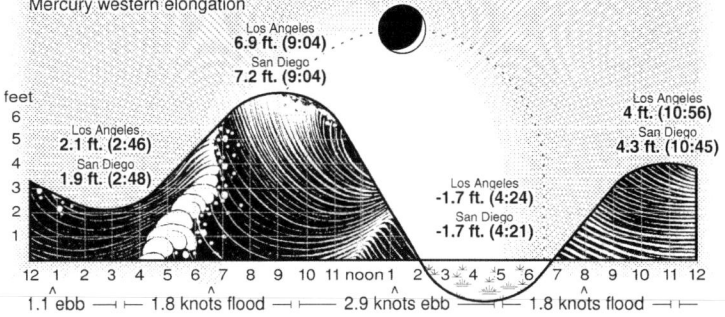

Los Angeles
6.9 ft. (9:04)
San Diego
7.2 ft. (9:04)

Los Angeles
4 ft. (10:56)
San Diego
4.3 ft. (10:45)

feet
6
5
4
3
2
1

Los Angeles
2.1 ft. (2:46)
San Diego
1.9 ft. (2:48)

Los Angeles
-1.7 ft. (4:24)
San Diego
-1.7 ft. (4:21)

12 1 2 3 4 5 6 7 8 9 10 11 noon 1 2 3 4 5 6 7 8 9 10 11 12

1.1 ebb ⟶ ⊢ 1.8 knots flood ⟶ ⊢ 2.9 knots ebb ⟶ ⊢ 1.8 knots flood ⟶ ⊢

SAT JAN 13

dawn 6:00 sunrise 6:58 sunset 5:06 dark 6:03
moonrise 9:01 a.m. moonset 7:53 p.m.

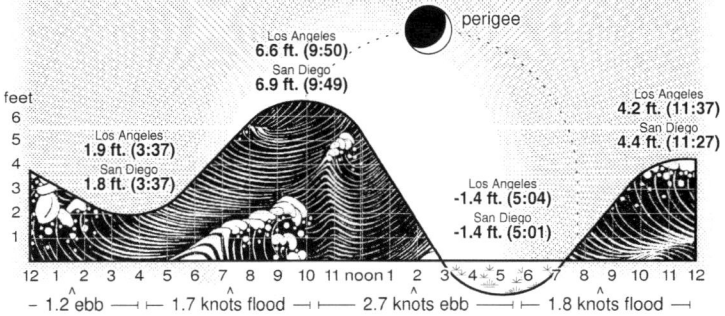

perigee

Los Angeles
6.6 ft. (9:50)
San Diego
6.9 ft. (9:49)

Los Angeles
4.2 ft. (11:37)
San Diego
4 ft. (11:27)

feet
6
5
4
3
2
1

Los Angeles
1.9 ft. (3:37)
San Diego
1.8 ft. (3:37)

Los Angeles
-1.4 ft. (5:04)
San Diego
-1.4 ft. (5:01)

12 1 2 3 4 5 6 7 8 9 10 11 noon 1 2 3 4 5 6 7 8 9 10 11 12

− 1.2 ebb ⊢ ⊢ 1.7 knots flood ⟶ ⊢ 2.7 knots ebb ⟶ ⊢ 1.8 knots flood ⟶

SUN JAN 14

dawn 6:00 sunrise 6:58 sunset 5:06 dark 6:04
moonrise 9:36 a.m. moonset 9:05 p.m.

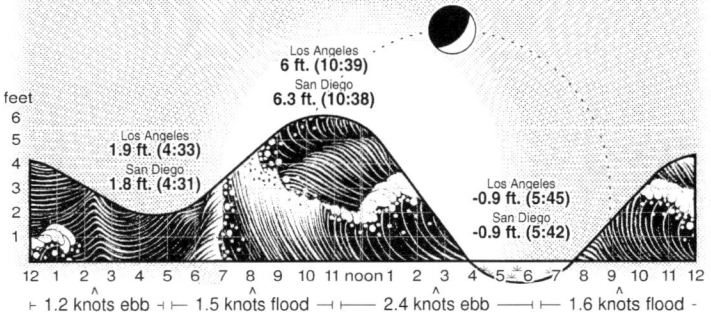

Los Angeles
6 ft. (10:39)
San Diego
6.3 ft. (10:38)

feet
6
5
4
3
2
1

Los Angeles
1.9 ft. (4:33)
San Diego
1.8 ft. (4:31)

Los Angeles
-0.9 ft. (5:45)
San Diego
-0.9 ft. (5:42)

12 1 2 3 4 5 6 7 8 9 10 11 noon 1 2 3 4 5 6 7 8 9 10 11 12

⊢ 1.2 knots ebb ⊣ ⊢ 1.5 knots flood ⟶ ⊢ 2.4 knots ebb ⟶ ⊢ 1.6 knots flood ⊣

(V) (m) (M) (S) (J)

MON JAN 15
dawn 6:00 sunrise 6:58 sunset 5:07 dark 6:05
moonrise 10:07 a.m. moonset 10:14 p.m.

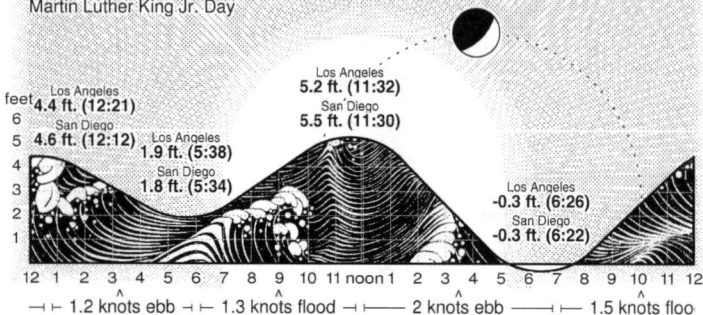

Martin Luther King Jr. Day

Los Angeles
4.4 ft. (12:21)
San Diego
4.6 ft. (12:12)
Los Angeles
5.2 ft. (11:32)
San Diego
5.5 ft. (11:30)
Los Angeles
1.9 ft. (5:38)
San Diego
1.8 ft. (5:34)
Los Angeles
-0.3 ft. (6:26)
San Diego
-0.3 ft. (6:22)

feet 6 5 4 3 2 1

12 1 2 3 4 5 6 7 8 9 10 11 noon 1 2 3 4 5 6 7 8 9 10 11 12

⊣ ⊢ 1.2 knots ebb ⊣ ⊢ 1.3 knots flood ⊣ ⊢ 2 knots ebb ⊣ ⊢ 1.5 knots floo

---

TUE JAN 16
dawn 6:00 sunrise 6:57 sunset 5:08 dark 6:06
moonrise 10:36 a.m. moonset 11:21 p.m.

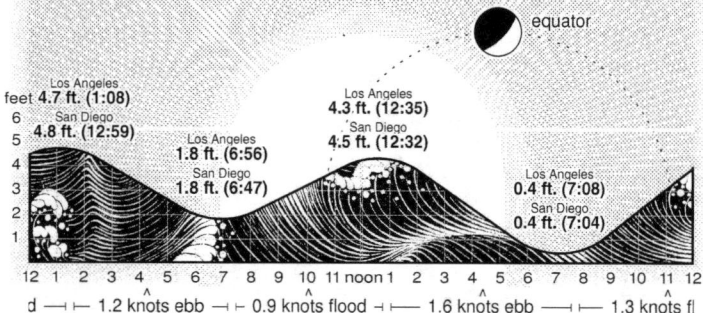

equator

Los Angeles **4.7 ft. (1:08)**
San Diego **4.8 ft. (12:59)**
Los Angeles **4.3 ft. (12:35)**
San Diego **4.5 ft. (12:32)**
Los Angeles **1.8 ft. (6:56)**
San Diego **1.8 ft. (6:47)**
Los Angeles **0.4 ft. (7:08)**
San Diego **0.4 ft. (7:04)**

feet 6 5 4 3 2 1

12 1 2 3 4 5 6 7 8 9 10 11 noon 1 2 3 4 5 6 7 8 9 10 11 12

d ⊣ ⊢ 1.2 knots ebb ⊣ ⊢ 0.9 knots flood ⊣ ⊢ 1.6 knots ebb ⊣ ⊢ 1.3 knots fl

---

WED JAN 17
dawn 6:00 sunrise 6:57 sunset 5:09 dark 6:07
moonrise 11:06 a.m.

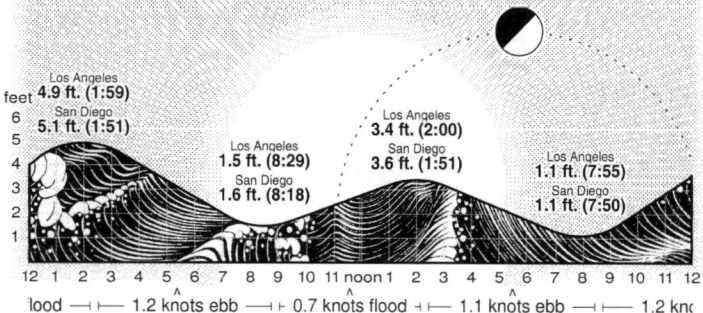

Los Angeles **4.9 ft. (1:59)**
San Diego **5.1 ft. (1:51)**
Los Angeles **3.4 ft. (2:00)**
San Diego **3.6 ft. (1:51)**
Los Angeles **1.5 ft. (8:29)**
San Diego **1.6 ft. (8:18)**
Los Angeles **1.1 ft. (7:55)**
San Diego **1.1 ft. (7:50)**

feet 6 5 4 3 2 1

12 1 2 3 4 5 6 7 8 9 10 11 noon 1 2 3 4 5 6 7 8 9 10 11 12

lood ⊣ ⊢ 1.2 knots ebb ⊣ ⊢ 0.7 knots flood ⊣ ⊢ 1.1 knots ebb ⊣ ⊢ 1.2 kno

---

THU JAN 18
dawn 6:00 sunrise 6:57 sunset 5:10 dark 6:08
moonset 12:28 a.m. moonrise 11:36 a.m.

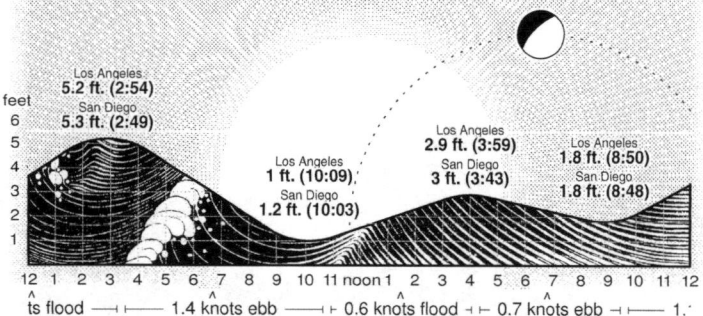

Los Angeles **5.2 ft. (2:54)**
San Diego **5.3 ft. (2:49)**
Los Angeles **2.9 ft. (3:59)**
San Diego **3 ft. (3:43)**
Los Angeles **1 ft. (10:09)**
San Diego **1.2 ft. (10:03)**
Los Angeles **1.8 ft. (8:50)**
San Diego **1.8 ft. (8:48)**

feet 6 5 4 3 2 1

12 1 2 3 4 5 6 7 8 9 10 11 noon 1 2 3 4 5 6 7 8 9 10 11 12

ts flood ⊣ ⊢ 1.4 knots ebb ⊣ ⊢ 0.6 knots flood ⊣ ⊢ 0.7 knots ebb ⊣ ⊢ 1.

FRI JAN 19

dawn 5:59 sunrise 6:57 sunset 5:11 dark 6:08
moonset 1:35 a.m. moonrise 12:10 p.m.

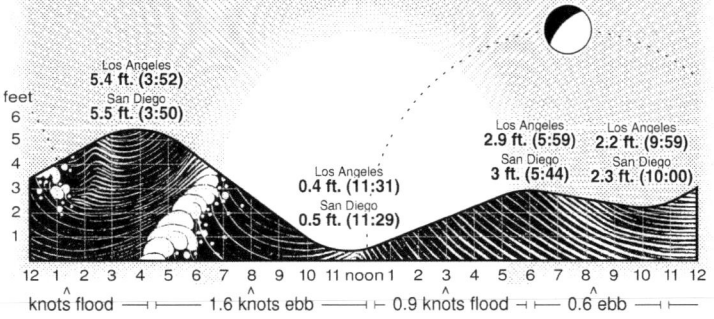

feet
6
5
4
3
2
1

Los Angeles
5.4 ft. (3:52)
San Diego
5.5 ft. (3:50)

Los Angeles
0.4 ft. (11:31)
San Diego
0.5 ft. (11:29)

Los Angeles
2.9 ft. (5:59)
San Diego
3 ft. (5:44)

Los Angeles
2.2 ft. (9:59)
San Diego
2.3 ft. (10:00)

12 1 2 3 4 5 6 7 8 9 10 11 noon 1 2 3 4 5 6 7 8 9 10 11 12

knots flood → ⊢ 1.6 knots ebb → ⊢ 0.9 knots flood → ⊢ 0.6 ebb → ⊢

SAT JAN 20

dawn 5:59 sunrise 6:56 sunset 5:12 dark 6:09
moonset 2:41 a.m. moonrise 12:49 p.m.

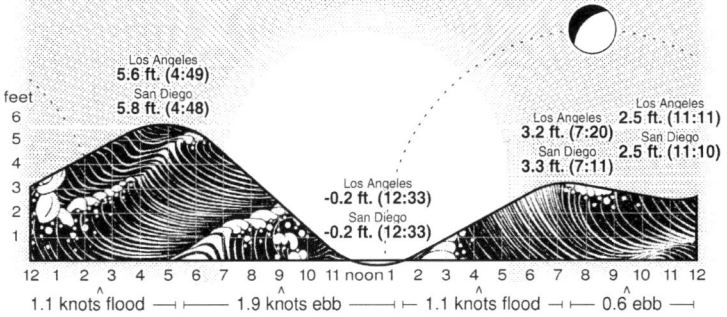

feet
6
5
4
3
2
1

Los Angeles
5.6 ft. (4:49)
San Diego
5.8 ft. (4:48)

Los Angeles
-0.2 ft. (12:33)
San Diego
-0.2 ft. (12:33)

Los Angeles
3.2 ft. (7:20)
San Diego
3.3 ft. (7:11)

Los Angeles
2.5 ft. (11:11)
San Diego
2.5 ft. (11:10)

12 1 2 3 4 5 6 7 8 9 10 11 noon 1 2 3 4 5 6 7 8 9 10 11 12

1.1 knots flood → ⊢ 1.9 knots ebb → ⊢ 1.1 knots flood → ⊢ 0.6 ebb →

SUN JAN 21

dawn 5:59 sunrise 6:56 sunset 5:13 dark 6:10
moonset 3:47 a.m. moonrise 1:33 p.m.

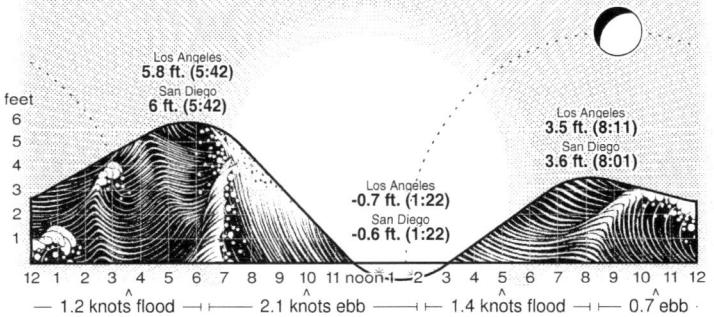

feet
6
5
4
3
2
1

Los Angeles
5.8 ft. (5:42)
San Diego
6 ft. (5:42)

Los Angeles
-0.7 ft. (1:22)
San Diego
-0.6 ft. (1:22)

Los Angeles
3.5 ft. (8:11)
San Diego
3.6 ft. (8:01)

12 1 2 3 4 5 6 7 8 9 10 11 noon 1 2 3 4 5 6 7 8 9 10 11 12

— 1.2 knots flood → ⊢ 2.1 knots ebb → ⊢ 1.4 knots flood → ⊢ 0.7 ebb ·

Ⓥ Ⓜ ⓜ Ⓢ Ⓙ

MON JAN 22
dawn 5:58 sunrise 6:55 sunset 5:14 dark 6:11
moonset 4:48 a.m. moonrise 2:24 p.m.

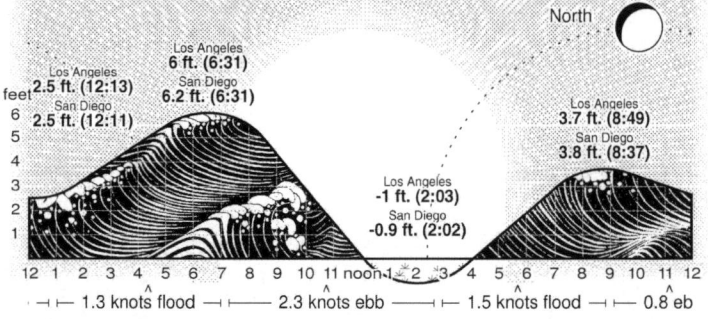

North

Los Angeles
6 ft. (6:31)
San Diego
6.2 ft. (6:31)

feet
Los Angeles
2.5 ft. (12:13)
San Diego
2.5 ft. (12:11)

Los Angeles
3.7 ft. (8:49)
San Diego
3.8 ft. (8:37)

Los Angeles
-1 ft. (2;03)
San Diego
-0.9 ft. (2:02)

12 1 2 3 4 5 6 7 8 9 10 11 noon 1 2 3 4 5 6 7 8 9 10 11 12

⊢ 1.3 knots flood ⊣ ⊢ 2.3 knots ebb ⊣ ⊢ 1.5 knots flood ⊣ ⊢ 0.8 eb

TUE JAN 23
dawn 5:58 sunrise 6:55 sunset 5:15 dark 6:12
moonset 5:44 a.m. moonrise 3:20 p.m.

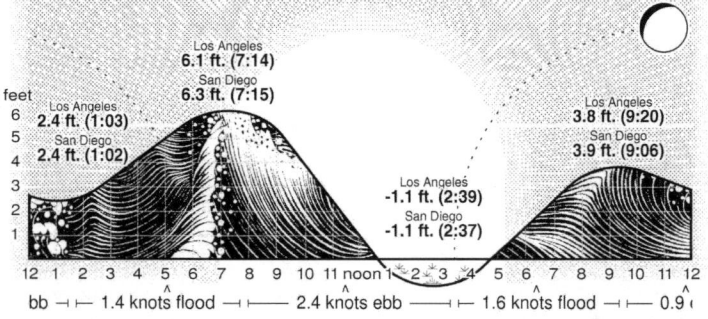

Los Angeles
6.1 ft. (7:14)
San Diego
6.3 ft. (7:15)

feet
Los Angeles
2.4 ft. (1:03)
San Diego
2.4 ft. (1:02)

Los Angeles
3.8 ft. (9:20)
San Diego
3.9 ft. (9:06)

Los Angeles
-1.1 ft. (2:39)
San Diego
-1.1 ft. (2:37)

12 1 2 3 4 5 6 7 8 9 10 11 noon 1 2 3 4 5 6 7 8 9 10 11 12

bb ⊢ 1.4 knots flood ⊣ ⊢ 2.4 knots ebb ⊣ ⊢ 1.6 knots flood ⊣ ⊢ 0.9

WED JAN 24
dawn 5:58 sunrise 6:55 sunset 5:16 dark 6:13
moonset 6:32 a.m. moonrise 4:20 p.m.

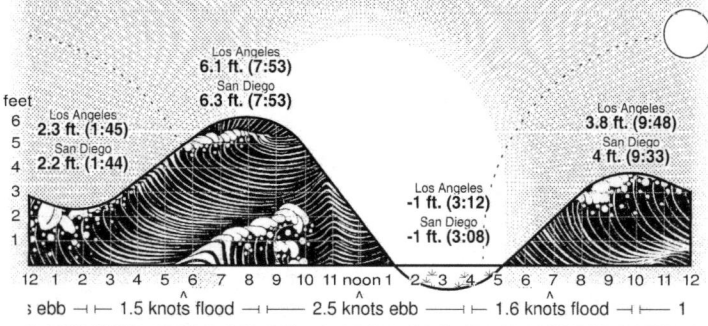

Los Angeles
6.1 ft. (7:53)
San Diego
6.3 ft. (7:53)

feet
Los Angeles
2.3 ft. (1:45)
San Diego
2.2 ft. (1:44)

Los Angeles
3.8 ft. (9:48)
San Diego
4 ft. (9:33)

Los Angeles
-1 ft. (3:12)
San Diego
-1 ft. (3:08)

12 1 2 3 4 5 6 7 8 9 10 11 noon 1 2 3 4 5 6 7 8 9 10 11 12

s ebb ⊣ ⊢ 1.5 knots flood ⊣ ⊢ 2.5 knots ebb ⊣ ⊢ 1.6 knots flood ⊣ ⊢ 1

THU JAN 25
dawn 5:57 sunrise 6:54 sunset 5:17 dark 6:14
moonset 7:13 a.m. moonrise 5:21 p.m.

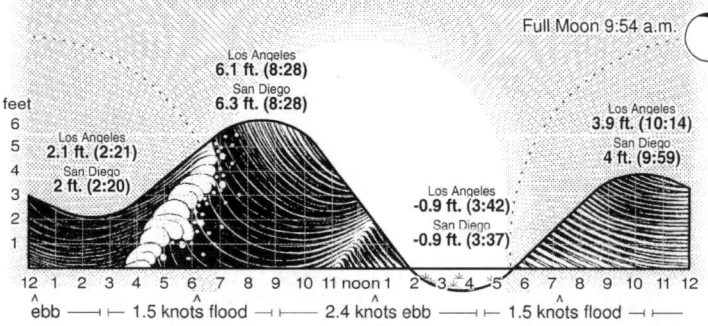

Full Moon 9:54 a.m.

Los Angeles
6.1 ft. (8:28)
San Diego
6.3 ft. (8:28)

feet
Los Angeles
2.1 ft. (2:21)
San Diego
2 ft. (2:20)

Los Angeles
3.9 ft. (10:14)
San Diego
4 ft. (9:59)

Los Angeles
-0.9 ft. (3:42)
San Diego
-0.9 ft. (3:37)

12 1 2 3 4 5 6 7 8 9 10 11 noon 1 2 3 4 5 6 7 8 9 10 11 12

ebb ⊢ 1.5 knots flood ⊣ ⊢ 2.4 knots ebb ⊣ ⊢ 1.5 knots flood ⊣ ⊢

FRI JAN 26

dawn 5:57 sunrise 6:54 sunset 5:18 dark 6:15
moonset 7:48 a.m. moonrise 6:20 p.m.

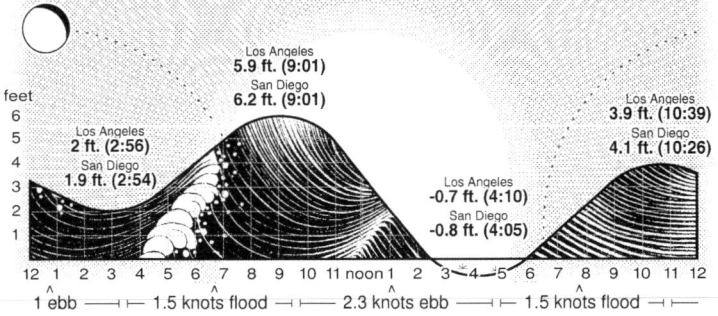

feet

Los Angeles
5.9 ft. (9:01)
San Diego
6.2 ft. (9:01)

Los Angeles
2 ft. (2:56)
San Diego
1.9 ft. (2:54)

Los Angeles
3.9 ft. (10:39)
San Diego
4.1 ft. (10:26)

Los Angeles
-0.7 ft. (4:10)
San Diego
-0.8 ft. (4:05)

12 1 2 3 4 5 6 7 8 9 10 11 noon 1 2 3 4 5 6 7 8 9 10 11 12

1 ebb ⊣ ⊢ 1.5 knots flood ⊣ ⊢ 2.3 knots ebb ⊣ ⊢ 1.5 knots flood ⊣ ⊢

SAT JAN 27

dawn 5:56 sunrise 6:53 sunset 5:19 dark 6:15
moonset 8:18 a.m. moonrise 7:18 p.m.

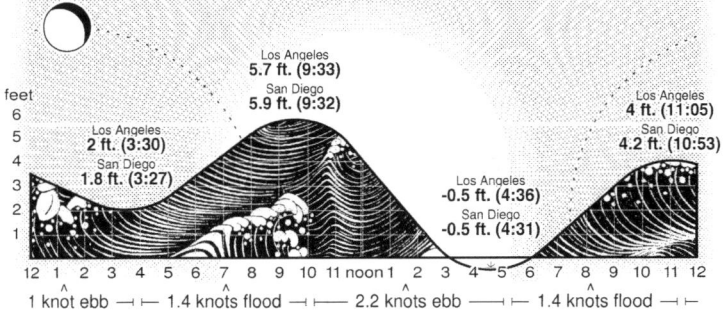

feet

Los Angeles
5.7 ft. (9:33)
San Diego
5.9 ft. (9:32)

Los Angeles
2 ft. (3:30)
San Diego
1.8 ft. (3:27)

Los Angeles
4 ft. (11:05)
San Diego
4.2 ft. (10:53)

Los Angeles
-0.5 ft. (4:36)
San Diego
-0.5 ft. (4:31)

12 1 2 3 4 5 6 7 8 9 10 11 noon 1 2 3 4 5 6 7 8 9 10 11 12

1 knot ebb ⊣ ⊢ 1.4 knots flood ⊣ ⊢ 2.2 knots ebb ⊣ ⊢ 1.4 knots flood ⊣ ⊢

SUN JAN 28

dawn 5:56 sunrise 6:52 sunset 5:20 dark 6:16
moonset 8:44 a.m. moonrise 8:14 p.m.

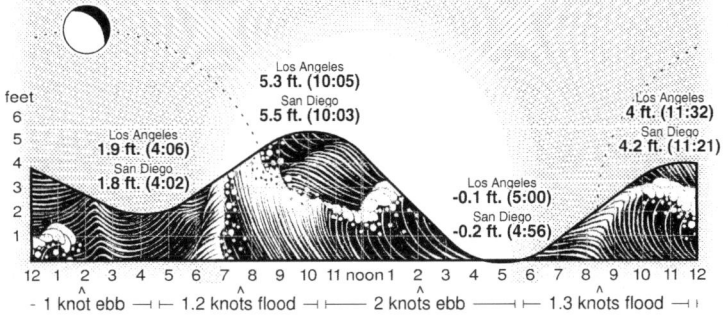

feet

Los Angeles
5.3 ft. (10:05)
San Diego
5.5 ft. (10:03)

Los Angeles
1.9 ft. (4:06)
San Diego
1.8 ft. (4:02)

Los Angeles
4 ft. (11:32)
San Diego
4.2 ft. (11:21)

Los Angeles
-0.1 ft. (5:00)
San Diego
-0.2 ft. (4:56)

12 1 2 3 4 5 6 7 8 9 10 11 noon 1 2 3 4 5 6 7 8 9 10 11 12

- 1 knot ebb ⊣ ⊢ 1.2 knots flood ⊣ ⊢ 2 knots ebb ⊣ ⊢ 1.3 knots flood ⊣ ⊢

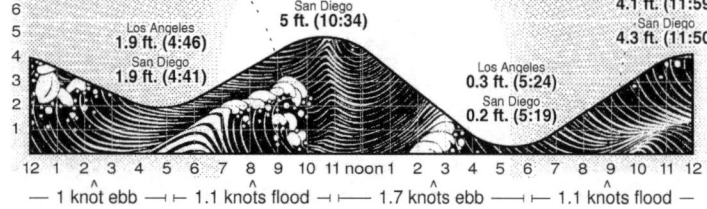

MON JAN 29
dawn 5:55 sunrise 6:52 sunset 5:21 dark 6:17
moonset 9:08 a.m. moonrise 9:10 p.m.

apogee

feet
6
5
4
3
2
1

Los Angeles **4.8 ft. (10:37)**
San Diego **5 ft. (10:34)**

Los Angeles **1.9 ft. (4:46)**
San Diego **1.9 ft. (4:41)**

Los Angeles **4.1 ft. (11:59)**
San Diego **4.3 ft. (11:50)**

Los Angeles **0.3 ft. (5:24)**
San Diego **0.2 ft. (5:19)**

12 1 2 3 4 5 6 7 8 9 10 11 noon 1 2 3 4 5 6 7 8 9 10 11 12

— 1 knot ebb — ⊢ 1.1 knots flood ⊣ ⊢ 1.7 knots ebb — ⊢ 1.1 knots flood —

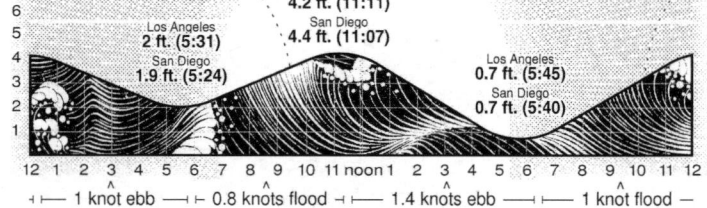

TUE JAN 30
dawn 5:55 sunrise 6:51 sunset 5:22 dark 6:18
moonset 9:32 a.m. moonrise 10:04 p.m.

equator

feet
6
5
4
3
2
1

Los Angeles **4.2 ft. (11:11)**
San Diego **4.4 ft. (11:07)**

Los Angeles **2 ft. (5:31)**
San Diego **1.9 ft. (5:24)**

Los Angeles **0.7 ft. (5:45)**
San Diego **0.7 ft. (5:40)**

12 1 2 3 4 5 6 7 8 9 10 11 noon 1 2 3 4 5 6 7 8 9 10 11 12

⊣ ⊢ 1 knot ebb — ⊢ 0.8 knots flood ⊣ ⊢ 1.4 knots ebb — ⊢ 1 knot flood —

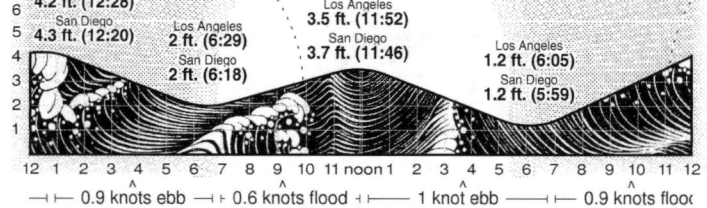

WED JAN 31
dawn 5:54 sunrise 6:50 sunset 5:23 dark 6:19
moonset 9:55 a.m. moonrise 11:00 p.m.

feet
6
5
4
3
2
1

Los Angeles **4.2 ft. (12:28)**
San Diego **4.3 ft. (12:20)**

Los Angeles **2 ft. (6:29)**
San Diego **2 ft. (6:18)**

Los Angeles **3.5 ft. (11:52)**
San Diego **3.7 ft. (11:46)**

Los Angeles **1.2 ft. (6:05)**
San Diego **1.2 ft. (5:59)**

12 1 2 3 4 5 6 7 8 9 10 11 noon 1 2 3 4 5 6 7 8 9 10 11 12

⊣ ⊢ 0.9 knots ebb — ⊢ 0.6 knots flood ⊣ ⊢ 1 knot ebb — ⊢ 0.9 knots flood

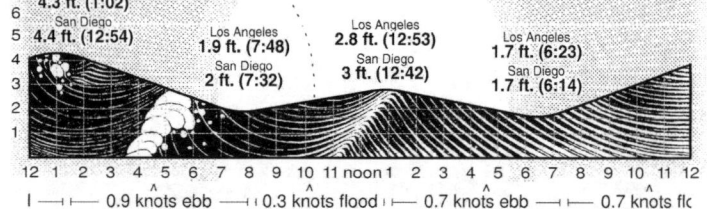

THU FEB 1
dawn 5:54 sunrise 6:50 sunset 5:24 dark 6:20
moonset 10:20 a.m. moonrise 11:58 p.m.

feet
6
5
4
3
2
1

Los Angeles **4.3 ft. (1:02)**
San Diego **4.4 ft. (12:54)**

Los Angeles **1.9 ft. (7:48)**
San Diego **2 ft. (7:32)**

Los Angeles **2.8 ft. (12:53)**
San Diego **3 ft. (12:42)**

Los Angeles **1.7 ft. (6:23)**
San Diego **1.7 ft. (6:14)**

12 1 2 3 4 5 6 7 8 9 10 11 noon 1 2 3 4 5 6 7 8 9 10 11 12

⊢ ⊣ ⊢ 0.9 knots ebb — ⊣ 0.3 knots flood ⊢ — 0.7 knots ebb — ⊣ ⊢ 0.7 knots flo

FRI FEB 2
dawn 5:53 sunrise 6:49 sunset 5:25 dark 6:21
moonset 10:48 a.m.

Groundhog Day

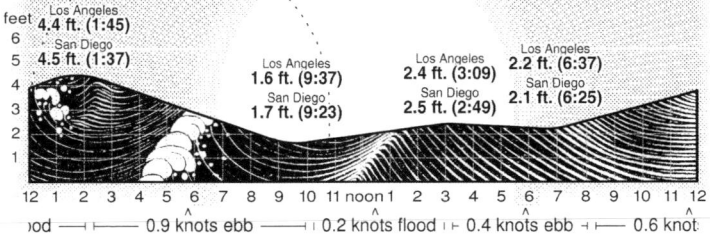

feet

Los Angeles
4.4 ft. (1:45)
San Diego
4.5 ft. (1:37)

Los Angeles
1.6 ft. (9:37)
San Diego
1.7 ft. (9:23)

Los Angeles
2.4 ft. (3:09)
San Diego
2.5 ft. (2:49)

Los Angeles
2.2 ft. (6:37)
San Diego
2.1 ft. (6:25)

12 1 2 3 4 5 6 7 8 9 10 11 noon 1 2 3 4 5 6 7 8 9 10 11 12

ood ⊢ ⊢—— 0.9 knots ebb ——⊣ ⊢ 0.2 knots flood ⊢ ⊢ 0.4 knots ebb ⊣ ⊢—— 0.6 knot

SAT FEB 3
dawn 5:53 sunrise 6:48 sunset 5:26 dark 6:22
moonrise 12:59 a.m. moonset 11:21 a.m.

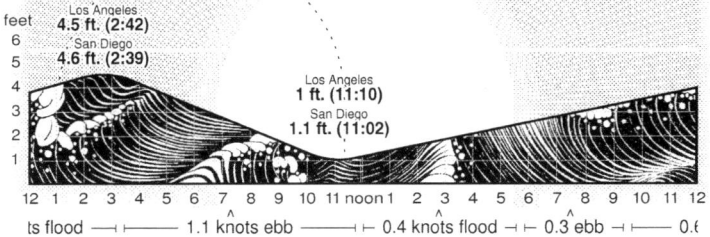

feet

Los Angeles
4.5 ft. (2:42)
San Diego
4.6 ft. (2:39)

Los Angeles
1 ft. (11:10)
San Diego
1.1 ft. (11:02)

12 1 2 3 4 5 6 7 8 9 10 11 noon 1 2 3 4 5 6 7 8 9 10 11 12

ts flood ——⊣ ⊢—— 1.1 knots ebb ———⊣ ⊢ 0.4 knots flood ⊣ ⊢ 0.3 ebb ⊣ ⊢—— 0.6

SUN FEB 4
dawn 5:52 sunrise 6:48 sunset 5:27 dark 6:22
moonrise 2:03 a.m. moonset 12:01 p.m.

Antares .6 degree S of Moon

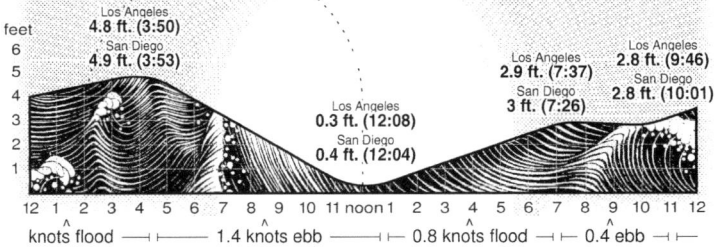

feet

Los Angeles
4.8 ft. (3:50)
San Diego
4.9 ft. (3:53)

Los Angeles
0.3 ft. (12:08)
San Diego
0.4 ft. (12:04)

Los Angeles
2.9 ft. (7:37)
San Diego
3 ft. (7:26)

Los Angeles
2.8 ft. (9:46)
San Diego
2.8 ft. (10:01)

12 1 2 3 4 5 6 7 8 9 10 11 noon 1 2 3 4 5 6 7 8 9 10 11 12

knots flood ——⊣ ⊢—— 1.4 knots ebb ———⊣ ⊢ 0.8 knots flood ⊣ ⊢ 0.4 ebb ⊣ ⊢—

Ⓥ Ⓜ ⓜ   Ⓢ   Ⓙ

Antares, the fire star The evening of Feb 4th, Antares will be
within a degree of the waning Moon. Antares is a red super giant star
located 550 light years from Earth. Antares is known as the "heart of
the Scorpion" in the constellation Scorpius. The ancient Chinese called
Antares the fire star. Antares is sometimes mistaken for Mars as it is
approximately the same hue and brightness.

MON FEB 5
dawn 5:51 sunrise 6:47 sunset 5:28 dark 6:23
moonrise 3:09 a.m. moonset 12:49 p.m.

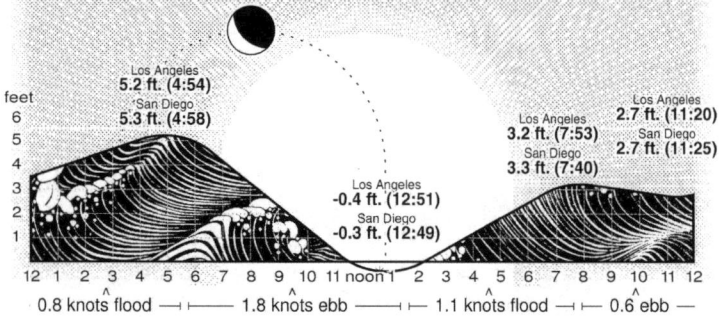

Los Angeles **5.2 ft. (4:54)**
San Diego **5.3 ft. (4:58)**

Los Angeles **2.7 ft. (11:20)**
San Diego **2.7 ft. (11:25)**

Los Angeles **3.2 ft. (7:53)**
San Diego **3.3 ft. (7:40)**

Los Angeles **-0.4 ft. (12:51)**
San Diego **-0.3 ft. (12:49)**

feet 6 5 4 3 2 1

12 1 2 3 4 5 6 7 8 9 10 11 noon 1 2 3 4 5 6 7 8 9 10 11 12

0.8 knots flood ⊢—⊣ 1.8 knots ebb ——— ⊢ 1.1 knots flood ⊣ ⊢ 0.6 ebb —

TUE FEB 6
dawn 5:50 sunrise 6:46 sunset 5:29 dark 6:24
moonrise 4:14 a.m. moonset 1:48 p.m.

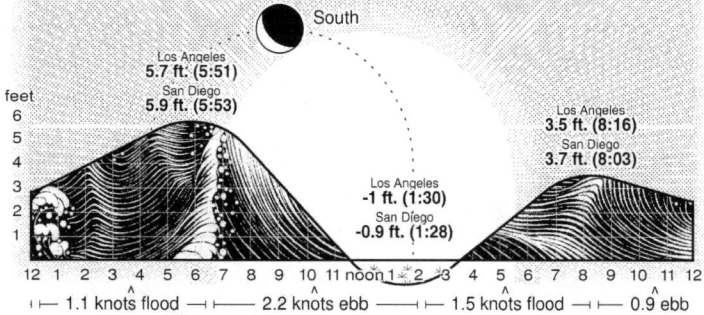

South

Los Angeles **5.7 ft. (5:51)**
San Diego **5.9 ft. (5:53)**

Los Angeles **3.5 ft. (8:16)**
San Diego **3.7 ft. (8:03)**

Los Angeles **-1 ft. (1:30)**
San Diego **-0.9 ft. (1:28)**

feet 6 5 4 3 2 1

12 1 2 3 4 5 6 7 8 9 10 11 noon 1 2 3 4 5 6 7 8 9 10 11 12

⊢—⊣ 1.1 knots flood —⊣ ⊢ 2.2 knots ebb ——— ⊢ 1.5 knots flood ⊣ ⊢ 0.9 ebb

WED FEB 7
dawn 5:50 sunrise 6:45 sunset 5:30 dark 6:25
moonrise 5:14 a.m. moonset 2:56 p.m.

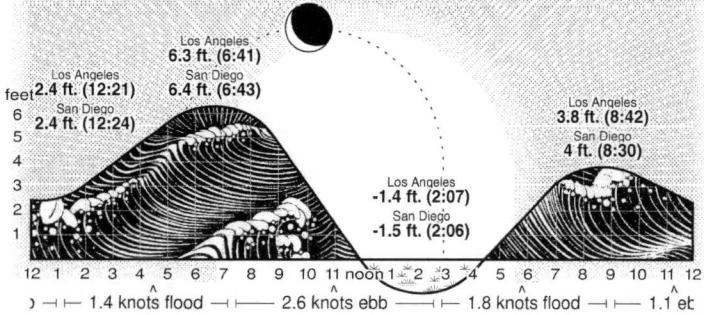

Los Angeles **6.3 ft. (6:41)**
San Diego **6.4 ft. (6:43)**

Los Angeles **2.4 ft. (12:21)**
San Diego **2.4 ft. (12:24)**

Los Angeles **3.8 ft. (8:42)**
San Diego **4 ft. (8:30)**

Los Angeles **-1.4 ft. (2:07)**
San Diego **-1.5 ft. (2:06)**

feet 6 5 4 3 2 1

12 1 2 3 4 5 6 7 8 9 10 11 noon 1 2 3 4 5 6 7 8 9 10 11 12

⊃ ⊣ ⊢ 1.4 knots flood —⊣ ⊢ 2.6 knots ebb ——— ⊢ 1.8 knots flood ⊣ ⊢ 1.1 eb

THU FEB 8
dawn 5:49 sunrise 6:44 sunset 5:31 dark 6:26
moonrise 6:07 a.m. moonset 4:10 p.m.

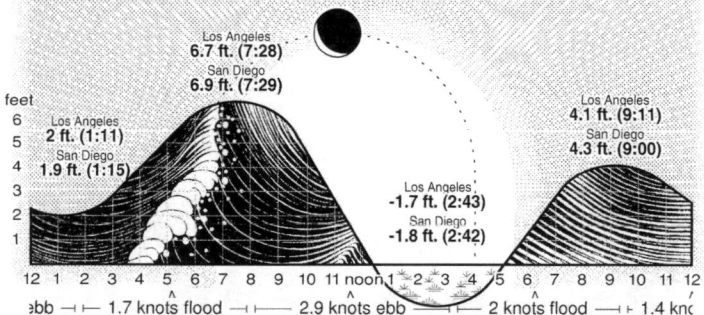

Los Angeles **6.7 ft. (7:28)**
San Diego **6.9 ft. (7:29)**

Los Angeles **2 ft. (1:11)**
San Diego **1.9 ft. (1:15)**

Los Angeles **4.1 ft. (9:11)**
San Diego **4.3 ft. (9:00)**

Los Angeles **-1.7 ft. (2:43)**
San Diego **-1.8 ft. (2:42)**

feet 6 5 4 3 2 1

12 1 2 3 4 5 6 7 8 9 10 11 noon 1 2 3 4 5 6 7 8 9 10 11 12

ebb —⊣ ⊢ 1.7 knots flood —⊣ ⊢ 2.9 knots ebb ——— ⊢ 2 knots flood ⊣ ⊢ 1.4 kn

FRI FEB 9

dawn 5:48 sunrise 6:43 sunset 5:32 dark 6:27
moonrise 6:52 a.m. moonset 5:27 p.m.

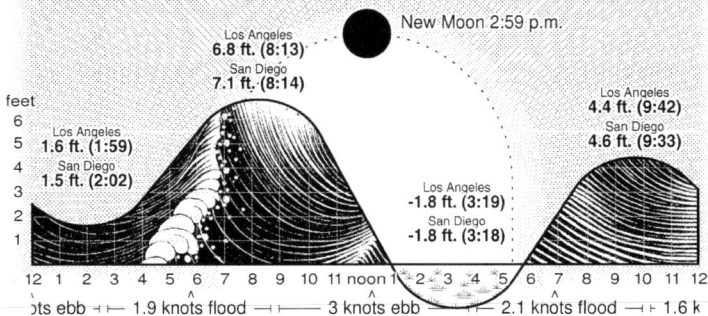

New Moon 2:59 p.m.

Los Angeles
6.8 ft. (8:13)
San Diego
7.1 ft. (8:14)

Los Angeles
4.4 ft. (9:42)
San Diego
4.6 ft. (9:33)

feet
Los Angeles
1.6 ft. (1:59)
San Diego
1.5 ft. (2:02)

Los Angeles
-1.8 ft. (3:19)
San Diego
-1.8 ft. (3:18)

12 1 2 3 4 5 6 7 8 9 10 11 noon 1 2 3 4 5 6 7 8 9 10 11 12

ots ebb ⊢ 1.9 knots flood ⟶ ⊢ 3 knots ebb ⟶ ⊢ 2.1 knots flood ⟶ ⊢ 1.6 k

SAT FEB 10

dawn 5:47 sunrise 6:42 sunset 5:32 dark 6:28
moonrise 7:31 a.m. moonset 6:42 p.m.

Chinese New Year

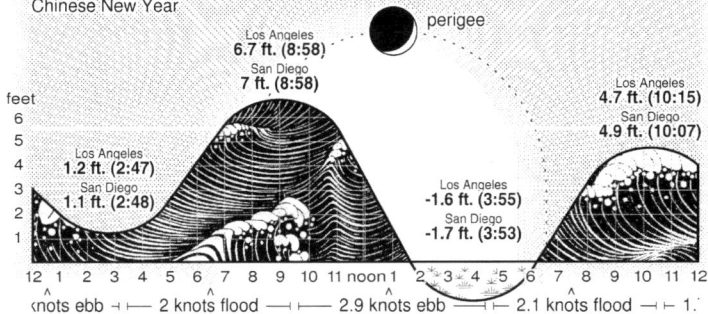

perigee

Los Angeles
6.7 ft. (8:58)
San Diego
7 ft. (8:58)

Los Angeles
4.7 ft. (10:15)
San Diego
4.9 ft. (10:07)

feet
Los Angeles
1.2 ft. (2:47)
San Diego
1.1 ft. (2:48)

Los Angeles
-1.6 ft. (3:55)
San Diego
-1.7 ft. (3:53)

12 1 2 3 4 5 6 7 8 9 10 11 noon 1 2 3 4 5 6 7 8 9 10 11 12

knots ebb ⊣ ⊢ 2 knots flood ⟶ ⊢ 2.9 knots ebb ⟶ ⊢ 2.1 knots flood ⟶ ⊢ 1.

SUN FEB 11

dawn 5:47 sunrise 6:42 sunset 5:33 dark 6:28
moonrise 8:04 a.m. moonset 7:55 p.m.

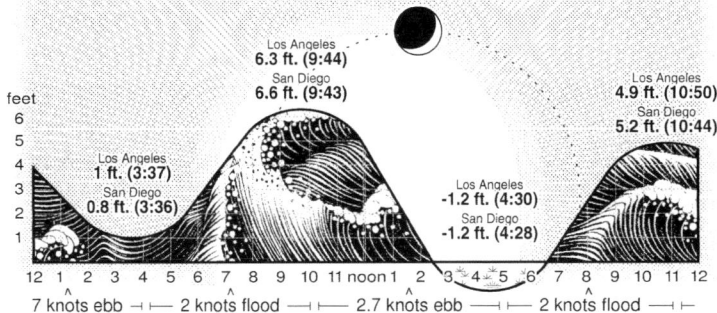

Los Angeles
6.3 ft. (9:44)
San Diego
6.6 ft. (9:43)

Los Angeles
4.9 ft. (10:50)
San Diego
5.2 ft. (10:44)

feet
Los Angeles
1 ft. (3:37)
San Diego
0.8 ft. (3:36)

Los Angeles
-1.2 ft. (4:30)
San Diego
-1.2 ft. (4:28)

12 1 2 3 4 5 6 7 8 9 10 11 noon 1 2 3 4 5 6 7 8 9 10 11 12

7 knots ebb ⊣ ⊢ 2 knots flood ⟶ ⊢ 2.7 knots ebb ⟶ ⊢ 2 knots flood ⟶ ⊢

Planets visible in morning and evening twilight:
Mercury will be visible in the morning from Jan 1st to Feb 16th, Apr 20th to Jun 7th, Aug 27th to Sep 20th and Dec 12th to 31st.
Venus will be visible in the morning from Jan 1st to Apr 28th and in the evenings from Jul 11th to Dec 31st.
Mars will be visible in the morning from Jan 10th to Dec 21st.
Jupiter will be visible in the morning from Jun 2nd to Dec 7th and in the evening from Jan 1st to May 5th and Dec 7th to 31st.
Saturn will be visible in the morning from Mar 17th to Sep 8th and in the evening from Sep 8th to Dec 31st.

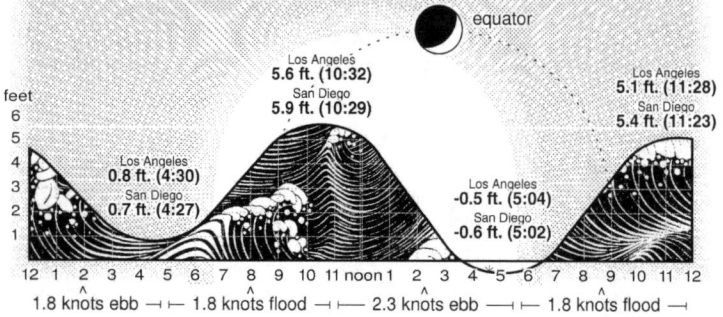

MON FEB 12

dawn 5:46 sunrise 6:41 sunset 5:34 dark 6:29
moonrise 8:35 a.m. moonset 9:06 p.m.

equator

Los Angeles
5.6 ft. (10:32)
San Diego
5.9 ft. (10:29)

Los Angeles
5.1 ft. (11:28)
San Diego
5.4 ft. (11:23)

feet
6
5
4
3
2
1

Los Angeles
0.8 ft. (4:30)
San Diego
0.7 ft. (4:27)

Los Angeles
-0.5 ft. (5:04)
San Diego
-0.6 ft. (5:02)

12 1 2 3 4 5 6 7 8 9 10 11 noon 1 2 3 4 5 6 7 8 9 10 11 12

1.8 knots ebb → ← 1.8 knots flood → ← 2.3 knots ebb → ← 1.8 knots flood →

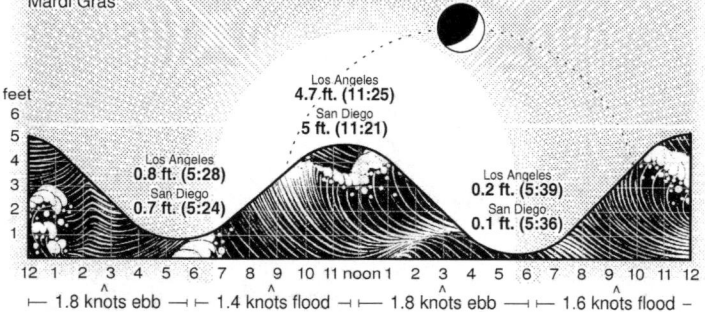

TUE FEB 13

dawn 5:45 sunrise 6:40 sunset 5:35 dark 6:30
moonrise 9:06 a.m. moonset 10:16 p.m.

Mardi Gras

Los Angeles
4.7 ft. (11:25)
San Diego
.5 ft. (11:21)

feet
6
5
4
3
2
1

Los Angeles
0.8 ft. (5:28)
San Diego
0.7 ft. (5:24)

Los Angeles
0.2 ft. (5:39)
San Diego
0.1 ft. (5:36)

12 1 2 3 4 5 6 7 8 9 10 11 noon 1 2 3 4 5 6 7 8 9 10 11 12

← 1.8 knots ebb → ← 1.4 knots flood → ← 1.8 knots ebb → ← 1.6 knots flood –

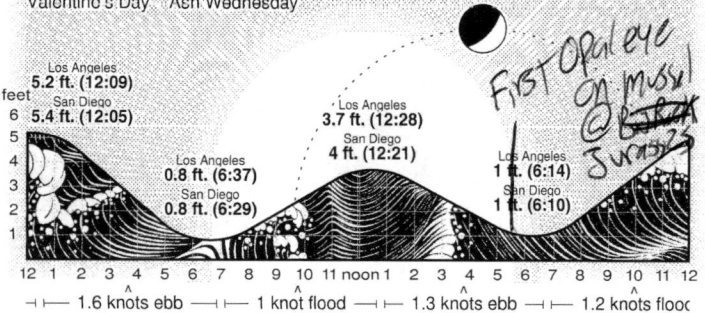

WED FEB 14

dawn 5:44 sunrise 6:39 sunset 5:36 dark 6:31
moonrise 9:37 a.m. moonset 11:25 p.m.

Valentine's Day   Ash Wednesday

Los Angeles
5.2 ft. (12:09)
San Diego
5.4 ft. (12:05)

Los Angeles
3.7 ft. (12:28)
San Diego
4 ft. (12:21)

First Opaleye
on mussel
@ Brick
Jures23

feet
6
5
4
3
2
1

Los Angeles
0.8 ft. (6:37)
San Diego
0.8 ft. (6:29)

Los Angeles
1 ft. (6:14)
San Diego
1 ft. (6:10)

12 1 2 3 4 5 6 7 8 9 10 11 noon 1 2 3 4 5 6 7 8 9 10 11 12

← 1.6 knots ebb → ← 1 knot flood → ← 1.3 knots ebb → ← 1.2 knots flood

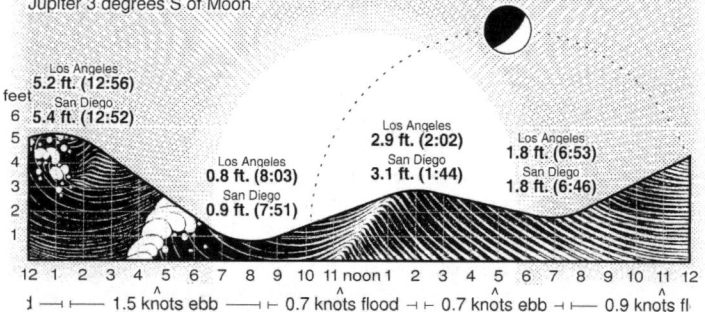

THU FEB 15

dawn 5:43 sunrise 6:38 sunset 5:37 dark 6:32
moonrise 10:10 a.m.

Jupiter 3 degrees S of Moon

Los Angeles
5.2 ft. (12:56)
San Diego
5.4 ft. (12:52)

Los Angeles
2.9 ft. (2:02)
San Diego
3.1 ft. (1:44)

Los Angeles
1.8 ft. (6:53)
San Diego
1.8 ft. (6:46)

feet
6
5
4
3
2
1

Los Angeles
0.8 ft. (8:03)
San Diego
0.9 ft. (7:51)

12 1 2 3 4 5 6 7 8 9 10 11 noon 1 2 3 4 5 6 7 8 9 10 11 12

← ← 1.5 knots ebb → ← 0.7 knots flood → ← 0.7 knots ebb → ← 0.9 knots fl

FRI FEB 16
dawn 5:42 sunrise 6:37 sunset 5:38 dark 6:33
moonset 12:33 a.m. moonrise 10:48 a.m.

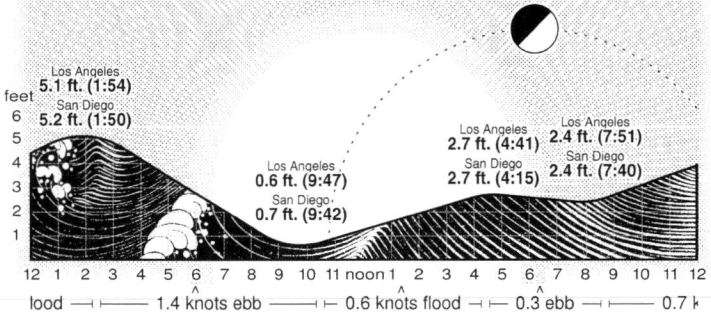

feet
6
5
4
3
2
1

Los Angeles
5.1 ft. (1:54)
San Diego
5.2 ft. (1:50)

Los Angeles
0.6 ft. (9:47)
San Diego
0.7 ft. (9:42)

Los Angeles
2.7 ft. (4:41)
San Diego
2.7 ft. (4:15)

Los Angeles
2.4 ft. (7:51)
San Diego
2.4 ft. (7:40)

12 1 2 3 4 5 6 7 8 9 10 11 noon 1 2 3 4 5 6 7 8 9 10 11 12

lood ⊢ ⊢ 1.4 knots ebb ⊢ ⊢ 0.6 knots flood ⊣ ⊢ 0.3 ebb ⊢ ⊢ 0.7 k

SAT FEB 17
dawn 5:41 sunrise 6:36 sunset 5:39 dark 6:34
moonset 1:40 a.m. moonrise 11:31 a.m.

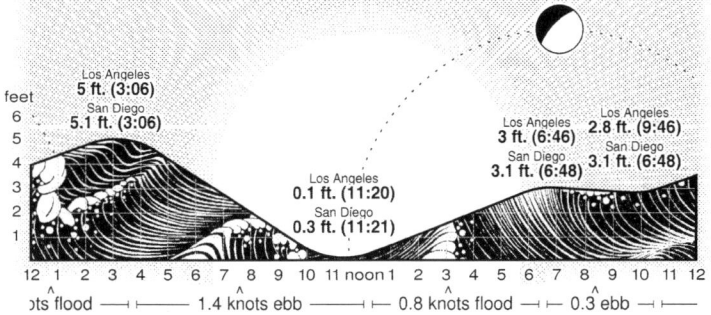

feet
6
5
4
3
2
1

Los Angeles
5 ft. (3:06)
San Diego
5.1 ft. (3:06)

Los Angeles
0.1 ft. (11:20)
San Diego
0.3 ft. (11:21)

Los Angeles
3 ft. (6:46)
San Diego
3.1 ft. (6:48)

Los Angeles
2.8 ft. (9:46)
San Diego
3.1 ft. (6:48)

12 1 2 3 4 5 6 7 8 9 10 11 noon 1 2 3 4 5 6 7 8 9 10 11 12

ots flood ⊢ ⊢ 1.4 knots ebb ⊢ ⊢ 0.8 knots flood ⊣ ⊢ 0.3 ebb ⊢ ⊢

SUN FEB 18
dawn 5:40 sunrise 6:35 sunset 5:40 dark 6:34
moonset 2:43 a.m. moonrise 12:20 p.m.

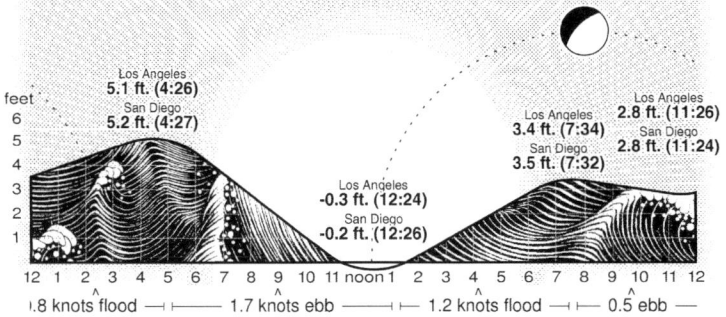

feet
6
5
4
3
2
1

Los Angeles
5.1 ft. (4:26)
San Diego
5.2 ft. (4:27)

Los Angeles
-0.3 ft. (12:24)
San Diego
-0.2 ft. (12:26)

Los Angeles
3.4 ft. (7:34)
San Diego
3.5 ft. (7:32)

Los Angeles
2.8 ft. (11:26)
San Diego
2.8 ft. (11:24)

12 1 2 3 4 5 6 7 8 9 10 11 noon 1 2 3 4 5 6 7 8 9 10 11 12

).8 knots flood ⊢ ⊢ 1.7 knots ebb ⊢ ⊢ 1.2 knots flood ⊣ ⊢ 0.5 ebb ⊢

MON FEB 19
dawn 5:39 sunrise 6:33 sunset 5:41 dark 6:35
moonset 3:41 a.m. moonrise 1:14 p.m.

Presidents' Day

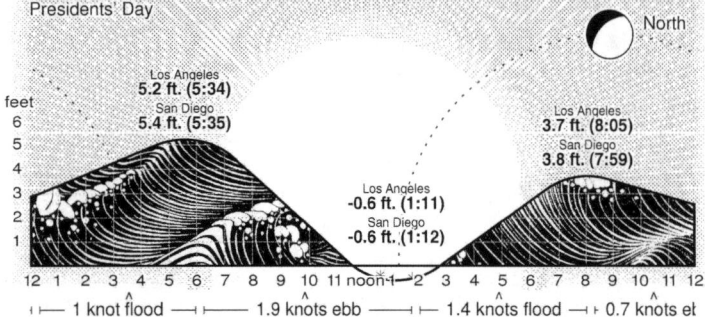

North

feet

Los Angeles
5.2 ft. (5:34)
San Diego
5.4 ft. (5:35)

Los Angeles
3.7 ft. (8:05)
San Diego
3.8 ft. (7:59)

Los Angeles
-0.6 ft. (1:11)
San Diego
-0.6 ft. (1:12)

12 1 2 3 4 5 6 7 8 9 10 11 noon 1 2 3 4 5 6 7 8 9 10 11 12

⊢ 1 knot flood ⊣ ⊢ 1.9 knots ebb ⊢ 1.4 knots flood ⊣ 0.7 knots el

TUE FEB 20
dawn 5:38 sunrise 6:32 sunset 5:42 dark 6:36
moonset 4:31 a.m. moonrise 2:13 p.m.

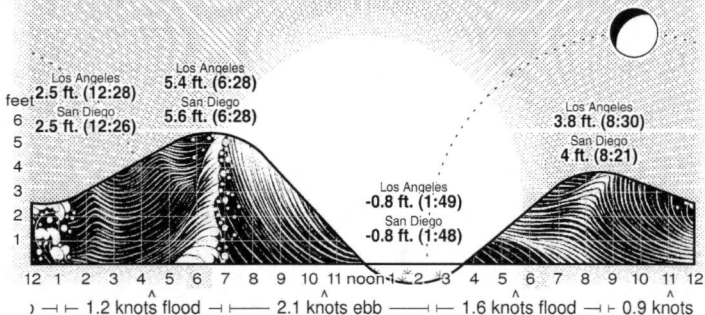

feet
Los Angeles
2.5 ft. (12:28)
San Diego
2.5 ft. (12:26)

Los Angeles
5.4 ft. (6:28)
San Diego
5.6 ft. (6:28)

Los Angeles
3.8 ft. (8:30)
San Diego
4 ft. (8:21)

Los Angeles
-0.8 ft. (1:49)
San Diego
-0.8 ft. (1:48)

12 1 2 3 4 5 6 7 8 9 10 11 noon 1 2 3 4 5 6 7 8 9 10 11 12

) ⊣ ⊢ 1.2 knots flood ⊣ ⊢ 2.1 knots ebb ⊢ 1.6 knots flood ⊣ ⊢ 0.9 knots

WED FEB 21
dawn 5:37 sunrise 6:31 sunset 5:43 dark 6:37
moonset 5:14 a.m. moonrise 3:13 p.m.

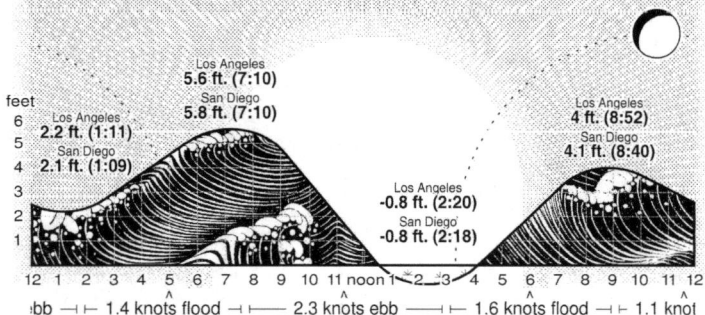

Los Angeles
5.6 ft. (7:10)
San Diego
5.8 ft. (7:10)

feet
Los Angeles
2.2 ft. (1:11)
San Diego
2.1 ft. (1:09)

Los Angeles
4 ft. (8:52)
San Diego
4.1 ft. (8:40)

Los Angeles
-0.8 ft. (2:20)
San Diego
-0.8 ft. (2:18)

12 1 2 3 4 5 6 7 8 9 10 11 noon 1 2 3 4 5 6 7 8 9 10 11 12

bb ⊣ ⊢ 1.4 knots flood ⊣ ⊢ 2.3 knots ebb ⊢ 1.6 knots flood ⊣ ⊢ 1.1 knot

THU FEB 22
dawn 5:36 sunrise 6:30 sunset 5:43 dark 6:38
moonset 5:50 a.m. moonrise 4:13 p.m.

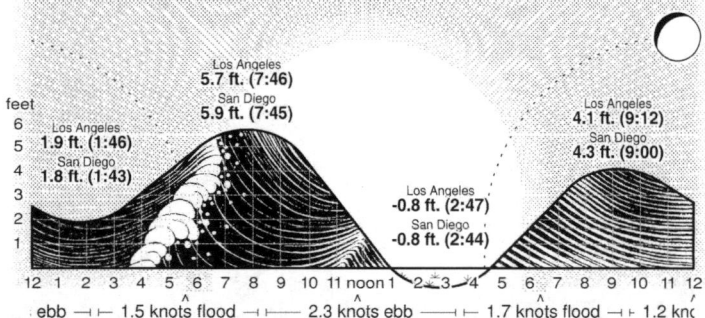

Los Angeles
5.7 ft. (7:46)
San Diego
5.9 ft. (7:45)

feet
Los Angeles
1.9 ft. (1:46)
San Diego
1.8 ft. (1:43)

Los Angeles
4.1 ft. (9:12)
San Diego
4.3 ft. (9:00)

Los Angeles
-0.8 ft. (2:47)
San Diego
-0.8 ft. (2:44)

12 1 2 3 4 5 6 7 8 9 10 11 noon 1 2 3 4 5 6 7 8 9 10 11 12

ebb ⊣ ⊢ 1.5 knots flood ⊣ ⊢ 2.3 knots ebb ⊢ 1.7 knots flood ⊣ ⊢ 1.2 knot

FRI FEB 23
dawn 5:35 sunrise 6:29 sunset 5:44 dark 6:38
moonset 6:20 a.m. moonrise 5:11 p.m.

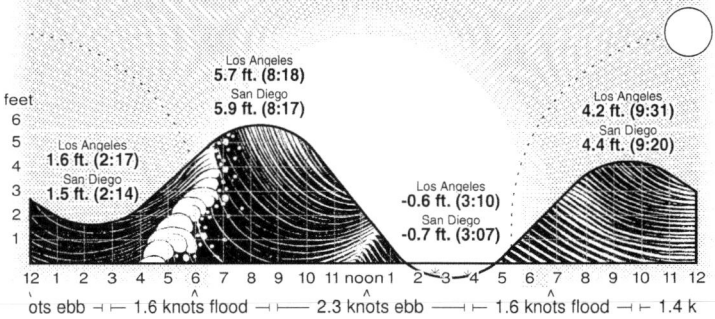

feet
6
5
4
3
2
1

Los Angeles **1.6 ft. (2:17)**
San Diego **1.5 ft. (2:14)**

Los Angeles **5.7 ft. (8:18)**
San Diego **5.9 ft. (8:17)**

Los Angeles **-0.6 ft. (3:10)**
San Diego **-0.7 ft. (3:07)**

Los Angeles **4.2 ft. (9:31)**
San Diego **4.4 ft. (9:20)**

12 1 2 3 4 5 6 7 8 9 10 11 noon 1 2 3 4 5 6 7 8 9 10 11 12

ots ebb →← 1.6 knots flood →←— 2.3 knots ebb ——← 1.6 knots flood →← 1.4 k

SAT FEB 24
dawn 5:34 sunrise 6:28 sunset 5:45 dark 6:39
moonset 6:48 a.m. moonrise 6:08 p.m.

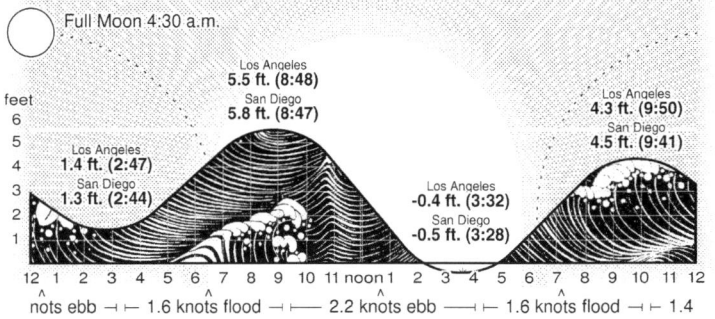

Full Moon 4:30 a.m.

feet
6
5
4
3
2
1

Los Angeles **1.4 ft. (2:47)**
San Diego **1.3 ft. (2:44)**

Los Angeles **5.5 ft. (8:48)**
San Diego **5.8 ft. (8:47)**

Los Angeles **-0.4 ft. (3:32)**
San Diego **-0.5 ft. (3:28)**

Los Angeles **4.3 ft. (9:50)**
San Diego **4.5 ft. (9:41)**

12 1 2 3 4 5 6 7 8 9 10 11 noon 1 2 3 4 5 6 7 8 9 10 11 12

nots ebb →← 1.6 knots flood →←— 2.2 knots ebb ——← 1.6 knots flood →← 1.4

SUN FEB 25
dawn 5:33 sunrise 6:27 sunset 5:46 dark 6:40
moonset 7:12 a.m. moonrise 7:03 p.m.

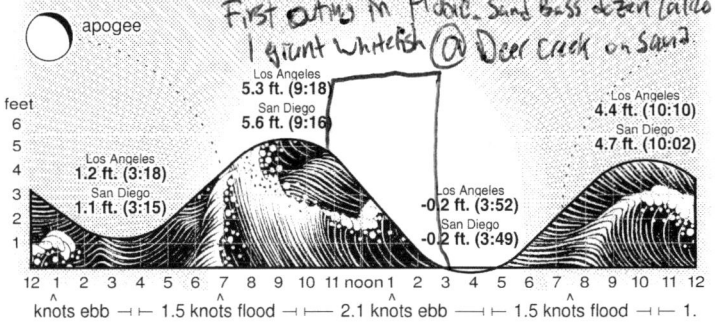

apogee

*First outing in Habia. Sand Bass dozen Calico
1 giant Whitefish @ Deer Creek on Sand*

feet
6
5
4
3
2
1

Los Angeles **1.2 ft. (3:18)**
San Diego **1.1 ft. (3:15)**

Los Angeles **5.3 ft. (9:18)**
San Diego **5.6 ft. (9:16)**

Los Angeles **-0.2 ft. (3:52)**
San Diego **-0.2 ft. (3:49)**

Los Angeles **4.4 ft. (10:10)**
San Diego **4.7 ft. (10:02)**

12 1 2 3 4 5 6 7 8 9 10 11 noon 1 2 3 4 5 6 7 8 9 10 11 12

knots ebb →← 1.5 knots flood →←— 2.1 knots ebb ——← 1.5 knots flood →← 1. -

MON FEB 26
dawn 5:32 sunrise 6:26 sunset 5:47 dark 6:41
moonset 7:36 a.m. moonrise 7:58 p.m.

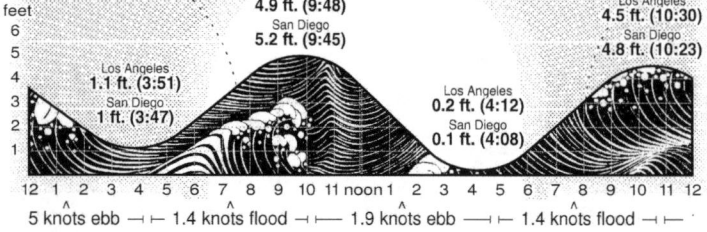

equator

feet

6
5
4
3
2
1

Los Angeles
4.9 ft. (9:48)
San Diego
5.2 ft. (9:45)

Los Angeles
4.5 ft. (10:30)
San Diego
4.8 ft. (10:23)

Los Angeles
1.1 ft. (3:51)
San Diego
1 ft. (3:47)

Los Angeles
0.2 ft. (4:12)
San Diego
0.1 ft. (4:08)

12 1 2 3 4 5 6 7 8 9 10 11 noon 1 2 3 4 5 6 7 8 9 10 11 12

5 knots ebb ⊢ ← 1.4 knots flood → ⊢ ← 1.9 knots ebb → ⊢ ← 1.4 knots flood → ⊢ ←

TUE FEB 27
dawn 5:30 sunrise 6:24 sunset 5:48 dark 6:42
moonset 7:59 a.m. moonrise 8:54 p.m.

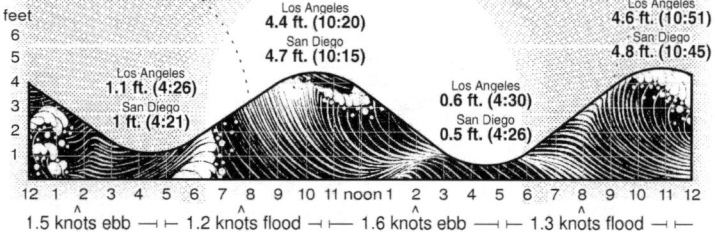

feet

6
5
4
3
2
1

Los Angeles
4.4 ft. (10:20)
San Diego
4.7 ft. (10:15)

Los Angeles
4.6 ft. (10:51)
San Diego
4.8 ft. (10:45)

Los Angeles
1.1 ft. (4:26)
San Diego
1 ft. (4:21)

Los Angeles
0.6 ft. (4:30)
San Diego
0.5 ft. (4:26)

12 1 2 3 4 5 6 7 8 9 10 11 noon 1 2 3 4 5 6 7 8 9 10 11 12

1.5 knots ebb → ⊢ ← 1.2 knots flood → ⊢ ← 1.6 knots ebb → ⊢ ← 1.3 knots flood → ⊢ ←

WED FEB 28
dawn 5:29 sunrise 6:23 sunset 5:49 dark 6:43
moonset 8:23 a.m. moonrise 9:51 p.m.

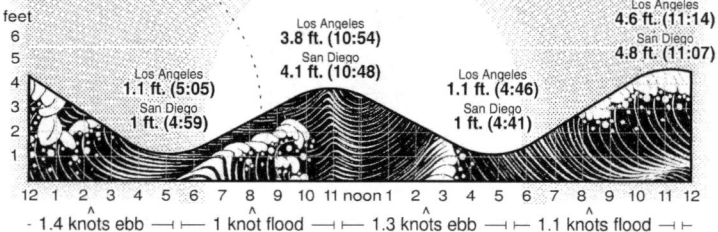

feet

6
5
4
3
2
1

Los Angeles
3.8 ft. (10:54)
San Diego
4.1 ft. (10:48)

Los Angeles
4.6 ft. (11:14)
San Diego
4.8 ft. (11:07)

Los Angeles
1.1 ft. (5:05)
San Diego
1 ft. (4:59)

Los Angeles
1.1 ft. (4:46)
San Diego
1 ft. (4:41)

12 1 2 3 4 5 6 7 8 9 10 11 noon 1 2 3 4 5 6 7 8 9 10 11 12

- 1.4 knots ebb → ⊢ ← 1 knot flood → ⊢ ← 1.3 knots ebb → ⊢ ← 1.1 knots flood → ⊢ ←

THU FEB 29
dawn 5:28 sunrise 6:22 sunset 5:49 dark 6:43
moonset 8:50 a.m. moonrise 10:50 p.m.

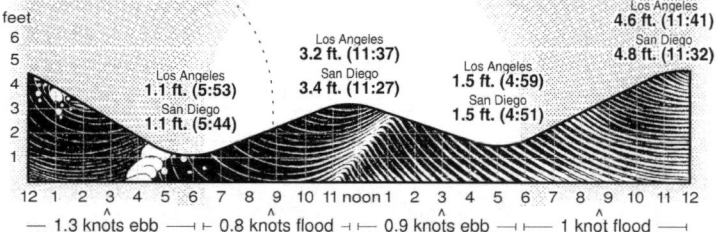

feet

6
5
4
3
2
1

Los Angeles
3.2 ft. (11:37)
San Diego
3.4 ft. (11:27)

Los Angeles
4.6 ft. (11:41)
San Diego
4.8 ft. (11:32)

Los Angeles
1.1 ft. (5:53)
San Diego
1.1 ft. (5:44)

Los Angeles
1.5 ft. (4:59)
San Diego
1.5 ft. (4:51)

12 1 2 3 4 5 6 7 8 9 10 11 noon 1 2 3 4 5 6 7 8 9 10 11 12

— 1.3 knots ebb → ⊢ ← 0.8 knots flood → ⊢ ← 0.9 knots ebb → ⊢ ← 1 knot flood —

FRI MAR 1

dawn 5:27 sunrise 6:21 sunset 5:50 dark 6:44
moonset 9:20 a.m. moonrise 11:52 p.m.

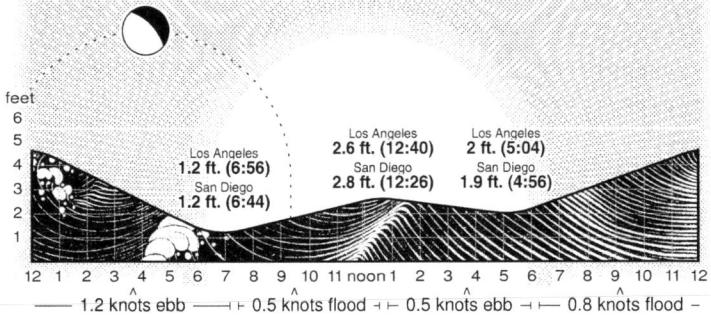

feet
6
5
4
3
2
1

Los Angeles 1.2 ft. (6:56)
San Diego 1.2 ft. (6:44)

Los Angeles 2.6 ft. (12:40)
San Diego 2.8 ft. (12:26)

Los Angeles 2 ft. (5:04)
San Diego 1.9 ft. (4:56)

12 1 2 3 4 5 6 7 8 9 10 11 noon 1 2 3 4 5 6 7 8 9 10 11 12

— 1.2 knots ebb → ⊢ 0.5 knots flood ⊣ ⊢ 0.5 knots ebb → ⊢ 0.8 knots flood –

SAT MAR 2

dawn 5:26 sunrise 6:19 sunset 5:51 dark 6:45
moonset 9:56 a.m.

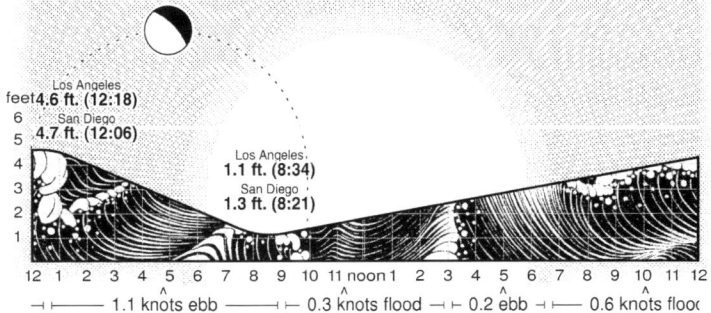

feet **Los Angeles 4.6 ft. (12:18)**
6 **San Diego 4.7 ft. (12:06)**
5
4
3
2
1

Los Angeles 1.1 ft. (8:34)
San Diego 1.3 ft. (8:21)

12 1 2 3 4 5 6 7 8 9 10 11 noon 1 2 3 4 5 6 7 8 9 10 11 12

⊣ ⊢ 1.1 knots ebb ——— ⊢ 0.3 knots flood ⊣ ⊢ 0.2 ebb ⊣ ⊢ 0.6 knots flood

SUN MAR 3

dawn 5:24 sunrise 6:18 sunset 5:52 dark 6:46
moonrise 12:55 a.m. moonset 10:39 a.m.

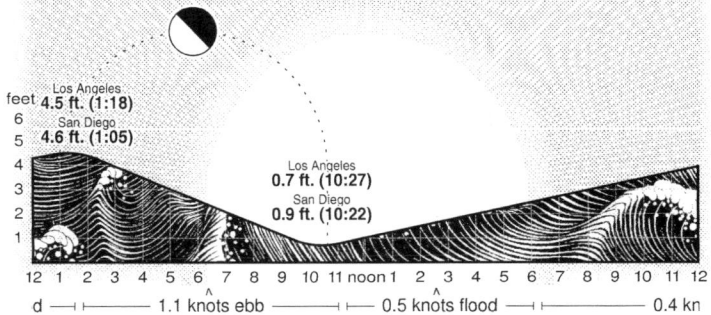

feet **Los Angeles 4.5 ft. (1:18)**
6 **San Diego 4.6 ft. (1:05)**
5
4
3
2
1

Los Angeles 0.7 ft. (10:27)
San Diego 0.9 ft. (10:22)

12 1 2 3 4 5 6 7 8 9 10 11 noon 1 2 3 4 5 6 7 8 9 10 11 12

d ⊣ ⊢——— 1.1 knots ebb ——— ⊢ 0.5 knots flood ——— ⊢ 0.4 kn

MON MAR 4 dawn 5:23 sunrise 6:17 sunset 5:53 dark 6:47
moonrise 1:59 a.m. moonset 11:31 a.m.

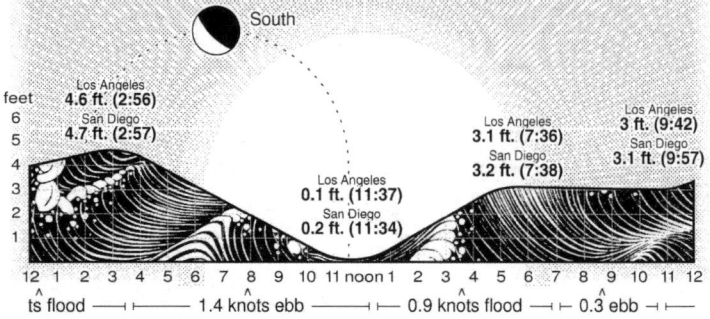

South

feet
6
5
4
3
2
1

Los Angeles
4.6 ft. (2:56)
San Diego
4.7 ft. (2:57)

Los Angeles
0.1 ft. (11:37)
San Diego
0.2 ft. (11:34)

Los Angeles
3.1 ft. (7:36)
San Diego
3.2 ft. (7:38)

Los Angeles
3 ft. (9:42)
San Diego
3.1 ft. (9:57)

12 1 2 3 4 5 6 7 8 9 10 11 noon 1 2 3 4 5 6 7 8 9 10 11 12

ts flood ⊢ ⊢ 1.4 knots ebb ⊢ ⊢ 0.9 knots flood ⊢ 0.3 ebb ⊣ ⊢

TUE MAR 5 dawn 5:22 sunrise 6:16 sunset 5:53 dark 6:47
moonrise 2:59 a.m. moonset 12:33 p.m.

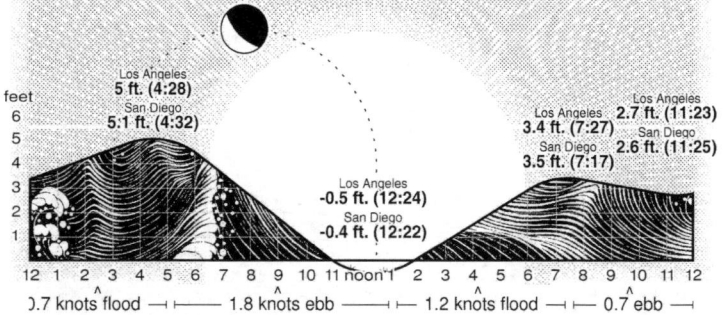

feet
6
5
4
3
2
1

Los Angeles
5 ft. (4:28)
San Diego
5.1 ft. (4:32)

Los Angeles
-0.5 ft. (12:24)
San Diego
-0.4 ft. (12:22)

Los Angeles 2.7 ft. (11:23)
San Diego 2.6 ft. (11:25)

Los Angeles
3.4 ft. (7:27)
San Diego
3.5 ft. (7:17)

12 1 2 3 4 5 6 7 8 9 10 11 noon 1 2 3 4 5 6 7 8 9 10 11 12

0.7 knots flood ⊢ ⊢ 1.8 knots ebb ⊢ ⊢ 1.2 knots flood ⊢ 0.7 ebb ⊣

WED MAR 6 dawn 5:21 sunrise 6:14 sunset 5:54 dark 6:48
moonrise 3:54 a.m. moonset 1:43 p.m.

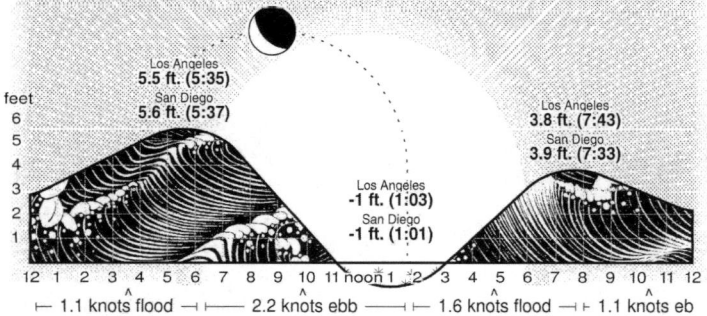

feet
6
5
4
3
2
1

Los Angeles
5.5 ft. (5:35)
San Diego
5.6 ft. (5:37)

Los Angeles
-1 ft. (1:03)
San Diego
-1 ft. (1:01)

Los Angeles
3.8 ft. (7:43)
San Diego
3.9 ft. (7:33)

12 1 2 3 4 5 6 7 8 9 10 11 noon 1 2 3 4 5 6 7 8 9 10 11 12

⊢ 1.1 knots flood ⊣ ⊢ 2.2 knots ebb ⊢ 1.6 knots flood ⊣ ⊢ 1.1 eb

THU MAR 7 dawn 5:19 sunrise 6:13 sunset 5:55 dark 6:49
moonrise 4:41 a.m. moonset 2:58 p.m.

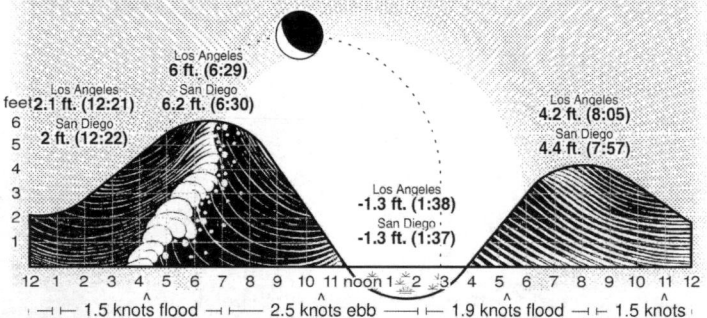

feet
6
5
4
3
2
1

Los Angeles
2.1 ft. (12:21)
San Diego
2 ft. (12:22)

Los Angeles
6 ft. (6:29)
San Diego
6.2 ft. (6:30)

Los Angeles
-1.3 ft. (1:38)
San Diego
-1.3 ft. (1:37)

Los Angeles
4.2 ft. (8:05)
San Diego
4.4 ft. (7:57)

12 1 2 3 4 5 6 7 8 9 10 11 noon 1 2 3 4 5 6 7 8 9 10 11 12

⊣ ⊢ 1.5 knots flood ⊣ ⊢ 2.5 knots ebb ⊢ 1.9 knots flood ⊣ ⊢ 1.5 knots

FRI MAR 8

dawn 5:18 sunrise 6:12 sunset 5:56 dark 6:50
moonrise 5:22 a.m. moonset 4:13 p.m.

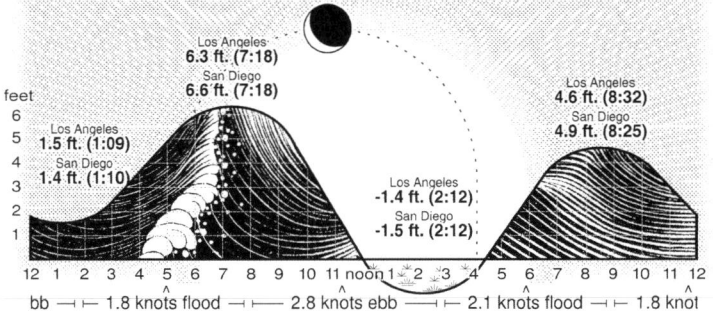

feet
6
5
4
3
2
1

Los Angeles
6.3 ft. (7:18)
San Diego
6.6 ft. (7:18)

Los Angeles
1.5 ft. (1:09)
San Diego
1.4 ft. (1:10)

Los Angeles
-1.4 ft. (2:12)
San Diego
-1.5 ft. (2:12)

Los Angeles
4.6 ft. (8:32)
San Diego
4.9 ft. (8:25)

12 1 2 3 4 5 6 7 8 9 10 11 noon 1 2 3 4 5 6 7 8 9 10 11 12

bb ⊢ ← 1.8 knots flood → ⊢ ← 2.8 knots ebb → ⊢ ← 2.1 knots flood → ⊢ ← 1.8 knot

SAT MAR 9

dawn 5:17 sunrise 6:11 sunset 5:57 dark 6:50
moonrise 5:58 a.m. moonset 5:28 p.m.

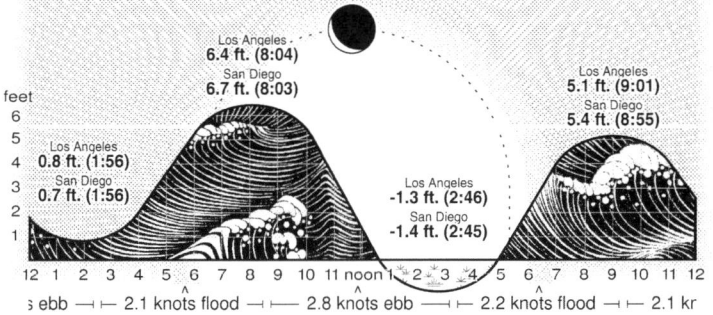

feet
6
5
4
3
2
1

Los Angeles
6.4 ft. (8:04)
San Diego
6.7 ft. (8:03)

Los Angeles
0.8 ft. (1:56)
San Diego
0.7 ft. (1:56)

Los Angeles
-1.3 ft. (2:46)
San Diego
-1.4 ft. (2:45)

Los Angeles
5.1 ft. (9:01)
San Diego
5.4 ft. (8:55)

12 1 2 3 4 5 6 7 8 9 10 11 noon 1 2 3 4 5 6 7 8 9 10 11 12

s ebb → ⊢ ← 2.1 knots flood → ⊢ ← 2.8 knots ebb → ⊢ ← 2.2 knots flood → ⊢ ← 2.1 kr

SUN MAR 10

dawn 6:16 sunrise 7:09 sunset 6:58 dark 7:51
moonrise 7:31 a.m. moonset 7:41 p.m.

Daylight Savings Time Begins   perigee   equator   New Moon 1:00 a.m.

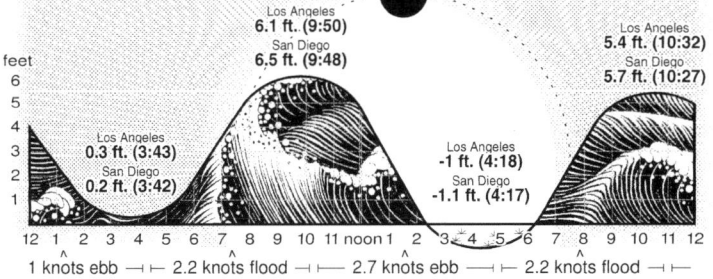

feet
6
5
4
3
2
1

Los Angeles
6.1 ft. (9:50)
San Diego
6.5 ft. (9:48)

Los Angeles
0.3 ft. (3:43)
San Diego
0.2 ft. (3:42)

Los Angeles
-1 ft. (4:18)
San Diego
-1.1 ft. (4:17)

Los Angeles
5.4 ft. (10:32)
San Diego
5.7 ft. (10:27)

12 1 2 3 4 5 6 7 8 9 10 11 noon 1 2 3 4 5 6 7 8 9 10 11 12

1 knots ebb → ⊢ ← 2.2 knots flood → ⊢ ← 2.7 knots ebb → ⊢ ← 2.2 knots flood → ⊢ ←

MON MAR 11
dawn 6:14 sunrise 7:08 sunset 6:58 dark 7:52
moonrise 8:02 a.m. moonset 8:53 p.m.

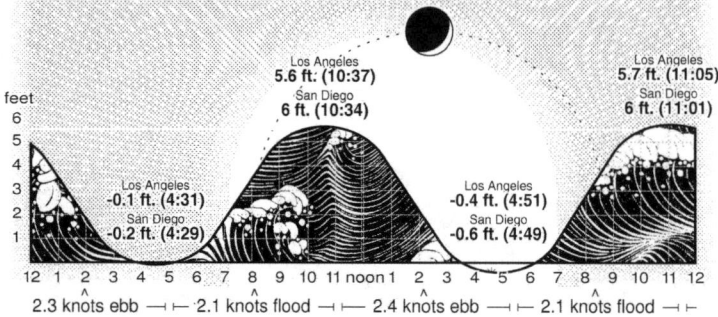

Los Angeles
5.6 ft. (10:37)
San Diego
6 ft. (10:34)

Los Angeles
5.7 ft. (11:05)
San Diego
6 ft. (11:01)

Los Angeles
-0.1 ft. (4:31)
San Diego
-0.2 ft. (4:29)

Los Angeles
-0.4 ft. (4:51)
San Diego
-0.6 ft. (4:49)

feet
6
5
4
3
2
1

12 1 2 3 4 5 6 7 8 9 10 11 noon 1 2 3 4 5 6 7 8 9 10 11 12

2.3 knots ebb → ← 2.1 knots flood → ← 2.4 knots ebb → ← 2.1 knots flood → ←

TUE MAR 12
dawn 6:13 sunrise 7:07 sunset 6:59 dark 7:53
moonrise 8:33 a.m. moonset 10:05 p.m.

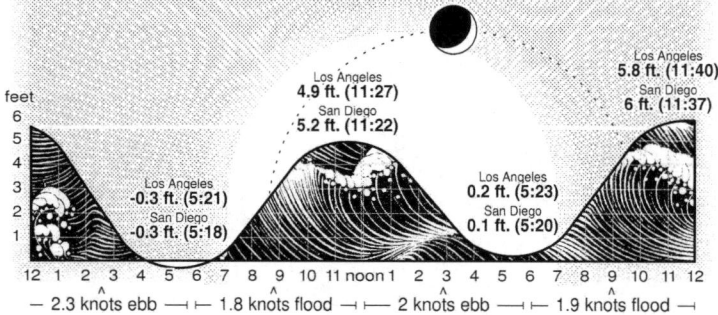

Los Angeles
4.9 ft. (11:27)
San Diego
5.2 ft. (11:22)

Los Angeles
5.8 ft. (11:40)
San Diego
6 ft. (11:37)

Los Angeles
-0.3 ft. (5:21)
San Diego
-0.3 ft. (5:18)

Los Angeles
0.2 ft. (5:23)
San Diego
0.1 ft. (5:20)

feet
6
5
4
3
2
1

12 1 2 3 4 5 6 7 8 9 10 11 noon 1 2 3 4 5 6 7 8 9 10 11 12

— 2.3 knots ebb → ← 1.8 knots flood → ← 2 knots ebb → ← 1.9 knots flood →

WED MAR 13
dawn 6:12 sunrise 7:05 sunset 7:00 dark 7:54
moonrise 9:06 a.m. moonset 11:17 p.m.

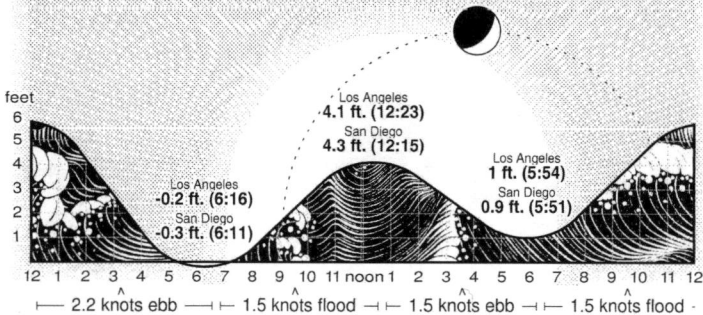

Los Angeles
4.1 ft. (12:23)
San Diego
4.3 ft. (12:15)

Los Angeles
1 ft. (5:54)
San Diego
0.9 ft. (5:51)

Los Angeles
-0.2 ft. (6:16)
San Diego
-0.3 ft. (6:11)

feet
6
5
4
3
2
1

12 1 2 3 4 5 6 7 8 9 10 11 noon 1 2 3 4 5 6 7 8 9 10 11 12

← 2.2 knots ebb → ← 1.5 knots flood → ← 1.5 knots ebb → ← 1.5 knots flood ·

THU MAR 14
dawn 6:10 sunrise 7:04 sunset 7:01 dark 7:54
moonrise 9:43 a.m.

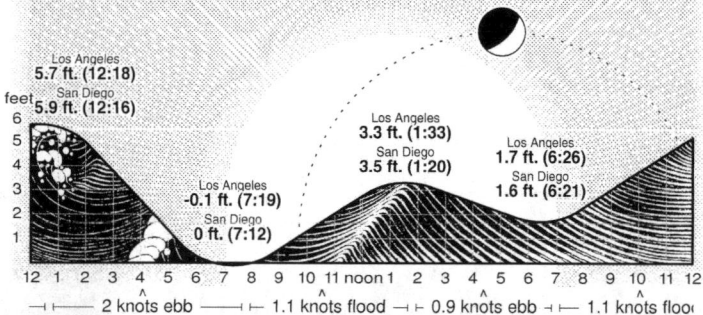

Los Angeles
5.7 ft. (12:18)
San Diego
5.9 ft. (12:16)

Los Angeles
3.3 ft. (1:33)
San Diego
3.5 ft. (1:20)

Los Angeles
1.7 ft. (6:26)
San Diego
1.6 ft. (6:21)

Los Angeles
-0.1 ft. (7:19)
San Diego
0 ft. (7:12)

feet
6
5
4
3
2
1

12 1 2 3 4 5 6 7 8 9 10 11 noon 1 2 3 4 5 6 7 8 9 10 11 12

→ ← 2 knots ebb → ← 1.1 knots flood → ← 0.9 knots ebb → ← 1.1 knots floo

FRI MAR 15
dawn 6:09 sunrise 7:03 sunset 7:01 dark 7:55
moonset 12:27 a.m. moonrise 10:26 a.m.

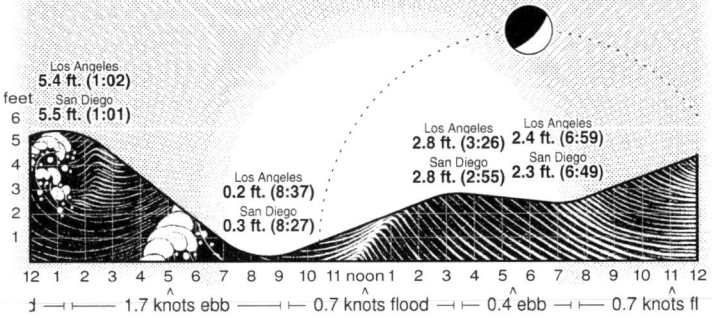

Los Angeles
5.4 ft. (1:02)
feet San Diego
6 **5.5 ft. (1:01)**

Los Angeles
2.8 ft. (3:26) Los Angeles
2.4 ft. (6:59)
San Diego
2.8 ft. (2:55) San Diego
2.3 ft. (6:49)

Los Angeles
0.2 ft. (8:37)
San Diego
0.3 ft. (8:27)

12 1 2 3 4 5 6 7 8 9 10 11 noon 1 2 3 4 5 6 7 8 9 10 11 12

⌐ ⊢ 1.7 knots ebb ⊢ 0.7 knots flood ⊣ ⊢ 0.4 ebb ⊢ 0.7 knots fl

SAT MAR 16
dawn 6:08 sunrise 7:01 sunset 7:02 dark 7:56
moonset 1:34 a.m. moonrise 11:14 a.m.

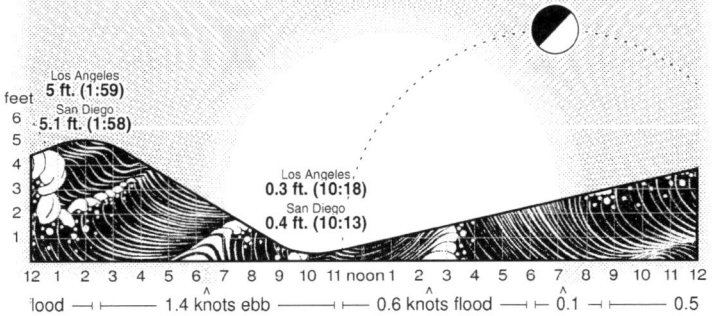

Los Angeles
feet **5 ft. (1:59)**
San Diego
6 **5.1 ft. (1:58)**

Los Angeles
0.3 ft. (10:18)
San Diego
0.4 ft. (10:13)

12 1 2 3 4 5 6 7 8 9 10 11 noon 1 2 3 4 5 6 7 8 9 10 11 12

flood ⊣ ⊢ 1.4 knots ebb ⊢ 0.6 knots flood ⊢ ⊢ 0.1 ⊣ ⊢ 0.5

SUN MAR 17
dawn 6:06 sunrise 7:00 sunset 7:03 dark 7:57
moonset 2:35 a.m. moonrise 12:08 p.m.

St. Patrick's Day

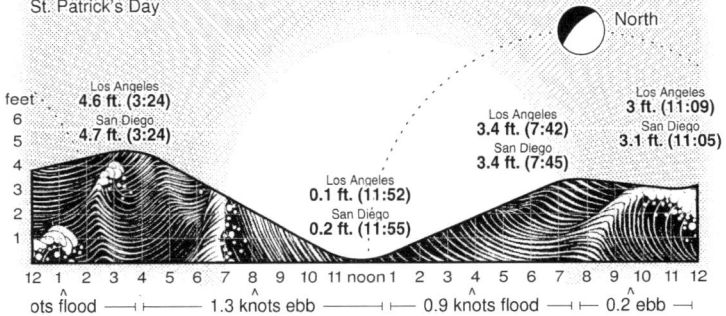

North

Los Angeles
feet **4.6 ft. (3:24)**
San Diego
4.7 ft. (3:24)

Los Angeles
3.4 ft. (7:42)
San Diego
3.4 ft. (7:45)

Los Angeles
3 ft. (11:09)
San Diego
3.1 ft. (11:05)

Los Angeles
0.1 ft. (11:52)
San Diego
0.2 ft. (11:55)

12 1 2 3 4 5 6 7 8 9 10 11 noon 1 2 3 4 5 6 7 8 9 10 11 12

ots flood ⊣ ⊢ 1.3 knots ebb ⊢ 0.9 knots flood ⊣ ⊢ 0.2 ebb ⊣

MON MAR 18
dawn 6:05 sunrise 6:59 sunset 7:04 dark 7:58
moonset 3:29 a.m. moonrise 1:06 p.m.

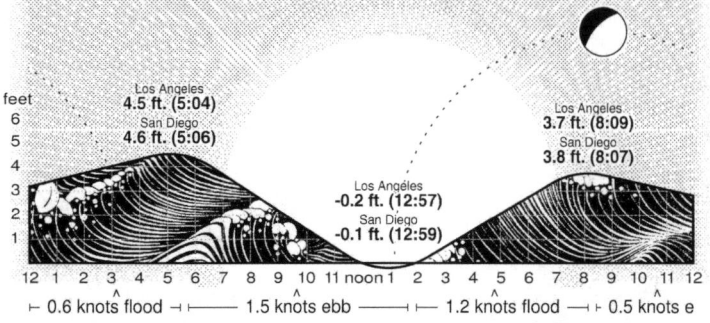

feet

Los Angeles
4.5 ft. (5:04)
San Diego
4.6 ft. (5:06)

Los Angeles
3.7 ft. (8:09)
San Diego
3.8 ft. (8:07)

Los Angeles
-0.2 ft. (12:57)
San Diego
-0.1 ft. (12:59)

6
5
4
3
2
1

12 1 2 3 4 5 6 7 8 9 10 11 noon 1 2 3 4 5 6 7 8 9 10 11 12

⊢ 0.6 knots flood ⊣ ⊢——— 1.5 knots ebb ——— ⊢ 1.2 knots flood ⊣ ⊢ 0.5 knots e

TUE MAR 19
dawn 6:03 sunrise 6:57 sunset 7:04 dark 7:58
moonset 4:14 a.m. moonrise 2:06 p.m.

Vernal Equinox 8:06 p.m.

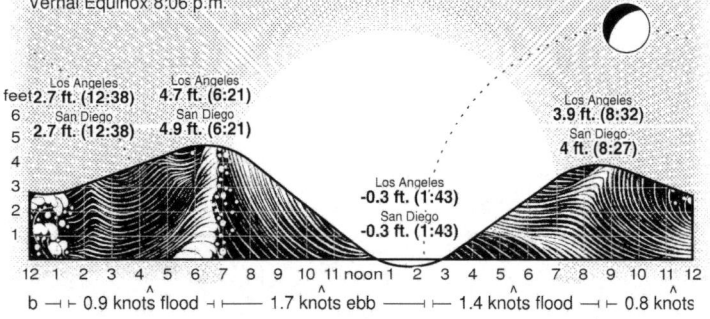

feet
Los Angeles
2.7 ft. (12:38)
San Diego
2.7 ft. (12:38)

Los Angeles
4.7 ft. (6:21)
San Diego
4.9 ft. (6:21)

Los Angeles
3.9 ft. (8:32)
San Diego
4 ft. (8:27)

Los Angeles
-0.3 ft. (1:43)
San Diego
-0.3 ft. (1:43)

6
5
4
3
2
1

12 1 2 3 4 5 6 7 8 9 10 11 noon 1 2 3 4 5 6 7 8 9 10 11 12

b ⊣ ⊢ 0.9 knots flood ⊣ ⊢——— 1.7 knots ebb ——— ⊢ 1.4 knots flood ⊣ ⊢ 0.8 knots

WED MAR 20
dawn 6:02 sunrise 6:56 sunset 7:05 dark 7:59
moonset 4:52 a.m. moonrise 3:06 p.m.

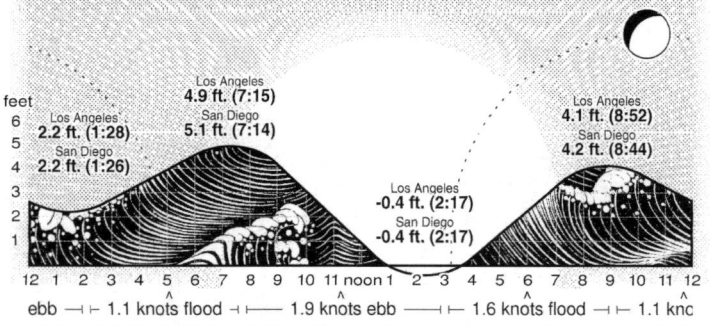

feet
Los Angeles
2.2 ft. (1:28)
San Diego
2.2 ft. (1:26)

Los Angeles
4.9 ft. (7:15)
San Diego
5.1 ft. (7:14)

Los Angeles
4.1 ft. (8:52)
San Diego
4.2 ft. (8:44)

Los Angeles
-0.4 ft. (2:17)
San Diego
-0.4 ft. (2:17)

6
5
4
3
2
1

12 1 2 3 4 5 6 7 8 9 10 11 noon 1 2 3 4 5 6 7 8 9 10 11 12

ebb ⊣ ⊢ 1.1 knots flood ⊣ ⊢——— 1.9 knots ebb ——— ⊢ 1.6 knots flood ⊣ ⊢ 1.1 knc

THU MAR 21
dawn 6:01 sunrise 6:55 sunset 7:06 dark 8:00
moonset 5:24 a.m. moonrise 4:05 p.m.

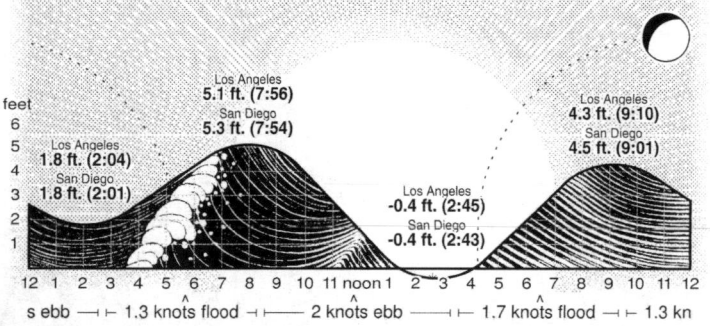

feet
Los Angeles
5.1 ft. (7:56)
San Diego
5.3 ft. (7:54)

Los Angeles
4.3 ft. (9:10)
San Diego
4.5 ft. (9:01)

Los Angeles
1.8 ft. (2:04)
San Diego
1.8 ft. (2:01)

Los Angeles
-0.4 ft. (2:45)
San Diego
-0.4 ft. (2:43)

6
5
4
3
2
1

12 1 2 3 4 5 6 7 8 9 10 11 noon 1 2 3 4 5 6 7 8 9 10 11 12

s ebb ⊣ ⊢ 1.3 knots flood ⊣ ⊢——— 2 knots ebb ——— ⊣ ⊢ 1.7 knots flood ⊣ ⊢ 1.3 kn

FRI MAR 22

dawn 5:59 sunrise 6:53 sunset 7:07 dark 8:01
moonset 5:52 a.m. moonrise 5:02 p.m.

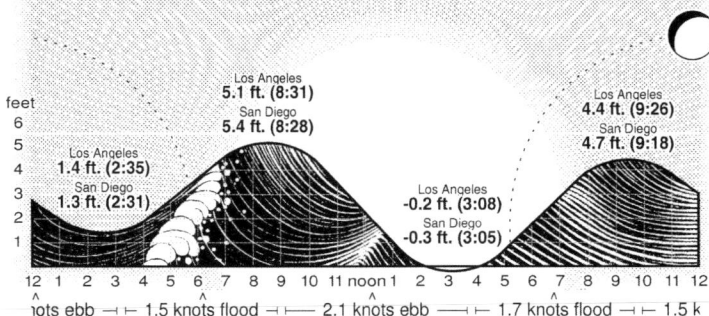

feet
6
5
4
3
2
1

Los Angeles
5.1 ft. (8:31)
San Diego
5.4 ft. (8:28)

Los Angeles
1.4 ft. (2:35)
San Diego
1.3 ft. (2:31)

Los Angeles
-0.2 ft. (3:08)
San Diego
-0.3 ft. (3:05)

Los Angeles
4.4 ft. (9:26)
San Diego
4.7 ft. (9:18)

12 1 2 3 4 5 6 7 8 9 10 11 noon 1 2 3 4 5 6 7 8 9 10 11 12

1ots ebb → ⊢ 1.5 knots flood → ⊢ 2.1 knots ebb —→ ⊢ 1.7 knots flood → ⊢ 1.5 k

SAT MAR 23

dawn 5:58 sunrise 6:52 sunset 7:07 dark 8:02
moonset 6:17 a.m. moonrise 5:58 p.m.

apogee

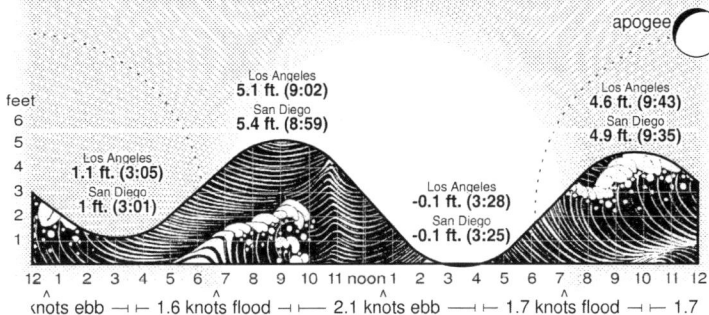

feet
6
5
4
3
2
1

Los Angeles
5.1 ft. (9:02)
San Diego
5.4 ft. (8:59)

Los Angeles
1.1 ft. (3:05)
San Diego
1 ft. (3:01)

Los Angeles
-0.1 ft. (3:28)
San Diego
-0.1 ft. (3:25)

Los Angeles
4.6 ft. (9:43)
San Diego
4.9 ft. (9:35)

12 1 2 3 4 5 6 7 8 9 10 11 noon 1 2 3 4 5 6 7 8 9 10 11 12

knots ebb —→ ⊢ 1.6 knots flood → ⊢ 2.1 knots ebb —→ ⊢ 1.7 knots flood → ⊢ 1.7

SUN MAR 24

dawn 5:56 sunrise 6:50 sunset 7:08 dark 8:02
moonset 6:40 a.m. moonrise 6:53 p.m.

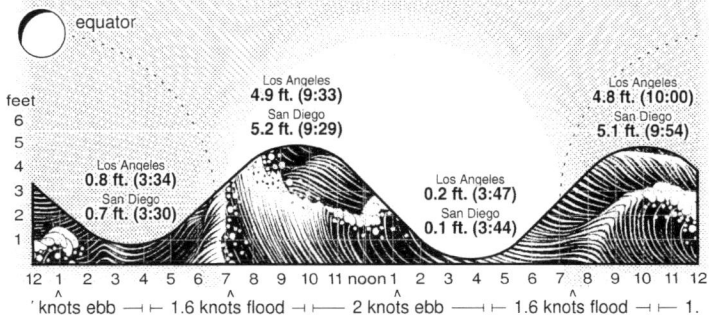 equator

feet
6
5
4
3
2
1

Los Angeles
4.9 ft. (9:33)
San Diego
5.2 ft. (9:29)

Los Angeles
0.8 ft. (3:34)
San Diego
0.7 ft. (3:30)

Los Angeles
0.2 ft. (3:47)
San Diego
0.1 ft. (3:44)

Los Angeles
4.8 ft. (10:00)
San Diego
5.1 ft. (9:54)

12 1 2 3 4 5 6 7 8 9 10 11 noon 1 2 3 4 5 6 7 8 9 10 11 12

' knots ebb —→ ⊢ 1.6 knots flood → ⊢ 2 knots ebb —→ ⊢ 1.6 knots flood → ⊢ 1.

Vernal Equinox The Vernal equinox occurs the moment when the Sun is exactly above the equator and periods of day and night are of approximately equal length. Equinox comes from Latin and means "equal nights." The equinox marks the first day of Spring in the Northern Hemisphere. copyright 2023 Pacific Publishers, L.L.C. WWW.TIDELOG.COM

MON MAR 25

dawn 5:55 sunrise 6:49 sunset 7:09 dark 8:03
moonset 7:04 a.m. moonrise 7:48 p.m.

Penumbral Lunar Eclipse

Full Moon 12:00 a.m.

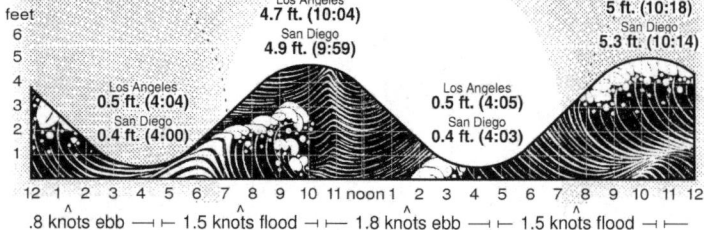

feet

6
5
4
3
2
1

Los Angeles
4.7 ft. (10:04)
San Diego
4.9 ft. (9:59)

Los Angeles
5 ft. (10:18)
San Diego
5.3 ft. (10:14)

Los Angeles
0.5 ft. (4:04)
San Diego
0.4 ft. (4:00)

Los Angeles
0.5 ft. (4:05)
San Diego
0.4 ft. (4:03)

12 1 2 3 4 5 6 7 8 9 10 11 noon 1 2 3 4 5 6 7 8 9 10 11 12

.8 knots ebb ⟶ ⊢ 1.5 knots flood ⟶ ⊢ 1.8 knots ebb ⟶ ⊢ 1.5 knots flood ⟶ ⊢

TUE MAR 26

dawn 5:54 sunrise 6:48 sunset 7:10 dark 8:04
moonset 7:27 a.m. moonrise 8:45 p.m.

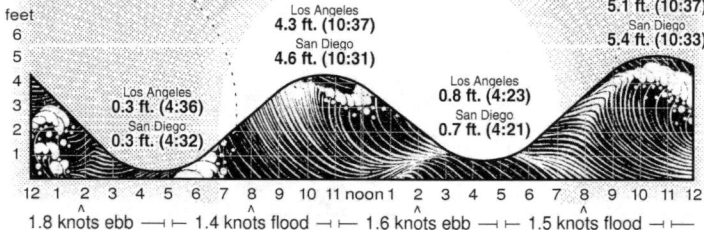

feet

6
5
4
3
2
1

Los Angeles
4.3 ft. (10:37)
San Diego
4.6 ft. (10:31)

Los Angeles
5.1 ft. (10:37)
San Diego
5.4 ft. (10:33)

Los Angeles
0.3 ft. (4:36)
San Diego
0.3 ft. (4:32)

Los Angeles
0.8 ft. (4:23)
San Diego
0.7 ft. (4:21)

12 1 2 3 4 5 6 7 8 9 10 11 noon 1 2 3 4 5 6 7 8 9 10 11 12

1.8 knots ebb ⟶ ⊢ 1.4 knots flood ⟶ ⊢ 1.6 knots ebb ⟶ ⊢ 1.5 knots flood ⟶ ⊢

WED MAR 27

dawn 5:52 sunrise 6:46 sunset 7:10 dark 8:05
moonset 7:53 a.m. moonrise 9:43 p.m.

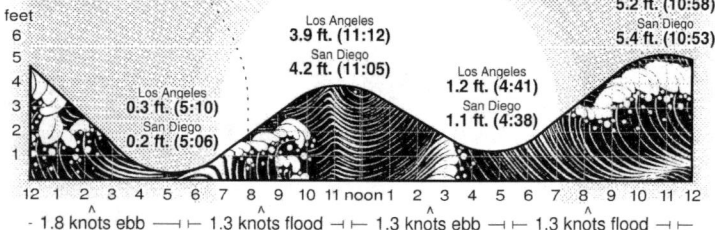

feet

6
5
4
3
2
1

Los Angeles
3.9 ft. (11:12)
San Diego
4.2 ft. (11:05)

Los Angeles
5.2 ft. (10:58)
San Diego
5.4 ft. (10:53)

Los Angeles
0.3 ft. (5:10)
San Diego
0.2 ft. (5:06)

Los Angeles
1.2 ft. (4:41)
San Diego
1.1 ft. (4:38)

12 1 2 3 4 5 6 7 8 9 10 11 noon 1 2 3 4 5 6 7 8 9 10 11 12

- 1.8 knots ebb ⟶ ⊢ 1.3 knots flood ⟶ ⊢ 1.3 knots ebb ⟶ ⊢ 1.3 knots flood ⟶ ⊢

THU MAR 28

dawn 5:51 sunrise 6:45 sunset 7:11 dark 8:06
moonset 8:22 a.m. moonrise 10:44 p.m.

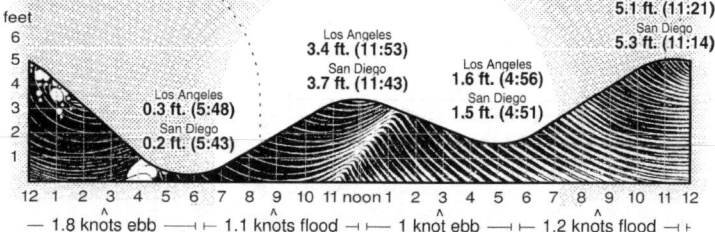

feet

6
5
4
3
2
1

Los Angeles
3.4 ft. (11:53)
San Diego
3.7 ft. (11:43)

Los Angeles
5.1 ft. (11:21)
San Diego
5.3 ft. (11:14)

Los Angeles
0.3 ft. (5:48)
San Diego
0.2 ft. (5:43)

Los Angeles
1.6 ft. (4:56)
San Diego
1.5 ft. (4:51)

12 1 2 3 4 5 6 7 8 9 10 11 noon 1 2 3 4 5 6 7 8 9 10 11 12

— 1.8 knots ebb ⟶ ⊢ 1.1 knots flood ⟶ ⊢ 1 knot ebb ⟶ ⊢ 1.2 knots flood ⟶ ⊢

FRI MAR 29

dawn 5:49 sunrise 6:44 sunset 7:12 dark 8:06
moonset 8:56 a.m. moonrise 11:47 p.m.

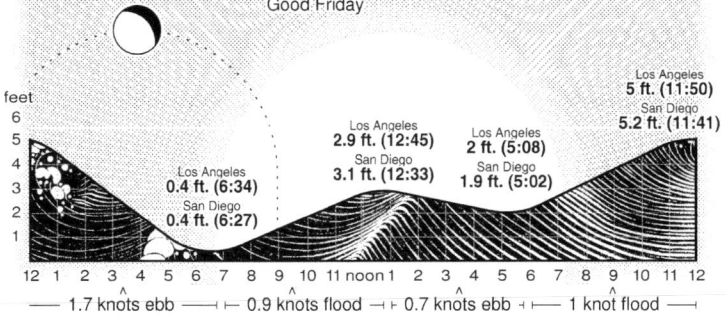

Good Friday

feet

Los Angeles
5 ft. (11:50)
San Diego
5.2 ft. (11:41)

Los Angeles
2.9 ft. (12:45)
San Diego
3.1 ft. (12:33)

Los Angeles
2 ft. (5:08)
San Diego
1.9 ft. (5:02)

Los Angeles
0.4 ft. (6:34)
San Diego
0.4 ft. (6:27)

12 1 2 3 4 5 6 7 8 9 10 11 noon 1 2 3 4 5 6 7 8 9 10 11 12

— 1.7 knots ebb — ⊢ 0.9 knots flood → ⊢ 0.7 knots ebb → ⊢— 1 knot flood —

SAT MAR 30

dawn 5:48 sunrise 6:42 sunset 7:13 dark 8:07
moonset 9:36 a.m.

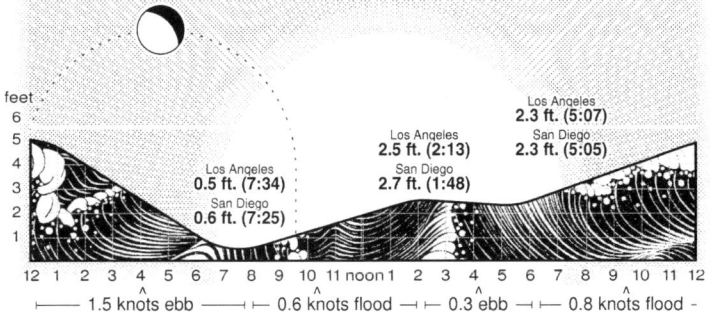

feet

Los Angeles
2.3 ft. (5:07)
San Diego
2.3 ft. (5:05)

Los Angeles
2.5 ft. (2:13)
San Diego
2.7 ft. (1:48)

Los Angeles
0.5 ft. (7:34)
San Diego
0.6 ft. (7:25)

12 1 2 3 4 5 6 7 8 9 10 11 noon 1 2 3 4 5 6 7 8 9 10 11 12

⊢— 1.5 knots ebb — ⊢ 0.6 knots flood → ⊢ 0.3 ebb → ⊢ 0.8 knots flood -

SUN MAR 31

dawn 5:47 sunrise 6:41 sunset 7:13 dark 8:08
moonrise 12:50 a.m. moonset 10:24 a.m.

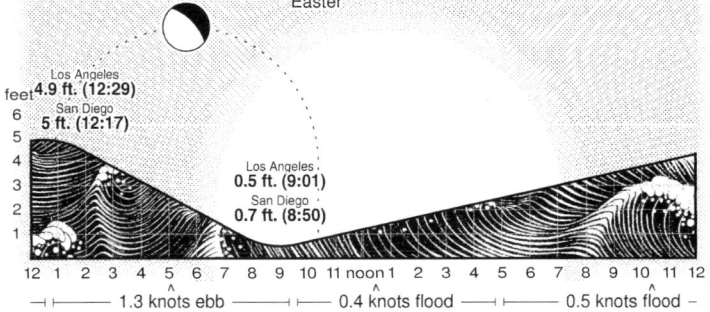

Easter

Los Angeles
4.9 ft. (12:29)
feet
San Diego
5 ft. (12:17)

Los Angeles
0.5 ft. (9:01)
San Diego
0.7 ft. (8:50)

12 1 2 3 4 5 6 7 8 9 10 11 noon 1 2 3 4 5 6 7 8 9 10 11 12

⊢⊢— 1.3 knots ebb — ⊢— 0.4 knots flood — ⊢— 0.5 knots flood -

Penumbral Lunar Eclipse The word penumbra is derived from the Latin phrase "paene" meaning "almost, nearly." The Mar 25th eclipse occurs as the Moon passes through the outer and fainter part of the Earth's shadow, resulting in a subtle and more difficult to observe darkening of the Moon. While the Moon will almost be completely in the Earth's shadow, some people may not be able to perceive any difference in the Moon's apperance. The eclipse will be visible all across the night side of the Earth. On the west coast, the Full Moon enters the penumbra on Mar 24 at 9:51 p.m. and reaches "maximum" eclipse on Mar 25 at 12:12 a.m. and exits the penumbra at 2:34 a.m.

MON APR 1
dawn 5:45 sunrise 6:40 sunset 7:14 dark 8:09
moonrise 1:50 a.m. moonset 11:21 a.m.

South

April Fools' Day

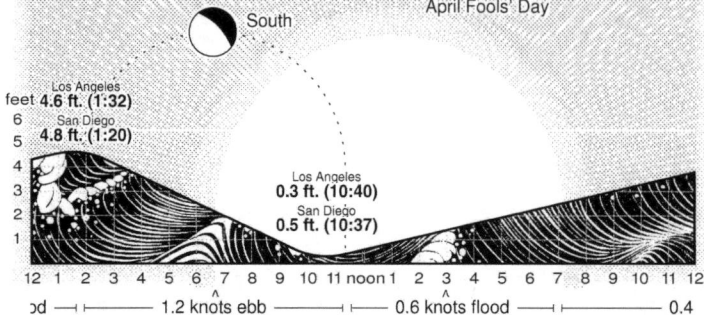

feet
Los Angeles
4.6 ft. (1:32)
San Diego
4.8 ft. (1:20)

Los Angeles
0.3 ft. (10:40)
San Diego
0.5 ft. (10:37)

12 1 2 3 4 5 6 7 8 9 10 11 noon 1 2 3 4 5 6 7 8 9 10 11 12

ood ⊢——— 1.2 knots ebb ———— ⊢— 0.6 knots flood ——— ⊢——— 0.4

TUE APR 2
dawn 5:44 sunrise 6:38 sunset 7:15 dark 8:10
moonrise 2:45 a.m. moonset 12:26 p.m.

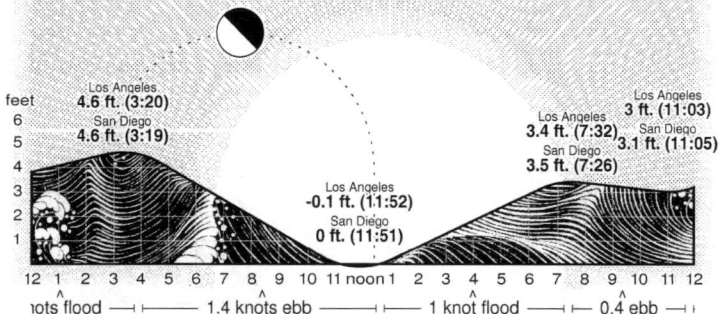

feet
Los Angeles
4.6 ft. (3:20)
San Diego
4.6 ft. (3:19)

Los Angeles
3.4 ft. (7:32)
San Diego
3.5 ft. (7:26)

Los Angeles
3 ft. (11:03)
San Diego
3.1 ft. (11:05)

Los Angeles
-0.1 ft. (11:52)
San Diego
0 ft. (11:51)

12 1 2 3 4 5 6 7 8 9 10 11 noon 1 2 3 4 5 6 7 8 9 10 11 12

nots flood —— ⊢—— 1.4 knots ebb ——— ⊢— 1 knot flood —— ⊢— 0.4 ebb —⊣

WED APR 3
dawn 5:42 sunrise 6:37 sunset 7:16 dark 8:11
moonrise 3:34 a.m. moonset 1:36 p.m.

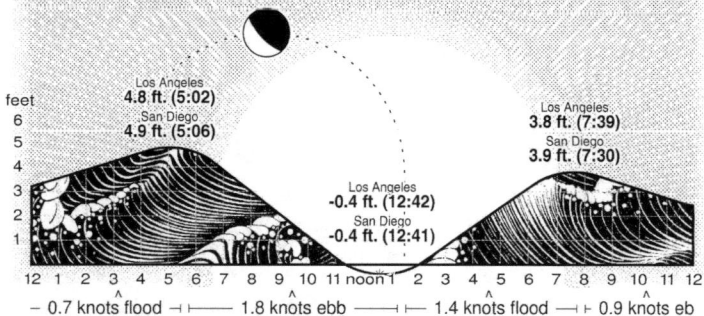

feet
Los Angeles
4.8 ft. (5:02)
San Diego
4.9 ft. (5:06)

Los Angeles
3.8 ft. (7:39)
San Diego
3.9 ft. (7:30)

Los Angeles
-0.4 ft. (12:42)
San Diego
-0.4 ft. (12:41)

12 1 2 3 4 5 6 7 8 9 10 11 noon 1 2 3 4 5 6 7 8 9 10 11 12

– 0.7 knots flood ⊣ ⊢—— 1.8 knots ebb ——— ⊣ ⊢— 1.4 knots flood —⊣ ⊢ 0.9 eb

THU APR 4
dawn 5:41 sunrise 6:36 sunset 7:16 dark 8:11
moonrise 4:16 a.m. moonset 2:49 p.m.

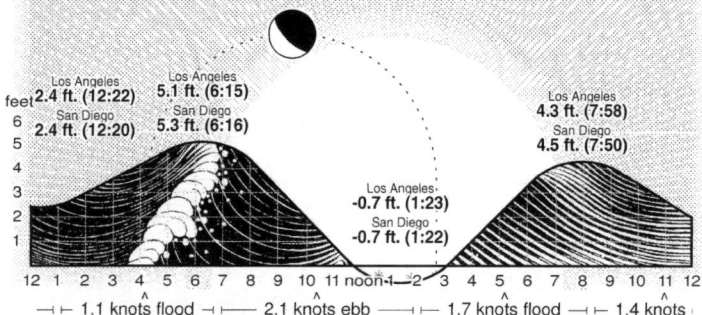

feet
Los Angeles
2.4 ft. (12:22)
San Diego
2.4 ft. (12:20)

Los Angeles
5.1 ft. (6:15)
San Diego
5.3 ft. (6:16)

Los Angeles
4.3 ft. (7:58)
San Diego
4.5 ft. (7:50)

Los Angeles
-0.7 ft. (1:23)
San Diego
-0.7 ft. (1:22)

12 1 2 3 4 5 6 7 8 9 10 11 noon 1 2 3 4 5 6 7 8 9 10 11 12

⊣ ⊢ 1.1 knots flood ⊣ ⊢—— 2.1 knots ebb ——— ⊣ ⊢ 1.7 knots flood —⊣ ⊢ 1.4 knots

FRI APR 5
dawn 5:39 sunrise 6:34 sunset 7:17 dark 8:12
moonrise 4:53 a.m. moonset 4:02 p.m.

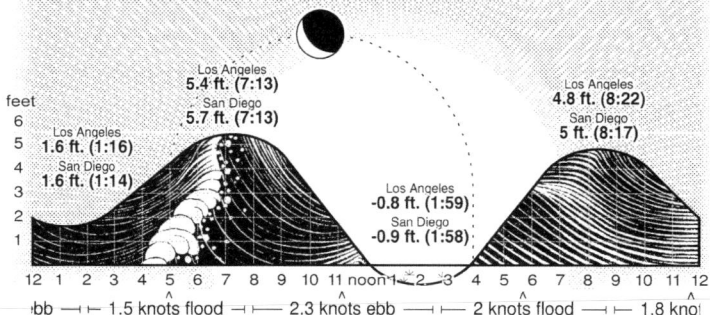

feet
6
5
4
3
2
1

Los Angeles
5.4 ft. (7:13)
San Diego
5.7 ft. (7:13)

Los Angeles
1.6 ft. (1:16)
San Diego
1.6 ft. (1:14)

Los Angeles
-0.8 ft. (1:59)
San Diego
-0.9 ft. (1:58)

Los Angeles
4.8 ft. (8:22)
San Diego
5 ft. (8:17)

12 1 2 3 4 5 6 7 8 9 10 11 noon 1 2 3 4 5 6 7 8 9 10 11 12

bb —⊢— 1.5 knots flood —⊣—— 2.3 knots ebb —— ⊢— 2 knots flood —⊣— 1.8 knot

SAT APR 6
dawn 5:38 sunrise 6:33 sunset 7:18 dark 8:13
moonrise 5:26 a.m. moonset 5:14 p.m.

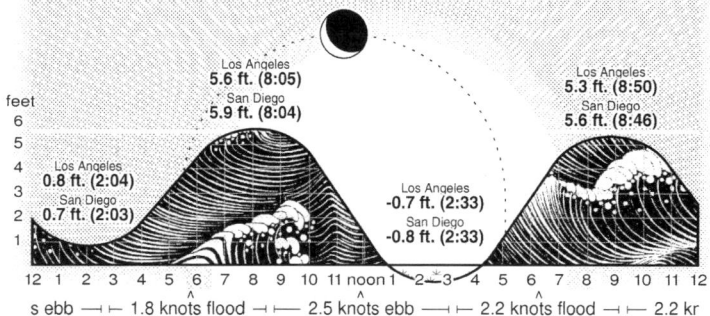

feet
6
5
4
3
2
1

Los Angeles
5.6 ft. (8:05)
San Diego
5.9 ft. (8:04)

Los Angeles
0.8 ft. (2:04)
San Diego
0.7 ft. (2:03)

Los Angeles
-0.7 ft. (2:33)
San Diego
-0.8 ft. (2:33)

Los Angeles
5.3 ft. (8:50)
San Diego
5.6 ft. (8:46)

12 1 2 3 4 5 6 7 8 9 10 11 noon 1 2 3 4 5 6 7 8 9 10 11 12

s ebb —⊣— 1.8 knots flood —⊣— 2.5 knots ebb —— ⊢— 2.2 knots flood —— 2.2 kr

SUN APR 7
dawn 5:37 sunrise 6:32 sunset 7:19 dark 8:14
moonrise 5:57 a.m. moonset 6:26 p.m.

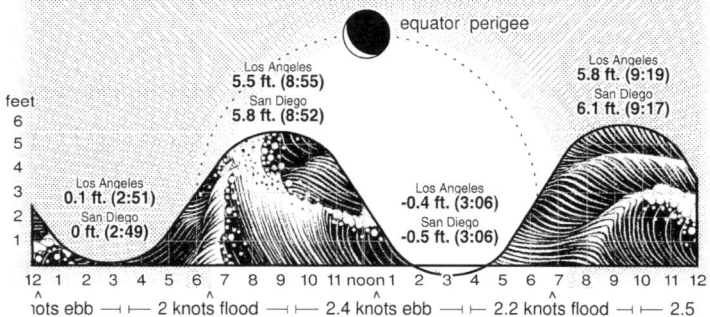

equator perigee

feet
6
5
4
3
2
1

Los Angeles
5.5 ft. (8:55)
San Diego
5.8 ft. (8:52)

Los Angeles
0.1 ft. (2:51)
San Diego
0 ft. (2:49)

Los Angeles
-0.4 ft. (3:06)
San Diego
-0.5 ft. (3:06)

Los Angeles
5.8 ft. (9:19)
San Diego
6.1 ft. (9:17)

12 1 2 3 4 5 6 7 8 9 10 11 noon 1 2 3 4 5 6 7 8 9 10 11 12

ots ebb —⊢— 2 knots flood —⊣— 2.4 knots ebb —— ⊢— 2.2 knots flood —⊣— 2.5

Ⓢ Ⓥ Ⓙ
Ⓜ

MON APR 8

dawn 5:35 sunrise 6:31 sunset 7:19 dark 8:15
moonrise 6:28 a.m. moonset 7:39 p.m.

Total Solar Eclipse

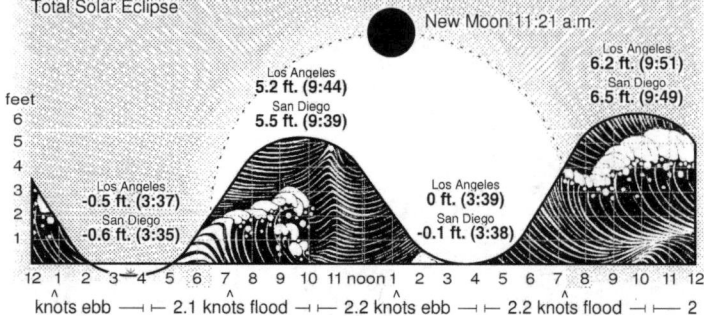

New Moon 11:21 a.m.

Los Angeles **5.2 ft. (9:44)**
San Diego **5.5 ft. (9:39)**

Los Angeles **6.2 ft. (9:51)**
San Diego **6.5 ft. (9:49)**

feet
6
5
4
3
2
1

Los Angeles **-0.5 ft. (3:37)**
San Diego **-0.6 ft. (3:35)**

Los Angeles **0 ft. (3:39)**
San Diego **-0.1 ft. (3:38)**

12 1 2 3 4 5 6 7 8 9 10 11 noon 1 2 3 4 5 6 7 8 9 10 11 12

knots ebb — ⊢ 2.1 knots flood — ⊢ 2.2 knots ebb — ⊢ 2.2 knots flood — ⊢ 2

TUE APR 9

dawn 5:34 sunrise 6:29 sunset 7:20 dark 8:16
moonrise 7:00 a.m. moonset 8:52 p.m.

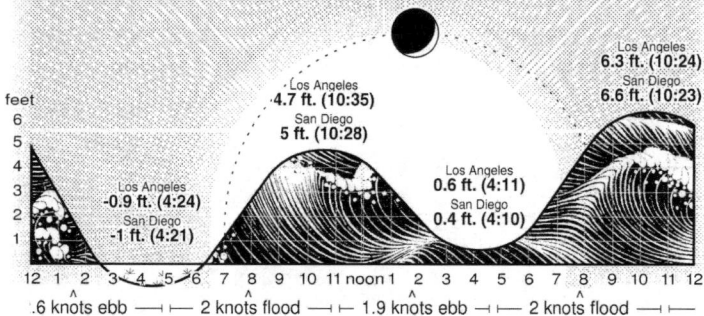

Los Angeles **4.7 ft. (10:35)**
San Diego **5 ft. (10:28)**

Los Angeles **6.3 ft. (10:24)**
San Diego **6.6 ft. (10:23)**

feet
6
5
4
3
2
1

Los Angeles **-0.9 ft. (4:24)**
San Diego **-1 ft. (4:21)**

Los Angeles **0.6 ft. (4:11)**
San Diego **0.4 ft. (4:10)**

12 1 2 3 4 5 6 7 8 9 10 11 noon 1 2 3 4 5 6 7 8 9 10 11 12

.6 knots ebb — ⊢ 2 knots flood — ⊢ 1.9 knots ebb — ⊢ 2 knots flood — ⊢

WED APR 10

dawn 5:32 sunrise 6:28 sunset 7:21 dark 8:17
moonrise 7:36 a.m. moonset 10:05 p.m.

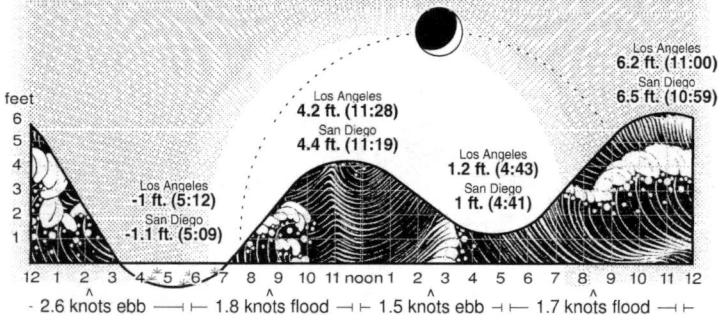

Los Angeles **4.2 ft. (11:28)**
San Diego **4.4 ft. (11:19)**

Los Angeles **6.2 ft. (11:00)**
San Diego **6.5 ft. (10:59)**

feet
6
5
4
3
2
1

Los Angeles **-1 ft. (5:12)**
San Diego **-1.1 ft. (5:09)**

Los Angeles **1.2 ft. (4:43)**
San Diego **1 ft. (4:41)**

12 1 2 3 4 5 6 7 8 9 10 11 noon 1 2 3 4 5 6 7 8 9 10 11 12

- 2.6 knots ebb — ⊢ 1.8 knots flood — ⊢ 1.5 knots ebb — ⊢ 1.7 knots flood — ⊢ ⊢

THU APR 11

dawn 5:31 sunrise 6:27 sunset 7:22 dark 8:17
moonrise 8:17 a.m. moonset 11:16 p.m.

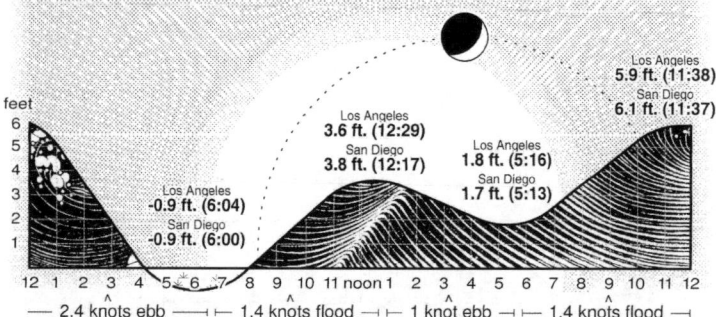

Los Angeles **3.6 ft. (12:29)**
San Diego **3.8 ft. (12:17)**

Los Angeles **5.9 ft. (11:38)**
San Diego **6.1 ft. (11:37)**

feet
6
5
4
3
2
1

Los Angeles **-0.9 ft. (6:04)**
San Diego **-0.9 ft. (6:00)**

Los Angeles **1.8 ft. (5:16)**
San Diego **1.7 ft. (5:13)**

12 1 2 3 4 5 6 7 8 9 10 11 noon 1 2 3 4 5 6 7 8 9 10 11 12

— 2.4 knots ebb — ⊢ 1.4 knots flood — ⊢ 1 knot ebb — ⊢ 1.4 knots flood — ⊣

FRI APR 12
dawn 5:30 sunrise 6:25 sunset 7:22 dark 8:18
moonrise 9:04 a.m.

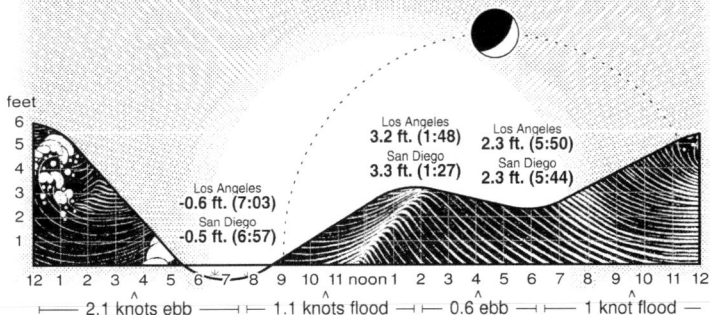

feet
6
5
4
3
2
1

Los Angeles
3.2 ft. (1:48)
San Diego
3.3 ft. (1:27)

Los Angeles
2.3 ft. (5:50)
San Diego
2.3 ft. (5:44)

Los Angeles
-0.6 ft. (7:03)
San Diego
-0.5 ft. (6:57)

12 1 2 3 4 5 6 7 8 9 10 11 noon 1 2 3 4 5 6 7 8 9 10 11 12

├── 2.1 knots ebb ──┤├── 1.1 knots flood ──┤├── 0.6 ebb ──┤├── 1 knot flood ──

SAT APR 13
dawn 5:28 sunrise 6:24 sunset 7:23 dark 8:19
moonset 12:22 a.m. moonrise 9:57 a.m.

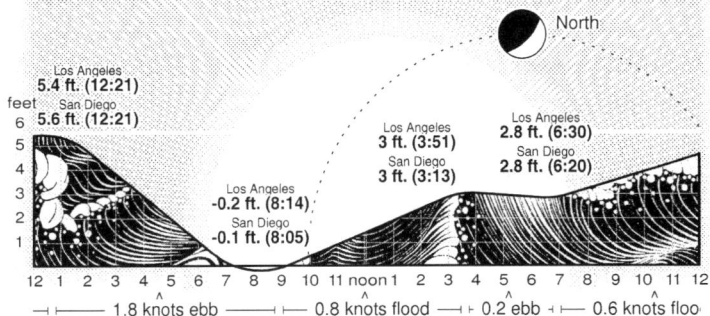

North

Los Angeles
5.4 ft. (12:21)
feet San Diego
6   **5.6 ft. (12:21)**
5
4
3
2
1

Los Angeles
3 ft. (3:51)
San Diego
3 ft. (3:13)

Los Angeles
2.8 ft. (6:30)
San Diego
2.8 ft. (6:20)

Los Angeles
-0.2 ft. (8:14)
San Diego
-0.1 ft. (8:05)

12 1 2 3 4 5 6 7 8 9 10 11 noon 1 2 3 4 5 6 7 8 9 10 11 12

├─┤├── 1.8 knots ebb ──┤├── 0.8 knots flood ──┤├ 0.2 ebb ─┤├── 0.6 knots floo

SUN APR 14
dawn 5:27 sunrise 6:23 sunset 7:24 dark 8:20
moonset 1:21 a.m. moonrise 10:55 a.m.

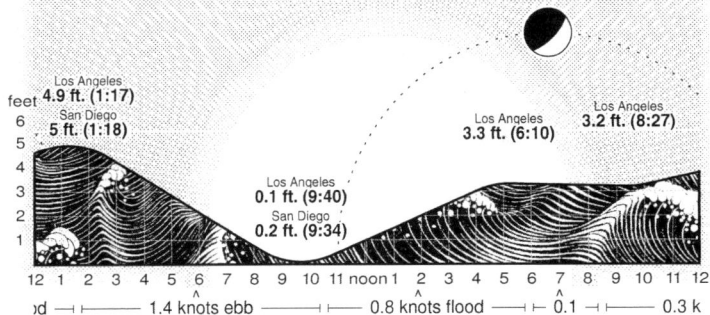

Los Angeles **4.9 ft. (1:17)**
feet San Diego
6   **5 ft. (1:18)**
5
4
3
2
1

Los Angeles
3.3 ft. (6:10)

Los Angeles
3.2 ft. (8:27)

Los Angeles
0.1 ft. (9:40)
San Diego
0.2 ft. (9:34)

12 1 2 3 4 5 6 7 8 9 10 11 noon 1 2 3 4 5 6 7 8 9 10 11 12

od ─┤├── 1.4 knots ebb ──┤├── 0.8 knots flood ──┤├ 0.1 ─┤├── 0.3 k

Total Solar Eclipse The April 8th eclipse presents an almost once in
a lifetime event for viewers in the eclipse's path of totality which
begins in the Pacific ocean below Baja and travels through the south
eastern U.S. on a north easterly path to Nova Scotia. Those of us out of
the path of totality will see a partial eclipse with the Moon partially
blocking out the Sun. On the west coast, the partial eclipse begins shortly
after noon, with the maximum eclipse at 1:14 p.m. and ending at 2:25 p.m.
for a duration of 2 hours 17 minutes with obsuration of 51.3%.
NOTE: As with all solar events, vision protection is warranted.

MON APR 15
dawn 5:26 sunrise 6:22 sunset 7:25 dark 8:21
moonset 2:10 a.m. moonrise 11:56 a.m.

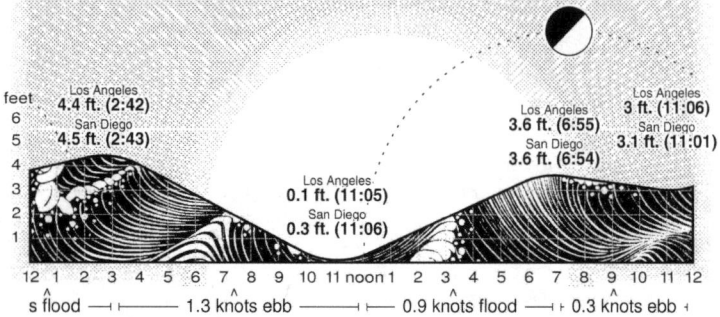

feet

Los Angeles
4.4 ft. (2:42)
San Diego
4.5 ft. (2:43)

Los Angeles
0.1 ft. (11:05)
San Diego
0.3 ft. (11:06)

Los Angeles
3.6 ft. (6:55)
San Diego
3.6 ft. (6:54)

Los Angeles
3 ft. (11:06)
San Diego
3.1 ft. (11:01)

6
5
4
3
2
1

12 1 2 3 4 5 6 7 8 9 10 11 noon 1 2 3 4 5 6 7 8 9 10 11 12

s flood ⊢ ⊢ 1.3 knots ebb ⊢ ⊢ 0.9 knots flood ⊣ ⊢ 0.3 knots ebb ⊣

TUE APR 16
dawn 5:24 sunrise 6:20 sunset 7:25 dark 8:22
moonset 2:51 a.m. moonrise 12:58 p.m.

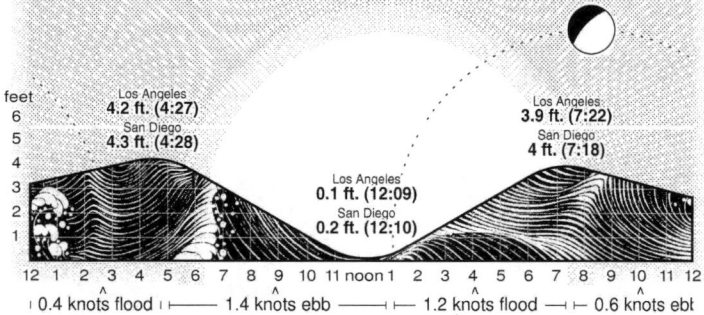

feet

Los Angeles
4.2 ft. (4:27)
San Diego
4.3 ft. (4:28)

Los Angeles
0.1 ft. (12:09)
San Diego
0.2 ft. (12:10)

Los Angeles
3.9 ft. (7:22)
San Diego
4 ft. (7:18)

6
5
4
3
2
1

12 1 2 3 4 5 6 7 8 9 10 11 noon 1 2 3 4 5 6 7 8 9 10 11 12

⊢ 0.4 knots flood ⊣ ⊢ 1.4 knots ebb ⊢ ⊢ 1.2 knots flood ⊣ ⊢ 0.6 knots ebb ⊦

WED APR 17
dawn 5:23 sunrise 6:19 sunset 7:26 dark 8:23
moonset 3:26 a.m. moonrise 1:57 p.m.

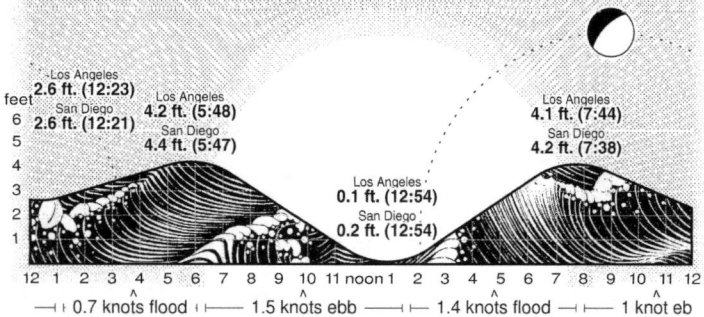

Los Angeles
2.6 ft. (12:23)
San Diego
2.6 ft. (12:21)

feet

Los Angeles
4.2 ft. (5:48)
San Diego
4.4 ft. (5:47)

Los Angeles
0.1 ft. (12:54)
San Diego
0.2 ft. (12:54)

Los Angeles
4.1 ft. (7:44)
San Diego
4.2 ft. (7:38)

6
5
4
3
2
1

12 1 2 3 4 5 6 7 8 9 10 11 noon 1 2 3 4 5 6 7 8 9 10 11 12

⊢ ⊣ 0.7 knots flood ⊢ ⊢ 1.5 knots ebb ⊢ ⊢ 1.4 knots flood ⊣ ⊢ 1 knot eb

THU APR 18
dawn 5:22 sunrise 6:18 sunset 7:27 dark 8:24
moonset 3:55 a.m. moonrise 2:55 p.m.

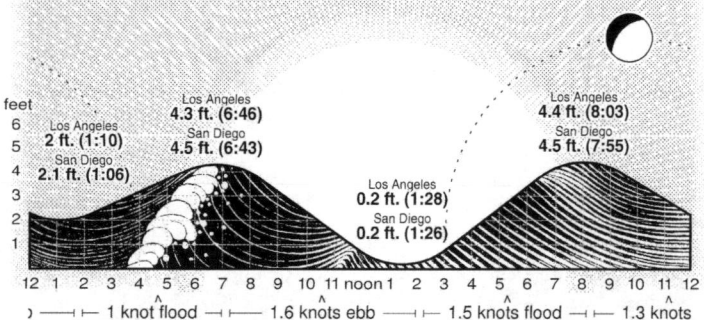

feet

Los Angeles
2 ft. (1:10)
San Diego
2.1 ft. (1:06)

Los Angeles
4.3 ft. (6:46)
San Diego
4.5 ft. (6:43)

Los Angeles
0.2 ft. (1:28)
San Diego
0.2 ft. (1:26)

Los Angeles
4.4 ft. (8:03)
San Diego
4.5 ft. (7:55)

6
5
4
3
2
1

12 1 2 3 4 5 6 7 8 9 10 11 noon 1 2 3 4 5 6 7 8 9 10 11 12

) ⊢ ⊢ 1 knot flood ⊣ ⊢ 1.6 knots ebb ⊢ ⊢ 1.5 knots flood ⊣ ⊢ 1.3 knots

FRI APR 19

dawn 5:20 sunrise 6:17 sunset 7:28 dark 8:25
moonset 4:21 a.m. moonrise 3:51 p.m.

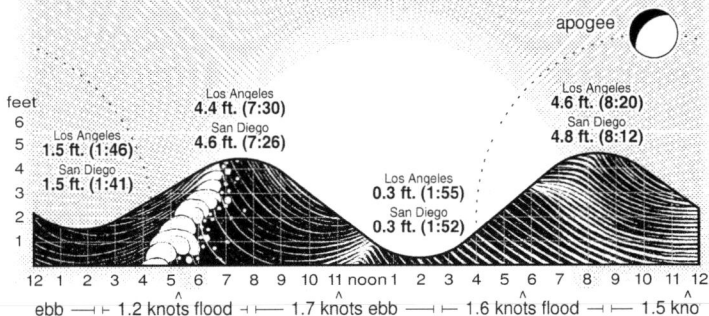

apogee

feet
6
5
4
3
2
1

Los Angeles
1.5 ft. (1:46)
San Diego
1.5 ft. (1:41)

Los Angeles
4.4 ft. (7:30)
San Diego
4.6 ft. (7:26)

Los Angeles
0.3 ft. (1:55)
San Diego
0.3 ft. (1:52)

Los Angeles
4.6 ft. (8:20)
San Diego
4.8 ft. (8:12)

12 1 2 3 4 5 6 7 8 9 10 11 noon 1 2 3 4 5 6 7 8 9 10 11 12

ebb ⊢ 1.2 knots flood ⊣ ⊢ 1.7 knots ebb ⊣ 1.6 knots flood ⊣ ⊢ 1.5 kno

SAT APR 20

dawn 5:19 sunrise 6:16 sunset 7:28 dark 8:25
moonset 4:45 a.m. moonrise 4:46 p.m.

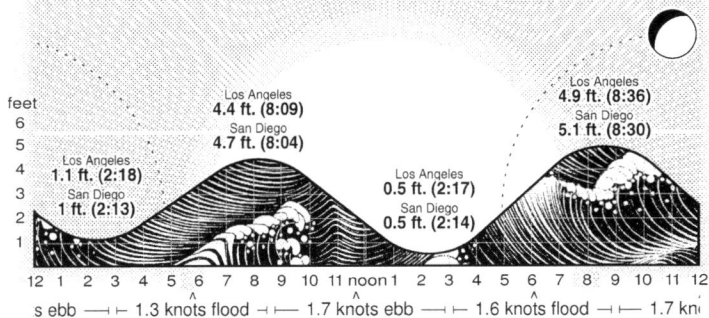

feet
6
5
4
3
2
1

Los Angeles
1.1 ft. (2:18)
San Diego
1 ft. (2:13)

Los Angeles
4.4 ft. (8:09)
San Diego
4.7 ft. (8:04)

Los Angeles
0.5 ft. (2:17)
San Diego
0.5 ft. (2:14)

Los Angeles
4.9 ft. (8:36)
San Diego
5.1 ft. (8:30)

12 1 2 3 4 5 6 7 8 9 10 11 noon 1 2 3 4 5 6 7 8 9 10 11 12

s ebb ⊢ 1.3 knots flood ⊣ ⊢ 1.7 knots ebb ⊣ 1.6 knots flood ⊣ ⊢ 1.7 kno

SUN APR 21

dawn 5:18 sunrise 6:15 sunset 7:29 dark 8:26
moonset 5:08 a.m. moonrise 5:41 p.m.

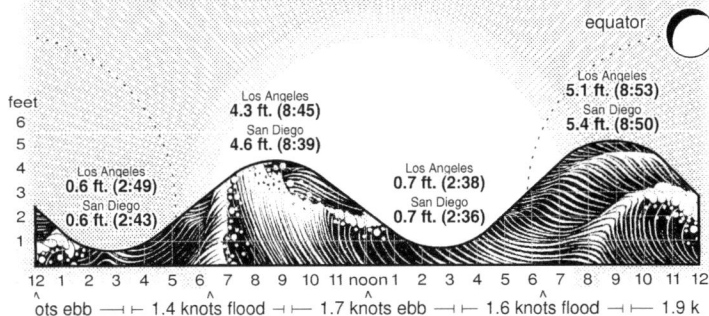

equator

feet
6
5
4
3
2
1

Los Angeles
0.6 ft. (2:49)
San Diego
0.6 ft. (2:43)

Los Angeles
4.3 ft. (8:45)
San Diego
4.6 ft. (8:39)

Los Angeles
0.7 ft. (2:38)
San Diego
0.7 ft. (2:36)

Los Angeles
5.1 ft. (8:53)
San Diego
5.4 ft. (8:50)

12 1 2 3 4 5 6 7 8 9 10 11 noon 1 2 3 4 5 6 7 8 9 10 11 12

ots ebb ⊢ 1.4 knots flood ⊣ ⊢ 1.7 knots ebb ⊣ 1.6 knots flood ⊣ ⊢ 1.9 k

Lyrids Meteor Shower The Lyrids active annually between Apr 16th - 25th with this year's peak the evening of the 21st and the following morning. The Lyrids are a well recognized shower even recorded in Chinese texts dating some 2,500 years ago. The Lyrids' radiant point, the constellation Lyra, the Harp, will rise above the eastern horizon on the 21st at approximately 10:00 p.m. The Lyrids, at peak, can produce upto 20 meteors per hour. With the waxing first quarter Moon that will be high in the sky all evening, the best opportunty to catch a glimpse of a bright fast Lyrid meteor would be after the early morning moonset and before dawn on the 22nd.

MON APR 22

dawn 5:16 sunrise 6:13 sunset 7:30 dark 8:27
moonset 5:32 a.m. moonrise 6:38 p.m.

Lyrid Meteor Peak   Earth Day

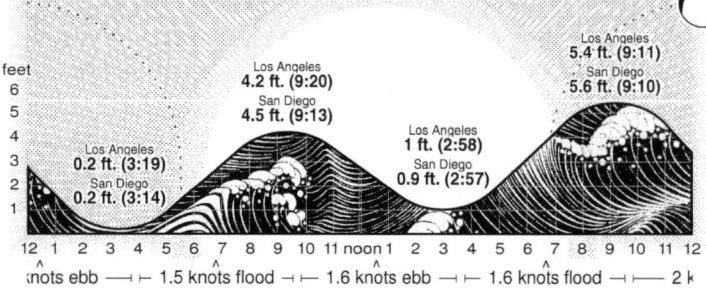

Los Angeles
5.4 ft. (9:11)
San Diego
5.6 ft. (9:10)

Los Angeles
4.2 ft. (9:20)
San Diego
4.5 ft. (9:13)

Los Angeles
1 ft. (2:58)
San Diego
0.9 ft. (2:57)

feet
6
5
4
3
2
1

Los Angeles
0.2 ft. (3:19)
San Diego
0.2 ft. (3:14)

12 1 2 3 4 5 6 7 8 9 10 11 noon 1 2 3 4 5 6 7 8 9 10 11 12

knots ebb ⟶ ⊢ 1.5 knots flood ⟶ ⊢ 1.6 knots ebb ⟶ ⊢ 1.6 knots flood ⟶ ⊢ 2 k

TUE APR 23

dawn 5:15 sunrise 6:12 sunset 7:31 dark 8:28
moonset 5:57 a.m. moonrise 7:36 p.m.

Passover

Full Moon 4:49 p.m.

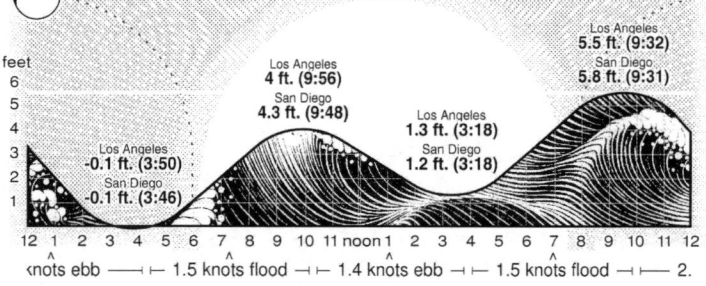

Los Angeles
5.5 ft. (9:32)
San Diego
5.8 ft. (9:31)

Los Angeles
4 ft. (9:56)
San Diego
4.3 ft. (9:48)

Los Angeles
1.3 ft. (3:18)
San Diego
1.2 ft. (3:18)

feet
6
5
4
3
2
1

Los Angeles
-0.1 ft. (3:50)
San Diego
-0.1 ft. (3:46)

12 1 2 3 4 5 6 7 8 9 10 11 noon 1 2 3 4 5 6 7 8 9 10 11 12

knots ebb ⟶ ⊢ 1.5 knots flood ⟶ ⊢ 1.4 knots ebb ⟶ ⊢ 1.5 knots flood ⟶ ⊢ 2.

WED APR 24

dawn 5:14 sunrise 6:11 sunset 7:32 dark 8:29
moonset 6:25 a.m. moonrise 8:37 p.m.

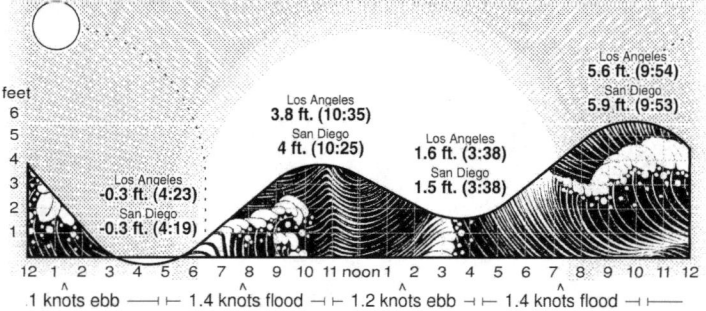

Los Angeles
5.6 ft. (9:54)
San Diego
5.9 ft. (9:53)

Los Angeles
3.8 ft. (10:35)
San Diego
4 ft. (10:25)

Los Angeles
1.6 ft. (3:38)
San Diego
1.5 ft. (3:38)

feet
6
5
4
3
2
1

Los Angeles
-0.3 ft. (4:23)
San Diego
-0.3 ft. (4:19)

12 1 2 3 4 5 6 7 8 9 10 11 noon 1 2 3 4 5 6 7 8 9 10 11 12

1 knots ebb ⟶ ⊢ 1.4 knots flood ⟶ ⊢ 1.2 knots ebb ⟶ ⊢ 1.4 knots flood ⟶ ⊢

THU APR 25

dawn 5:12 sunrise 6:10 sunset 7:32 dark 8:30
moonset 6:57 a.m. moonrise 9:40 p.m.

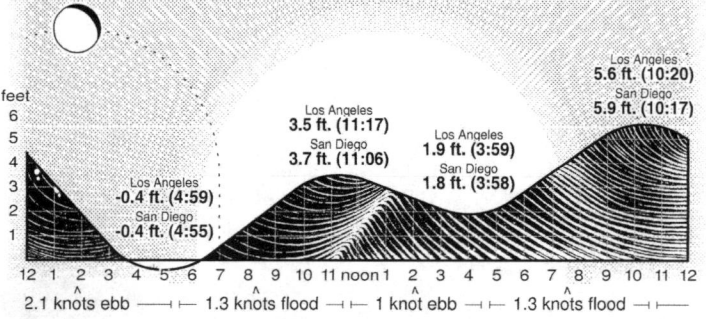

Los Angeles
5.6 ft. (10:20)
San Diego
5.9 ft. (10:17)

Los Angeles
3.5 ft. (11:17)
San Diego
3.7 ft. (11:06)

Los Angeles
1.9 ft. (3:59)
San Diego
1.8 ft. (3:58)

feet
6
5
4
3
2
1

Los Angeles
-0.4 ft. (4:59)
San Diego
-0.4 ft. (4:55)

12 1 2 3 4 5 6 7 8 9 10 11 noon 1 2 3 4 5 6 7 8 9 10 11 12

2.1 knots ebb ⟶ ⊢ 1.3 knots flood ⟶ ⊢ 1 knot ebb ⟶ ⊢ 1.3 knots flood ⟶ ⊢

FRI APR 26
dawn 5:11 sunrise 6:09 sunset 7:33 dark 8:31
moonset 7:35 a.m. moonrise 10:43 p.m.

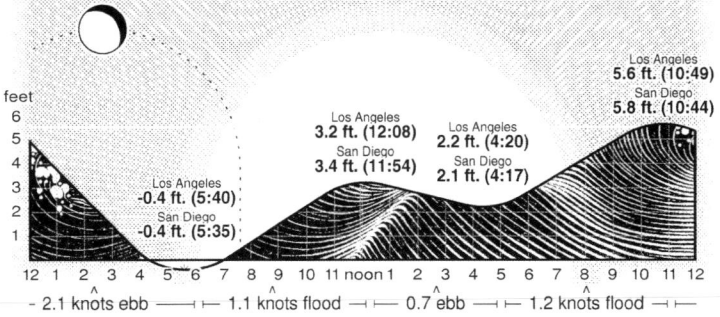

Los Angeles
5.6 ft. (10:49)
San Diego
5.8 ft. (10:44)

Los Angeles
3.2 ft. (12:08)
San Diego
3.4 ft. (11:54)

Los Angeles
2.2 ft. (4:20)
San Diego
2.1 ft. (4:17)

Los Angeles
-0.4 ft. (5:40)
San Diego
-0.4 ft. (5:35)

feet
6
5
4
3
2
1

12 1 2 3 4 5 6 7 8 9 10 11 noon 1 2 3 4 5 6 7 8 9 10 11 12

— 2.1 knots ebb ——⊢— 1.1 knots flood —⊣— 0.7 ebb —⊢— 1.2 knots flood —⊣⊢—

SAT APR 27
dawn 5:10 sunrise 6:08 sunset 7:34 dark 8:32
moonset 8:21 a.m. moonrise 11:45 p.m.

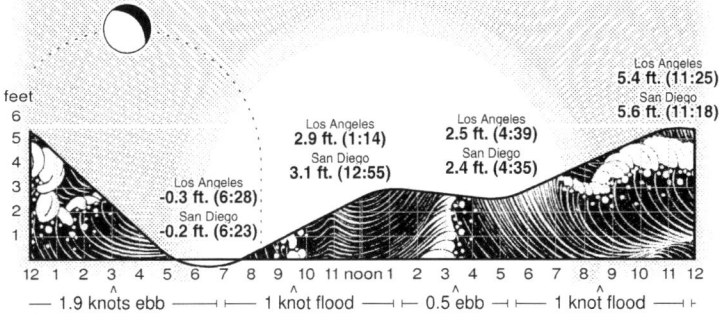

Los Angeles
5.4 ft. (11:25)
San Diego
5.6 ft. (11:18)

Los Angeles
2.9 ft. (1:14)
San Diego
3.1 ft. (12:55)

Los Angeles
2.5 ft. (4:39)
San Diego
2.4 ft. (4:35)

Los Angeles
-0.3 ft. (6:28)
San Diego
-0.2 ft. (6:23)

feet
6
5
4
3
2
1

12 1 2 3 4 5 6 7 8 9 10 11 noon 1 2 3 4 5 6 7 8 9 10 11 12

— 1.9 knots ebb ———⊢— 1 knot flood —⊣—⊢— 0.5 ebb —⊣—⊢— 1 knot flood —⊣⊢

SUN APR 28
dawn 5:09 sunrise 6:07 sunset 7:35 dark 8:33
moonset 9:15 a.m.

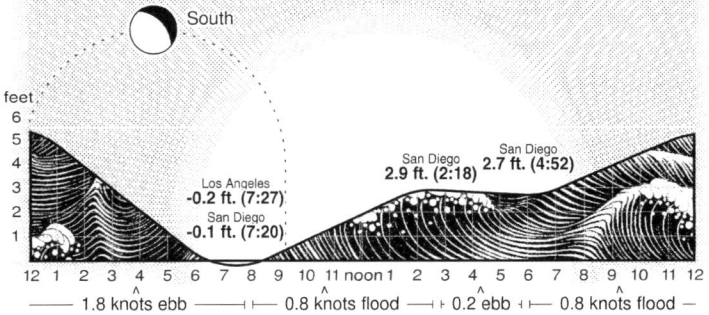

South

San Diego
2.9 ft. (2:18)
San Diego
2.7 ft. (4:52)

Los Angeles
-0.2 ft. (7:27)
San Diego
-0.1 ft. (7:20)

feet
6
5
4
3
2
1

12 1 2 3 4 5 6 7 8 9 10 11 noon 1 2 3 4 5 6 7 8 9 10 11 12

—— 1.8 knots ebb ———⊢— 0.8 knots flood —⊣—⊢ 0.2 ebb ⊣—⊢— 0.8 knots flood —

MON APR 29 — dawn 5:08 sunrise 6:06 sunset 7:35 dark 8:34
moonrise 12:41 a.m. moonset 10:17 a.m.

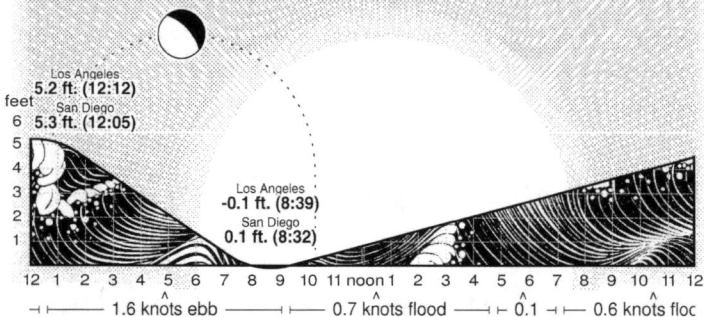

Los Angeles **5.2 ft. (12:12)**
San Diego **5.3 ft. (12:05)**
feet 6

Los Angeles **-0.1 ft. (8:39)**
San Diego **0.1 ft. (8:32)**

12 1 2 3 4 5 6 7 8 9 10 11 noon 1 2 3 4 5 6 7 8 9 10 11 12

1.6 knots ebb — 0.7 knots flood — 0.1 — 0.6 knots floc

TUE APR 30 — dawn 5:06 sunrise 6:05 sunset 7:36 dark 8:35
moonrise 1:31 a.m. moonset 11:25 a.m.

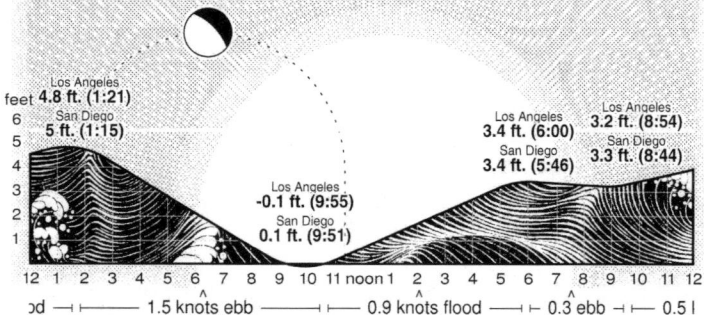

Los Angeles **4.8 ft. (1:21)**
feet 6 San Diego **5 ft. (1:15)**

Los Angeles **3.4 ft. (6:00)**
San Diego **3.4 ft. (5:46)**

Los Angeles **3.2 ft. (8:54)**
San Diego **3.3 ft. (8:44)**

Los Angeles **-0.1 ft. (9:55)**
San Diego **0.1 ft. (9:51)**

12 1 2 3 4 5 6 7 8 9 10 11 noon 1 2 3 4 5 6 7 8 9 10 11 12

od — 1.5 knots ebb — 0.9 knots flood — 0.3 ebb — 0.5 l

WED MAY 1 — dawn 5:05 sunrise 6:04 sunset 7:37 dark 8:36
moonrise 2:14 a.m. moonset 12:35 p.m.

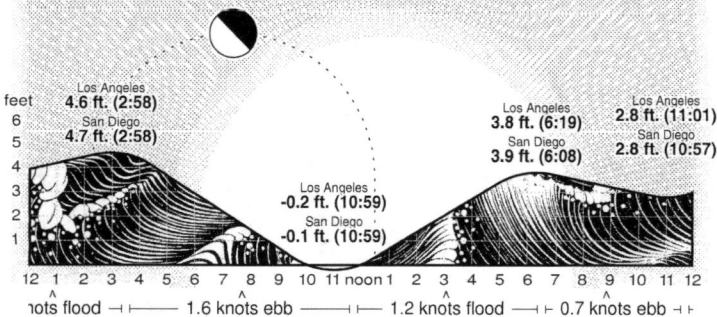

Los Angeles **4.6 ft. (2:58)**
feet 6 San Diego **4.7 ft. (2:58)**

Los Angeles **3.8 ft. (6:19)**
San Diego **3.9 ft. (6:08)**

Los Angeles **2.8 ft. (11:01)**
San Diego **2.8 ft. (10:57)**

Los Angeles **-0.2 ft. (10:59)**
San Diego **-0.1 ft. (10:59)**

12 1 2 3 4 5 6 7 8 9 10 11 noon 1 2 3 4 5 6 7 8 9 10 11 12

nots flood — 1.6 knots ebb — 1.2 knots flood — 0.7 knots ebb —

THU MAY 2 — dawn 5:04 sunrise 6:03 sunset 7:38 dark 8:37
moonrise 2:51 a.m. moonset 1:45 p.m.

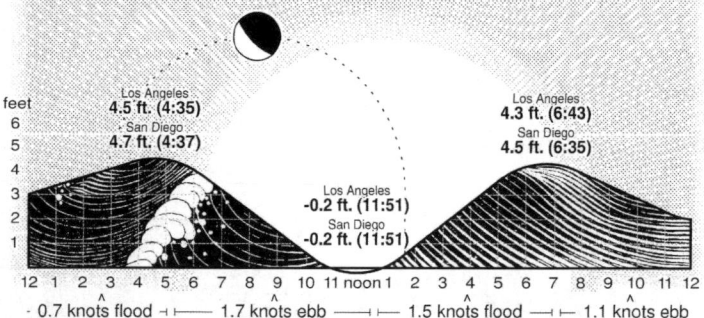

Los Angeles **4.5 ft. (4:35)**
feet 6 San Diego **4.7 ft. (4:37)**

Los Angeles **4.3 ft. (6:43)**
San Diego **4.5 ft. (6:35)**

Los Angeles **-0.2 ft. (11:51)**
San Diego **-0.2 ft. (11:51)**

12 1 2 3 4 5 6 7 8 9 10 11 noon 1 2 3 4 5 6 7 8 9 10 11 12

0.7 knots flood — 1.7 knots ebb — 1.5 knots flood — 1.1 knots ebb

FRI MAY 3
dawn 5:03 sunrise 6:02 sunset 7:38 dark 8:37
moonrise 3:24 a.m. moonset 2:55 p.m.

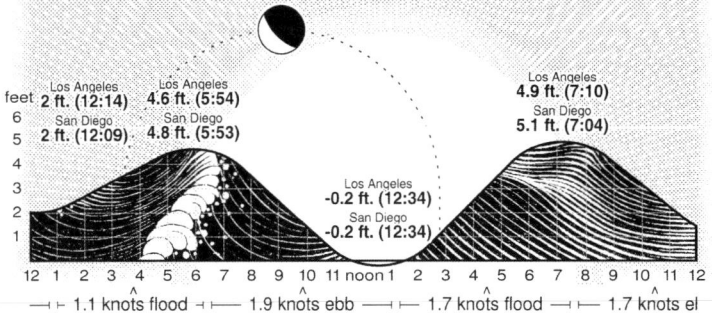

feet

Los Angeles
2 ft. (12:14)
San Diego
2 ft. (12:09)

Los Angeles
4.6 ft. (5:54)
San Diego
4.8 ft. (5:53)

Los Angeles
4.9 ft. (7:10)
San Diego
5.1 ft. (7:04)

Los Angeles
-0.2 ft. (12:34)
San Diego
-0.2 ft. (12:34)

6
5
4
3
2
1

12 1 2 3 4 5 6 7 8 9 10 11 noon 1 2 3 4 5 6 7 8 9 10 11 12

⊢ 1.1 knots flood ⊣ ⊢ 1.9 knots ebb ⊣ ⊢ 1.7 knots flood ⊣ ⊢ 1.7 knots el

SAT MAY 4
dawn 5:02 sunrise 6:01 sunset 7:39 dark 8:38
moonrise 3:55 a.m. moonset 4:05 p.m.

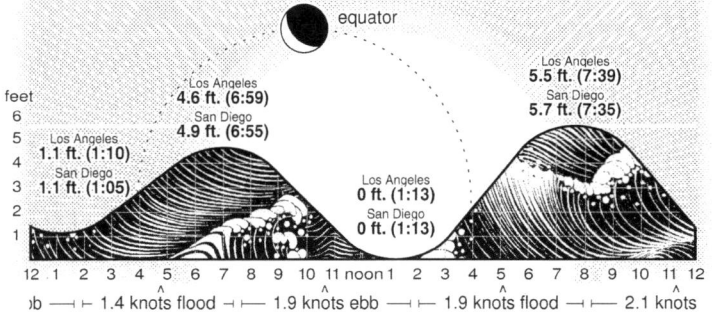

equator

feet

Los Angeles
1.1 ft. (1:10)
San Diego
1.1 ft. (1:05)

Los Angeles
4.6 ft. (6:59)
San Diego
4.9 ft. (6:55)

Los Angeles
5.5 ft. (7:39)
San Diego
5.7 ft. (7:35)

Los Angeles
0 ft. (1:13)
San Diego
0 ft. (1:13)

6
5
4
3
2
1

12 1 2 3 4 5 6 7 8 9 10 11 noon 1 2 3 4 5 6 7 8 9 10 11 12

ob ⊢ 1.4 knots flood ⊣ ⊢ 1.9 knots ebb ⊣ ⊢ 1.9 knots flood ⊣ ⊢ 2.1 knots

SUN MAY 5
dawn 5:01 sunrise 6:00 sunset 7:40 dark 8:39
moonrise 4:25 a.m. moonset 5:15 p.m.

Cinco de Mayo   perigee   Eta Aquarids Peak

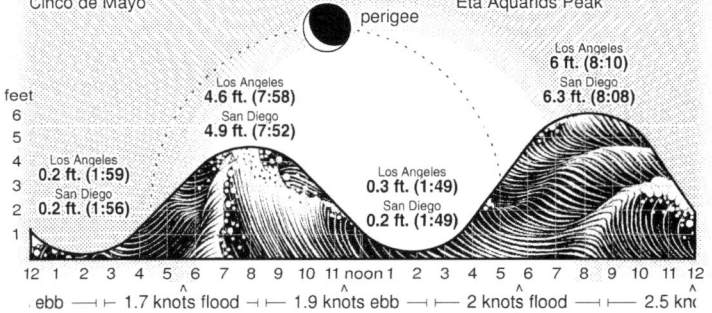

feet

Los Angeles
0.2 ft. (1:59)
San Diego
0.2 ft. (1:56)

Los Angeles
4.6 ft. (7:58)
San Diego
4.9 ft. (7:52)

Los Angeles
6 ft. (8:10)
San Diego
6.3 ft. (8:08)

Los Angeles
0.3 ft. (1:49)
San Diego
0.2 ft. (1:49)

6
5
4
3
2
1

12 1 2 3 4 5 6 7 8 9 10 11 noon 1 2 3 4 5 6 7 8 9 10 11 12

ebb ⊢ 1.7 knots flood ⊣ ⊢ 1.9 knots ebb ⊣ ⊢ 2 knots flood ⊣ ⊢ 2.5 kno

Eta Aquarids Meteor Shower The Eta Aquarids run annually between
Apr 15th to May 27th and at peak produce 10 to 20 meteors per hour.
This shower's peak can stretch over several days with the most promising
viewing before dawn on May 5th and 6th. The Eta Aquarids' radiant point,
the constellation Aquarius, the water jar, will rise above the eastern
horizon at approximately 2:30 a.m. The Moon will have set by early
evening providing ideal viewing condtions before dawn to catch an Eta
Aquarids meteor.

MON MAY 6
dawn 5:00 sunrise 5:59 sunset 7:41 dark 8:40
moonrise 4:55 a.m. moonset 6:27 p.m.

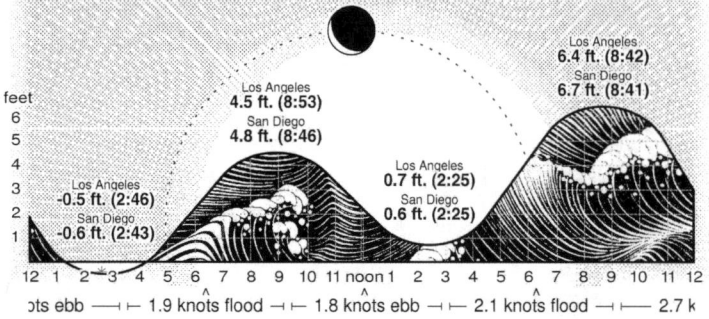

Los Angeles
6.4 ft. (8:42)
San Diego
6.7 ft. (8:41)

Los Angeles
4.5 ft. (8:53)
San Diego
4.8 ft. (8:46)

Los Angeles
0.7 ft. (2:25)
San Diego
0.6 ft. (2:25)

Los Angeles
-0.5 ft. (2:46)
San Diego
-0.6 ft. (2:43)

feet
6
5
4
3
2
1

12 1 2 3 4 5 6 7 8 9 10 11 noon 1 2 3 4 5 6 7 8 9 10 11 12

ots ebb ⊢ 1.9 knots flood ⊣ ⊢ 1.8 knots ebb ⊣ ⊢ 2.1 knots flood ⊣ ⊢ 2.7 k

TUE MAY 7
dawn 4:59 sunrise 5:58 sunset 7:42 dark 8:41
moonrise 5:29 a.m. moonset 7:39 p.m.

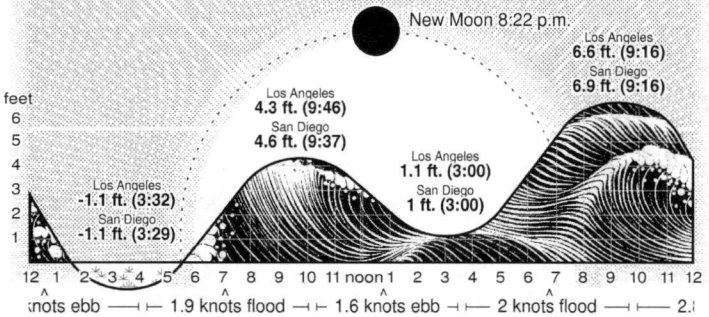

New Moon 8:22 p.m.

Los Angeles
6.6 ft. (9:16)
San Diego
6.9 ft. (9:16)

Los Angeles
4.3 ft. (9:46)
San Diego
4.6 ft. (9:37)

Los Angeles
1.1 ft. (3:00)
San Diego
1 ft. (3:00)

Los Angeles
-1.1 ft. (3:32)
San Diego
-1.1 ft. (3:29)

feet
6
5
4
3
2
1

12 1 2 3 4 5 6 7 8 9 10 11 noon 1 2 3 4 5 6 7 8 9 10 11 12

knots ebb ⊢ 1.9 knots flood ⊣ ⊢ 1.6 knots ebb ⊣ ⊢ 2 knots flood ⊣ ⊢ 2.

WED MAY 8
dawn 4:57 sunrise 5:57 sunset 7:42 dark 8:42
moonrise 6:07 a.m. moonset 8:52 p.m.

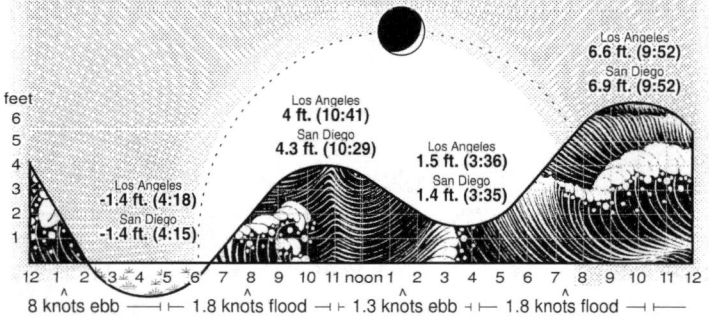

Los Angeles
6.6 ft. (9:52)
San Diego
6.9 ft. (9:52)

Los Angeles
4 ft. (10:41)
San Diego
4.3 ft. (10:29)

Los Angeles
1.5 ft. (3:36)
San Diego
1.4 ft. (3:35)

Los Angeles
-1.4 ft. (4:18)
San Diego
-1.4 ft. (4:15)

feet
6
5
4
3
2
1

12 1 2 3 4 5 6 7 8 9 10 11 noon 1 2 3 4 5 6 7 8 9 10 11 12

8 knots ebb ⊢ 1.8 knots flood ⊣ ⊢ 1.3 knots ebb ⊣ ⊢ 1.8 knots flood ⊣ ⊢

THU MAY 9
dawn 4:56 sunrise 5:56 sunset 7:43 dark 8:43
moonrise 6:51 a.m. moonset 10:03 p.m.

Mercury western elongation

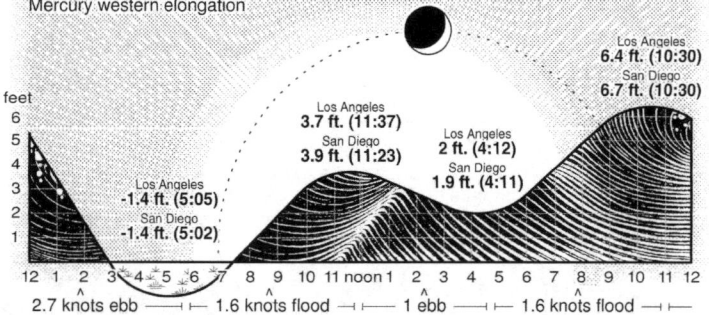

Los Angeles
6.4 ft. (10:30)
San Diego
6.7 ft. (10:30)

Los Angeles
3.7 ft. (11:37)
San Diego
3.9 ft. (11:23)

Los Angeles
2 ft. (4:12)
San Diego
1.9 ft. (4:11)

Los Angeles
-1.4 ft. (5:05)
San Diego
-1.4 ft. (5:02)

feet
6
5
4
3
2
1

12 1 2 3 4 5 6 7 8 9 10 11 noon 1 2 3 4 5 6 7 8 9 10 11 12

2.7 knots ebb ⊢ 1.6 knots flood ⊣ ⊢ 1 ebb ⊣ ⊢ 1.6 knots flood ⊣ ⊢

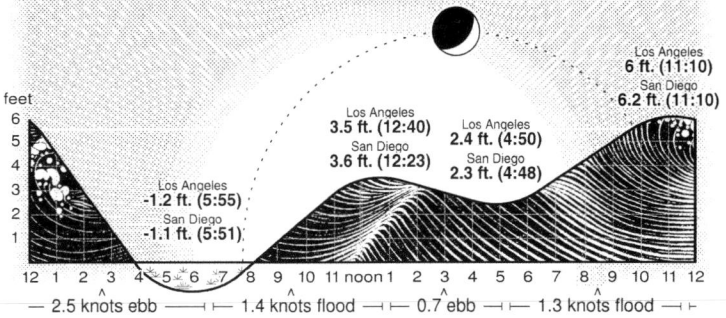

FRI MAY 10 dawn 4:55 sunrise 5:56 sunset 7:44 dark 8:44
moonrise 7:43 a.m. moonset 11:06 p.m.

feet

Los Angeles
6 ft. (11:10)
San Diego
6.2 ft. (11:10)

Los Angeles
3.5 ft. (12:40)
San Diego
3.6 ft. (12:23)

Los Angeles
2.4 ft. (4:50)
San Diego
2.3 ft. (4:48)

Los Angeles
-1.2 ft. (5:55)
San Diego
-1.1 ft. (5:51)

— 2.5 knots ebb —⊢ 1.4 knots flood —⊢ 0.7 ebb —⊣ 1.3 knots flood —⊢

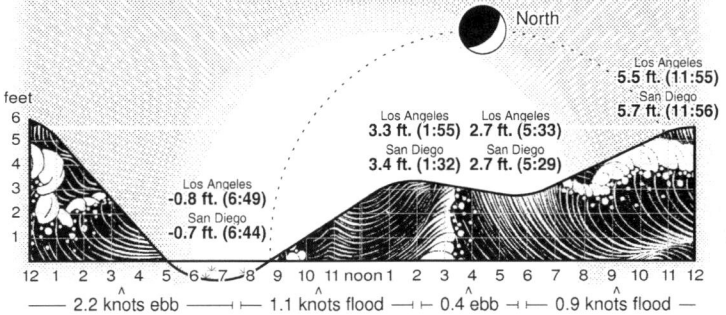

SAT MAY 11 dawn 4:54 sunrise 5:55 sunset 7:45 dark 8:45
moonrise 8:41 a.m.

North

feet

Los Angeles
5.5 ft. (11:55)
San Diego
5.7 ft. (11:56)

Los Angeles
3.3 ft. (1:55)
San Diego
3.4 ft. (1:32)

Los Angeles
2.7 ft. (5:33)
San Diego
2.7 ft. (5:29)

Los Angeles
-0.8 ft. (6:49)
San Diego
-0.7 ft. (6:44)

— 2.2 knots ebb —⊢ 1.1 knots flood —⊢ 0.4 ebb —⊣ 0.9 knots flood —

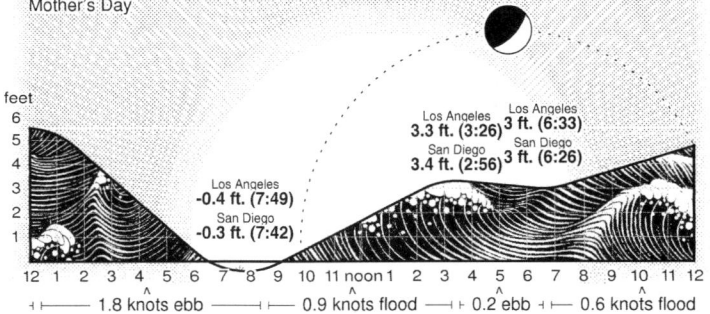

SUN MAY 12 dawn 4:54 sunrise 5:54 sunset 7:45 dark 8:46
moonset 12:01 a.m. moonrise 9:42 a.m.

Mother's Day

feet

Los Angeles
3.3 ft. (3:26)
San Diego
3.4 ft. (2:56)

Los Angeles
3 ft. (6:33)
San Diego
3 ft. (6:26)

Los Angeles
-0.4 ft. (7:49)
San Diego
-0.3 ft. (7:42)

⊢ — 1.8 knots ebb — ⊢ — 0.9 knots flood —⊣ ⊢ 0.2 ebb ⊣ ⊢— 0.6 knots flood —

MON MAY 13
dawn 4:53 sunrise 5:53 sunset 7:46 dark 8:47
moonset 12:47 a.m. moonrise 10:45 a.m.

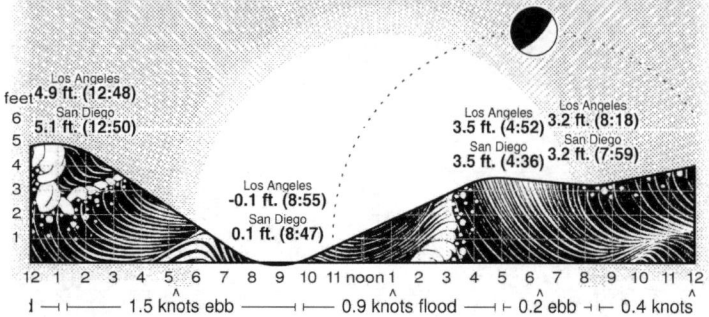

feet
6
5
4
3
2
1

Los Angeles
4.9 ft. (12:48)
San Diego
5.1 ft. (12:50)

Los Angeles
-0.1 ft. (8:55)
San Diego
0.1 ft. (8:47)

Los Angeles
3.5 ft. (4:52)
San Diego
3.5 ft. (4:36)

Los Angeles
3.2 ft. (8:18)
San Diego
3.2 ft. (7:59)

12 1 2 3 4 5 6 7 8 9 10 11 noon 1 2 3 4 5 6 7 8 9 10 11 12

⊦ ⊢ ⊢ 1.5 knots ebb ⎯⎯⎯ ⊢ 0.9 knots flood ⎯ ⊦ 0.2 ebb ⊣ ⊢ 0.4 knots

TUE MAY 14
dawn 4:52 sunrise 5:52 sunset 7:47 dark 8:48
moonset 1:24 a.m. moonrise 11:46 a.m.

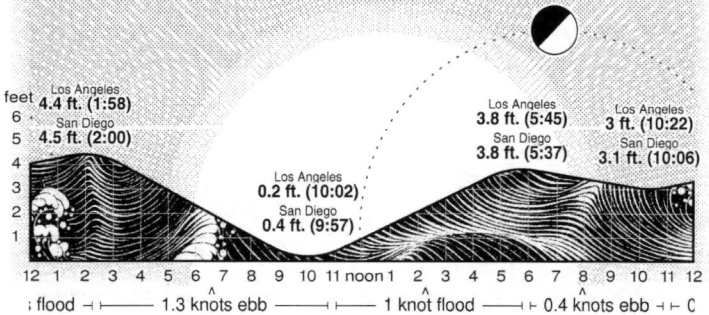

feet
6
5
4
3
2
1

Los Angeles
4.4 ft. (1:58)
San Diego
4.5 ft. (2:00)

Los Angeles
0.2 ft. (10:02)
San Diego
0.4 ft. (9:57)

Los Angeles
3.8 ft. (5:45)
San Diego
3.8 ft. (5:37)

Los Angeles
3 ft. (10:22)
San Diego
3.1 ft. (10:06)

12 1 2 3 4 5 6 7 8 9 10 11 noon 1 2 3 4 5 6 7 8 9 10 11 12

⊦ flood ⊣ ⊢ 1.3 knots ebb ⎯⎯⎯ ⊢ 1 knot flood ⎯ ⊢ 0.4 knots ebb ⊣ ⊢ C

WED MAY 15
dawn 4:51 sunrise 5:52 sunset 7:48 dark 8:49
moonset 1:56 a.m. moonrise 12:46 p.m.

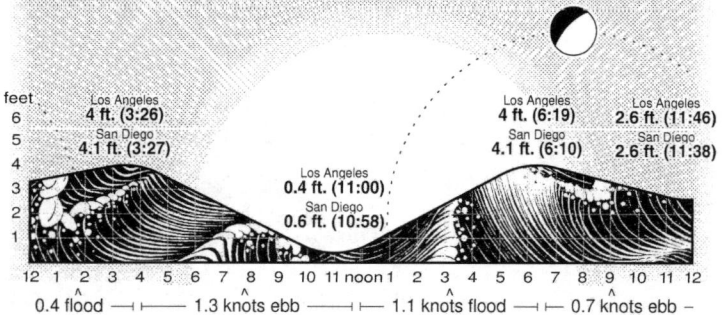

feet
6
5
4
3
2
1

Los Angeles
4 ft. (3:26)
San Diego
4.1 ft. (3:27)

Los Angeles
0.4 ft. (11:00)
San Diego
0.6 ft. (10:58)

Los Angeles
4 ft. (6:19)
San Diego
4.1 ft. (6:10)

Los Angeles
2.6 ft. (11:46)
San Diego
2.6 ft. (11:38)

12 1 2 3 4 5 6 7 8 9 10 11 noon 1 2 3 4 5 6 7 8 9 10 11 12

0.4 flood ⎯ ⊦ ⊢ 1.3 knots ebb ⎯⎯⎯ ⊢ 1.1 knots flood ⎯ ⊢ 0.7 knots ebb ⎯

THU MAY 16
dawn 4:50 sunrise 5:51 sunset 7:48 dark 8:50
moonset 2:23 a.m. moonrise 1:42 p.m.

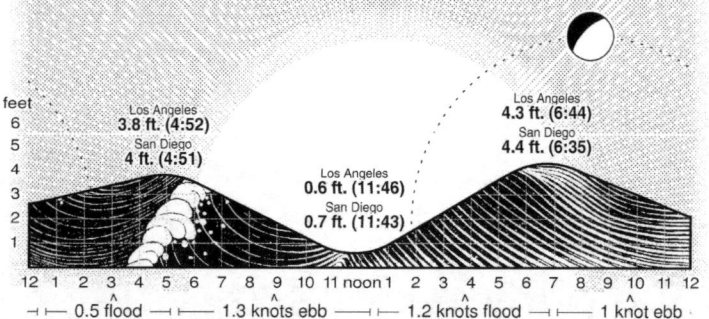

feet
6
5
4
3
2
1

Los Angeles
3.8 ft. (4:52)
San Diego
4 ft. (4:51)

Los Angeles
0.6 ft. (11:46)
San Diego
0.7 ft. (11:43)

Los Angeles
4.3 ft. (6:44)
San Diego
4.4 ft. (6:35)

12 1 2 3 4 5 6 7 8 9 10 11 noon 1 2 3 4 5 6 7 8 9 10 11 12

⊣ ⊢ 0.5 flood ⎯ ⊦ ⊢ 1.3 knots ebb ⎯ ⊦ ⊢ 1.2 knots flood ⎯ ⊦ ⊢ 1 knot ebb

FRI MAY 17
dawn 4:49 sunrise 5:50 sunset 7:49 dark 8:51
moonset 2:48 a.m. moonrise 2:38 p.m.

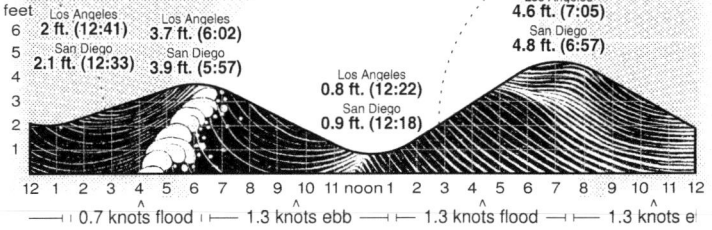

apogee

feet
6
5
4
3
2
1

Los Angeles
2 ft. (12:41)
San Diego
2.1 ft. (12:33)

Los Angeles
3.7 ft. (6:02)
San Diego
3.9 ft. (5:57)

Los Angeles
0.8 ft. (12:22)
San Diego
0.9 ft. (12:18)

Los Angeles
4.6 ft. (7:05)
San Diego
4.8 ft. (6:57)

12 1 2 3 4 5 6 7 8 9 10 11 noon 1 2 3 4 5 6 7 8 9 10 11 12

0.7 knots flood — 1.3 knots ebb — 1.3 knots flood — 1.3 knots e

SAT MAY 18
dawn 4:48 sunrise 5:50 sunset 7:50 dark 8:51
moonset 3:11 a.m. moonrise 3:33 p.m.

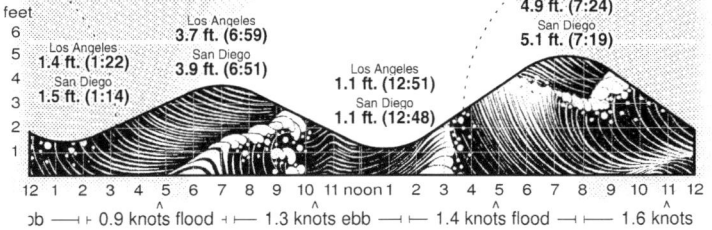

equator

feet
6
5
4
3
2
1

Los Angeles
1.4 ft. (1:22)
San Diego
1.5 ft. (1:14)

Los Angeles
3.7 ft. (6:59)
San Diego
3.9 ft. (6:51)

Los Angeles
1.1 ft. (12:51)
San Diego
1.1 ft. (12:48)

Los Angeles
4.9 ft. (7:24)
San Diego
5.1 ft. (7:19)

12 1 2 3 4 5 6 7 8 9 10 11 noon 1 2 3 4 5 6 7 8 9 10 11 12

b — 0.9 knots flood — 1.3 knots ebb — 1.4 knots flood — 1.6 knots

SUN MAY 19
dawn 4:47 sunrise 5:49 sunset 7:50 dark 8:52
moonset 3:35 a.m. moonrise 4:29 p.m.

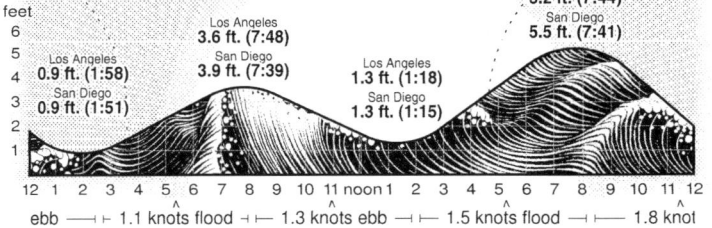

feet
6
5
4
3
2
1

Los Angeles
0.9 ft. (1:58)
San Diego
0.9 ft. (1:51)

Los Angeles
3.6 ft. (7:48)
San Diego
3.9 ft. (7:39)

Los Angeles
1.3 ft. (1:18)
San Diego
1.3 ft. (1:15)

Los Angeles
5.2 ft. (7:44)
San Diego
5.5 ft. (7:41)

12 1 2 3 4 5 6 7 8 9 10 11 noon 1 2 3 4 5 6 7 8 9 10 11 12

ebb — 1.1 knots flood — 1.3 knots ebb — 1.5 knots flood — 1.8 knot

Ⓢ Ⓜ ⑾

MON MAY 20
dawn 4:47 sunrise 5:49 sunset 7:51 dark 8:53
moonset 3:59 a.m. moonrise 5:26 p.m.

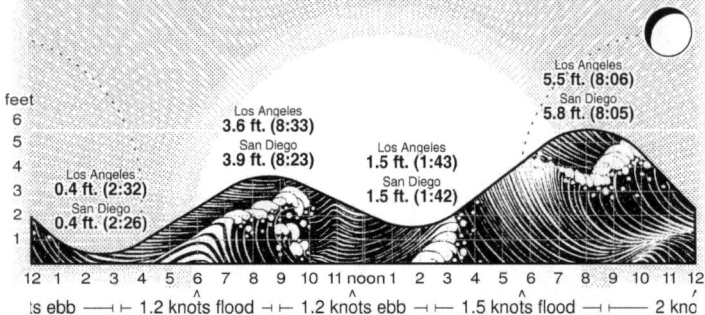

Los Angeles
5.5 ft. (8:06)
San Diego
5.8 ft. (8:05)

feet
6
5
Los Angeles
3.6 ft. (8:33)
San Diego
3.9 ft. (8:23)
4
Los Angeles
1.5 ft. (1:43)
San Diego
1.5 ft. (1:42)
3
Los Angeles
0.4 ft. (2:32)
San Diego
0.4 ft. (2:26)
2
1

12 1 2 3 4 5 6 7 8 9 10 11 noon 1 2 3 4 5 6 7 8 9 10 11 12

ts ebb ⟶ ⊢ 1.2 knots flood ⟶ ⊢ 1.2 knots ebb ⟶ ⊢ 1.5 knots flood ⟶ ⊢ 2 kno

TUE MAY 21
dawn 4:46 sunrise 5:48 sunset 7:52 dark 8:54
moonset 4:26 a.m. moonrise 6:27 p.m.

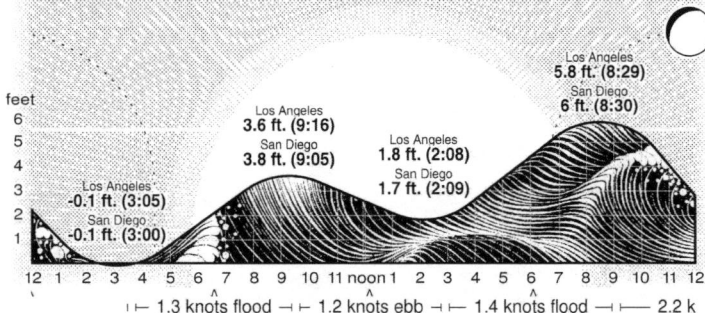

Los Angeles
5.8 ft. (8:29)
San Diego
6 ft. (8:30)

feet
6
5
Los Angeles
3.6 ft. (9:16)
San Diego
3.8 ft. (9:05)
4
Los Angeles
1.8 ft. (2:08)
San Diego
1.7 ft. (2:09)
3
2
Los Angeles
-0.1 ft. (3:05)
San Diego
-0.1 ft. (3:00)
1

12 1 2 3 4 5 6 7 8 9 10 11 noon 1 2 3 4 5 6 7 8 9 10 11 12

⊢ 1.3 knots flood ⟶ ⊢ 1.2 knots ebb ⟶ ⊢ 1.4 knots flood ⟶ ⊢ 2.2 k

WED MAY 22
dawn 4:45 sunrise 5:47 sunset 7:53 dark 8:55
moonset 4:57 a.m. moonrise 7:29 p.m.

National Maritime Day

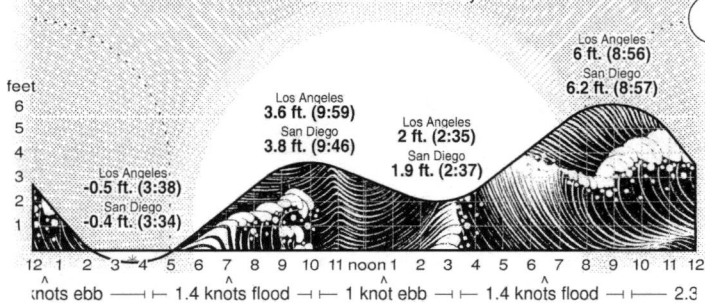

Los Angeles
6 ft. (8:56)
San Diego
6.2 ft. (8:57)

feet
6
5
Los Angeles
3.6 ft. (9:59)
San Diego
3.8 ft. (9:46)
4
Los Angeles
2 ft. (2:35)
San Diego
1.9 ft. (2:37)
3
2
Los Angeles
-0.5 ft. (3:38)
San Diego
-0.4 ft. (3:34)
1

12 1 2 3 4 5 6 7 8 9 10 11 noon 1 2 3 4 5 6 7 8 9 10 11 12

knots ebb ⟶ ⊢ 1.4 knots flood ⟶ ⊢ 1 knot ebb ⟶ ⊢ 1.4 knots flood ⟶ ⊢ 2.3

THU MAY 23
dawn 4:45 sunrise 5:47 sunset 7:53 dark 8:56
moonset 5:33 a.m. moonrise 8:34 p.m.

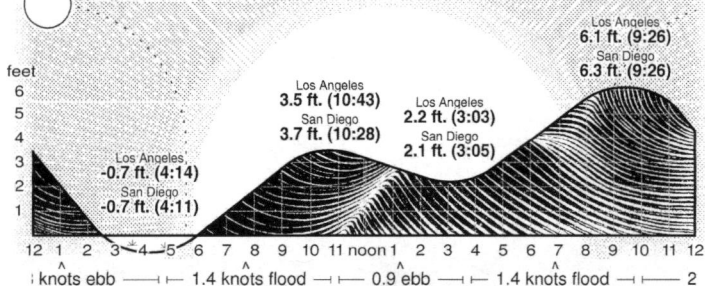

Full Moon 6:33 a.m.

Los Angeles
6.1 ft. (9:26)
San Diego
6.3 ft. (9:26)

feet
6
5
Los Angeles
3.5 ft. (10:43)
San Diego
3.7 ft. (10:28)
4
Los Angeles
2.2 ft. (3:03)
San Diego
2.1 ft. (3:05)
3
Los Angeles
-0.7 ft. (4:14)
San Diego
-0.7 ft. (4:11)
2
1

12 1 2 3 4 5 6 7 8 9 10 11 noon 1 2 3 4 5 6 7 8 9 10 11 12

knots ebb ⟶ ⊢ 1.4 knots flood ⟶ ⊢ 0.9 ebb ⟶ ⊢ 1.4 knots flood ⟶ ⊢ 2

FRI MAY 24

dawn 4:44 sunrise 5:46 sunset 7:54 dark 8:57
moonset 6:17 a.m. moonrise 9:37 p.m.

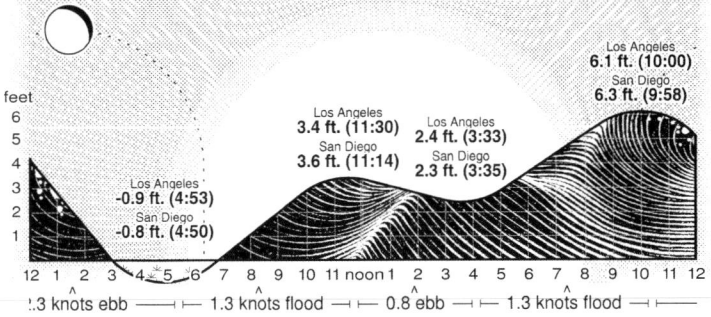

Los Angeles
6.1 ft. (10:00)
San Diego
6.3 ft. (9:58)

Los Angeles
3.4 ft. (11:30)
San Diego
3.6 ft. (11:14)

Los Angeles
2.4 ft. (3:33)
San Diego
2.3 ft. (3:35)

feet
6
5
4
3
2
1

Los Angeles
-0.9 ft. (4:53)
San Diego
-0.8 ft. (4:50)

12 1 2 3 4 5 6 7 8 9 10 11 noon 1 2 3 4 5 6 7 8 9 10 11 12

.3 knots ebb ⊢— 1.3 knots flood —⊣ ⊢ 0.8 ebb —⊣ ⊢ 1.3 knots flood —⊣ ⊢

SAT MAY 25

dawn 4:43 sunrise 5:46 sunset 7:55 dark 8:57
moonset 7:10 a.m. moonrise 10:36 p.m.

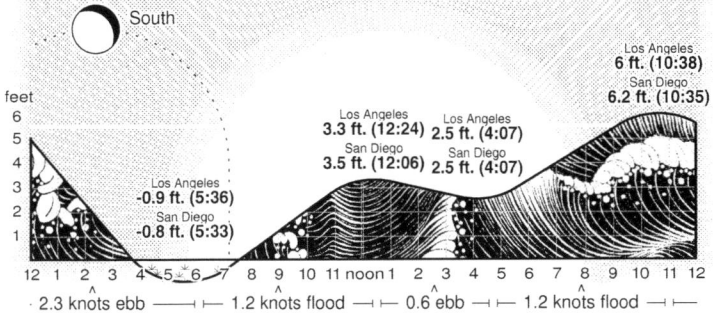

South

Los Angeles
6 ft. (10:38)
San Diego
6.2 ft. (10:35)

Los Angeles
3.3 ft. (12:24)
San Diego
3.5 ft. (12:06)

Los Angeles
2.5 ft. (4:07)
San Diego
2.5 ft. (4:07)

feet
6
5
4
3
2
1

Los Angeles
-0.9 ft. (5:36)
San Diego
-0.8 ft. (5:33)

12 1 2 3 4 5 6 7 8 9 10 11 noon 1 2 3 4 5 6 7 8 9 10 11 12

2.3 knots ebb ——⊣ ⊢ 1.2 knots flood —⊣ ⊢ 0.6 ebb —⊣ ⊢ 1.2 knots flood —⊣ ⊢

SUN MAY 26

dawn 4:43 sunrise 5:46 sunset 7:55 dark 8:58
moonset 8:10 a.m. moonrise 11:29 p.m.

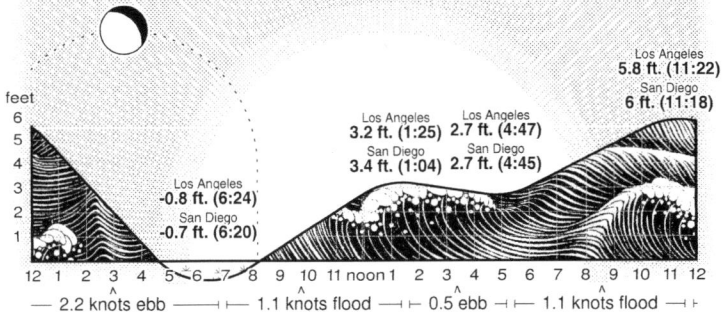

Los Angeles
5.8 ft. (11:22)
San Diego
6 ft. (11:18)

Los Angeles
3.2 ft. (1:25)
San Diego
3.4 ft. (1:04)

Los Angeles
2.7 ft. (4:47)
San Diego
2.7 ft. (4:45)

feet
6
5
4
3
2
1

Los Angeles
-0.8 ft. (6:24)
San Diego
-0.7 ft. (6:20)

12 1 2 3 4 5 6 7 8 9 10 11 noon 1 2 3 4 5 6 7 8 9 10 11 12

— 2.2 knots ebb ——⊣ ⊢ 1.1 knots flood —⊣ ⊢ 0.5 ebb —⊣ ⊢ 1.1 knots flood —⊣ ⊢

Ⓢ Ⓜ ⓜ

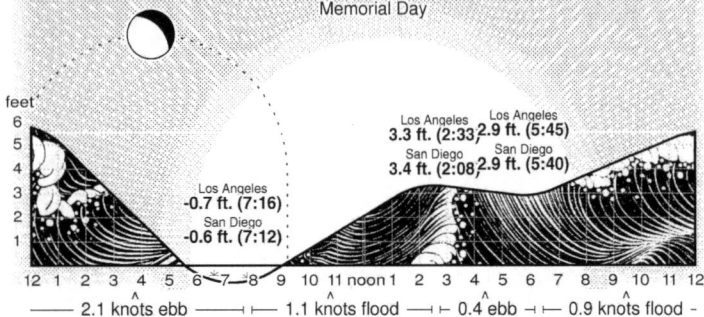

MON MAY 27 dawn 4:42 sunrise 5:45 sunset 7:56 dark 8:59
moonset 9:17 a.m.
Memorial Day

feet
6
5
4
3
2
1

Los Angeles 3.3 ft. (2:33) Los Angeles 2.9 ft. (5:45)
San Diego 3.4 ft. (2:08) San Diego 2.9 ft. (5:40)

Los Angeles -0.7 ft. (7:16)
San Diego -0.6 ft. (7:12)

12 1 2 3 4 5 6 7 8 9 10 11 noon 1 2 3 4 5 6 7 8 9 10 11 12

— 2.1 knots ebb — ⊢ 1.1 knots flood — ⊢ 0.4 ebb ⊣ ⊢ 0.9 knots flood -

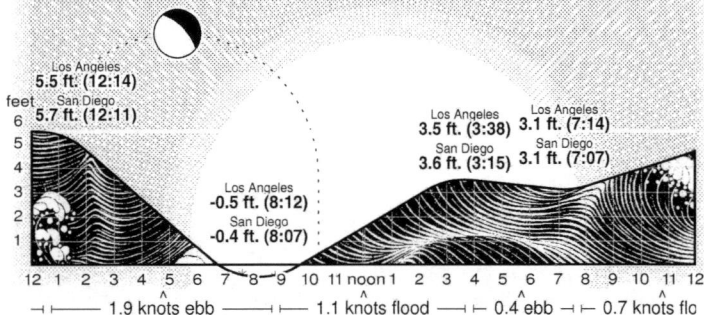

TUE MAY 28 dawn 4:42 sunrise 5:45 sunset 7:56 dark 9:00
moonrise 12:14 a.m. moonset 10:27 a.m.

Los Angeles 5.5 ft. (12:14)
San Diego 5.7 ft. (12:11)

feet
6
5
4
3
2
1

Los Angeles 3.5 ft. (3:38) Los Angeles 3.1 ft. (7:14)
San Diego 3.6 ft. (3:15) San Diego 3.1 ft. (7:07)

Los Angeles -0.5 ft. (8:12)
San Diego -0.4 ft. (8:07)

12 1 2 3 4 5 6 7 8 9 10 11 noon 1 2 3 4 5 6 7 8 9 10 11 12

⊢⊣ 1.9 knots ebb — ⊢ 1.1 knots flood — ⊢ 0.4 ebb ⊣ ⊢ 0.7 knots flo

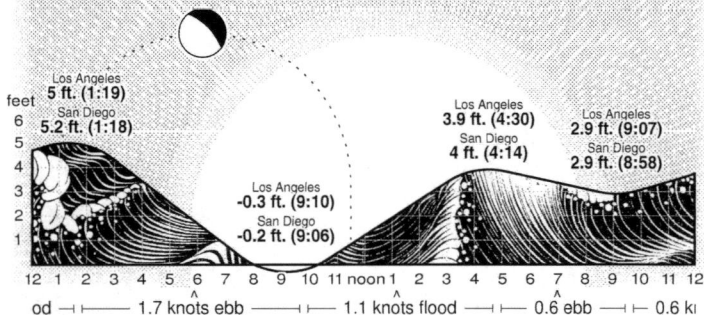

WED MAY 29 dawn 4:41 sunrise 5:44 sunset 7:57 dark 9:00
moonrise 12:52 a.m. moonset 11:36 a.m.

Los Angeles 5 ft. (1:19)
San Diego 5.2 ft. (1:18)

feet
6
5
4
3
2
1

Los Angeles 3.9 ft. (4:30) Los Angeles 2.9 ft. (9:07)
San Diego 4 ft. (4:14) San Diego 2.9 ft. (8:58)

Los Angeles -0.3 ft. (9:10)
San Diego -0.2 ft. (9:06)

12 1 2 3 4 5 6 7 8 9 10 11 noon 1 2 3 4 5 6 7 8 9 10 11 12

od ⊣ ⊢ 1.7 knots ebb — ⊢ 1.1 knots flood — ⊢ 0.6 ebb — ⊢ 0.6 k⊢

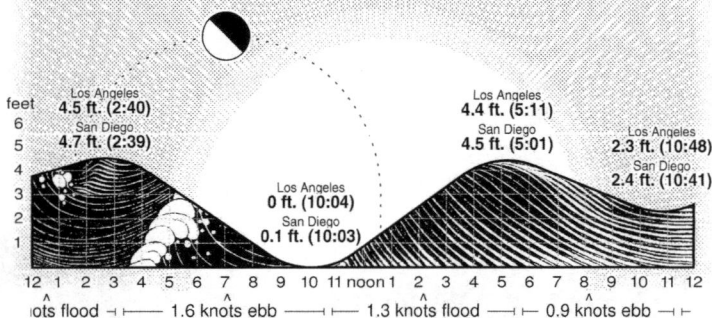

THU MAY 30 dawn 4:41 sunrise 5:44 sunset 7:58 dark 9:01
moonrise 1:26 a.m. moonset 12:45 p.m.

feet
6
5
4
3
2
1

Los Angeles 4.5 ft. (2:40) Los Angeles 4.4 ft. (5:11)
San Diego 4.7 ft. (2:39) San Diego 4.5 ft. (5:01)

Los Angeles 2.3 ft. (10:48)
San Diego 2.4 ft. (10:41)

Los Angeles 0 ft. (10:04)
San Diego 0.1 ft. (10:03)

12 1 2 3 4 5 6 7 8 9 10 11 noon 1 2 3 4 5 6 7 8 9 10 11 12

⊢ots flood ⊣ ⊢ 1.6 knots ebb — ⊢ 1.3 knots flood — ⊢ 0.9 knots ebb ⊣ ⊢

FRI MAY 31

dawn 4:40 sunrise 5:44 sunset 7:58 dark 9:02
moonrise 1:56 a.m. moonset 1:53 p.m.

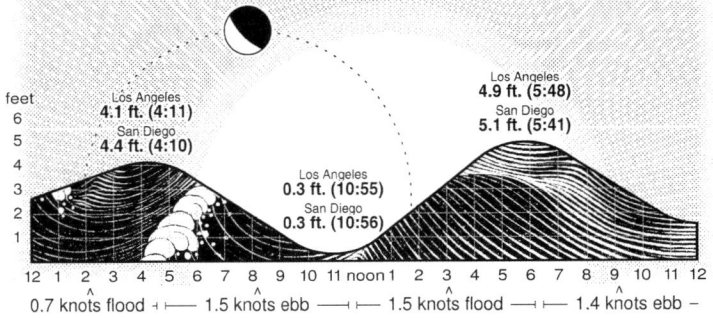

Los Angeles
4.9 ft. (5:48)
San Diego
5.1 ft. (5:41)

Los Angeles
4.1 ft. (4:11)
San Diego
4.4 ft. (4:10)

Los Angeles
0.3 ft. (10:55)
San Diego
0.3 ft. (10:56)

feet
6
5
4
3
2
1

12 1 2 3 4 5 6 7 8 9 10 11 noon 1 2 3 4 5 6 7 8 9 10 11 12

0.7 knots flood ⊣ ⊢— 1.5 knots ebb —⊣ ⊢— 1.5 knots flood —⊣ ⊢— 1.4 knots ebb –

SAT JUN 1

dawn 4:40 sunrise 5:43 sunset 7:59 dark 9:03
moonrise 2:26 a.m. moonset 3:01 p.m.

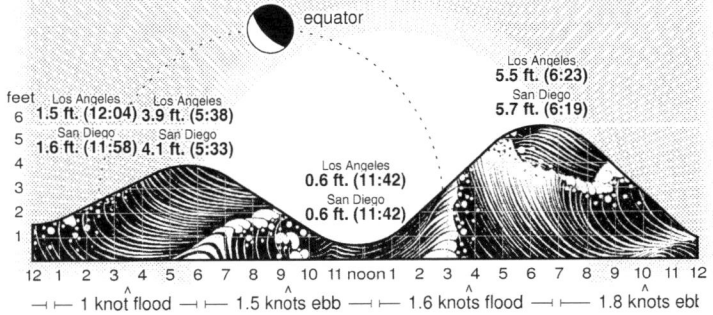

equator

Los Angeles
5.5 ft. (6:23)
San Diego
5.7 ft. (6:19)

Los Angeles
1.5 ft. (12:04)
San Diego
1.6 ft. (11:58)

Los Angeles
3.9 ft. (5:38)
San Diego
4.1 ft. (5:33)

Los Angeles
0.6 ft. (11:42)
San Diego
0.6 ft. (11:42)

feet
6
5
4
3
2
1

12 1 2 3 4 5 6 7 8 9 10 11 noon 1 2 3 4 5 6 7 8 9 10 11 12

⊣ ⊢ 1 knot flood ⊣ ⊢ 1.5 knots ebb —⊣ ⊢— 1.6 knots flood —⊣ ⊢— 1.8 knots ebt

SUN JUN 2

dawn 4:39 sunrise 5:43 sunset 7:59 dark 9:03
moonrise 2:55 a.m. moonset 4:09 p.m.

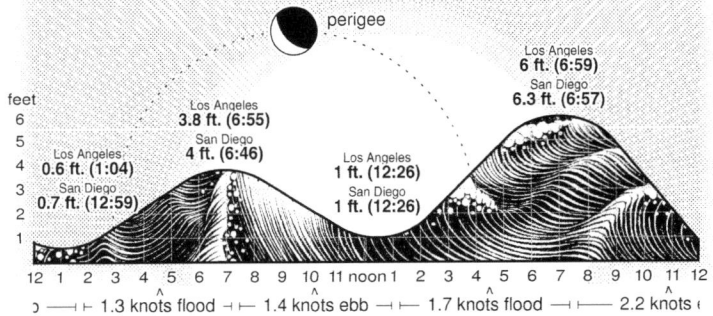

perigee

Los Angeles
6 ft. (6:59)
San Diego
6.3 ft. (6:57)

Los Angeles
3.8 ft. (6:55)
San Diego
4 ft. (6:46)

Los Angeles
0.6 ft. (1:04)
San Diego
0.7 ft. (12:59)

Los Angeles
1 ft. (12:26)
San Diego
1 ft. (12:26)

feet
6
5
4
3
2
1

12 1 2 3 4 5 6 7 8 9 10 11 noon 1 2 3 4 5 6 7 8 9 10 11 12

⊃ —⊢ 1.3 knots flood ⊣ ⊢ 1.4 knots ebb —⊣ ⊢ 1.7 knots flood —⊣ ⊢— 2.2 knots

Ⓢ   Ⓜ   ⓜ

MON JUN 3
dawn 4:39 sunrise 5:43 sunset 8:00 dark 9:04
moonrise 3:26 a.m. moonset 5:20 p.m.

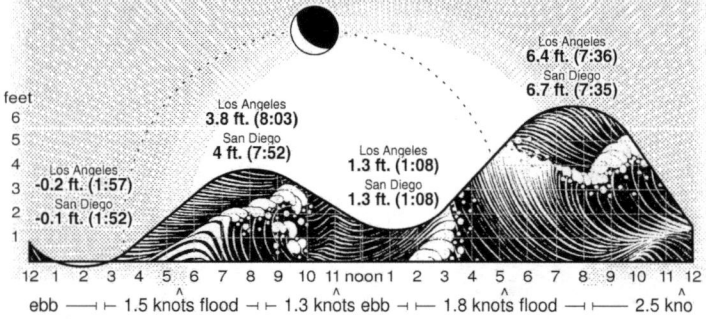

Los Angeles
6.4 ft. (7:36)
San Diego
6.7 ft. (7:35)

Los Angeles
3.8 ft. (8:03)
San Diego
4 ft. (7:52)

Los Angeles
1.3 ft. (1:08)
San Diego
1.3 ft. (1:08)

feet
Los Angeles
-0.2 ft. (1:57)
San Diego
-0.1 ft. (1:52)

12 1 2 3 4 5 6 7 8 9 10 11 noon 1 2 3 4 5 6 7 8 9 10 11 12

ebb ⊢— 1.5 knots flood —⊣ ⊢— 1.3 knots ebb —⊣ ⊢— 1.8 knots flood —⊣ ⊢— 2.5 kno

TUE JUN 4
dawn 4:39 sunrise 5:43 sunset 8:01 dark 9:05
moonrise 4:01 a.m. moonset 6:31 p.m.

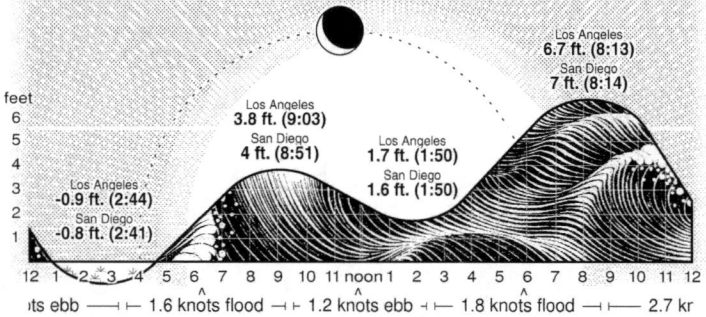

Los Angeles
6.7 ft. (8:13)
San Diego
7 ft. (8:14)

Los Angeles
3.8 ft. (9:03)
San Diego
4 ft. (8:51)

Los Angeles
1.7 ft. (1:50)
San Diego
1.6 ft. (1:50)

feet
Los Angeles
-0.9 ft. (2:44)
San Diego
-0.8 ft. (2:41)

12 1 2 3 4 5 6 7 8 9 10 11 noon 1 2 3 4 5 6 7 8 9 10 11 12

ts ebb —⊣ ⊢— 1.6 knots flood —⊣ ⊢— 1.2 knots ebb —⊣ ⊢— 1.8 knots flood —⊣ ⊢— 2.7 kr

WED JUN 5
dawn 4:38 sunrise 5:43 sunset 8:01 dark 9:05
moonrise 4:42 a.m. moonset 7:42 p.m.

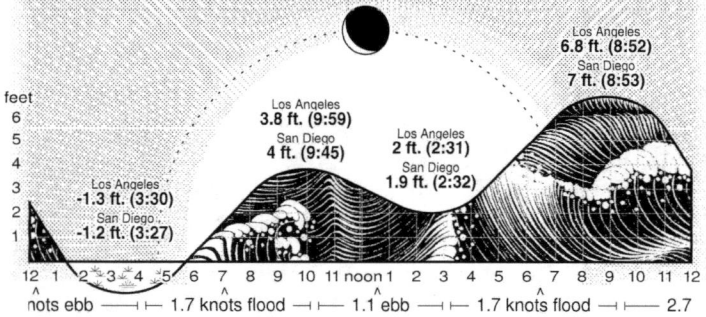

Los Angeles
6.8 ft. (8:52)
San Diego
7 ft. (8:53)

Los Angeles
3.8 ft. (9:59)
San Diego
4 ft. (9:45)

Los Angeles
2 ft. (2:31)
San Diego
1.9 ft. (2:32)

feet
Los Angeles
-1.3 ft. (3:30)
San Diego
-1.2 ft. (3:27)

12 1 2 3 4 5 6 7 8 9 10 11 noon 1 2 3 4 5 6 7 8 9 10 11 12

nots ebb —⊣ ⊢— 1.7 knots flood —⊣ ⊢— 1.1 ebb —⊣ ⊢— 1.7 knots flood —⊣ ⊢— 2.7

THU JUN 6
dawn 4:38 sunrise 5:42 sunset 8:02 dark 9:06
moonrise 5:30 a.m. moonset 8:49 p.m.

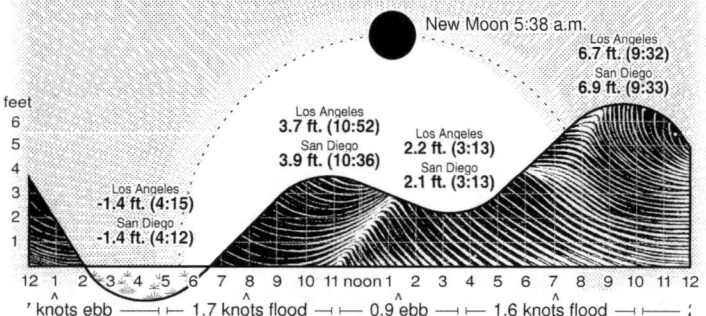

New Moon 5:38 a.m.

Los Angeles
6.7 ft. (9:32)
San Diego
6.9 ft. (9:33)

Los Angeles
3.7 ft. (10:52)
San Diego
3.9 ft. (10:36)

Los Angeles
2.2 ft. (3:13)
San Diego
2.1 ft. (3:13)

feet
Los Angeles
-1.4 ft. (4:15)
San Diego
-1.4 ft. (4:12)

12 1 2 3 4 5 6 7 8 9 10 11 noon 1 2 3 4 5 6 7 8 9 10 11 12

' knots ebb —⊣ ⊢— 1.7 knots flood —⊣ ⊢— 0.9 ebb —⊣ ⊢— 1.6 knots flood —⊣ ⊢—

FRI JUN 7 dawn 4:38 sunrise 5:42 sunset 8:02 dark 9:06
moonrise 6:25 a.m. moonset 9:48 p.m.

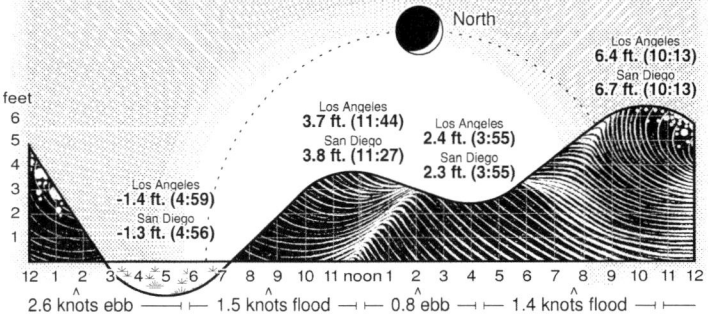

North

feet
6
5
4
3
2
1

Los Angeles
6.4 ft. (10:13)
San Diego
6.7 ft. (10:13)

Los Angeles
3.7 ft. (11:44)
San Diego
3.8 ft. (11:27)

Los Angeles
2.4 ft. (3:55)
San Diego
2.3 ft. (3:55)

Los Angeles
-1.4 ft. (4:59)
San Diego
-1.3 ft. (4:56)

12 1 2 3 4 5 6 7 8 9 10 11 noon 1 2 3 4 5 6 7 8 9 10 11 12

2.6 knots ebb ⊢—⊢ 1.5 knots flood —⊣ ⊢ 0.8 ebb —⊣ ⊢ 1.4 knots flood —⊣ ⊢

SAT JUN 8 dawn 4:38 sunrise 5:42 sunset 8:03 dark 9:07
moonrise 7:26 a.m. moonset 10:38 p.m.

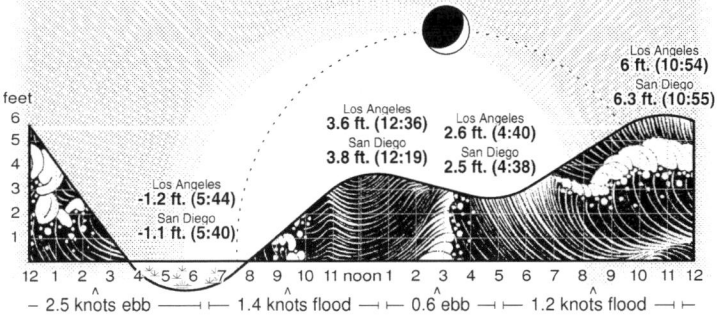

feet
6
5
4
3
2
1

Los Angeles
6 ft. (10:54)
San Diego
6.3 ft. (10:55)

Los Angeles
3.6 ft. (12:36)
San Diego
3.8 ft. (12:19)

Los Angeles
2.6 ft. (4:40)
San Diego
2.5 ft. (4:38)

Los Angeles
-1.2 ft. (5:44)
San Diego
-1.1 ft. (5:40)

12 1 2 3 4 5 6 7 8 9 10 11 noon 1 2 3 4 5 6 7 8 9 10 11 12

— 2.5 knots ebb ——⊣ ⊢ 1.4 knots flood —⊣ ⊢ 0.6 ebb —⊣ ⊢ 1.2 knots flood —⊣ ⊢

SUN JUN 9 dawn 4:38 sunrise 5:42 sunset 8:03 dark 9:08
moonrise 8:30 a.m. moonset 11:20 p.m.

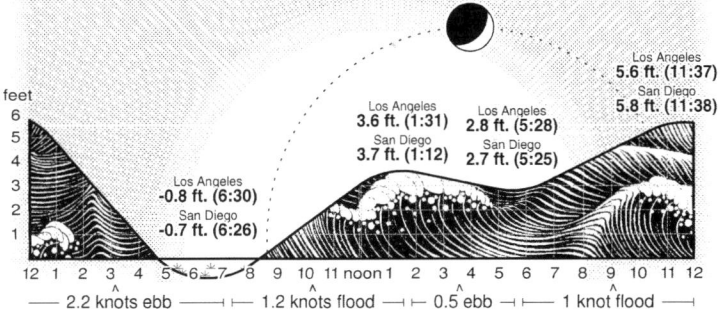

feet
6
5
4
3
2
1

Los Angeles
5.6 ft. (11:37)
San Diego
5.8 ft. (11:38)

Los Angeles
3.6 ft. (1:31)
San Diego
3.7 ft. (1:12)

Los Angeles
2.8 ft. (5:28)
San Diego
2.7 ft. (5:25)

Los Angeles
-0.8 ft. (6:30)
San Diego
-0.7 ft. (6:26)

12 1 2 3 4 5 6 7 8 9 10 11 noon 1 2 3 4 5 6 7 8 9 10 11 12

—— 2.2 knots ebb ——⊣ ⊢ 1.2 knots flood —⊣ ⊢ 0.5 ebb —⊣ ⊢ 1 knot flood ——⊣

Ⓢ Ⓙ
Ⓜ

copyright 2023 Pacific Publishers, L.L.C. WWW.TIDELOG.COM

MON JUN 10

dawn 4:38 sunrise 5:42 sunset 8:03 dark 9:08
moonrise 9:33 a.m. moonset 11:54 p.m.

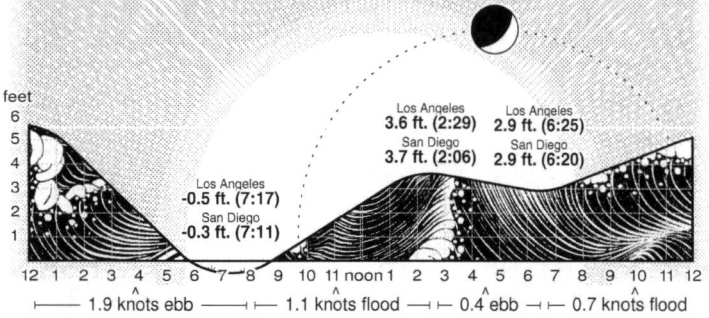

feet

Los Angeles
3.6 ft. (2:29)
San Diego
3.7 ft. (2:06)

Los Angeles
2.9 ft. (6:25)
San Diego
2.9 ft. (6:20)

Los Angeles
-0.5 ft. (7:17)
San Diego
-0.3 ft. (7:11)

12 1 2 3 4 5 6 7 8 9 10 11 noon 1 2 3 4 5 6 7 8 9 10 11 12

⊢——— 1.9 knots ebb ———⊣ ⊢— 1.1 knots flood —⊣ ⊢— 0.4 ebb —⊣ ⊢— 0.7 knots flood

TUE JUN 11

dawn 4:37 sunrise 5:42 sunset 8:04 dark 9:09
moonrise 10:34 a.m.

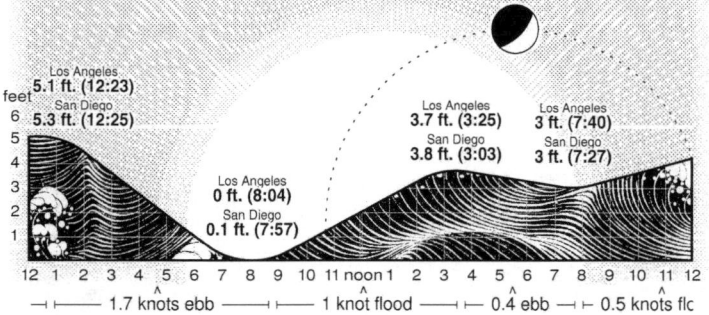

Los Angeles
5.1 ft. (12:23)
San Diego
5.3 ft. (12:25)

feet

Los Angeles
3.7 ft. (3:25)
San Diego
3.8 ft. (3:03)

Los Angeles
3 ft. (7:40)
San Diego
3 ft. (7:27)

Los Angeles
0 ft. (8:04)
San Diego
0.1 ft. (7:57)

12 1 2 3 4 5 6 7 8 9 10 11 noon 1 2 3 4 5 6 7 8 9 10 11 12

⊢⊣ 1.7 knots ebb ———⊣ ⊢— 1 knot flood —⊣ ⊢— 0.4 ebb —⊣ ⊢ 0.5 knots flc

WED JUN 12

dawn 4:37 sunrise 5:42 sunset 8:04 dark 9:09
moonset 12:24 a.m. moonrise 11:32 a.m.

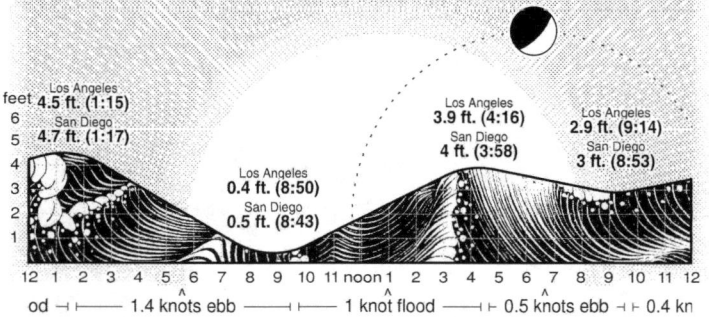

Los Angeles
4.5 ft. (1:15)
San Diego
4.7 ft. (1:17)

feet

Los Angeles
3.9 ft. (4:16)
San Diego
4 ft. (3:58)

Los Angeles
2.9 ft. (9:14)
San Diego
3 ft. (8:53)

Los Angeles
0.4 ft. (8:50)
San Diego
0.5 ft. (8:43)

12 1 2 3 4 5 6 7 8 9 10 11 noon 1 2 3 4 5 6 7 8 9 10 11 12

od ⊣ ⊢— 1.4 knots ebb ———⊣ ⊢— 1 knot flood ———⊣ ⊢ 0.5 knots ebb ⊣ ⊢ 0.4 kn

THU JUN 13

dawn 4:37 sunrise 5:42 sunset 8:05 dark 9:09
moonset 12:50 a.m. moonrise 12:28 p.m.

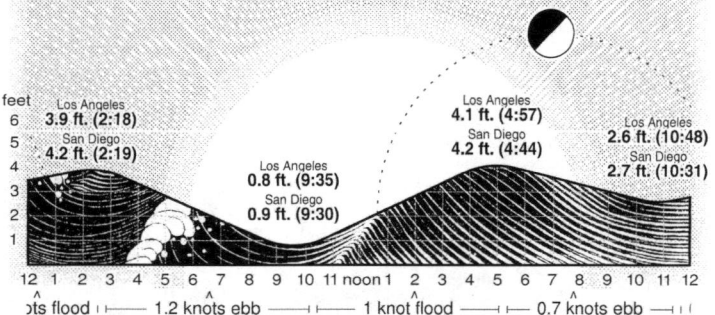

Los Angeles
3.9 ft. (2:18)
San Diego
4.2 ft. (2:19)

feet

Los Angeles
4.1 ft. (4:57)
San Diego
4.2 ft. (4:44)

Los Angeles
2.6 ft. (10:48)
San Diego
2.7 ft. (10:31)

Los Angeles
0.8 ft. (9:35)
San Diego
0.9 ft. (9:30)

12 1 2 3 4 5 6 7 8 9 10 11 noon 1 2 3 4 5 6 7 8 9 10 11 12

ots flood ⊢—— 1.2 knots ebb ———⊣ ⊢— 1 knot flood ———⊣ ⊢ 0.7 knots ebb —⊣⊣

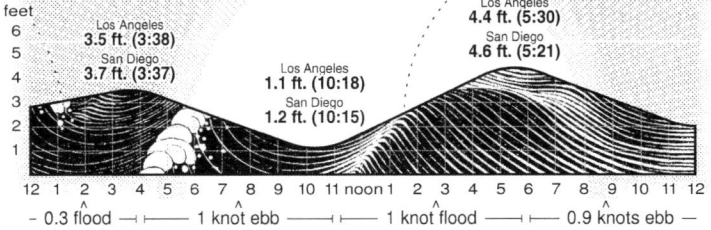

FRI JUN 14

dawn 4:37 sunrise 5:42 sunset 8:05 dark 9:10
moonset 1:13 a.m. moonrise 1:23 p.m.

Flag Day

apogee equator

feet
6
5
4
3
2
1

Los Angeles
3.5 ft. (3:38)
San Diego
3.7 ft. (3:37)

Los Angeles
1.1 ft. (10:18)
San Diego
1.2 ft. (10:15)

Los Angeles
4.4 ft. (5:30)
San Diego
4.6 ft. (5:21)

12 1 2 3 4 5 6 7 8 9 10 11 noon 1 2 3 4 5 6 7 8 9 10 11 12

– 0.3 flood ⊢→ ⊢— 1 knot ebb ——→ ⊢— 1 knot flood ——→ ⊢— 0.9 knots ebb —

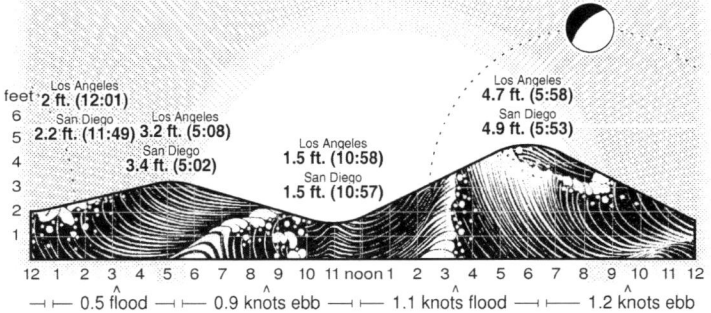

SAT JUN 15

dawn 4:37 sunrise 5:42 sunset 8:05 dark 9:10
moonset 1:37 a.m. moonrise 2:18 p.m.

feet
6
5
4
3
2
1

Los Angeles
2 ft. (12:01)
San Diego
2.2 ft. (11:49)

Los Angeles
3.2 ft. (5:08)
San Diego
3.4 ft. (5:02)

Los Angeles
1.5 ft. (10:58)
San Diego
1.5 ft. (10:57)

Los Angeles
4.7 ft. (5:58)
San Diego
4.9 ft. (5:53)

12 1 2 3 4 5 6 7 8 9 10 11 noon 1 2 3 4 5 6 7 8 9 10 11 12

⊢— 0.5 flood —→ ⊢— 0.9 knots ebb ——→ ⊢— 1.1 knots flood ——→ ⊢— 1.2 knots ebb

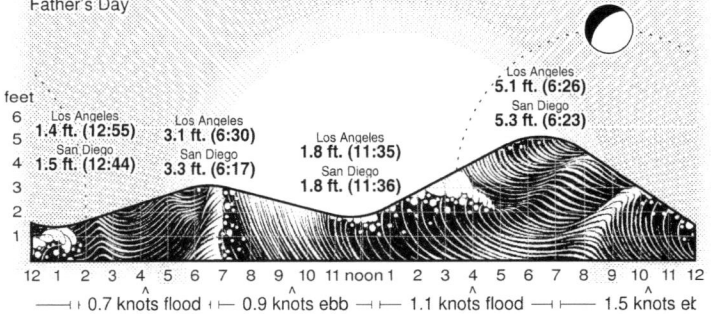

SUN JUN 16

dawn 4:37 sunrise 5:42 sunset 8:06 dark 9:11
moonset 2:01 a.m. moonrise 3:15 p.m.

Father's Day

feet
6
5
4
3
2
1

Los Angeles
1.4 ft. (12:55)
San Diego
1.5 ft. (12:44)

Los Angeles
3.1 ft. (6:30)
San Diego
3.3 ft. (6:17)

Los Angeles
1.8 ft. (11:35)
San Diego
1.8 ft. (11:36)

Los Angeles
5.1 ft. (6:26)
San Diego
5.3 ft. (6:23)

12 1 2 3 4 5 6 7 8 9 10 11 noon 1 2 3 4 5 6 7 8 9 10 11 12

——→⊢ 0.7 knots flood ⊢— 0.9 knots ebb —→ ⊢— 1.1 knots flood ——→ ⊢— 1.5 knots et

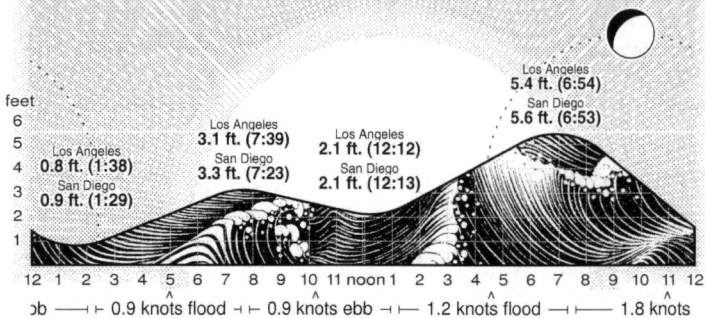

MON JUN 17 dawn 4:38 sunrise 5:42 sunset 8:06 dark 9:11
moonset 2:26 a.m. moonrise 4:14 p.m.

Los Angeles
5.4 ft. (6:54)
San Diego
5.6 ft. (6:53)

feet
6
5
Los Angeles
0.8 ft. (1:38)
San Diego
0.9 ft. (1:29)

Los Angeles
3.1 ft. (7:39)
San Diego
3.3 ft. (7:23)

Los Angeles
2.1 ft. (12:12)
San Diego
2.1 ft. (12:13)

4
3
2
1

12 1 2 3 4 5 6 7 8 9 10 11 noon 1 2 3 4 5 6 7 8 9 10 11 12

ob ⊢ 0.9 knots flood ⊣ ⊢ 0.9 knots ebb ⊣ ⊢ 1.2 knots flood ⊣ ⊢ 1.8 knots

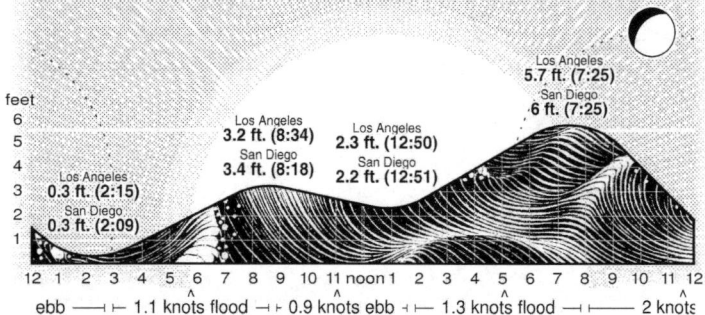

TUE JUN 18 dawn 4:38 sunrise 5:43 sunset 8:06 dark 9:11
moonset 2:55 a.m. moonrise 5:15 p.m.

Los Angeles
5.7 ft. (7:25)
San Diego
6 ft. (7:25)

feet
6
5
4
Los Angeles
0.3 ft. (2:15)
San Diego
0.3 ft. (2:09)

Los Angeles
3.2 ft. (8:34)
San Diego
3.4 ft. (8:18)

Los Angeles
2.3 ft. (12:50)
San Diego
2.2 ft. (12:51)

3
2
1

12 1 2 3 4 5 6 7 8 9 10 11 noon 1 2 3 4 5 6 7 8 9 10 11 12

ebb ⊢ 1.1 knots flood ⊣ ⊢ 0.9 knots ebb ⊣ ⊢ 1.3 knots flood ⊣ ⊢ 2 knots

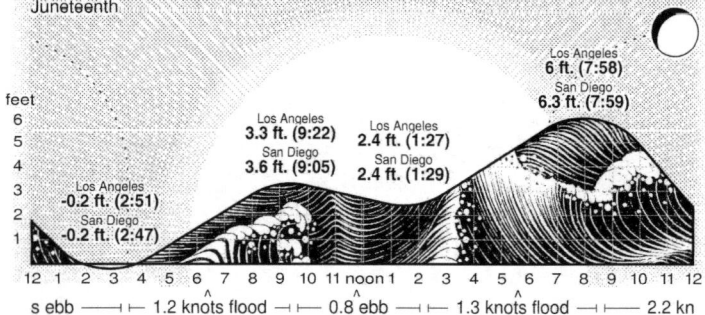

WED JUN 19 dawn 4:38 sunrise 5:43 sunset 8:07 dark 9:11
moonset 3:29 a.m. moonrise 6:19 p.m.

Juneteenth

Los Angeles
6 ft. (7:58)
San Diego
6.3 ft. (7:59)

feet
6
5
4
Los Angeles
3.3 ft. (9:22)
San Diego
3.6 ft. (9:05)

Los Angeles
2.4 ft. (1:27)
San Diego
2.4 ft. (1:29)

3
Los Angeles
-0.2 ft. (2:51)
San Diego
-0.2 ft. (2:47)

2
1

12 1 2 3 4 5 6 7 8 9 10 11 noon 1 2 3 4 5 6 7 8 9 10 11 12

s ebb ⊢ 1.2 knots flood ⊣ ⊢ 0.8 ebb ⊣ ⊢ 1.3 knots flood ⊣ ⊢ 2.2 kn

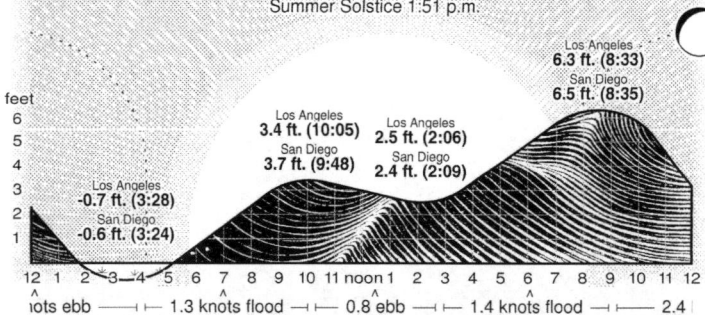

THU JUN 20 dawn 4:38 sunrise 5:43 sunset 8:07 dark 9:12
moonset 4:11 a.m. moonrise 7:24 p.m.

Summer Solstice 1:51 p.m.

Los Angeles
6.3 ft. (8:33)
San Diego
6.5 ft. (8:35)

feet
6
5
Los Angeles
3.4 ft. (10:05)
San Diego
3.7 ft. (9:48)

Los Angeles
2.5 ft. (2:06)
San Diego
2.4 ft. (2:09)

4
3
Los Angeles
-0.7 ft. (3:28)
San Diego
-0.6 ft. (3:24)

2
1

12 1 2 3 4 5 6 7 8 9 10 11 noon 1 2 3 4 5 6 7 8 9 10 11 12

ots ebb ⊢ 1.3 knots flood ⊣ ⊢ 0.8 ebb ⊣ ⊢ 1.4 knots flood ⊣ ⊢ 2.4

FRI JUN 21

dawn 4:38 sunrise 5:43 sunset 8:07 dark 9:12
moonset 5:00 a.m. moonrise 8:26 p.m.

Full Moon 6:08 p.m.

South

Los Angeles
6.5 ft. (9:11)
San Diego
6.7 ft. (9:13)

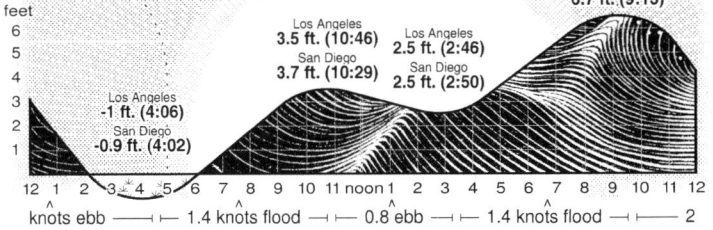

Los Angeles
3.5 ft. (10:46)
San Diego
3.7 ft. (10:29)

Los Angeles
2.5 ft. (2:46)
San Diego
2.5 ft. (2:50)

feet
6
5
4
3
2
1

Los Angeles
-1 ft. (4:06)
San Diego
-0.9 ft. (4:02)

12 1 2 3 4 5 6 7 8 9 10 11 noon 1 2 3 4 5 6 7 8 9 10 11 12

knots ebb ⟶ ⊢ 1.4 knots flood ⟶ ⊢ 0.8 ebb ⟶ ⊢ 1.4 knots flood ⟶ ⊢ 2

SAT JUN 22

dawn 4:39 sunrise 5:43 sunset 8:07 dark 9:12
moonset 5:59 a.m. moonrise 9:22 p.m.

Los Angeles
6.5 ft. (9:52)
San Diego
6.8 ft. (9:52)

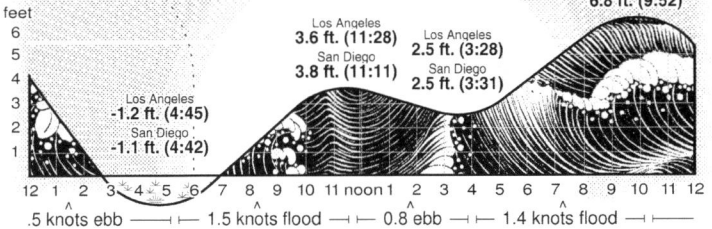

Los Angeles
3.6 ft. (11:28)
San Diego
3.8 ft. (11:11)

Los Angeles
2.5 ft. (3:28)
San Diego
2.5 ft. (3:31)

feet
6
5
4
3
2
1

Los Angeles
-1.2 ft. (4:45)
San Diego
-1.1 ft. (4:42)

12 1 2 3 4 5 6 7 8 9 10 11 noon 1 2 3 4 5 6 7 8 9 10 11 12

.5 knots ebb ⟶ ⊢ 1.5 knots flood ⟶ ⊢ 0.8 ebb ⟶ ⊢ 1.4 knots flood ⟶ ⊢

SUN JUN 23

dawn 4:39 sunrise 5:44 sunset 8:07 dark 9:12
moonset 7:06 a.m. moonrise 10:11 p.m.

Los Angeles
6.4 ft. (10:35)
San Diego
6.7 ft. (10:35)

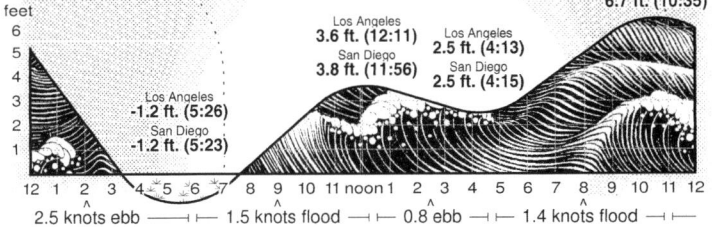

Los Angeles
3.6 ft. (12:11)
San Diego
3.8 ft. (11:56)

Los Angeles
2.5 ft. (4:13)
San Diego
2.5 ft. (4:15)

feet
6
5
4
3
2
1

Los Angeles
-1.2 ft. (5:26)
San Diego
-1.2 ft. (5:23)

12 1 2 3 4 5 6 7 8 9 10 11 noon 1 2 3 4 5 6 7 8 9 10 11 12

2.5 knots ebb ⟶ ⊢ 1.5 knots flood ⟶ ⊢ 0.8 ebb ⟶ ⊢ 1.4 knots flood ⟶ ⊢

Ⓢ   Ⓙ
 Ⓜ
      ⓜ

Summer Solstice The solstice marks the first day of summer in the
northern hemisphere. The solstice occurs the moment the Earth's tilt
towards the Sun is at its maximum when the sun is directly over the Tropic
of Cancer. For every place north of the Tropic of Cancer, the Sun is at
its highest point in the sky and this is the longest day of the year.

MON JUN 24

dawn 4:39 sunrise 5:44 sunset 8:07 dark 9:12
moonset 8:16 a.m. moonrise 10:52 p.m.

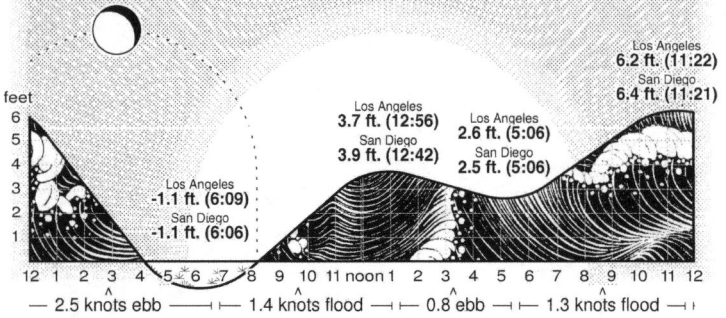

feet

Los Angeles
6.2 ft. (11:22)
San Diego
6.4 ft. (11:21)

Los Angeles
3.7 ft. (12:56)
San Diego
3.9 ft. (12:42)

Los Angeles
2.6 ft. (5:06)
San Diego
2.5 ft. (5:06)

Los Angeles
-1.1 ft. (6:09)
San Diego
-1.1 ft. (6:06)

12 1 2 3 4 5 6 7 8 9 10 11 noon 1 2 3 4 5 6 7 8 9 10 11 12

— 2.5 knots ebb — ⊢— 1.4 knots flood —⊣ ⊢ 0.8 ebb ⊣ ⊢ 1.3 knots flood —⊣

TUE JUN 25

dawn 4:39 sunrise 5:44 sunset 8:07 dark 9:12
moonset 9:27 a.m. moonrise 11:28 p.m.

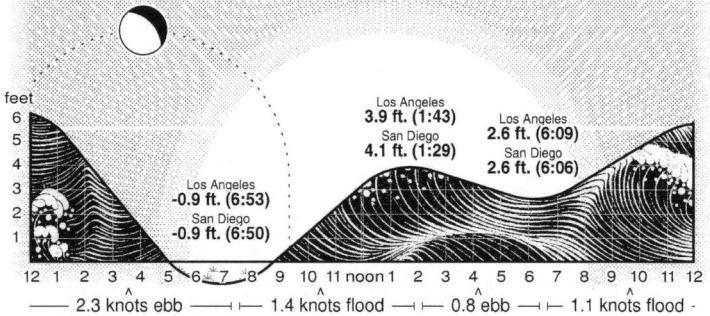

feet

Los Angeles
3.9 ft. (1:43)
San Diego
4.1 ft. (1:29)

Los Angeles
2.6 ft. (6:09)
San Diego
2.6 ft. (6:06)

Los Angeles
-0.9 ft. (6:53)
San Diego
-0.9 ft. (6:50)

12 1 2 3 4 5 6 7 8 9 10 11 noon 1 2 3 4 5 6 7 8 9 10 11 12

— 2.3 knots ebb — ⊢— 1.4 knots flood —⊣ ⊢ 0.8 ebb ⊣ ⊢ 1.1 knots flood ·

WED JUN 26

dawn 4:40 sunrise 5:45 sunset 8:08 dark 9:12
moonset 10:37 a.m. moonrise 11:59 p.m.

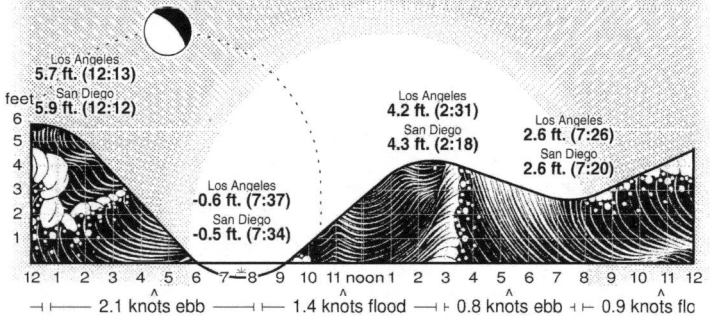

Los Angeles
5.7 ft. (12:13)
San Diego
5.9 ft. (12:12)
feet

Los Angeles
4.2 ft. (2:31)
San Diego
4.3 ft. (2:18)

Los Angeles
2.6 ft. (7:26)
San Diego
2.6 ft. (7:20)

Los Angeles
-0.6 ft. (7:37)
San Diego
-0.5 ft. (7:34)

12 1 2 3 4 5 6 7 8 9 10 11 noon 1 2 3 4 5 6 7 8 9 10 11 12

⊣ ⊢— 2.1 knots ebb —— ⊢— 1.4 knots flood —⊣ ⊢ 0.8 knots ebb ⊣ ⊢ 0.9 knots flo

THU JUN 27

dawn 4:40 sunrise 5:45 sunset 8:08 dark 9:12
moonset 11:46 a.m.

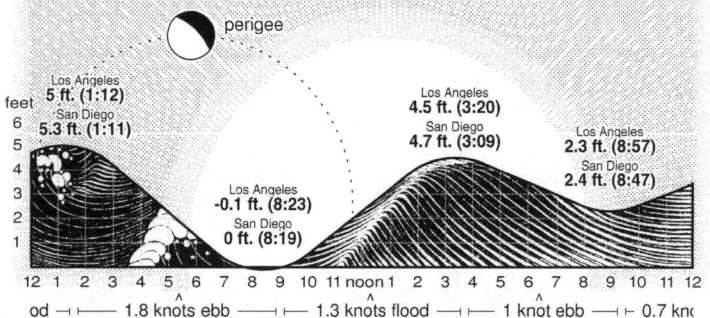

perigee

Los Angeles
5 ft. (1:12)
San Diego
5.3 ft. (1:11)
feet

Los Angeles
4.5 ft. (3:20)
San Diego
4.7 ft. (3:09)

Los Angeles
2.3 ft. (8:57)
San Diego
2.4 ft. (8:47)

Los Angeles
-0.1 ft. (8:23)
San Diego
0 ft. (8:19)

12 1 2 3 4 5 6 7 8 9 10 11 noon 1 2 3 4 5 6 7 8 9 10 11 12

od ⊣ ⊢— 1.8 knots ebb ——— ⊢— 1.3 knots flood —⊣ ⊢— 1 knot ebb —⊣ ⊢ 0.7 kn

FRI JUN 28
dawn 4:41 sunrise 5:45 sunset 8:08 dark 9:12
moonrise 12:29 a.m. moonset 12:53 p.m.

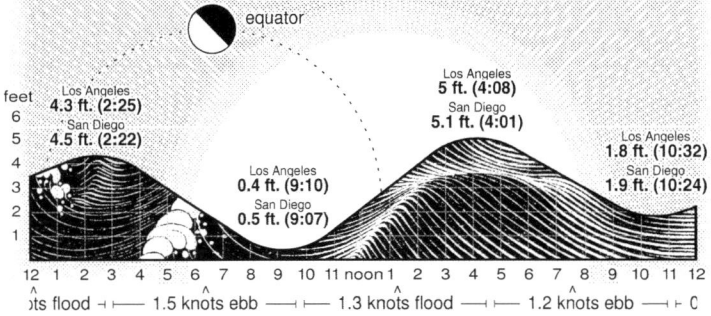

equator

feet
6
5
4
3
2
1

Los Angeles
4.3 ft. (2:25)
San Diego
4.5 ft. (2:22)

Los Angeles
0.4 ft. (9:10)
San Diego
0.5 ft. (9:07)

Los Angeles
5 ft. (4:08)
San Diego
5.1 ft. (4:01)

Los Angeles
1.8 ft. (10:32)
San Diego
1.9 ft. (10:24)

12 1 2 3 4 5 6 7 8 9 10 11 noon 1 2 3 4 5 6 7 8 9 10 11 12

ots flood ⊣ ⊢ 1.5 knots ebb ⟶ ⊢ 1.3 knots flood ⟶ ⊢ 1.2 knots ebb ⟶ ⊢ C

SAT JUN 29
dawn 4:41 sunrise 5:46 sunset 8:08 dark 9:12
moonrise 12:57 a.m. moonset 2:00 p.m.

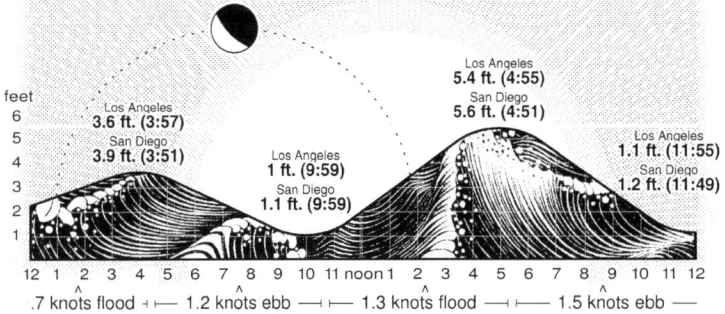

feet
6
5
4
3
2
1

Los Angeles
3.6 ft. (3:57)
San Diego
3.9 ft. (3:51)

Los Angeles
1 ft. (9:59)
San Diego
1.1 ft. (9:59)

Los Angeles
5.4 ft. (4:55)
San Diego
5.6 ft. (4:51)

Los Angeles
1.1 ft. (11:55)
San Diego
1.2 ft. (11:49)

12 1 2 3 4 5 6 7 8 9 10 11 noon 1 2 3 4 5 6 7 8 9 10 11 12

.7 knots flood ⊣ ⊢ 1.2 knots ebb ⟶ ⊢ 1.3 knots flood ⟶ ⊢ 1.5 knots ebb ⟶

SUN JUN 30
dawn 4:42 sunrise 5:46 sunset 8:08 dark 9:12
moonrise 1:27 a.m. moonset 3:09 p.m.

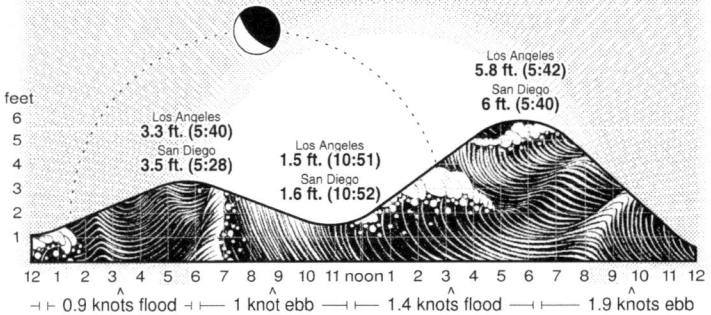

feet
6
5
4
3
2
1

Los Angeles
3.3 ft. (5:40)
San Diego
3.5 ft. (5:28)

Los Angeles
1.5 ft. (10:51)
San Diego
1.6 ft. (10:52)

Los Angeles
5.8 ft. (5:42)
San Diego
6 ft. (5:40)

12 1 2 3 4 5 6 7 8 9 10 11 noon 1 2 3 4 5 6 7 8 9 10 11 12

⊣ ⊢ 0.9 knots flood ⊣ ⊢ 1 knot ebb ⟶ ⊢ 1.4 knots flood ⟶ ⊢ 1.9 knots ebb

Ⓢ Ⓙ Ⓜ Ⓜ

MON JUL 1
dawn 4:42 sunrise 5:47 sunset 8:08 dark 9:12
moonrise 2:00 a.m. moonset 4:18 p.m.

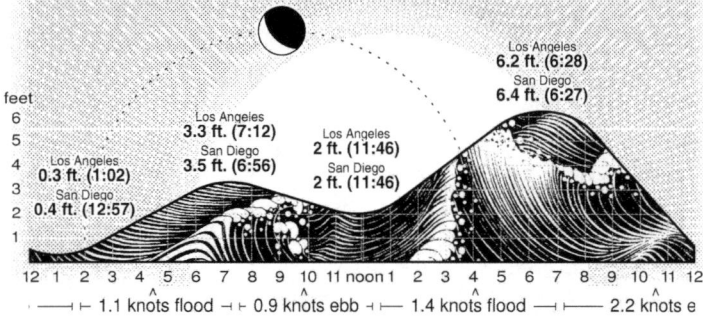

Los Angeles
6.2 ft. (6:28)
San Diego
6.4 ft. (6:27)

Los Angeles
3.3 ft. (7:12)
San Diego
3.5 ft. (6:56)

Los Angeles
2 ft. (11:46)
San Diego
2 ft. (11:46)

Los Angeles
0.3 ft. (1:02)
San Diego
0.4 ft. (12:57)

feet
6
5
4
3
2
1

12 1 2 3 4 5 6 7 8 9 10 11 noon 1 2 3 4 5 6 7 8 9 10 11 12

├─ 1.1 knots flood ─┤ ├ 0.9 knots ebb ┤ ├ 1.4 knots flood ─┤ ├── 2.2 knots e

TUE JUL 2
dawn 4:43 sunrise 5:47 sunset 8:07 dark 9:12
moonrise 2:38 a.m. moonset 5:28 p.m.

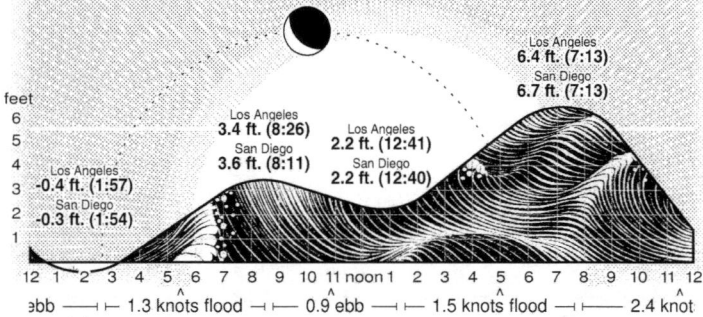

Los Angeles
6.4 ft. (7:13)
San Diego
6.7 ft. (7:13)

Los Angeles
3.4 ft. (8:26)
San Diego
3.6 ft. (8:11)

Los Angeles
2.2 ft. (12:41)
San Diego
2.2 ft. (12:40)

Los Angeles
-0.4 ft. (1:57)
San Diego
-0.3 ft. (1:54)

feet
6
5
4
3
2
1

12 1 2 3 4 5 6 7 8 9 10 11 noon 1 2 3 4 5 6 7 8 9 10 11 12

ebb ──┤ ├ 1.3 knots flood ─┤ ├ 0.9 ebb ─┤ ├ 1.5 knots flood ─┤ ├── 2.4 knot

WED JUL 3
dawn 4:43 sunrise 5:47 sunset 8:07 dark 9:12
moonrise 3:22 a.m. moonset 6:35 p.m.

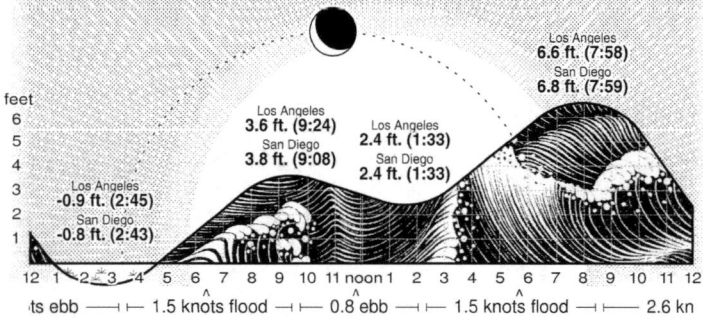

Los Angeles
6.6 ft. (7:58)
San Diego
6.8 ft. (7:59)

Los Angeles
3.6 ft. (9:24)
San Diego
3.8 ft. (9:08)

Los Angeles
2.4 ft. (1:33)
San Diego
2.4 ft. (1:33)

Los Angeles
-0.9 ft. (2:45)
San Diego
-0.8 ft. (2:43)

feet
6
5
4
3
2
1

12 1 2 3 4 5 6 7 8 9 10 11 noon 1 2 3 4 5 6 7 8 9 10 11 12

ts ebb ──┤ ├ 1.5 knots flood ─┤ ├ 0.8 ebb ─┤ ├ 1.5 knots flood ─┤ ├── 2.6 kn

THU JUL 4
dawn 4:44 sunrise 5:48 sunset 8:07 dark 9:11
moonrise 4:14 a.m. moonset 7:37 p.m.

Independence Day   Earth at Aphelion 10:06 p.m.

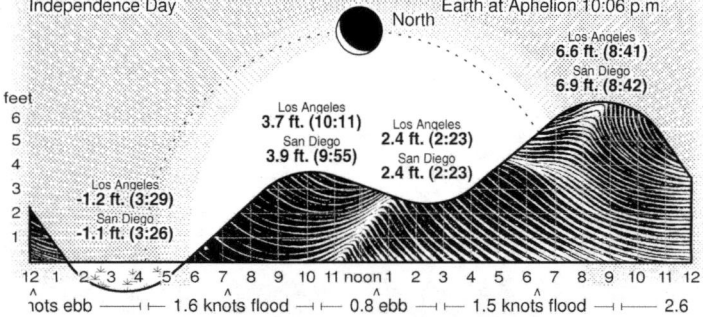

North

Los Angeles
6.6 ft. (8:41)
San Diego
6.9 ft. (8:42)

Los Angeles
3.7 ft. (10:11)
San Diego
3.9 ft. (9:55)

Los Angeles
2.4 ft. (2:23)
San Diego
2.4 ft. (2:23)

Los Angeles
-1.2 ft. (3:29)
San Diego
-1.1 ft. (3:26)

feet
6
5
4
3
2
1

12 1 2 3 4 5 6 7 8 9 10 11 noon 1 2 3 4 5 6 7 8 9 10 11 12

nots ebb ──┤ ├ 1.6 knots flood ─┤ ├ 0.8 ebb ─┤ ├ 1.5 knots flood ─┤ ├── 2.6

FRI JUL 5

dawn 4:44 sunrise 5:48 sunset 8:07 dark 9:11
moonrise 5:12 a.m. moonset 8:30 p.m.

New Moon 3:57 p.m.

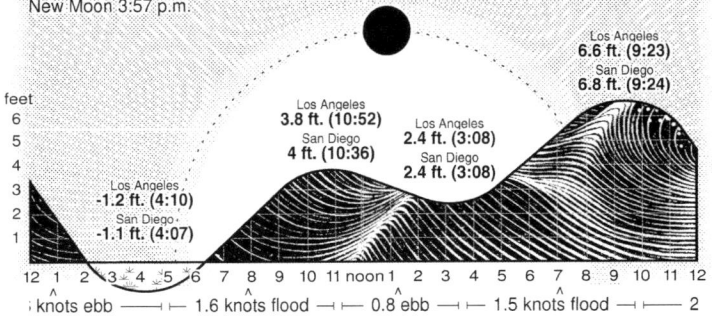

Los Angeles
6.6 ft. (9:23)
San Diego
6.8 ft. (9:24)

Los Angeles
3.8 ft. (10:52)
San Diego
4 ft. (10:36)

Los Angeles
2.4 ft. (3:08)
San Diego
2.4 ft. (3:08)

feet
6
5
4
3
2
1

Los Angeles
-1.2 ft. (4:10)
San Diego
-1.1 ft. (4:07)

12 1 2 3 4 5 6 7 8 9 10 11 noon 1 2 3 4 5 6 7 8 9 10 11 12

knots ebb ⟶ ⊢⟶ 1.6 knots flood ⟶ ⊢ 0.8 ebb ⟶ ⊢ 1.5 knots flood ⟶ ⊢⟶ 2

SAT JUL 6

dawn 4:45 sunrise 5:49 sunset 8:07 dark 9:11
moonrise 6:15 a.m. moonset 9:15 p.m.

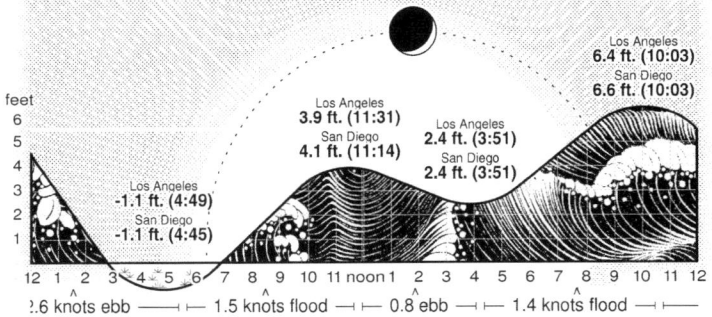

Los Angeles
6.4 ft. (10:03)
San Diego
6.6 ft. (10:03)

Los Angeles
3.9 ft. (11:31)
San Diego
4.1 ft. (11:14)

Los Angeles
2.4 ft. (3:51)
San Diego
2.4 ft. (3:51)

feet
6
5
4
3
2
1

Los Angeles
-1.1 ft. (4:49)
San Diego
-1.1 ft. (4:45)

12 1 2 3 4 5 6 7 8 9 10 11 noon 1 2 3 4 5 6 7 8 9 10 11 12

2.6 knots ebb ⟶ ⊢⟶ 1.5 knots flood ⟶ ⊢ 0.8 ebb ⟶ ⊢ 1.4 knots flood ⟶ ⊢

SUN JUL 7

dawn 4:45 sunrise 5:49 sunset 8:07 dark 9:11
moonrise 7:18 a.m. moonset 9:52 p.m.

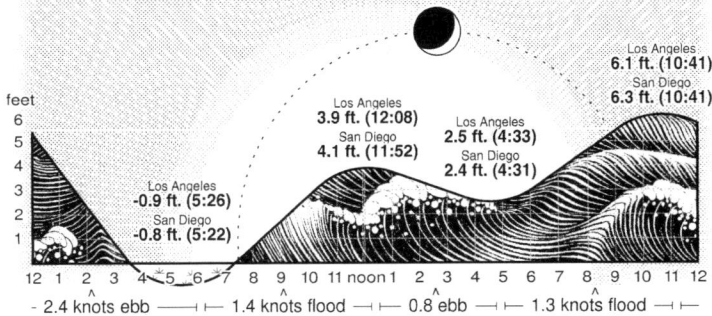

Los Angeles
6.1 ft. (10:41)
San Diego
6.3 ft. (10:41)

Los Angeles
3.9 ft. (12:08)
San Diego
4.1 ft. (11:52)

Los Angeles
2.5 ft. (4:33)
San Diego
2.4 ft. (4:31)

feet
6
5
4
3
2
1

Los Angeles
-0.9 ft. (5:26)
San Diego
-0.8 ft. (5:22)

12 1 2 3 4 5 6 7 8 9 10 11 noon 1 2 3 4 5 6 7 8 9 10 11 12

- 2.4 knots ebb ⟶ ⊢⟶ 1.4 knots flood ⟶ ⊢ 0.8 ebb ⟶ ⊢ 1.3 knots flood ⟶ ⊢

Ⓢ Ⓙ Ⓥ
Ⓜ   ⓜ

MON JUL 8 dawn 4:46 sunrise 5:50 sunset 8:06 dark 9:10
moonrise 8:21 a.m. moonset 10:23 p.m.

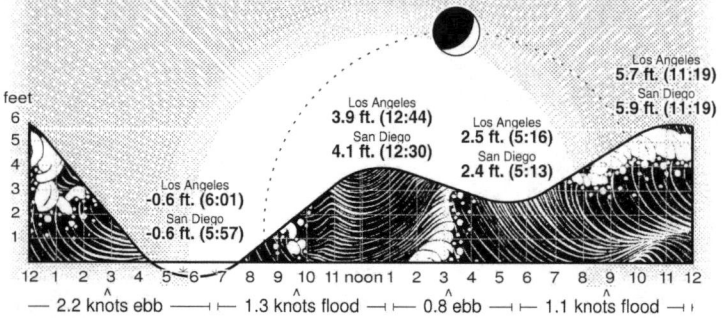

feet

Los Angeles
5.7 ft. (11:19)
San Diego
5.9 ft. (11:19)

Los Angeles
3.9 ft. (12:44)
San Diego
4.1 ft. (12:30)

Los Angeles
2.5 ft. (5:16)
San Diego
2.4 ft. (5:13)

Los Angeles
-0.6 ft. (6:01)
San Diego
-0.6 ft. (5:57)

— 2.2 knots ebb —|— 1.3 knots flood —|— 0.8 ebb —|— 1.1 knots flood —|

TUE JUL 9 dawn 4:47 sunrise 5:51 sunset 8:06 dark 9:10
moonrise 9:21 a.m. moonset 10:51 p.m.

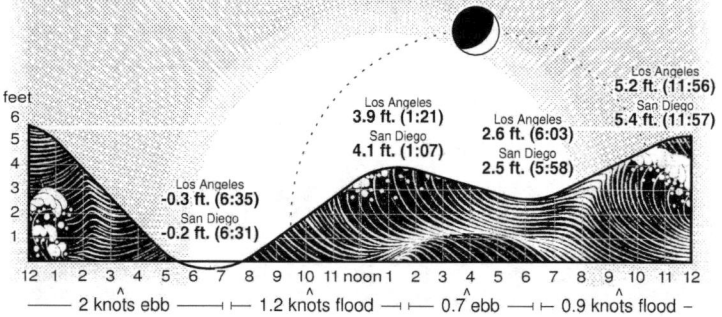

feet

Los Angeles
5.2 ft. (11:56)
San Diego
5.4 ft. (11:57)

Los Angeles
3.9 ft. (1:21)
San Diego
4.1 ft. (1:07)

Los Angeles
2.6 ft. (6:03)
San Diego
2.5 ft. (5:58)

Los Angeles
-0.3 ft. (6:35)
San Diego
-0.2 ft. (6:31)

— 2 knots ebb —|— 1.2 knots flood —|— 0.7 ebb —|— 0.9 knots flood –

WED JUL 10 dawn 4:47 sunrise 5:51 sunset 8:06 dark 9:09
moonrise 10:18 a.m. moonset 11:15 p.m.

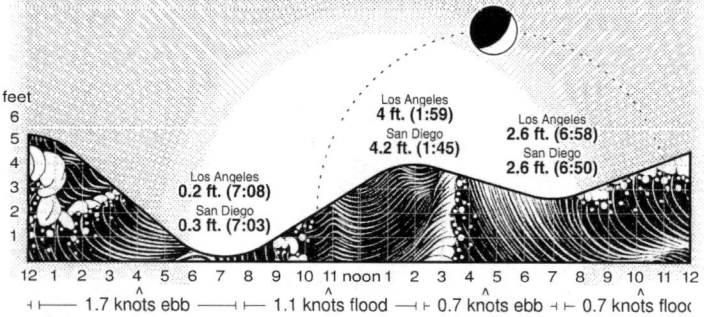

feet

Los Angeles
4 ft. (1:59)
San Diego
4.2 ft. (1:45)

Los Angeles
2.6 ft. (6:58)
San Diego
2.6 ft. (6:50)

Los Angeles
0.2 ft. (7:08)
San Diego
0.3 ft. (7:03)

–|— 1.7 knots ebb —|— 1.1 knots flood —|– 0.7 knots ebb –|– 0.7 knots flood

THU JUL 11 dawn 4:48 sunrise 5:52 sunset 8:06 dark 9:09
moonrise 11:14 a.m. moonset 11:39 p.m.

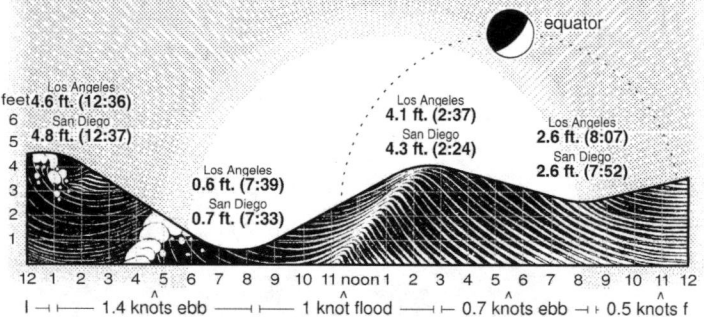

equator

feet
Los Angeles
4.6 ft. (12:36)
San Diego
4.8 ft. (12:37)

Los Angeles
4.1 ft. (2:37)
San Diego
4.3 ft. (2:24)

Los Angeles
2.6 ft. (8:07)
San Diego
2.6 ft. (7:52)

Los Angeles
0.6 ft. (7:39)
San Diego
0.7 ft. (7:33)

|—|— 1.4 knots ebb —|—|— 1 knot flood —|– 0.7 knots ebb –|– 0.5 knots f

FRI JUL 12 dawn 4:49 sunrise 5:52 sunset 8:05 dark 9:08
moonrise 12:08 p.m.

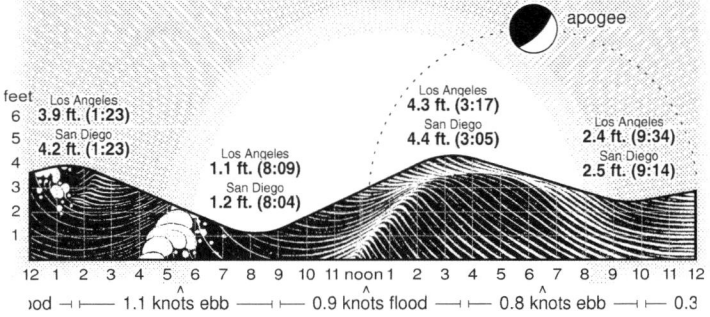

apogee

feet
6
5
4
3
2
1

Los Angeles
3.9 ft. (1:23)
San Diego
4.2 ft. (1:23)

Los Angeles
1.1 ft. (8:09)
San Diego
1.2 ft. (8:04)

Los Angeles
4.3 ft. (3:17)
San Diego
4.4 ft. (3:05)

Los Angeles
2.4 ft. (9:34)
San Diego
2.5 ft. (9:14)

12 1 2 3 4 5 6 7 8 9 10 11 noon 1 2 3 4 5 6 7 8 9 10 11 12

od ⊢⊣ 1.1 knots ebb ⊢⊣ 0.9 knots flood ⊢⊣ 0.8 knots ebb ⊢⊣ 0.3

SAT JUL 13 dawn 4:50 sunrise 5:53 sunset 8:05 dark 9:08
moonset 12:02 a.m. moonrise 1:04 p.m.

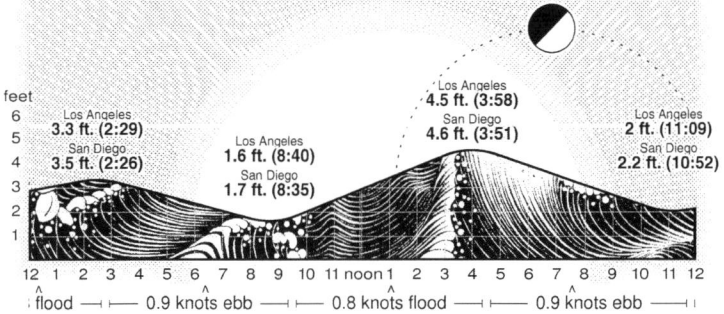

feet
6
5
4
3
2
1

Los Angeles
3.3 ft. (2:29)
San Diego
3.5 ft. (2:26)

Los Angeles
1.6 ft. (8:40)
San Diego
1.7 ft. (8:35)

Los Angeles
4.5 ft. (3:58)
San Diego
4.6 ft. (3:51)

Los Angeles
2 ft. (11:09)
San Diego
2.2 ft. (10:52)

12 1 2 3 4 5 6 7 8 9 10 11 noon 1 2 3 4 5 6 7 8 9 10 11 12

flood ⊢⊣ 0.9 knots ebb ⊢⊣ 0.8 knots flood ⊢⊣ 0.9 knots ebb ⊢⊣

SUN JUL 14 dawn 4:50 sunrise 5:53 sunset 8:04 dark 9:07
moonset 12:26 a.m. moonrise 2:01 p.m.

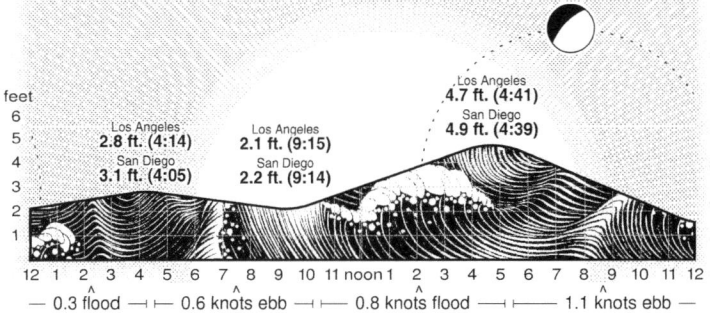

feet
6
5
4
3
2
1

Los Angeles
2.8 ft. (4:14)
San Diego
3.1 ft. (4:05)

Los Angeles
2.1 ft. (9:15)
San Diego
2.2 ft. (9:14)

Los Angeles
4.7 ft. (4:41)
San Diego
4.9 ft. (4:39)

12 1 2 3 4 5 6 7 8 9 10 11 noon 1 2 3 4 5 6 7 8 9 10 11 12

— 0.3 flood ⊢⊣ 0.6 knots ebb ⊢⊣ 0.8 knots flood ⊢⊣ 1.1 knots ebb —

Ⓢ Ⓙ Ⓥ
Ⓜ   ⓜ

copyright 2023 Pacific Publishers, L.L.C. WWW.TIDELOG.COM

MON JUL 15
dawn 4:51 sunrise 5:54 sunset 8:04 dark 9:07
moonset 12:54 a.m. moonrise 3:01 p.m.

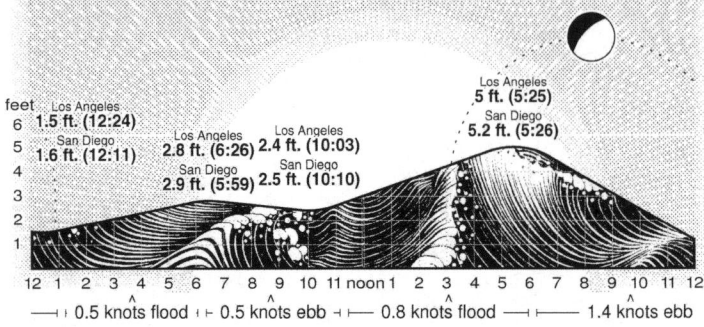

feet
Los Angeles
1.5 ft. (12:24)
San Diego
1.6 ft. (12:11)

Los Angeles
2.8 ft. (6:26)
San Diego
2.9 ft. (5:59)

Los Angeles
2.4 ft. (10:03)
San Diego
2.5 ft. (10:10)

Los Angeles
5 ft. (5:25)
San Diego
5.2 ft. (5:26)

⊢—⊣ 0.5 knots flood ⊢⊢ 0.5 knots ebb ⊣⊢ 0.8 knots flood ⊢⊢ 1.4 knots ebb

TUE JUL 16
dawn 4:52 sunrise 5:55 sunset 8:03 dark 9:06
moonset 1:25 a.m. moonrise 4:03 p.m.

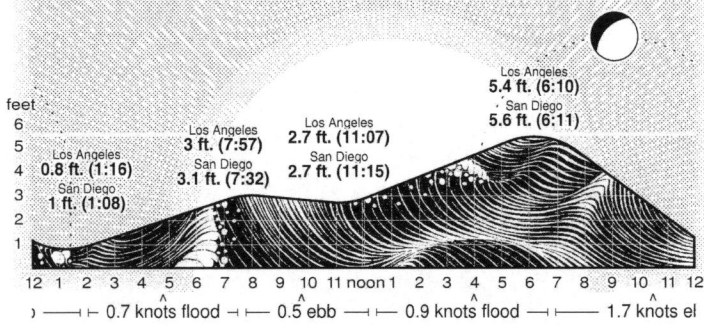

feet
Los Angeles
0.8 ft. (1:16)
San Diego
1 ft. (1:08)

Los Angeles
3 ft. (7:57)
San Diego
3.1 ft. (7:32)

Los Angeles
2.7 ft. (11:07)
San Diego
2.7 ft. (11:15)

Los Angeles
5.4 ft. (6:10)
San Diego
5.6 ft. (6:11)

⟩ ⊢—⊣ 0.7 knots flood ⊣⊢ 0.5 ebb ⊢— 0.9 knots flood ⊢—⊣ 1.7 knots el

WED JUL 17
dawn 4:53 sunrise 5:55 sunset 8:03 dark 9:06
moonset 2:03 a.m. moonrise 5:07 p.m.

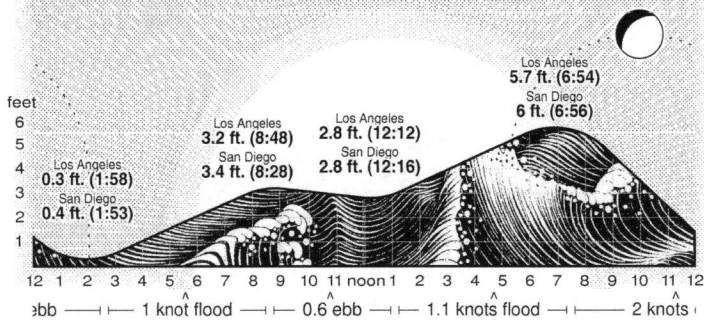

feet
Los Angeles
0.3 ft. (1:58)
San Diego
0.4 ft. (1:53)

Los Angeles
3.2 ft. (8:48)
San Diego
3.4 ft. (8:28)

Los Angeles
2.8 ft. (12:12)
San Diego
2.8 ft. (12:16)

Los Angeles
5.7 ft. (6:54)
San Diego
6 ft. (6:56)

ebb ⊢— 1 knot flood ⊢—⊣ 0.6 ebb ⊣⊢ 1.1 knots flood ⊢—⊣ 2 knots ⟨

THU JUL 18
dawn 4:53 sunrise 5:56 sunset 8:02 dark 9:05
moonset 2:48 a.m. moonrise 6:11 p.m.

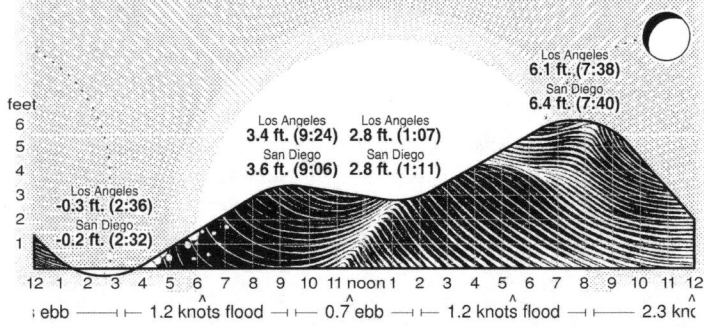

feet
Los Angeles
-0.3 ft. (2:36)
San Diego
-0.2 ft. (2:32)

Los Angeles
3.4 ft. (9:24)
San Diego
3.6 ft. (9:06)

Los Angeles
2.8 ft. (1:07)
San Diego
2.8 ft. (1:11)

Los Angeles
6.1 ft. (7:38)
San Diego
6.4 ft. (7:40)

⟨ ebb ⊣—⊣ 1.2 knots flood ⊢—⊣ 0.7 ebb ⊢— 1.2 knots flood ⊢—⊣ 2.3 knots ⟨

FRI JUL 19

dawn 4:54 sunrise 5:57 sunset 8:02 dark 9:04
moonset 3:43 a.m. moonrise 7:10 p.m.

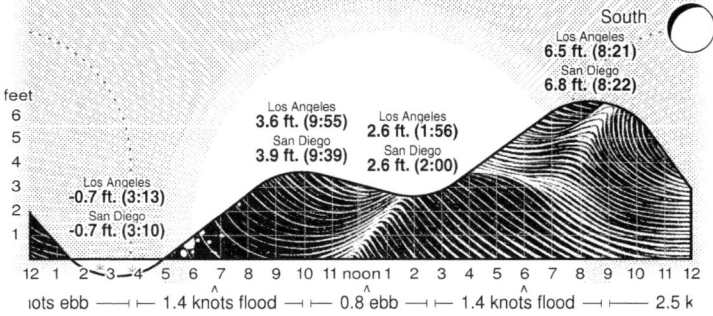

South

Los Angeles
6.5 ft. (8:21)
San Diego
6.8 ft. (8:22)

Los Angeles
3.6 ft. (9:55)
San Diego
3.9 ft. (9:39)

Los Angeles
2.6 ft. (1:56)
San Diego
2.6 ft. (2:00)

Los Angeles
-0.7 ft. (3:13)
San Diego
-0.7 ft. (3:10)

feet
6
5
4
3
2
1

12 1 2 3 4 5 6 7 8 9 10 11 noon 1 2 3 4 5 6 7 8 9 10 11 12

knots ebb —— ├— 1.4 knots flood —┤ ├— 0.8 ebb —┤ ├— 1.4 knots flood —┤ ├— 2.5 k

SAT JUL 20

dawn 4:55 sunrise 5:57 sunset 8:01 dark 9:03
moonset 4:47 a.m. moonrise 8:03 p.m.

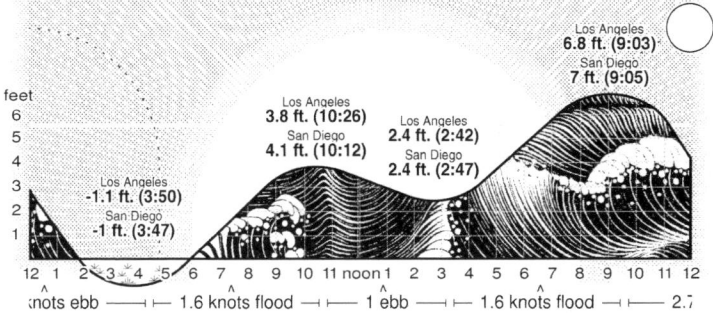

Los Angeles
6.8 ft. (9:03)
San Diego
7 ft. (9:05)

Los Angeles
3.8 ft. (10:26)
San Diego
4.1 ft. (10:12)

Los Angeles
2.4 ft. (2:42)
San Diego
2.4 ft. (2:47)

Los Angeles
-1.1 ft. (3:50)
San Diego
-1 ft. (3:47)

feet
6
5
4
3
2
1

12 1 2 3 4 5 6 7 8 9 10 11 noon 1 2 3 4 5 6 7 8 9 10 11 12

knots ebb —— ├— 1.6 knots flood —┤ ├— 1 ebb —┤ ├— 1.6 knots flood —┤ ├— 2.7

SUN JUL 21

dawn 4:56 sunrise 5:58 sunset 8:01 dark 9:03
moonset 5:58 a.m. moonrise 8:48 p.m.

Mercury eastern elongation

Full Moon 3:17 a.m.

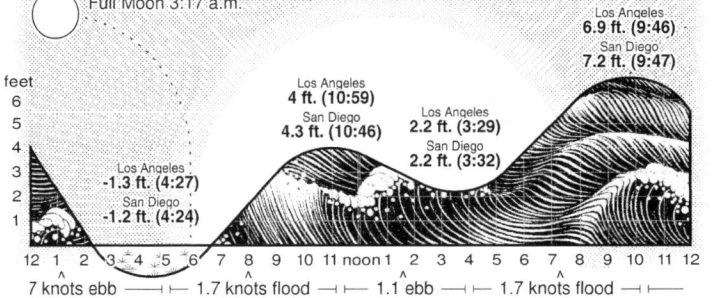

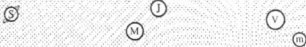

Los Angeles
6.9 ft. (9:46)
San Diego
7.2 ft. (9:47)

Los Angeles
4 ft. (10:59)
San Diego
4.3 ft. (10:46)

Los Angeles
2.2 ft. (3:29)
San Diego
2.2 ft. (3:32)

Los Angeles
-1.3 ft. (4:27)
San Diego
-1.2 ft. (4:24)

feet
6
5
4
3
2
1

12 1 2 3 4 5 6 7 8 9 10 11 noon 1 2 3 4 5 6 7 8 9 10 11 12

7 knots ebb —— ├— 1.7 knots flood —┤ ├— 1.1 ebb —┤ ├— 1.7 knots flood —┤ ├—

Ⓢ   Ⓙ   Ⓥ
  Ⓜ   ⓜ

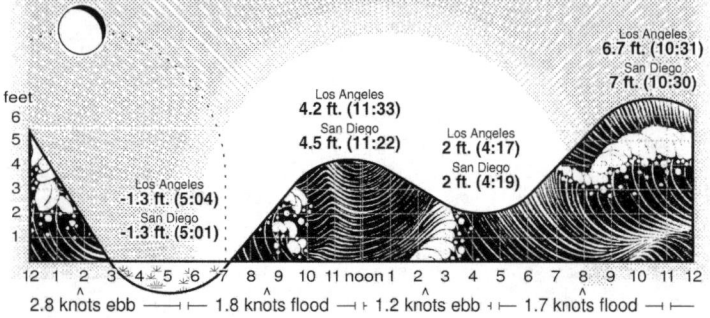

MON JUL 22
dawn 4:57 sunrise 5:59 sunset 8:00 dark 9:02
moonset 7:11 a.m. moonrise 9:26 p.m.

feet

Los Angeles
6.7 ft. (10:31)
San Diego
7 ft. (10:30)

Los Angeles
4.2 ft. (11:33)
San Diego
4.5 ft. (11:22)

Los Angeles
2 ft. (4:17)
San Diego
2 ft. (4:19)

Los Angeles
-1.3 ft. (5:04)
San Diego
-1.3 ft. (5:01)

12 1 2 3 4 5 6 7 8 9 10 11 noon 1 2 3 4 5 6 7 8 9 10 11 12

2.8 knots ebb ⊢—⊣ 1.8 knots flood → ⊢ 1.2 knots ebb ⊣ ⊦— 1.7 knots flood —⊣ ⊦

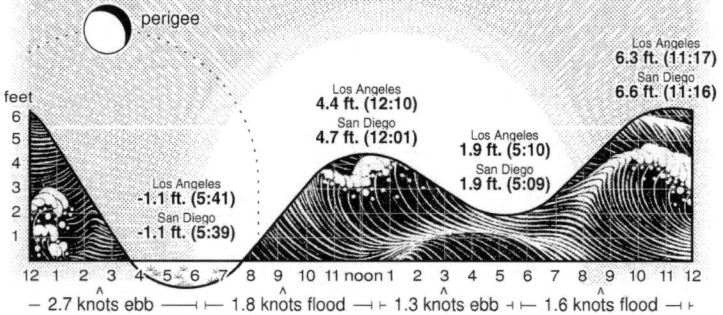

TUE JUL 23
dawn 4:58 sunrise 5:59 sunset 8:00 dark 9:01
moonset 8:24 a.m. moonrise 10:00 p.m.

perigee

feet

Los Angeles
6.3 ft. (11:17)
San Diego
6.6 ft. (11:16)

Los Angeles
4.4 ft. (12:10)
San Diego
4.7 ft. (12:01)

Los Angeles
1.9 ft. (5:10)
San Diego
1.9 ft. (5:09)

Los Angeles
-1.1 ft. (5:41)
San Diego
-1.1 ft. (5:39)

12 1 2 3 4 5 6 7 8 9 10 11 noon 1 2 3 4 5 6 7 8 9 10 11 12

− 2.7 knots ebb —⊣ ⊢ 1.8 knots flood → ⊢ 1.3 knots ebb ⊣ ⊦ 1.6 knots flood —⊦

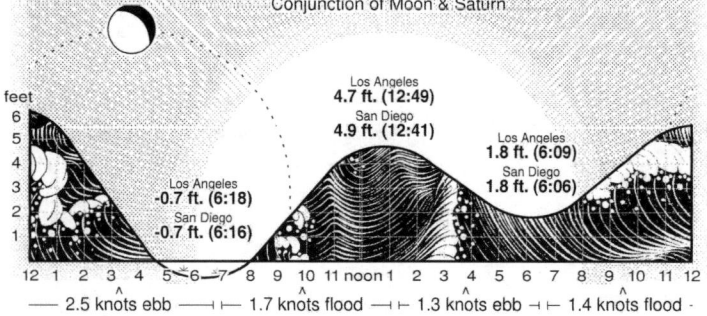

WED JUL 24
dawn 4:58 sunrise 6:00 sunset 7:59 dark 9:00
moonset 9:35 a.m. moonrise 10:31 p.m.

Conjunction of Moon & Saturn

feet

Los Angeles
4.7 ft. (12:49)
San Diego
4.9 ft. (12:41)

Los Angeles
1.8 ft. (6:09)
San Diego
1.8 ft. (6:06)

Los Angeles
-0.7 ft. (6:18)
San Diego
-0.7 ft. (6:16)

12 1 2 3 4 5 6 7 8 9 10 11 noon 1 2 3 4 5 6 7 8 9 10 11 12

— 2.5 knots ebb —⊣ ⊦ 1.7 knots flood —⊣ ⊢ 1.3 knots ebb ⊣ ⊦ 1.4 knots flood -

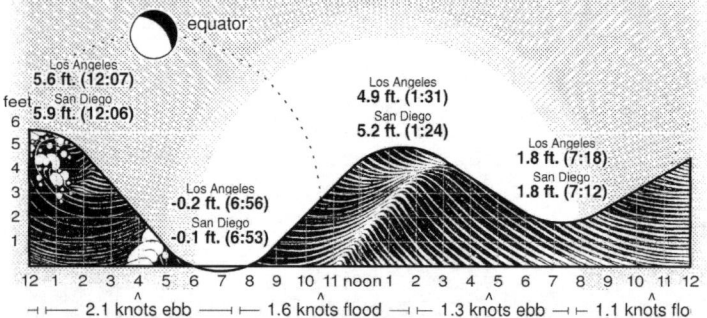

THU JUL 25
dawn 4:59 sunrise 6:01 sunset 7:58 dark 8:59
moonset 10:44 a.m. moonrise 11:00 p.m.

equator

feet

Los Angeles
5.6 ft. (12:07)
San Diego
5.9 ft. (12:06)

Los Angeles
4.9 ft. (1:31)
San Diego
5.2 ft. (1:24)

Los Angeles
1.8 ft. (7:18)
San Diego
1.8 ft. (7:12)

Los Angeles
-0.2 ft. (6:56)
San Diego
-0.1 ft. (6:53)

12 1 2 3 4 5 6 7 8 9 10 11 noon 1 2 3 4 5 6 7 8 9 10 11 12

⊣ ⊦— 2.1 knots ebb —⊣ ⊦ 1.6 knots flood —⊣ ⊦ 1.3 knots ebb ⊣ ⊦ 1.1 knots flo

FRI JUL 26
dawn 5:00 sunrise 6:01 sunset 7:57 dark 8:58
moonset 11:52 a.m. moonrise 11:30 p.m.

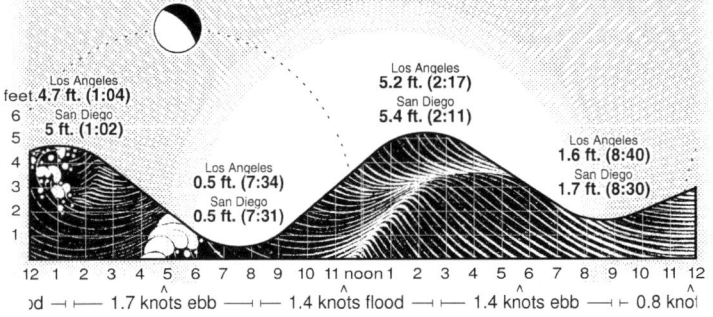

Los Angeles **4.7 ft. (1:04)**
San Diego **5 ft. (1:02)**

Los Angeles **0.5 ft. (7:34)**
San Diego **0.5 ft. (7:31)**

Los Angeles **5.2 ft. (2:17)**
San Diego **5.4 ft. (2:11)**

Los Angeles **1.6 ft. (8:40)**
San Diego **1.7 ft. (8:30)**

feet 6 5 4 3 2 1

12 1 2 3 4 5 6 7 8 9 10 11 noon 1 2 3 4 5 6 7 8 9 10 11 12

od → ├── 1.7 knots ebb ──→ ├── 1.4 knots flood ──→ ├── 1.4 knots ebb ──→ ├─ 0.8 knot

SAT JUL 27
dawn 5:01 sunrise 6:02 sunset 7:57 dark 8:58
moonset 1:01 p.m.

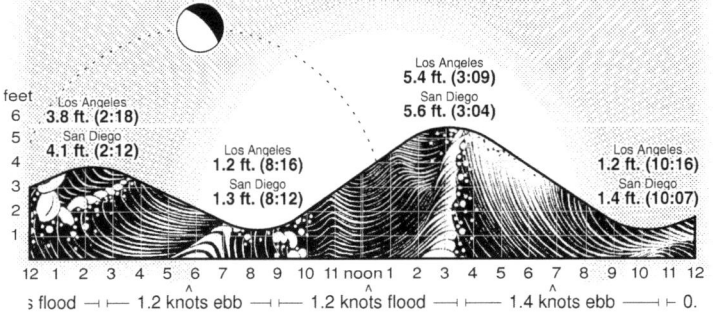

Los Angeles **3.8 ft. (2:18)**
San Diego **4.1 ft. (2:12)**

Los Angeles **1.2 ft. (8:16)**
San Diego **1.3 ft. (8:12)**

Los Angeles **5.4 ft. (3:09)**
San Diego **5.6 ft. (3:04)**

Los Angeles **1.2 ft. (10:16)**
San Diego **1.4 ft. (10:07)**

feet 6 5 4 3 2 1

12 1 2 3 4 5 6 7 8 9 10 11 noon 1 2 3 4 5 6 7 8 9 10 11 12

s flood → ├── 1.2 knots ebb ──→ ├── 1.2 knots flood ──→ ├── 1.4 knots ebb ──→ ├─ 0.

SUN JUL 28
dawn 5:02 sunrise 6:03 sunset 7:56 dark 8:57
moonrise 12:02 a.m. moonset 2:10 p.m.

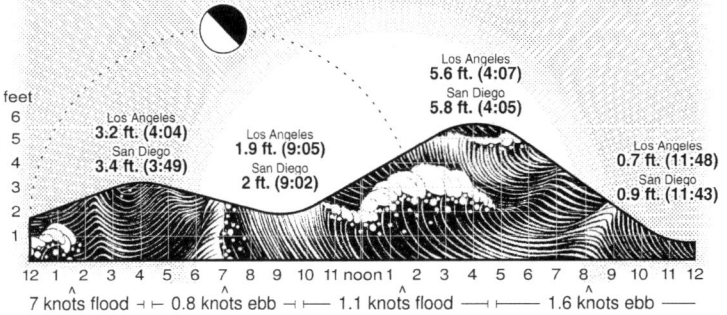

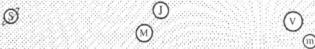

Los Angeles **3.2 ft. (4:04)**
San Diego **3.4 ft. (3:49)**

Los Angeles **1.9 ft. (9:05)**
San Diego **2 ft. (9:02)**

Los Angeles **5.6 ft. (4:07)**
San Diego **5.8 ft. (4:05)**

Los Angeles **0.7 ft. (11:48)**
San Diego **0.9 ft. (11:43)**

feet 6 5 4 3 2 1

12 1 2 3 4 5 6 7 8 9 10 11 noon 1 2 3 4 5 6 7 8 9 10 11 12

7 knots flood → ├─ 0.8 knots ebb ──→ ├── 1.1 knots flood ──→ ├── 1.6 knots ebb ──→

Ⓢ   Ⓙ   Ⓥ
     Ⓜ   ⓜ

MON JUL 29
dawn 5:03 sunrise 6:03 sunset 7:55 dark 8:56
moonrise 12:38 a.m. moonset 3:20 p.m.

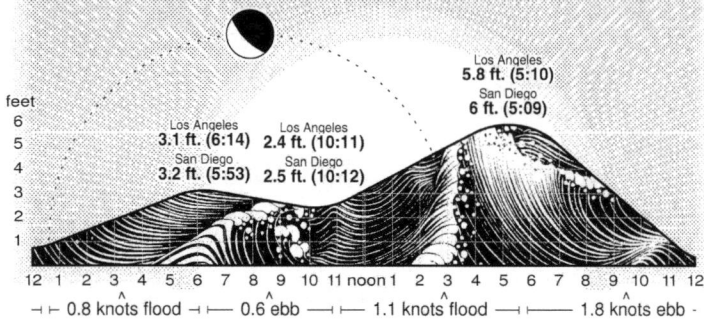

feet

Los Angeles
5.8 ft. (5:10)
San Diego
6 ft. (5:09)

Los Angeles
3.1 ft. (6:14)
San Diego
3.2 ft. (5:53)

Los Angeles
2.4 ft. (10:11)
San Diego
2.5 ft. (10:12)

6
5
4
3
2
1

12 1 2 3 4 5 6 7 8 9 10 11 noon 1 2 3 4 5 6 7 8 9 10 11 12

⊢ 0.8 knots flood ⊣ ⊢ 0.6 ebb ⊣ ⊢ 1.1 knots flood ⊣ ⊢ 1.8 knots ebb

TUE JUL 30
dawn 5:04 sunrise 6:04 sunset 7:54 dark 8:55
moonrise 1:19 a.m. moonset 4:27 p.m.

Conjunction of Moon, Mars & Jupiter

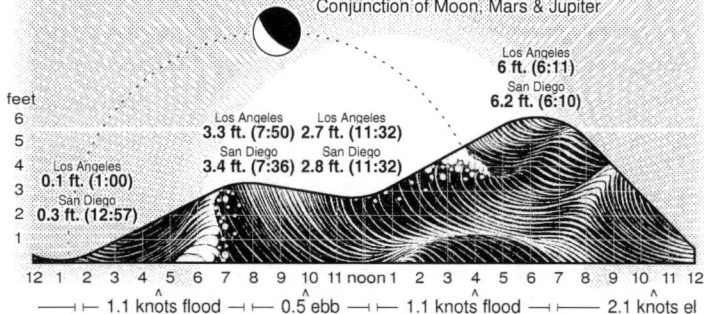

feet

Los Angeles
6 ft. (6:11)
San Diego
6.2 ft. (6:10)

Los Angeles
3.3 ft. (7:50)
San Diego
3.4 ft. (7:36)

Los Angeles
2.7 ft. (11:32)
San Diego
2.8 ft. (11:32)

Los Angeles
0.1 ft. (1:00)
San Diego
0.3 ft. (12:57)

6
5
4
3
2
1

12 1 2 3 4 5 6 7 8 9 10 11 noon 1 2 3 4 5 6 7 8 9 10 11 12

⊢ 1.1 knots flood ⊣ ⊢ 0.5 ebb ⊣ ⊢ 1.1 knots flood ⊣ ⊢ 2.1 knots el

WED JUL 31
dawn 5:05 sunrise 6:05 sunset 7:54 dark 8:54
moonrise 2:08 a.m. moonset 5:30 p.m.

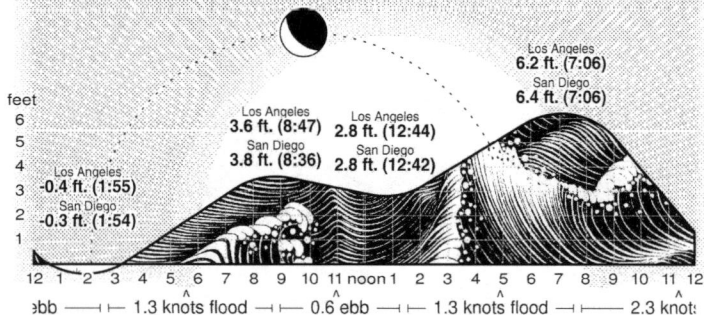

feet

Los Angeles
6.2 ft. (7:06)
San Diego
6.4 ft. (7:06)

Los Angeles
3.6 ft. (8:47)
San Diego
3.8 ft. (8:36)

Los Angeles
2.8 ft. (12:44)
San Diego
2.8 ft. (12:42)

Los Angeles
-0.4 ft. (1:55)
San Diego
-0.3 ft. (1:54)

6
5
4
3
2
1

12 1 2 3 4 5 6 7 8 9 10 11 noon 1 2 3 4 5 6 7 8 9 10 11 12

ebb ⊣ ⊢ 1.3 knots flood ⊣ ⊢ 0.6 ebb ⊣ ⊢ 1.3 knots flood ⊣ ⊢ 2.3 knots

THU AUG 1
dawn 5:05 sunrise 6:06 sunset 7:53 dark 8:53
moonrise 3:03 a.m. moonset 6:25 p.m.

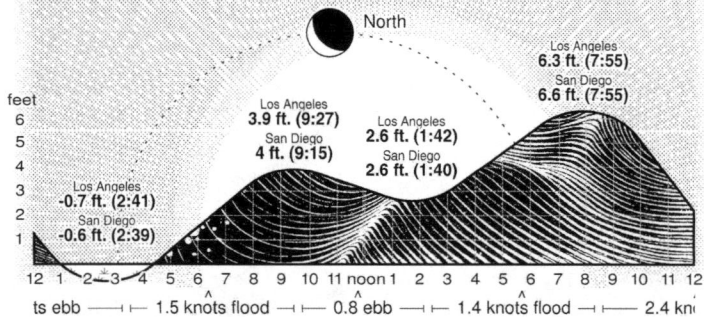

North

feet

Los Angeles
6.3 ft. (7:55)
San Diego
6.6 ft. (7:55)

Los Angeles
3.9 ft. (9:27)
San Diego
4 ft. (9:15)

Los Angeles
2.6 ft. (1:42)
San Diego
2.6 ft. (1:40)

Los Angeles
-0.7 ft. (2:41)
San Diego
-0.6 ft. (2:39)

6
5
4
3
2
1

12 1 2 3 4 5 6 7 8 9 10 11 noon 1 2 3 4 5 6 7 8 9 10 11 12

ts ebb ⊣ ⊢ 1.5 knots flood ⊣ ⊢ 0.8 ebb ⊣ ⊢ 1.4 knots flood ⊣ ⊢ 2.4 kn

FRI AUG 2
dawn 5:06 sunrise 6:06 sunset 7:52 dark 8:52
moonrise 4:04 a.m. moonset 7:12 p.m.

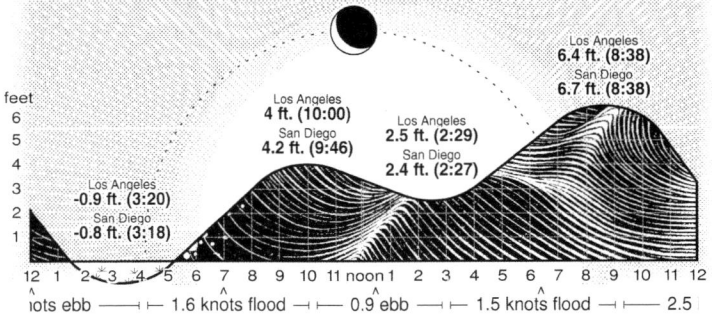

Los Angeles
6.4 ft. (8:38)
San Diego
6.7 ft. (8:38)

Los Angeles
4 ft. (10:00)
San Diego
4.2 ft. (9:46)

Los Angeles
2.5 ft. (2:29)
San Diego
2.4 ft. (2:27)

Los Angeles
-0.9 ft. (3:20)
San Diego
-0.8 ft. (3:18)

feet
6
5
4
3
2
1

12 1 2 3 4 5 6 7 8 9 10 11 noon 1 2 3 4 5 6 7 8 9 10 11 12

ots ebb ─── ├─ 1.6 knots flood ─┤ ├─ 0.9 ebb ─┤ ├─ 1.5 knots flood ─┤ ├─ 2.5

SAT AUG 3
dawn 5:07 sunrise 6:07 sunset 7:51 dark 8:51
moonrise 5:07 a.m. moonset 7:51 p.m.

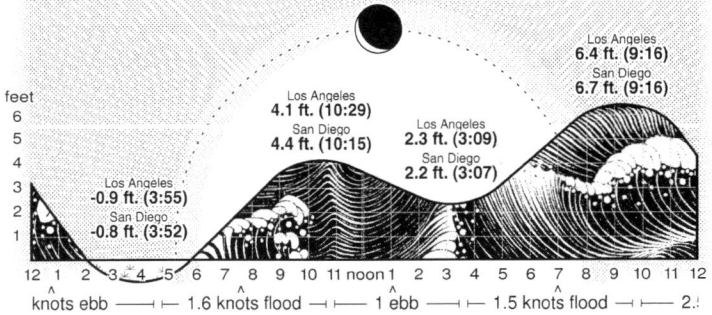

Los Angeles
6.4 ft. (9:16)
San Diego
6.7 ft. (9:16)

Los Angeles
4.1 ft. (10:29)
San Diego
4.4 ft. (10:15)

Los Angeles
2.3 ft. (3:09)
San Diego
2.2 ft. (3:07)

Los Angeles
-0.9 ft. (3:55)
San Diego
-0.8 ft. (3:52)

feet
6
5
4
3
2
1

12 1 2 3 4 5 6 7 8 9 10 11 noon 1 2 3 4 5 6 7 8 9 10 11 12

knots ebb ─── ├─ 1.6 knots flood ─┤ ├─ 1 ebb ─┤ ├─ 1.5 knots flood ─┤ ├─ 2.5

SUN AUG 4
dawn 5:08 sunrise 6:08 sunset 7:50 dark 8:49
moonrise 6:10 a.m. moonset 8:24 p.m.

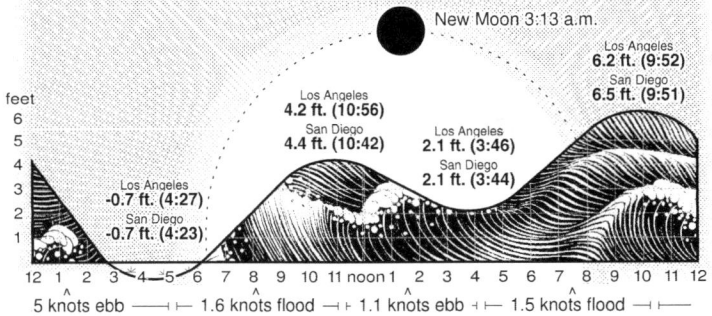

New Moon 3:13 a.m.

Los Angeles
6.2 ft. (9:52)
San Diego
6.5 ft. (9:51)

Los Angeles
4.2 ft. (10:56)
San Diego
4.4 ft. (10:42)

Los Angeles
2.1 ft. (3:46)
San Diego
2.1 ft. (3:44)

Los Angeles
-0.7 ft. (4:27)
San Diego
-0.7 ft. (4:23)

feet
6
5
4
3
2
1

12 1 2 3 4 5 6 7 8 9 10 11 noon 1 2 3 4 5 6 7 8 9 10 11 12

5 knots ebb ───┤ ├─ 1.6 knots flood ─┤ ├ 1.1 knots ebb ┤ ├─ 1.5 knots flood ─┤ ├─

MON AUG 5 dawn 5:09 sunrise 6:08 sunset 7:49 dark 8:48
moonrise 7:10 a.m. moonset 8:52 p.m.

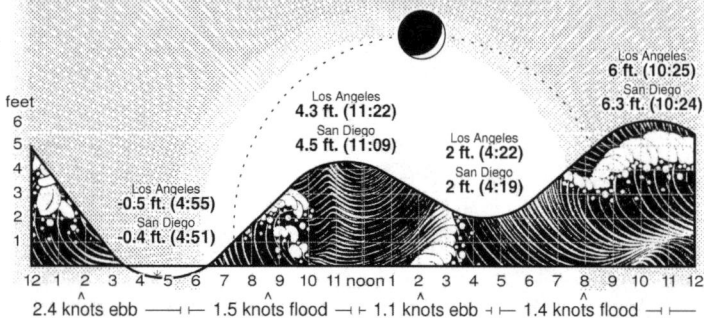

feet

Los Angeles
6 ft. (10:25)
San Diego
6.3 ft. (10:24)

Los Angeles
4.3 ft. (11:22)
San Diego
4.5 ft. (11:09)

Los Angeles
2 ft. (4:22)
San Diego
2 ft. (4:19)

Los Angeles
-0.5 ft. (4:55)
San Diego
-0.4 ft. (4:51)

12 1 2 3 4 5 6 7 8 9 10 11 noon 1 2 3 4 5 6 7 8 9 10 11 12

2.4 knots ebb ⊢ 1.5 knots flood ⊢ 1.1 knots ebb ⊣ 1.4 knots flood ⊣ ⊢

TUE AUG 6 dawn 5:10 sunrise 6:09 sunset 7:48 dark 8:47
moonrise 8:09 a.m. moonset 9:18 p.m.

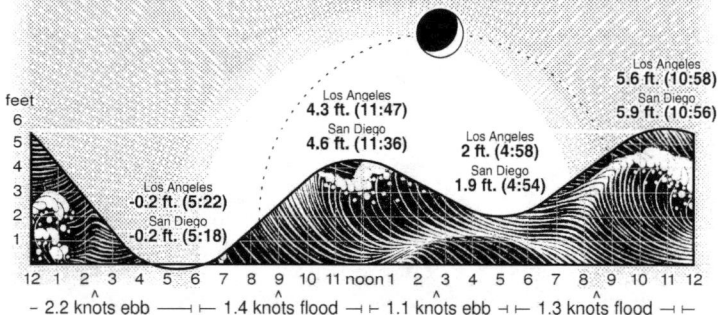

feet

Los Angeles
5.6 ft. (10:58)
San Diego
5.9 ft. (10:56)

Los Angeles
4.3 ft. (11:47)
San Diego
4.6 ft. (11:36)

Los Angeles
2 ft. (4:58)
San Diego
1.9 ft. (4:54)

Los Angeles
-0.2 ft. (5:22)
San Diego
-0.2 ft. (5:18)

12 1 2 3 4 5 6 7 8 9 10 11 noon 1 2 3 4 5 6 7 8 9 10 11 12

– 2.2 knots ebb ⊢ 1.4 knots flood ⊣ ⊢ 1.1 knots ebb ⊢ 1.3 knots flood ⊣ ⊢

WED AUG 7 dawn 5:11 sunrise 6:10 sunset 7:47 dark 8:46
moonrise 9:05 a.m. moonset 9:41 p.m.

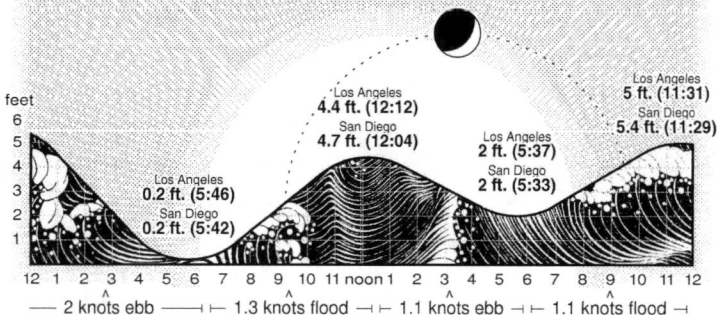

feet

Los Angeles
5 ft. (11:31)
San Diego
5.4 ft. (11:29)

Los Angeles
4.4 ft. (12:12)
San Diego
4.7 ft. (12:04)

Los Angeles
2 ft. (5:37)
San Diego
2 ft. (5:33)

Los Angeles
0.2 ft. (5:46)
San Diego
0.2 ft. (5:42)

12 1 2 3 4 5 6 7 8 9 10 11 noon 1 2 3 4 5 6 7 8 9 10 11 12

2 knots ebb ⊢ 1.3 knots flood ⊣ ⊢ 1.1 knots ebb ⊣ ⊢ 1.1 knots flood ⊣

THU AUG 8 dawn 5:12 sunrise 6:11 sunset 7:46 dark 8:45
moonrise 10:00 a.m. moonset 10:04 p.m.

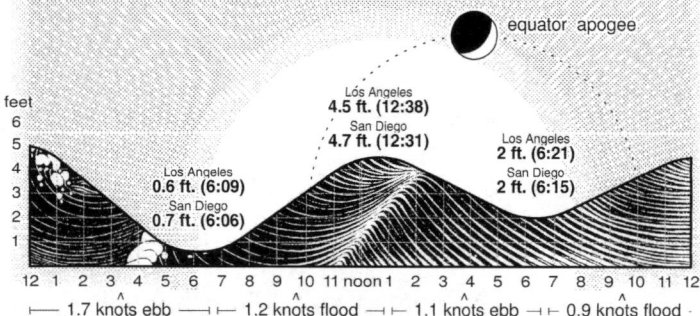

equator apogee

feet

Los Angeles
4.5 ft. (12:38)
San Diego
4.7 ft. (12:31)

Los Angeles
2 ft. (6:21)
San Diego
2 ft. (6:15)

Los Angeles
0.6 ft. (6:09)
San Diego
0.7 ft. (6:06)

12 1 2 3 4 5 6 7 8 9 10 11 noon 1 2 3 4 5 6 7 8 9 10 11 12

⊢ 1.7 knots ebb ⊣ ⊢ 1.2 knots flood ⊣ ⊢ 1.1 knots ebb ⊣ ⊢ 0.9 knots flood ·

FRI AUG 9

dawn 5:13 sunrise 6:11 sunset 7:45 dark 8:44
moonrise 10:55 a.m. moonset 10:28 p.m.

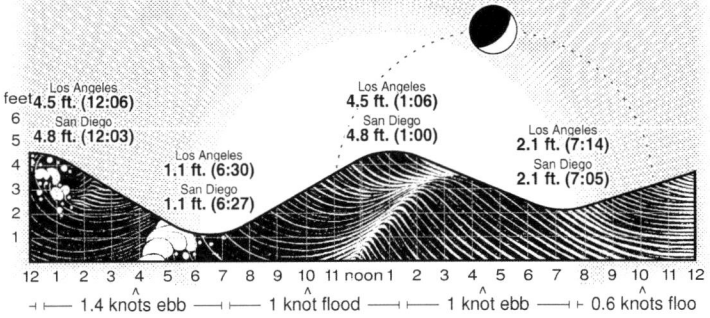

feet

Los Angeles
4.5 ft. (12:06)
San Diego
4.8 ft. (12:03)

Los Angeles
4.5 ft. (1:06)
San Diego
4.8 ft. (1:00)

Los Angeles
2.1 ft. (7:14)
San Diego
2.1 ft. (7:05)

Los Angeles
1.1 ft. (6:30)
San Diego
1.1 ft. (6:27)

12 1 2 3 4 5 6 7 8 9 10 11 noon 1 2 3 4 5 6 7 8 9 10 11 12

⊢ 1.4 knots ebb ⟶ ⊢ 1 knot flood ⟶ ⊢ 1 knot ebb ⟶ ⊢ 0.6 knots floo

SAT AUG 10

dawn 5:13 sunrise 6:12 sunset 7:44 dark 8:43
moonrise 11:51 a.m. moonset 10:54 p.m.

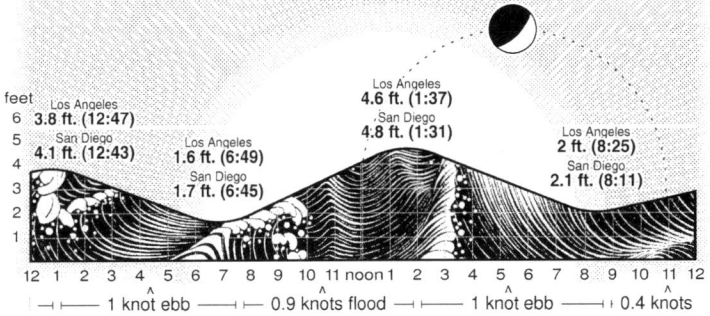

feet

Los Angeles
3.8 ft. (12:47)
San Diego
4.1 ft. (12:43)

Los Angeles
4.6 ft. (1:37)
San Diego
4.8 ft. (1:31)

Los Angeles
2 ft. (8:25)
San Diego
2.1 ft. (8:11)

Los Angeles
1.6 ft. (6:49)
San Diego
1.7 ft. (6:45)

12 1 2 3 4 5 6 7 8 9 10 11 noon 1 2 3 4 5 6 7 8 9 10 11 12

⊢ 1 knot ebb ⟶ ⊢ 0.9 knots flood ⟶ ⊢ 1 knot ebb ⟶ ⊢ 0.4 knots

SUN AUG 11

dawn 5:14 sunrise 6:13 sunset 7:43 dark 8:41
moonrise 12:49 p.m. moonset 11:23 p.m.

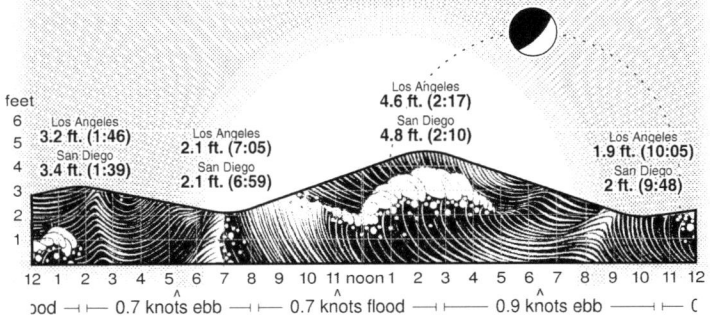

feet

Los Angeles
3.2 ft. (1:46)
San Diego
3.4 ft. (1:39)

Los Angeles
4.6 ft. (2:17)
San Diego
4.8 ft. (2:10)

Los Angeles
1.9 ft. (10:05)
San Diego
2 ft. (9:48)

Los Angeles
2.1 ft. (7:05)
San Diego
2.1 ft. (6:59)

12 1 2 3 4 5 6 7 8 9 10 11 noon 1 2 3 4 5 6 7 8 9 10 11 12

ood ⟶ ⊢ 0.7 knots ebb ⟶ ⊢ 0.7 knots flood ⟶ ⊢ 0.9 knots ebb ⟶ ⊢ 0

MON AUG 12

dawn 5:15 sunrise 6:13 sunset 7:42 dark 8:40
moonrise 1:49 p.m. moonset 11:57 p.m.

Perseid Meteor Peak

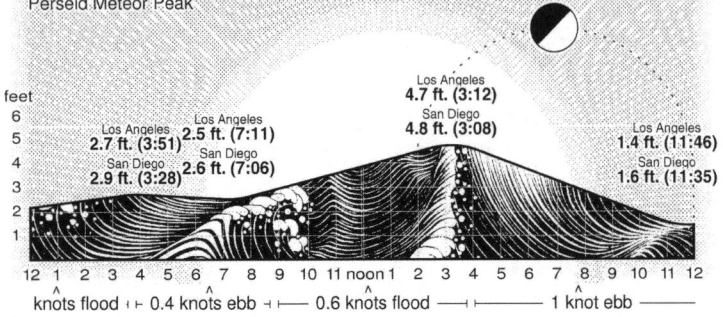

feet

Los Angeles
4.7 ft. (3:12)
San Diego
4.8 ft. (3:08)

Los Angeles 2.5 ft. (7:11)
Los Angeles 2.7 ft. (3:51)
San Diego 2.6 ft. (7:06)
San Diego 2.9 ft. (3:28)

Los Angeles
1.4 ft. (11:46)
San Diego
1.6 ft. (11:35)

6
5
4
3
2
1

12 1 2 3 4 5 6 7 8 9 10 11 noon 1 2 3 4 5 6 7 8 9 10 11 12

knots flood ⊢ 0.4 knots ebb ⊣ ⊢ 0.6 knots flood ⊣ ⊢ 1 knot ebb ⊣

TUE AUG 13

dawn 5:16 sunrise 6:14 sunset 7:41 dark 8:39
moonrise 2:52 p.m.

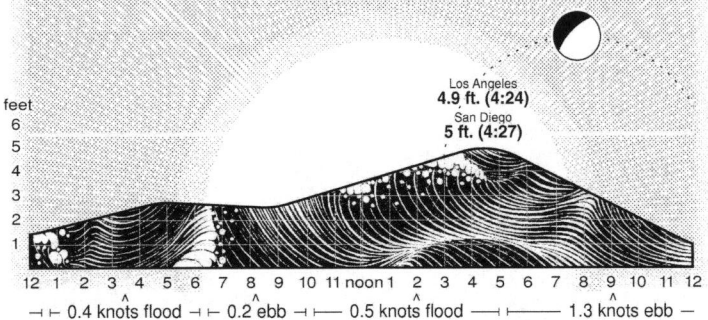

Los Angeles
4.9 ft. (4:24)
San Diego
5 ft. (4:27)

feet
6
5
4
3
2
1

12 1 2 3 4 5 6 7 8 9 10 11 noon 1 2 3 4 5 6 7 8 9 10 11 12

⊢⊢ 0.4 knots flood ⊣ ⊢ 0.2 ebb ⊢ 0.5 knots flood ⊣ ⊢ 1.3 knots ebb ⊣

WED AUG 14

dawn 5:17 sunrise 6:15 sunset 7:40 dark 8:38
moonset 12:38 a.m. moonrise 3:54 p.m.

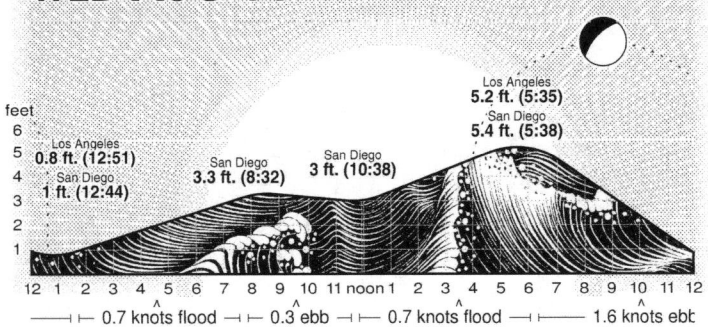

Los Angeles
5.2 ft. (5:35)
San Diego
5.4 ft. (5:38)

Los Angeles 0.8 ft. (12:51)
San Diego 1 ft. (12:44)

San Diego 3.3 ft. (8:32)
San Diego 3 ft. (10:38)

feet
6
5
4
3
2
1

12 1 2 3 4 5 6 7 8 9 10 11 noon 1 2 3 4 5 6 7 8 9 10 11 12

⊢⊢ 0.7 knots flood ⊣ ⊢ 0.3 ebb ⊢⊢ 0.7 knots flood ⊣ ⊢ 1.6 knots ebb

THU AUG 15

dawn 5:18 sunrise 6:16 sunset 7:39 dark 8:36
moonset 1:28 a.m. moonrise 4:55 p.m.

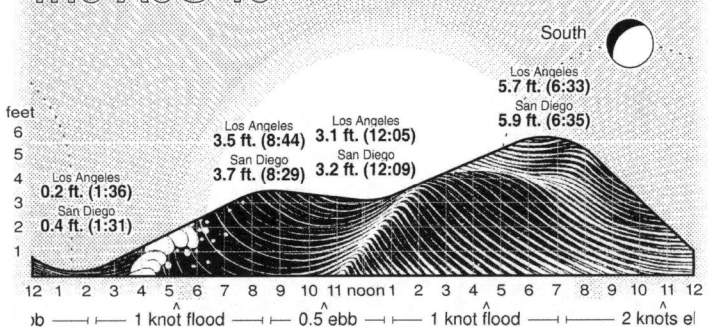

South

Los Angeles
5.7 ft. (6:33)
San Diego
5.9 ft. (6:35)

Los Angeles 3.5 ft. (8:44)
Los Angeles 3.1 ft. (12:05)
San Diego 3.7 ft. (8:29)
San Diego 3.2 ft. (12:09)

Los Angeles 0.2 ft. (1:36)
San Diego 0.4 ft. (1:31)

feet
6
5
4
3
2
1

12 1 2 3 4 5 6 7 8 9 10 11 noon 1 2 3 4 5 6 7 8 9 10 11 12

b ⊣ ⊢ 1 knot flood ⊣ ⊢ 0.5 ebb ⊢ ⊢ 1 knot flood ⊣ ⊢ 2 knots e

FRI AUG 16
dawn 5:19 sunrise 6:16 sunset 7:38 dark 8:35
moonset 2:27 a.m. moonrise 5:50 p.m.

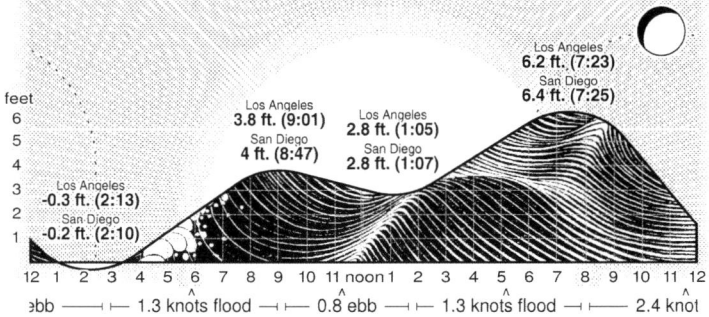

Los Angeles
6.2 ft. (7:23)
San Diego
6.4 ft. (7:25)

Los Angeles
3.8 ft. (9:01)
San Diego
4 ft. (8:47)

Los Angeles
2.8 ft. (1:05)
San Diego
2.8 ft. (1:07)

feet
6
5
4
3
2
1

Los Angeles
-0.3 ft. (2:13)
San Diego
-0.2 ft. (2:10)

12 1 2 3 4 5 6 7 8 9 10 11 noon 1 2 3 4 5 6 7 8 9 10 11 12

ebb ⟶ ⊢ 1.3 knots flood ⟶ ⊣ 0.8 ebb ⊢ ⊢ 1.3 knots flood ⟶ ⊢ 2.4 knot

SAT AUG 17
dawn 5:20 sunrise 6:17 sunset 7:36 dark 8:34
moonset 3:34 a.m. moonrise 6:39 p.m.

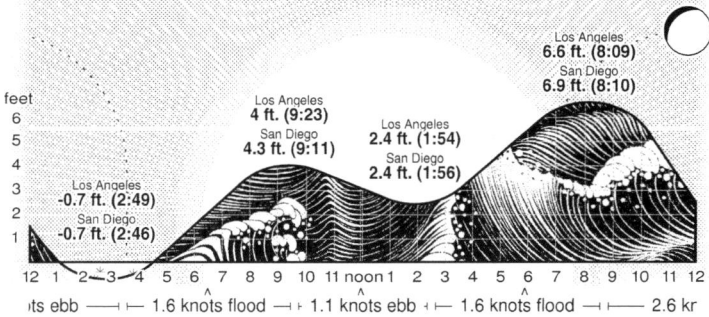

Los Angeles
6.6 ft. (8:09)
San Diego
6.9 ft. (8:10)

Los Angeles
4 ft. (9:23)
San Diego
4.3 ft. (9:11)

Los Angeles
2.4 ft. (1:54)
San Diego
2.4 ft. (1:56)

feet
6
5
4
3
2
1

Los Angeles
-0.7 ft. (2:49)
San Diego
-0.7 ft. (2:46)

12 1 2 3 4 5 6 7 8 9 10 11 noon 1 2 3 4 5 6 7 8 9 10 11 12

its ebb ⟶ ⊢ 1.6 knots flood ⟶ ⊢ 1.1 knots ebb ⊣ ⊢ 1.6 knots flood ⟶ ⊢ 2.6 kr

SUN AUG 18
dawn 5:20 sunrise 6:18 sunset 7:35 dark 8:32
moonset 4:47 a.m. moonrise 7:21 p.m.

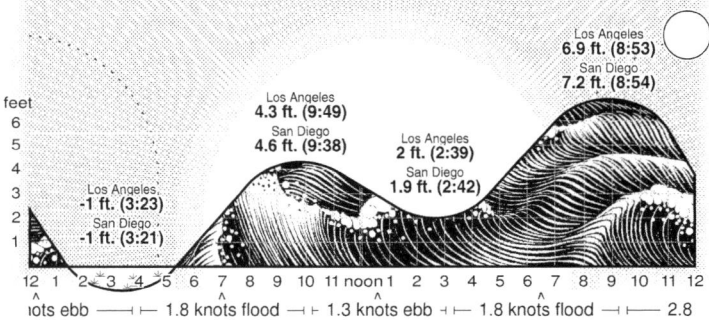

Los Angeles
6.9 ft. (8:53)
San Diego
7.2 ft. (8:54)

Los Angeles
4.3 ft. (9:49)
San Diego
4.6 ft. (9:38)

Los Angeles
2 ft. (2:39)
San Diego
1.9 ft. (2:42)

feet
6
5
4
3
2
1

Los Angeles
-1 ft. (3:23)
San Diego
-1 ft. (3:21)

12 1 2 3 4 5 6 7 8 9 10 11 noon 1 2 3 4 5 6 7 8 9 10 11 12

ots ebb ⟶ ⊢ 1.8 knots flood ⟶ ⊢ 1.3 knots ebb ⊣ ⊢ 1.8 knots flood ⟶ ⊢ 2.8

Perseid Meteor Shower The Perseids are active from Jul 17th to Aug 24th with its peak predicted Monday, Aug 12th. At peak, the shower has been known to produce over a 100 meteors per hour. The shower's radiant point is the constellation Perseus that will rise above the eastern horizon by 10:00 p.m. The first quarter Moon will compete with the shower until its sets near midnight. The best viewing will be after moonset and as the constellation Pereus continues to rise to its highest point in the night sky just before dawn. Perseids meteors tend to be very fast, possess an average magnitude of 2.3 and about 45% leave persistent trains.

MON AUG 19
dawn 5:21 sunrise 6:18 sunset 7:34 dark 8:31
moonset 6:01 a.m. moonrise 7:57 p.m.

Full Super Moon 11:26 a.m.

Los Angeles
6.9 ft. (9:37)
San Diego
7.2 ft. (9:36)

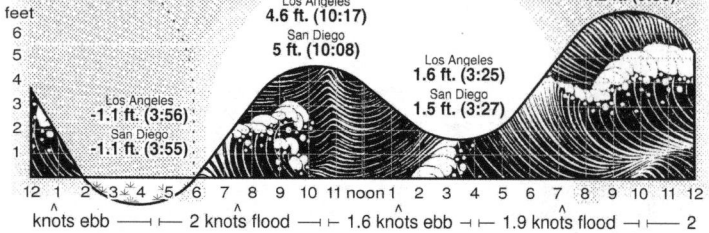

Los Angeles
4.6 ft. (10:17)
San Diego
5 ft. (10:08)

Los Angeles
1.6 ft. (3:25)
San Diego
1.5 ft. (3:27)

Los Angeles
-1.1 ft. (3:56)
San Diego
-1.1 ft. (3:55)

feet
6
5
4
3
2
1

12 1 2 3 4 5 6 7 8 9 10 11 noon 1 2 3 4 5 6 7 8 9 10 11 12

knots ebb — ⊢ 2 knots flood — ⊢ 1.6 knots ebb ⊣ ⊢ 1.9 knots flood ⊣ ⊢ 2

TUE AUG 20
dawn 5:22 sunrise 6:19 sunset 7:33 dark 8:30
moonset 7:15 a.m. moonrise 8:29 p.m.

perigee

Los Angeles
6.6 ft. (10:22)
San Diego
6.9 ft. (10:20)

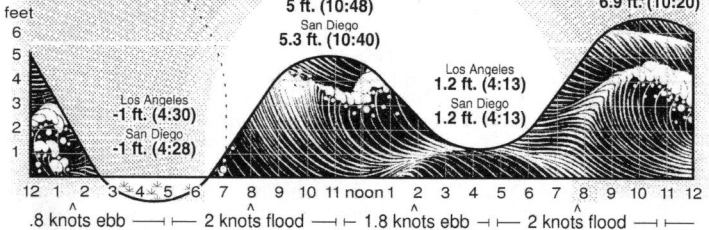

Los Angeles
5 ft. (10:48)
San Diego
5.3 ft. (10:40)

Los Angeles
1.2 ft. (4:13)
San Diego
1.2 ft. (4:13)

Los Angeles
-1 ft. (4:30)
San Diego
-1 ft. (4:28)

feet
6
5
4
3
2
1

12 1 2 3 4 5 6 7 8 9 10 11 noon 1 2 3 4 5 6 7 8 9 10 11 12

.8 knots ebb — ⊢ 2 knots flood — ⊢ 1.8 knots ebb ⊣ ⊢ 2 knots flood ⊣ ⊢

WED AUG 21
dawn 5:23 sunrise 6:20 sunset 7:32 dark 8:28
moonset 8:27 a.m. moonrise 9:00 p.m.

equator

Los Angeles
6 ft. (11:09)
San Diego
6.3 ft. (11:06)

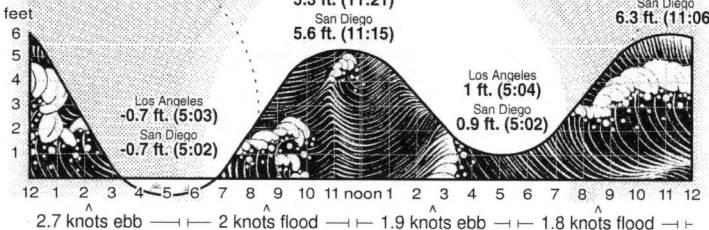

Los Angeles
5.3 ft. (11:21)
San Diego
5.6 ft. (11:15)

Los Angeles
1 ft. (5:04)
San Diego
0.9 ft. (5:02)

Los Angeles
-0.7 ft. (5:03)
San Diego
-0.7 ft. (5:02)

feet
6
5
4
3
2
1

12 1 2 3 4 5 6 7 8 9 10 11 noon 1 2 3 4 5 6 7 8 9 10 11 12

2.7 knots ebb — ⊢ 2 knots flood — ⊢ 1.9 knots ebb ⊣ ⊢ 1.8 knots flood ⊣ ⊢

THU AUG 22
dawn 5:24 sunrise 6:21 sunset 7:30 dark 8:27
moonset 9:38 a.m. moonrise 9:30 p.m.

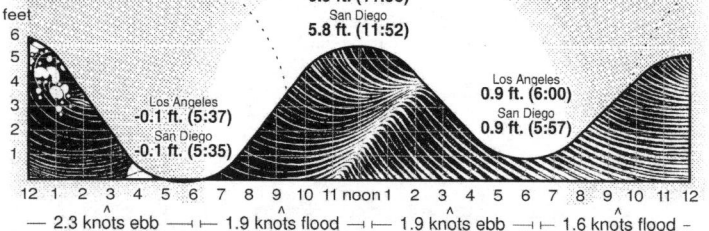

Los Angeles
5.5 ft. (11:56)
San Diego
5.8 ft. (11:52)

Los Angeles
0.9 ft. (6:00)
San Diego
0.9 ft. (5:57)

Los Angeles
-0.1 ft. (5:37)
San Diego
-0.1 ft. (5:35)

feet
6
5
4
3
2
1

12 1 2 3 4 5 6 7 8 9 10 11 noon 1 2 3 4 5 6 7 8 9 10 11 12

— 2.3 knots ebb — ⊢ 1.9 knots flood — ⊢ 1.9 knots ebb ⊣ ⊢ 1.6 knots flood -

FRI AUG 23
dawn 5:25 sunrise 6:21 sunset 7:29 dark 8:26
moonset 10:49 a.m. moonrise 10:02 p.m.

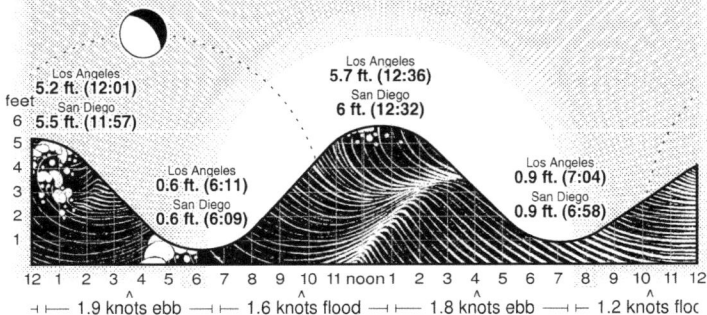

Los Angeles
5.2 ft. (12:01)
San Diego
5.5 ft. (11:57)

Los Angeles
5.7 ft. (12:36)
San Diego
6 ft. (12:32)

Los Angeles
0.6 ft. (6:11)
San Diego
0.6 ft. (6:09)

Los Angeles
0.9 ft. (7:04)
San Diego
0.9 ft. (6:58)

feet
6
5
4
3
2
1

12 1 2 3 4 5 6 7 8 9 10 11 noon 1 2 3 4 5 6 7 8 9 10 11 12

⊣ ⊢ 1.9 knots ebb ⟶ ⊢ 1.6 knots flood ⟶ ⊢ 1.8 knots ebb ⟶ ⊢ 1.2 knots flood

SAT AUG 24
dawn 5:25 sunrise 6:22 sunset 7:28 dark 8:24
moonset 12:00 noon moonrise 10:37 p.m.

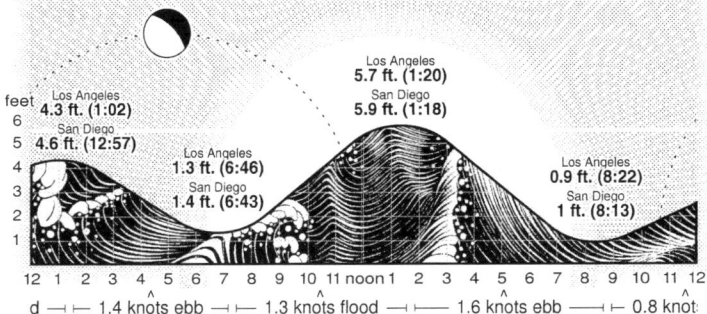

Los Angeles
4.3 ft. (1:02)
San Diego
4.6 ft. (12:57)

Los Angeles
5.7 ft. (1:20)
San Diego
5.9 ft. (1:18)

Los Angeles
1.3 ft. (6:46)
San Diego
1.4 ft. (6:43)

Los Angeles
0.9 ft. (8:22)
San Diego
1 ft. (8:13)

feet
6
5
4
3
2
1

12 1 2 3 4 5 6 7 8 9 10 11 noon 1 2 3 4 5 6 7 8 9 10 11 12

d ⟶ ⊢ 1.4 knots ebb ⟶ ⊢ 1.3 knots flood ⟶ ⊢ 1.6 knots ebb ⟶ ⊢ 0.8 knots

SUN AUG 25
dawn 5:26 sunrise 6:23 sunset 7:27 dark 8:23
moonset 1:11 p.m. moonrise 11:18 p.m.

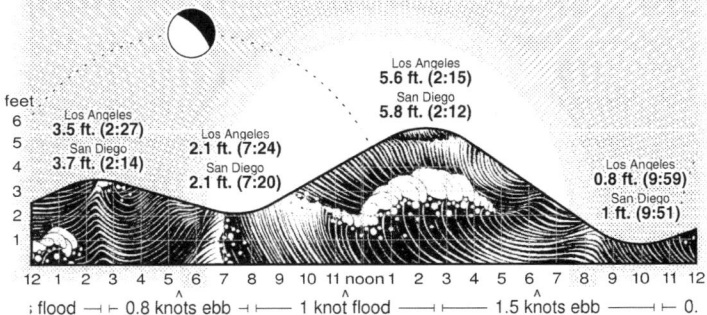

Los Angeles
3.5 ft. (2:27)
San Diego
3.7 ft. (2:14)

Los Angeles
5.6 ft. (2:15)
San Diego
5.8 ft. (2:12)

Los Angeles
2.1 ft. (7:24)
San Diego
2.1 ft. (7:20)

Los Angeles
0.8 ft. (9:59)
San Diego
1 ft. (9:51)

feet
6
5
4
3
2
1

12 1 2 3 4 5 6 7 8 9 10 11 noon 1 2 3 4 5 6 7 8 9 10 11 12

; flood ⟶ ⊢ 0.8 knots ebb ⊣ ⊢ 1 knot flood ⟶ ⊢ 1.5 knots ebb ⟶ ⊢ 0.

☿ ♃ Ⓜ ♀

Full Super Moon: The Full Moon on the 19th is the eighth in 2024 and is also called the Full Sturgeon Moon. By some accounts, this is the first of 4 Super Moons in 2024; the others fall on Sept 18th, Oct 17th and Nov 15th. When the moon is nearing its perigee it is closest to Earth in its elliptical orbit. The Moon can be as close as 223,354 miles to the Earth. Some observers contend that when a Super Moon is close to the horizon it appears larger than a typical full moon, hence the Super Moon label.

MON AUG 26
dawn 5:27 sunrise 6:23 sunset 7:25 dark 8:22
moonset 2:20 p.m.

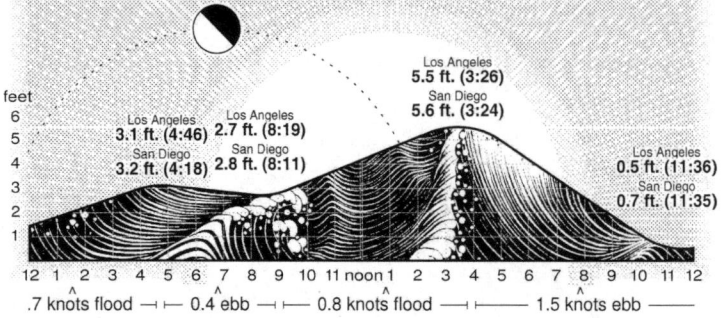

feet
6
5
4
3
2
1

Los Angeles
3.1 ft. (4:46)
San Diego
3.2 ft. (4:18)

Los Angeles
2.7 ft. (8:19)
San Diego
2.8 ft. (8:11)

Los Angeles
5.5 ft. (3:26)
San Diego
5.6 ft. (3:24)

Los Angeles
0.5 ft. (11:36)
San Diego
0.7 ft. (11:35)

12 1 2 3 4 5 6 7 8 9 10 11 noon 1 2 3 4 5 6 7 8 9 10 11 12

.7 knots flood → ⊢ 0.4 ebb ⊢ → 0.8 knots flood → ⊢ 1.5 ebb ——

TUE AUG 27
dawn 5:28 sunrise 6:24 sunset 7:24 dark 8:20
moonrise 12:05 a.m. moonset 3:25 p.m.

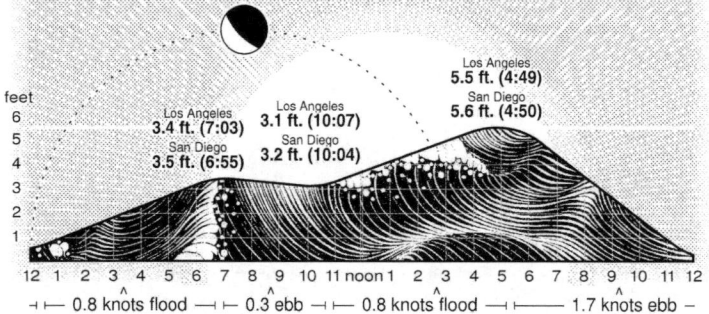

feet
6
5
4
3
2
1

Los Angeles
3.4 ft. (7:03)
San Diego
3.5 ft. (6:55)

Los Angeles
3.1 ft. (10:07)
San Diego
3.2 ft. (10:04)

Los Angeles
5.5 ft. (4:49)
San Diego
5.6 ft. (4:50)

12 1 2 3 4 5 6 7 8 9 10 11 noon 1 2 3 4 5 6 7 8 9 10 11 12

⊢⊢ 0.8 knots flood ⊢ → 0.3 ebb ⊢ → 0.8 knots flood ⊢ ⊢ 1.7 knots ebb →

WED AUG 28
dawn 5:29 sunrise 6:25 sunset 7:23 dark 8:19
moonrise 12:58 a.m. moonset 4:22 p.m.

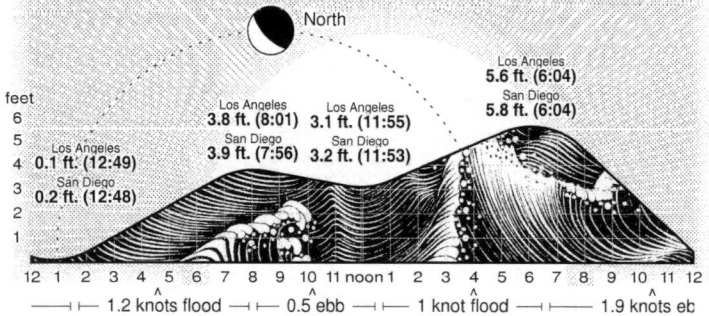

North

feet
6
5
4
3
2
1

Los Angeles
0.1 ft. (12:49)
San Diego
0.2 ft. (12:48)

Los Angeles
3.8 ft. (8:01)
San Diego
3.9 ft. (7:56)

Los Angeles
3.1 ft. (11:55)
San Diego
3.2 ft. (11:53)

Los Angeles
5.6 ft. (6:04)
San Diego
5.8 ft. (6:04)

12 1 2 3 4 5 6 7 8 9 10 11 noon 1 2 3 4 5 6 7 8 9 10 11 12

⊢ 1.2 knots flood ⊢ → 0.5 ebb → ⊢ 1 knot flood → ⊢ 1.9 knots eb

THU AUG 29
dawn 5:30 sunrise 6:25 sunset 7:22 dark 8:17
moonrise 1:57 a.m. moonset 5:11 p.m.

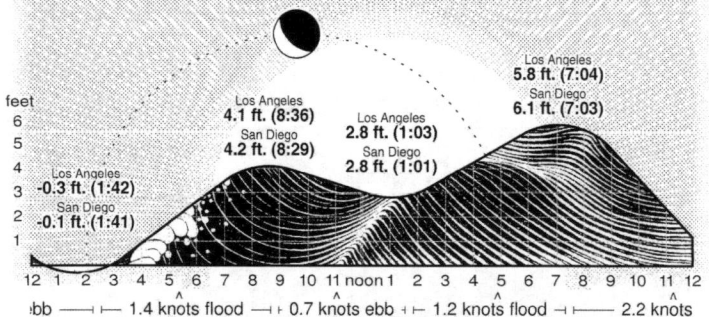

feet
6
5
4
3
2
1

Los Angeles
-0.3 ft. (1:42)
San Diego
-0.1 ft. (1:41)

Los Angeles
4.1 ft. (8:36)
San Diego
4.2 ft. (8:29)

Los Angeles
2.8 ft. (1:03)
San Diego
2.8 ft. (1:01)

Los Angeles
5.8 ft. (7:04)
San Diego
6.1 ft. (7:03)

12 1 2 3 4 5 6 7 8 9 10 11 noon 1 2 3 4 5 6 7 8 9 10 11 12

ebb ⊢ → 1.4 knots flood ⊢ → 0.7 knots ebb ⊢ ⊢ 1.2 knots flood ⊢ ⊢ 2.2 knots

FRI AUG 30
dawn 5:30 sunrise 6:26 sunset 7:20 dark 8:16
moonrise 2:59 a.m. moonset 5:52 p.m.

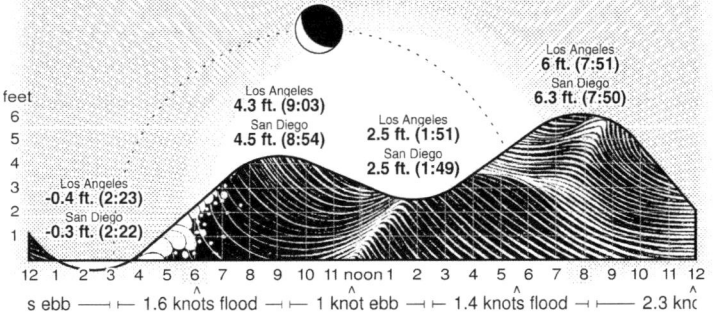

feet
6
5
4
3
2
1

Los Angeles
-0.4 ft. (2:23)
San Diego
-0.3 ft. (2:22)

Los Angeles
4.3 ft. (9:03)
San Diego
4.5 ft. (8:54)

Los Angeles
2.5 ft. (1:51)
San Diego
2.5 ft. (1:49)

Los Angeles
6 ft. (7:51)
San Diego
6.3 ft. (7:50)

12 1 2 3 4 5 6 7 8 9 10 11 noon 1 2 3 4 5 6 7 8 9 10 11 12

s ebb ⟶ ⊢ 1.6 knots flood ⟶ ⊢ 1 knot ebb ⟶ ⊢ 1.4 knots flood ⟶ ⊢ 2.3 kno

SAT AUG 31
dawn 5:31 sunrise 6:27 sunset 7:19 dark 8:14
moonrise 4:01 a.m. moonset 6:26 p.m.

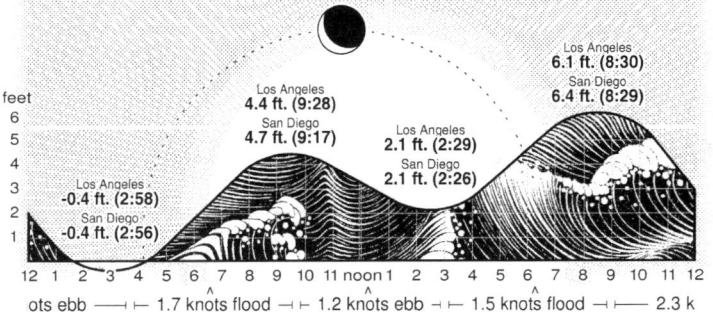

feet
6
5
4
3
2
1

Los Angeles
-0.4 ft. (2:58)
San Diego
-0.4 ft. (2:56)

Los Angeles
4.4 ft. (9:28)
San Diego
4.7 ft. (9:17)

Los Angeles
2.1 ft. (2:29)
San Diego
2.1 ft. (2:26)

Los Angeles
6.1 ft. (8:30)
San Diego
6.4 ft. (8:29)

12 1 2 3 4 5 6 7 8 9 10 11 noon 1 2 3 4 5 6 7 8 9 10 11 12

ots ebb ⟶ ⊢ 1.7 knots flood ⟶ ⊢ 1.2 knots ebb ⟶ ⊢ 1.5 knots flood ⟶ ⊢ 2.3 k

SUN SEP 1
dawn 5:32 sunrise 6:27 sunset 7:18 dark 8:13
moonrise 5:02 a.m. moonset 6:55 p.m.

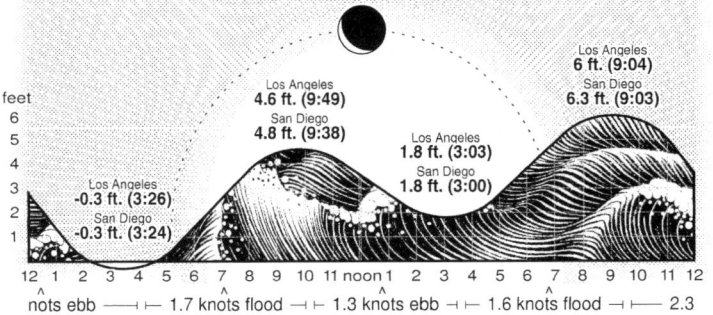

feet
6
5
4
3
2
1

Los Angeles
-0.3 ft. (3:26)
San Diego
-0.3 ft. (3:24)

Los Angeles
4.6 ft. (9:49)
San Diego
4.8 ft. (9:38)

Los Angeles
1.8 ft. (3:03)
San Diego
1.8 ft. (3:00)

Los Angeles
6 ft. (9:04)
San Diego
6.3 ft. (9:03)

12 1 2 3 4 5 6 7 8 9 10 11 noon 1 2 3 4 5 6 7 8 9 10 11 12

nots ebb ⟶ ⊢ 1.7 knots flood ⟶ ⊢ 1.3 knots ebb ⟶ ⊢ 1.6 knots flood ⟶ ⊢ 2.3

Ⓢ   Ⓙ   Ⓥ
         Ⓜ   ⓜ

MON SEP 2

dawn 5:33 sunrise 6:28 sunset 7:16 dark 8:12
moonrise 6:01 a.m. moonset 7:21 p.m.

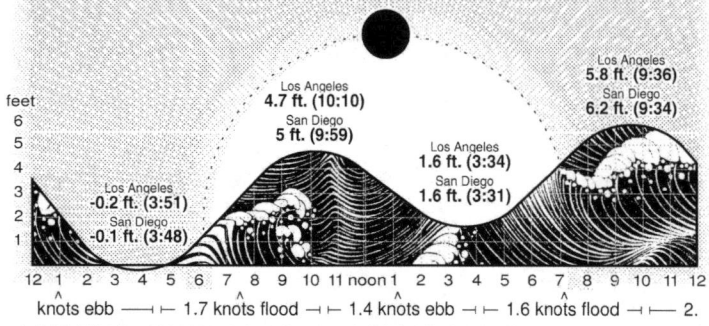

Los Angeles
5.8 ft. (9:36)
San Diego
6.2 ft. (9:34)

Los Angeles
4.7 ft. (10:10)
San Diego
5 ft. (9:59)

Los Angeles
1.6 ft. (3:34)
San Diego
1.6 ft. (3:31)

feet
6
5
4
3
2
1

Los Angeles
-0.2 ft. (3:51)
San Diego
-0.1 ft. (3:48)

12 1 2 3 4 5 6 7 8 9 10 11 noon 1 2 3 4 5 6 7 8 9 10 11 12

knots ebb ⟶ ⊢ 1.7 knots flood ⟶ ⊢ 1.4 knots ebb ⟶ ⊢ 1.6 knots flood ⟶ ⊢ 2.

TUE SEP 3

dawn 5:34 sunrise 6:29 sunset 7:15 dark 8:10
moonrise 6:58 a.m. moonset 7:45 p.m.

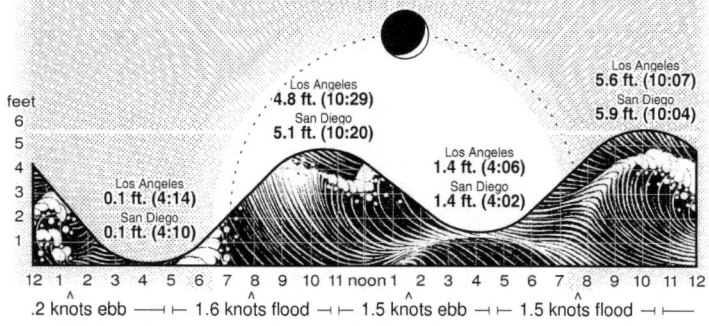

Los Angeles
4.8 ft. (10:29)
San Diego
5.1 ft. (10:20)

Los Angeles
5.6 ft. (10:07)
San Diego
5.9 ft. (10:04)

Los Angeles
1.4 ft. (4:06)
San Diego
1.4 ft. (4:02)

feet
6
5
4
3
2
1

Los Angeles
0.1 ft. (4:14)
San Diego
0.1 ft. (4:10)

12 1 2 3 4 5 6 7 8 9 10 11 noon 1 2 3 4 5 6 7 8 9 10 11 12

.2 knots ebb ⟶ ⊢ 1.6 knots flood ⟶ ⊢ 1.5 knots ebb ⟶ ⊢ 1.5 knots flood ⟶ ⊢

WED SEP 4

dawn 5:34 sunrise 6:29 sunset 7:14 dark 8:09
moonrise 7:53 a.m. moonset 8:08 p.m.

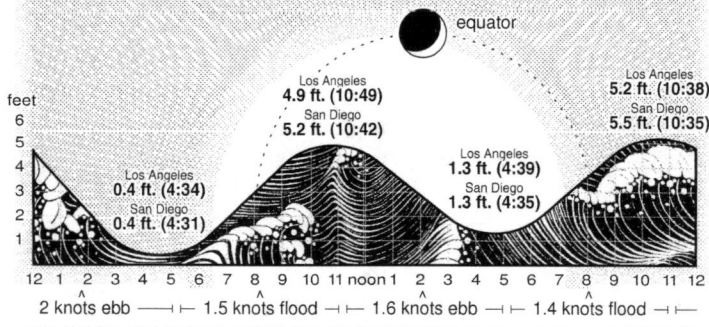

equator

Los Angeles
4.9 ft. (10:49)
San Diego
5.2 ft. (10:42)

Los Angeles
5.2 ft. (10:38)
San Diego
5.5 ft. (10:35)

Los Angeles
1.3 ft. (4:39)
San Diego
1.3 ft. (4:35)

feet
6
5
4
3
2
1

Los Angeles
0.4 ft. (4:34)
San Diego
0.4 ft. (4:31)

12 1 2 3 4 5 6 7 8 9 10 11 noon 1 2 3 4 5 6 7 8 9 10 11 12

2 knots ebb ⟶ ⊢ 1.5 knots flood ⟶ ⊢ 1.6 knots ebb ⟶ ⊢ 1.4 knots flood ⟶ ⊢

THU SEP 5

dawn 5:35 sunrise 6:30 sunset 7:12 dark 8:07
moonrise 8:48 a.m. moonset 8:32 p.m.

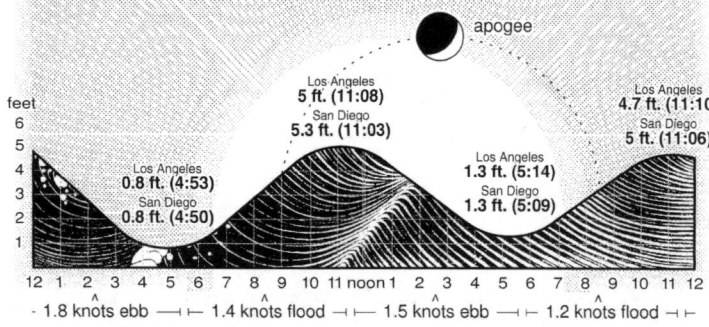

apogee

Los Angeles
5 ft. (11:08)
San Diego
5.3 ft. (11:03)

Los Angeles
4.7 ft. (11:10)
San Diego
5 ft. (11:06)

Los Angeles
1.3 ft. (5:14)
San Diego
1.3 ft. (5:09)

feet
6
5
4
3
2
1

Los Angeles
0.8 ft. (4:53)
San Diego
0.8 ft. (4:50)

12 1 2 3 4 5 6 7 8 9 10 11 noon 1 2 3 4 5 6 7 8 9 10 11 12

- 1.8 knots ebb ⟶ ⊢ 1.4 knots flood ⟶ ⊢ 1.5 knots ebb ⟶ ⊢ 1.2 knots flood ⟶ ⊢

FRI SEP 6
dawn 5:36 sunrise 6:31 sunset 7:11 dark 8:06
moonrise 9:43 a.m. moonset 8:56 p.m.

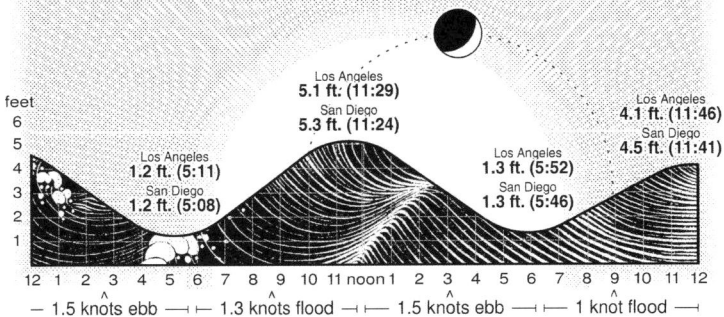

feet
6
5
4
3
2
1

Los Angeles
5.1 ft: (11:29)
San Diego
5.3 ft. (11:24)

Los Angeles
1.2 ft. (5:11)
San Diego
1.2 ft. (5:08)

Los Angeles
1.3 ft. (5:52)
San Diego
1.3 ft. (5:46)

Los Angeles
4.1 ft. (11:46)
San Diego
4.5 ft. (11:41)

12 1 2 3 4 5 6 7 8 9 10 11 noon 1 2 3 4 5 6 7 8 9 10 11 12

— 1.5 knots ebb — ├— 1.3 knots flood — ├— 1.5 knots ebb —┤ ├— 1 knot flood —┤

SAT SEP 7
dawn 5:37 sunrise 6:31 sunset 7:10 dark 8:04
moonrise 10:40 a.m. moonset 9:24 p.m.

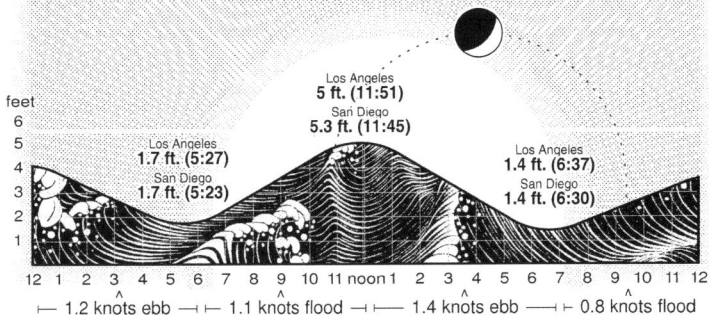

feet
6
5
4
3
2
1

Los Angeles
5 ft. (11:51)
San Diego
5.3 ft. (11:45)

Los Angeles
1.7 ft. (5:27)
San Diego
1.7 ft. (5:23)

Los Angeles
1.4 ft. (6:37)
San Diego
1.4 ft. (6:30)

12 1 2 3 4 5 6 7 8 9 10 11 noon 1 2 3 4 5 6 7 8 9 10 11 12

├— 1.2 knots ebb —┤ ├— 1.1 knots flood —┤ ├— 1.4 knots ebb —— ├ 0.8 knots flood

SUN SEP 8
dawn 5:37 sunrise 6:32 sunset 7:08 dark 8:03
moonrise 11:39 a.m. moonset 9:55 p.m.

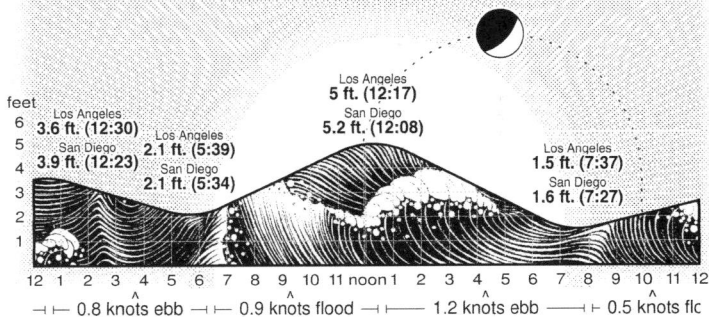

feet
6
5
4
3
2
1

Los Angeles
5 ft. (12:17)
San Diego
5.2 ft. (12:08)

Los Angeles
3.6 ft. (12:30)
San Diego
3.9 ft. (12:23)

Los Angeles
2.1 ft. (5:39)
San Diego
2.1 ft. (5:34)

Los Angeles
1.5 ft. (7:37)
San Diego
1.6 ft. (7:27)

12 1 2 3 4 5 6 7 8 9 10 11 noon 1 2 3 4 5 6 7 8 9 10 11 12

┤ ├— 0.8 knots ebb —┤ ├— 0.9 knots flood —┤ ├—— 1.2 knots ebb —— ├ 0.5 knots flc

MON SEP 9 dawn 5:38 sunrise 6:33 sunset 7:07 dark 8:01
moonrise 12:40 p.m. moonset 10:32 p.m.

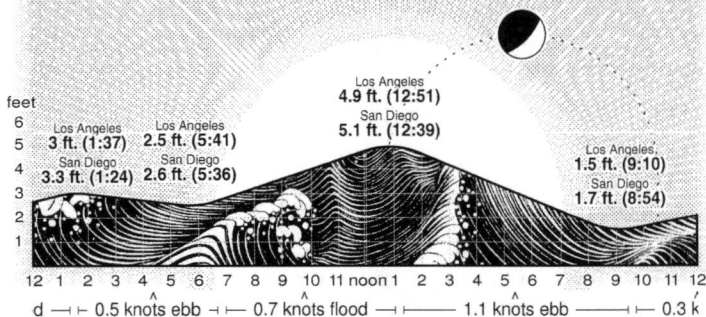

feet
6
5
4
3
2
1

Los Angeles
3 ft. (1:37)
San Diego
3.3 ft. (1:24)

Los Angeles
2.5 ft. (5:41)
San Diego
2.6 ft. (5:36)

Los Angeles
4.9 ft. (12:51)
San Diego
5.1 ft. (12:39)

Los Angeles
1.5 ft. (9:10)
San Diego
1.7 ft. (8:54)

12 1 2 3 4 5 6 7 8 9 10 11 noon 1 2 3 4 5 6 7 8 9 10 11 12

d ⊢ 0.5 knots ebb ⊣ ⊢ 0.7 knots flood ⊣ ⊢ 1.1 knots ebb ⊣ ⊢ 0.3 k

TUE SEP 10 dawn 5:39 sunrise 6:34 sunset 7:05 dark 8:00
moonrise 1:41 p.m. moonset 11:17 p.m.

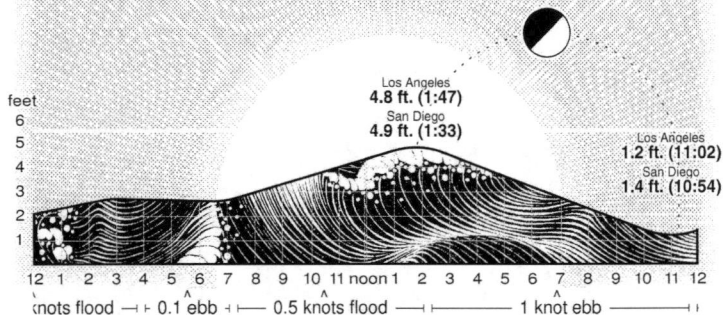

feet
6
5
4
3
2
1

Los Angeles
4.8 ft. (1:47)
San Diego
4.9 ft. (1:33)

Los Angeles
1.2 ft. (11:02)
San Diego
1.4 ft. (10:54)

12 1 2 3 4 5 6 7 8 9 10 11 noon 1 2 3 4 5 6 7 8 9 10 11 12

knots flood ⊣ ⊢ 0.1 ebb ⊣ ⊢ 0.5 knots flood ⊣ ⊢ 1 knot ebb ⊣

WED SEP 11 dawn 5:40 sunrise 6:34 sunset 7:04 dark 7:59
moonrise 2:42 p.m.

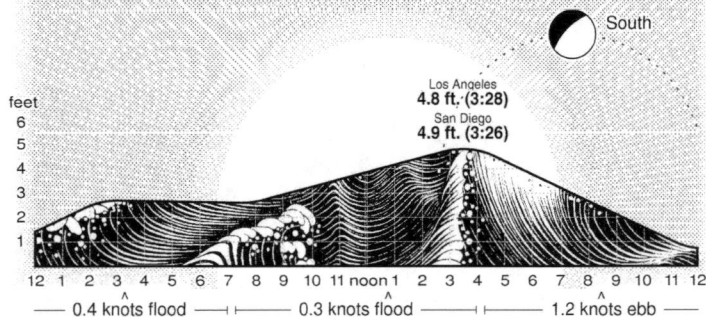

South

feet
6
5
4
3
2
1

Los Angeles
4.8 ft. (3:28)
San Diego
4.9 ft. (3:26)

12 1 2 3 4 5 6 7 8 9 10 11 noon 1 2 3 4 5 6 7 8 9 10 11 12

⊢ 0.4 knots flood ⊣ ⊢ 0.3 knots flood ⊣ ⊢ 1.2 knots ebb ⊣

THU SEP 12 dawn 5:40 sunrise 6:35 sunset 7:03 dark 7:57
moonset 12:11 a.m. moonrise 3:38 p.m.

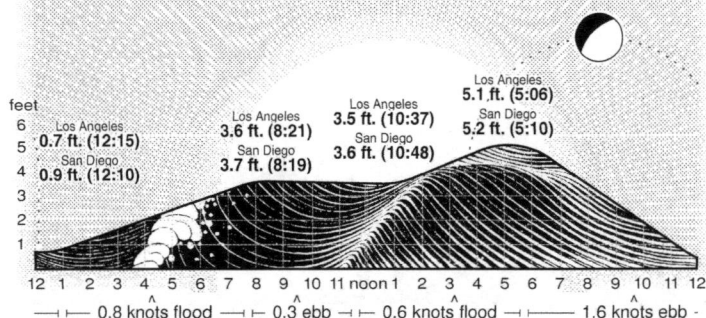

feet
6
5
4
3
2
1

Los Angeles
0.7 ft. (12:15)
San Diego
0.9 ft. (12:10)

Los Angeles
3.6 ft. (8:21)
San Diego
3.7 ft. (8:19)

Los Angeles
3.5 ft. (10:37)
San Diego
3.6 ft. (10:48)

Los Angeles
5.1 ft. (5:06)
San Diego
5.2 ft. (5:10)

12 1 2 3 4 5 6 7 8 9 10 11 noon 1 2 3 4 5 6 7 8 9 10 11 12

⊣ ⊢ 0.8 knots flood ⊣ ⊢ 0.3 ebb ⊣ ⊢ 0.6 knots flood ⊣ ⊢ 1.6 knots ebb ·

FRI SEP 13

dawn 5:41 sunrise 6:36 sunset 7:01 dark 7:56
moonset 1:13 a.m. moonrise 4:28 p.m.

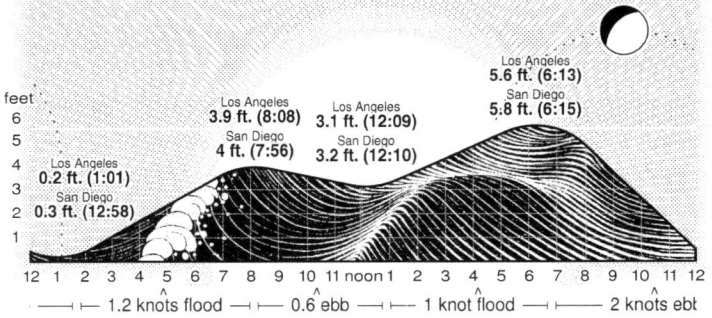

feet

Los Angeles
5.6 ft. (6:13)
San Diego
5.8 ft. (6:15)

Los Angeles
3.9 ft. (8:08)
San Diego
4 ft. (7:56)

Los Angeles
3.1 ft. (12:09)
San Diego
3.2 ft. (12:10)

Los Angeles
0.2 ft. (1:01)
San Diego
0.3 ft. (12:58)

12 1 2 3 4 5 6 7 8 9 10 11 noon 1 2 3 4 5 6 7 8 9 10 11 12

⊢— ⊢ 1.2 knots flood —⊢ ⊢ 0.6 ebb ⊢ ⊢— 1 knot flood —⊢ ⊢ 2 knots ebt

SAT SEP 14

dawn 5:42 sunrise 6:36 sunset 7:00 dark 7:54
moonset 2:22 a.m. moonrise 5:12 p.m.

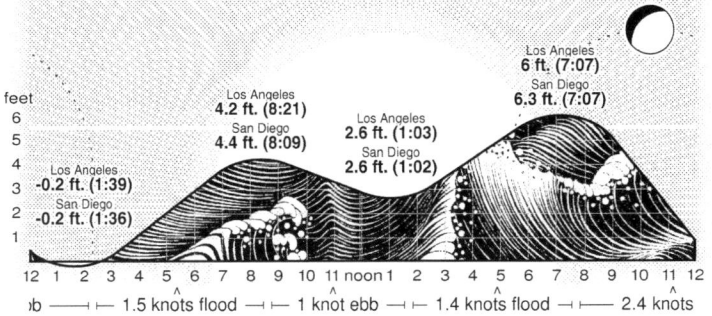

feet

Los Angeles
6 ft. (7:07)
San Diego
6.3 ft. (7:07)

Los Angeles
4.2 ft. (8:21)
San Diego
4.4 ft. (8:09)

Los Angeles
2.6 ft. (1:03)
San Diego
2.6 ft. (1:02)

Los Angeles
-0.2 ft. (1:39)
San Diego
-0.2 ft. (1:36)

12 1 2 3 4 5 6 7 8 9 10 11 noon 1 2 3 4 5 6 7 8 9 10 11 12

⊣b — ⊢ 1.5 knots flood —⊣ ⊢ 1 knot ebb —⊢ ⊢ 1.4 knots flood —⊣ ⊢ 2.4 knots

SUN SEP 15

dawn 5:43 sunrise 6:37 sunset 6:59 dark 7:53
moonset 3:35 a.m. moonrise 5:50 p.m.

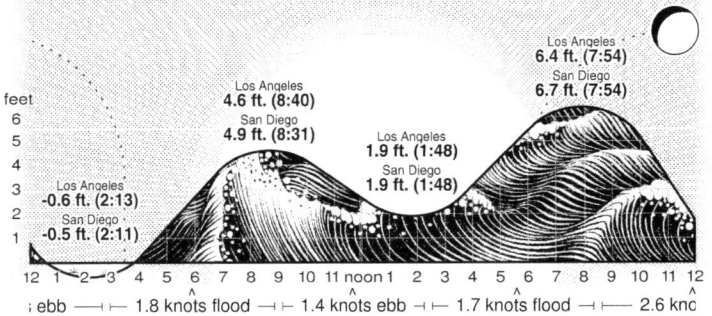

feet

Los Angeles
6.4 ft. (7:54)
San Diego
6.7 ft. (7:54)

Los Angeles
4.6 ft. (8:40)
San Diego
4.9 ft. (8:31)

Los Angeles
1.9 ft. (1:48)
San Diego
1.9 ft. (1:48)

Los Angeles
-0.6 ft. (2:13)
San Diego
-0.5 ft. (2:11)

12 1 2 3 4 5 6 7 8 9 10 11 noon 1 2 3 4 5 6 7 8 9 10 11 12

⊢ ebb —⊣ ⊢ 1.8 knots flood —⊣ ⊢ 1.4 knots ebb —⊣ ⊢ 1.7 knots flood —⊣ ⊢ 2.6 knc

Partial Lunar Eclipse The Sep 17th partial lunar eclipse will be visible throughout the United States. During the eclipse the Moon will pass through the Earth's shadow called the penumbra and barely enters the umbra. The eclipse will partially block the Sun's light making the Moon appear less bright than usual. On the west coast, the moon enters the umbra at approximately 7:11 p.m. with the maximum eclipse at 7:44 p.m. The eclipse ends at 9:49 p.m. as the Moon exits penumbra.

MON SEP 16
dawn 5:43 sunrise 6:38 sunset 6:57 dark 7:51
moonset 4:48 a.m. moonrise 6:24 p.m.

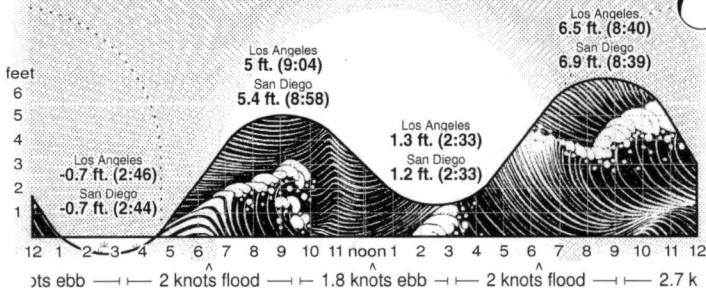

Los Angeles
6.5 ft. (8:40)
San Diego
6.9 ft. (8:39)

Los Angeles
5 ft. (9:04)
San Diego
5.4 ft. (8:58)

Los Angeles
1.3 ft. (2:33)
San Diego
1.2 ft. (2:33)

Los Angeles
-0.7 ft. (2:46)
San Diego
-0.7 ft. (2:44)

feet
6
5
4
3
2
1

12 1 2 3 4 5 6 7 8 9 10 11 noon 1 2 3 4 5 6 7 8 9 10 11 12

)ts ebb ⊢—⊣ 2 knots flood ⊣ ⊢ 1.8 knots ebb ⊣ ⊢ 2 knots flood ⊣ ⊢ 2.7 k

TUE SEP 17
dawn 5:44 sunrise 6:38 sunset 6:56 dark 7:50
moonset 6:02 a.m. moonrise 6:56 p.m.

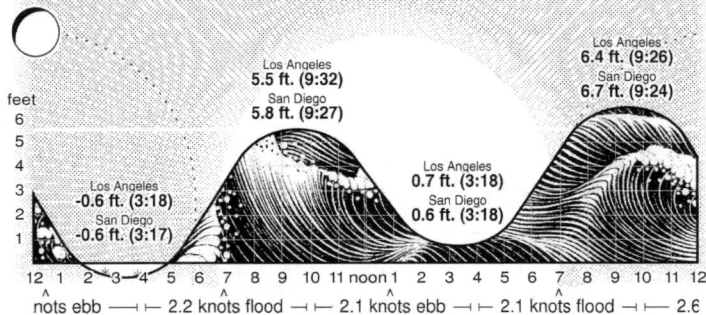

Los Angeles
6.4 ft. (9:26)
San Diego
6.7 ft. (9:24)

Los Angeles
5.5 ft. (9:32)
San Diego
5.8 ft. (9:27)

Los Angeles
0.7 ft. (3:18)
San Diego
0.6 ft. (3:18)

Los Angeles
-0.6 ft. (3:18)
San Diego
-0.6 ft. (3:17)

feet
6
5
4
3
2
1

12 1 2 3 4 5 6 7 8 9 10 11 noon 1 2 3 4 5 6 7 8 9 10 11 12

nots ebb ⊢—⊣ 2.2 knots flood ⊣ ⊢ 2.1 knots ebb ⊣ ⊢ 2.1 knots flood ⊣ ⊢ 2.6

WED SEP 18
dawn 5:45 sunrise 6:39 sunset 6:54 dark 7:48
moonset 7:14 a.m. moonrise 7:27 p.m.

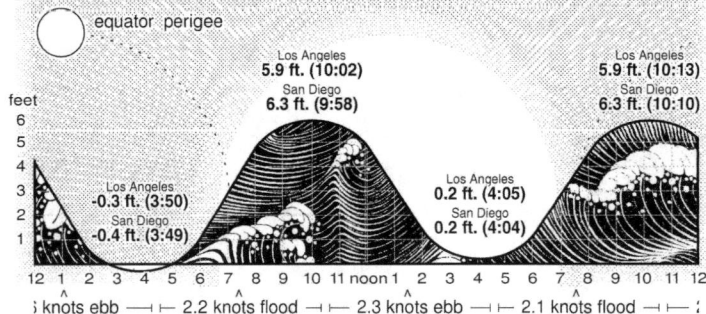

equator perigee

Los Angeles
5.9 ft. (10:02)
San Diego
6.3 ft. (9:58)

Los Angeles
5.9 ft. (10:13)
San Diego
6.3 ft. (10:10)

Los Angeles
0.2 ft. (4:05)
San Diego
0.2 ft. (4:04)

Los Angeles
-0.3 ft. (3:50)
San Diego
-0.4 ft. (3:49)

feet
6
5
4
3
2
1

12 1 2 3 4 5 6 7 8 9 10 11 noon 1 2 3 4 5 6 7 8 9 10 11 12

; knots ebb ⊣ ⊢ 2.2 knots flood ⊣ ⊢ 2.3 knots ebb ⊣ ⊢ 2.1 knots flood ⊣ ⊢ ;

THU SEP 19
dawn 5:46 sunrise 6:40 sunset 6:53 dark 7:47
moonset 8:27 a.m. moonrise 7:59 p.m.

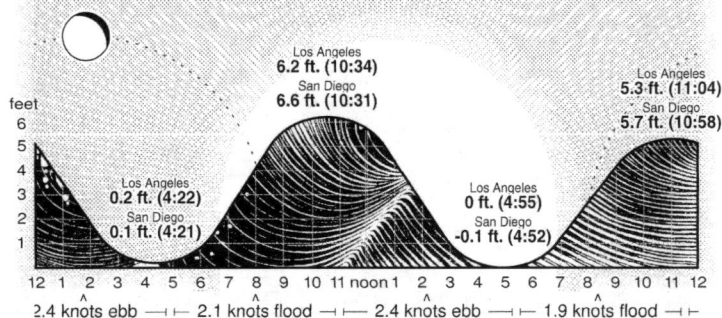

Los Angeles
6.2 ft. (10:34)
San Diego
6.6 ft. (10:31)

Los Angeles
5.3 ft. (11:04)
San Diego
5.7 ft. (10:58)

Los Angeles
0.2 ft. (4:22)
San Diego
0.1 ft. (4:21)

Los Angeles
0 ft. (4:55)
San Diego
-0.1 ft. (4:52)

feet
6
5
4
3
2
1

12 1 2 3 4 5 6 7 8 9 10 11 noon 1 2 3 4 5 6 7 8 9 10 11 12

2.4 knots ebb ⊣ ⊢ 2.1 knots flood ⊣ ⊢ 2.4 knots ebb ⊣ ⊢ 1.9 knots flood ⊣ ⊢

FRI SEP 20
dawn 5:46 sunrise 6:40 sunset 6:52 dark 7:46
moonset 9:41 a.m. moonrise 8:34 p.m.

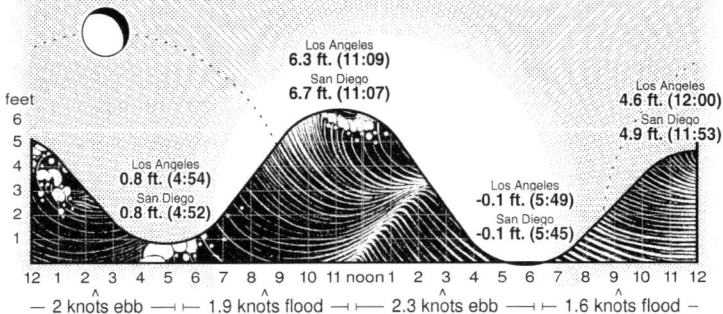

feet

Los Angeles
6.3 ft. (11:09)
San Diego
6.7 ft. (11:07)

Los Angeles
4.6 ft. (12:00)
San Diego
4.9 ft. (11:53)

Los Angeles
0.8 ft. (4:54)
San Diego
0.8 ft. (4:52)

Los Angeles
-0.1 ft. (5:49)
San Diego
-0.1 ft. (5:45)

12 1 2 3 4 5 6 7 8 9 10 11 noon 1 2 3 4 5 6 7 8 9 10 11 12

— 2 knots ebb — 1.9 knots flood — 2.3 knots ebb — 1.6 knots flood —

SAT SEP 21
dawn 5:47 sunrise 6:41 sunset 6:50 dark 7:44
moonset 10:55 a.m. moonrise 9:13 p.m.

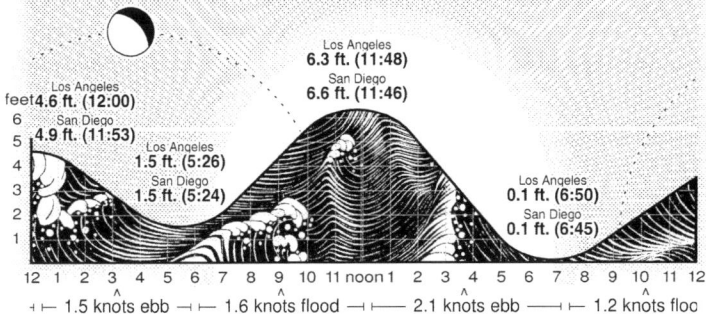

Los Angeles
6.3 ft. (11:48)
San Diego
6.6 ft. (11:46)

feet Los Angeles 4.6 ft. (12:00)
San Diego
4.9 ft. (11:53)

Los Angeles
1.5 ft. (5:26)
San Diego
1.5 ft. (5:24)

Los Angeles
0.1 ft. (6:50)
San Diego
0.1 ft. (6:45)

12 1 2 3 4 5 6 7 8 9 10 11 noon 1 2 3 4 5 6 7 8 9 10 11 12

— 1.5 knots ebb — 1.6 knots flood — 2.1 knots ebb — 1.2 knots floo

SUN SEP 22
dawn 5:48 sunrise 6:42 sunset 6:49 dark 7:43
moonset 12:08 p.m. moonrise 9:59 p.m.

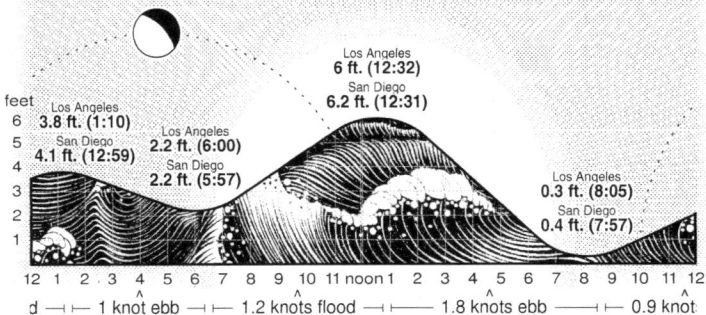

Los Angeles
6 ft. (12:32)
San Diego
6.2 ft. (12:31)

feet
Los Angeles
3.8 ft. (1:10)
San Diego
4.1 ft. (12:59)

Los Angeles
2.2 ft. (6:00)
San Diego
2.2 ft. (5:57)

Los Angeles
0.3 ft. (8:05)
San Diego
0.4 ft. (7:57)

12 1 2 3 4 5 6 7 8 9 10 11 noon 1 2 3 4 5 6 7 8 9 10 11 12

d — 1 knot ebb — 1.2 knots flood — 1.8 knots ebb — 0.9 knot

J
M
V
S

Autumnal Equinox The Sep 22nd equinox marks the first day of Fall
in the northern hemisphere as the Sun crosses the celestial equator going
south. With the equinox, the days become shorter and the nights longer.
This continues until the winter solstice where thereafter the days begin
to grow longer.

MON SEP 23
dawn 5:48 sunrise 6:42 sunset 6:47 dark 7:41
moonset 1:16 p.m. moonrise 10:52 p.m.

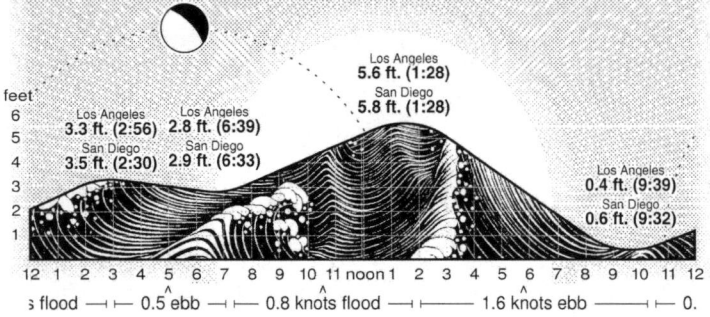

feet
6
5
4
3
2
1

Los Angeles
3.3 ft. (2:56)
San Diego
3.5 ft. (2:30)

Los Angeles
2.8 ft. (6:39)
San Diego
2.9 ft. (6:33)

Los Angeles
5.6 ft. (1:28)
San Diego
5.8 ft. (1:28)

Los Angeles
0.4 ft. (9:39)
San Diego
0.6 ft. (9:32)

12 1 2 3 4 5 6 7 8 9 10 11 noon 1 2 3 4 5 6 7 8 9 10 11 12

s flood —→ ⊢ 0.5 ebb ⊢—→ ⊢— 0.8 knots flood —→ ⊢ 1.6 ebb ——→ ⊢ 0.

TUE SEP 24
dawn 5:49 sunrise 6:43 sunset 6:46 dark 7:40
moonset 2:17 p.m. moonrise 11:50 p.m.

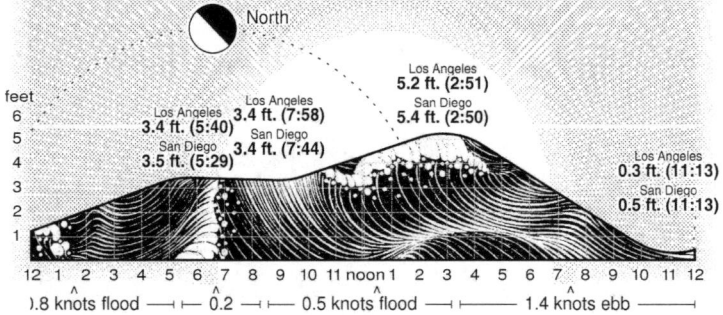

North

feet
6
5
4
3
2
1

Los Angeles
3.4 ft. (5:40)
San Diego
3.5 ft. (5:29)

Los Angeles
3.4 ft. (7:58)
San Diego
3.4 ft. (7:44)

Los Angeles
5.2 ft. (2:51)
San Diego
5.4 ft. (2:50)

Los Angeles
0.3 ft. (11:13)
San Diego
0.5 ft. (11:13)

12 1 2 3 4 5 6 7 8 9 10 11 noon 1 2 3 4 5 6 7 8 9 10 11 12

.8 knots flood —→ ⊢ 0.2 ⊣ ⊢— 0.5 knots flood —→ ⊢ 1.4 knots ebb ——→ ⊣

WED SEP 25
dawn 5:50 sunrise 6:44 sunset 6:45 dark 7:38
moonset 3:09 p.m.

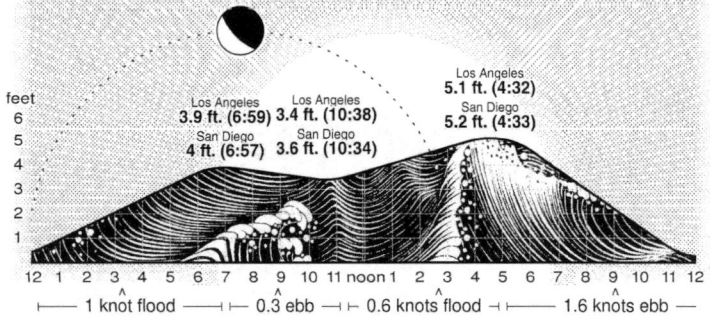

feet
6
5
4
3
2
1

Los Angeles
3.9 ft. (6:59)
San Diego
4 ft. (6:57)

Los Angeles
3.4 ft. (10:38)
San Diego
3.6 ft. (10:34)

Los Angeles
5.1 ft. (4:32)
San Diego
5.2 ft. (4:33)

12 1 2 3 4 5 6 7 8 9 10 11 noon 1 2 3 4 5 6 7 8 9 10 11 12

⊢— 1 knot flood —→ ⊢— 0.3 ebb ⊣ ⊢ 0.6 knots flood ⊣ ⊢— 1.6 knots ebb —

THU SEP 26
dawn 5:51 sunrise 6:44 sunset 6:43 dark 7:37
moonrise 12:52 a.m. moonset 3:53 p.m.

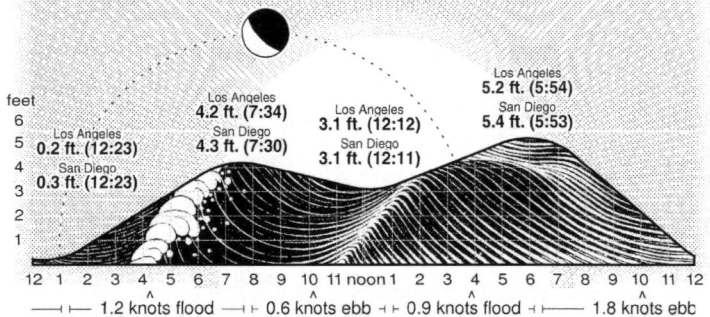

feet
6
5
4
3
2
1

Los Angeles
0.2 ft. (12:23)
San Diego
0.3 ft. (12:23)

Los Angeles
4.2 ft. (7:34)
San Diego
4.3 ft. (7:30)

Los Angeles
3.1 ft. (12:12)
San Diego
3.1 ft. (12:11)

Los Angeles
5.2 ft. (5:54)
San Diego
5.4 ft. (5:53)

12 1 2 3 4 5 6 7 8 9 10 11 noon 1 2 3 4 5 6 7 8 9 10 11 12

——⊢ 1.2 knots flood —⊣ ⊢ 0.6 knots ebb ⊣ ⊢ 0.9 knots flood ⊣ ⊢— 1.8 knots ebb —

FRI SEP 27

dawn 5:51 sunrise 6:45 sunset 6:42 dark 7:36
moonrise 1:55 a.m. moonset 4:29 p.m.

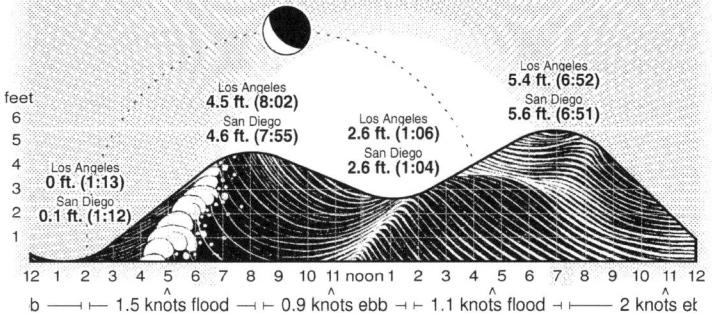

feet
6
5
4
3
2
1

Los Angeles
0 ft. (1:13)
San Diego
0.1 ft. (1:12)

Los Angeles
4.5 ft. (8:02)
San Diego
4.6 ft. (7:55)

Los Angeles
2.6 ft. (1:06)
San Diego
2.6 ft. (1:04)

Los Angeles
5.4 ft. (6:52)
San Diego
5.6 ft. (6:51)

12 1 2 3 4 5 6 7 8 9 10 11 noon 1 2 3 4 5 6 7 8 9 10 11 12

b ⟶ ⊢ 1.5 knots flood ⟶ ⊣ 0.9 knots ebb ⟶ ⊢ 1.1 knots flood ⟶ ⊢⟶ 2 knots et

SAT SEP 28

dawn 5:52 sunrise 6:46 sunset 6:41 dark 7:34
moonrise 2:56 a.m. moonset 4:59 p.m.

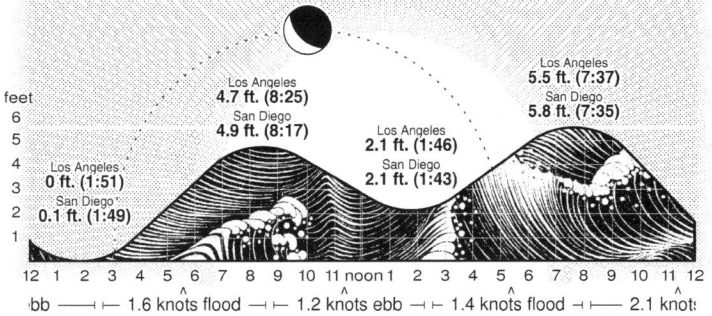

feet
6
5
4
3
2
1

Los Angeles
0 ft. (1:51)
San Diego
0.1 ft. (1:49)

Los Angeles
4.7 ft. (8:25)
San Diego
4.9 ft. (8:17)

Los Angeles
2.1 ft. (1:46)
San Diego
2.1 ft. (1:43)

Los Angeles
5.5 ft. (7:37)
San Diego
5.8 ft. (7:35)

12 1 2 3 4 5 6 7 8 9 10 11 noon 1 2 3 4 5 6 7 8 9 10 11 12

bb ⟶ ⊢ 1.6 knots flood ⟶ ⊣ 1.2 knots ebb ⟶ ⊢ 1.4 knots flood ⟶ ⊢⟶ 2.1 knots

SUN SEP 29

dawn 5:53 sunrise 6:47 sunset 6:39 dark 7:33
moonrise 3:55 a.m. moonset 5:26 p.m.

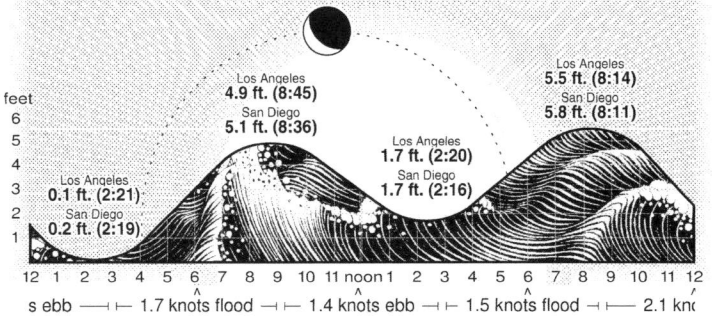

feet
6
5
4
3
2
1

Los Angeles
0.1 ft. (2:21)
San Diego
0.2 ft. (2:19)

Los Angeles
4.9 ft. (8:45)
San Diego
5.1 ft. (8:36)

Los Angeles
1.7 ft. (2:20)
San Diego
1.7 ft. (2:16)

Los Angeles
5.5 ft. (8:14)
San Diego
5.8 ft. (8:11)

12 1 2 3 4 5 6 7 8 9 10 11 noon 1 2 3 4 5 6 7 8 9 10 11 12

s ebb ⟶ ⊢ 1.7 knots flood ⟶ ⊣ 1.4 knots ebb ⟶ ⊢ 1.5 knots flood ⟶ ⊢⟶ 2.1 kno

Ⓙ
Ⓜ
Ⓥ
Ⓢ

MON SEP 30 dawn 5:53 sunrise 6:47 sunset 6:38 dark 7:32
moonrise 4:52 a.m. moonset 5:50 p.m.

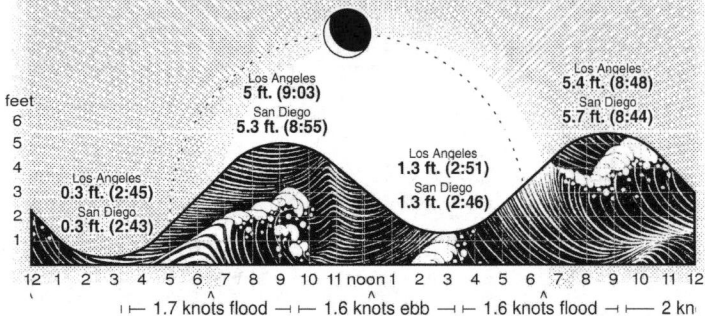

Los Angeles 5 ft. (9:03)
San Diego 5.3 ft. (8:55)

Los Angeles 5.4 ft. (8:48)
San Diego 5.7 ft. (8:44)

Los Angeles 1.3 ft. (2:51)
San Diego 1.3 ft. (2:46)

Los Angeles 0.3 ft. (2:45)
San Diego 0.3 ft. (2:43)

feet 6 5 4 3 2 1

12 1 2 3 4 5 6 7 8 9 10 11 noon 1 2 3 4 5 6 7 8 9 10 11 12

⊢ 1.7 knots flood → ⊢ 1.6 knots ebb → ⊢ 1.6 knots flood → ⊢ 2 kn

TUE OCT 1 dawn 5:54 sunrise 6:48 sunset 6:36 dark 7:30
moonrise 5:47 a.m. moonset 6:13 p.m.

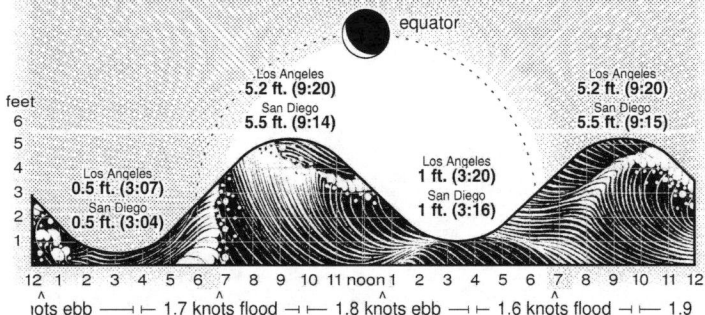

equator

Los Angeles 5.2 ft. (9:20)
San Diego 5.5 ft. (9:14)

Los Angeles 5.2 ft. (9:20)
San Diego 5.5 ft. (9:15)

Los Angeles 1 ft. (3:20)
San Diego 1 ft. (3:16)

Los Angeles 0.5 ft. (3:07)
San Diego 0.5 ft. (3:04)

feet 6 5 4 3 2 1

12 1 2 3 4 5 6 7 8 9 10 11 noon 1 2 3 4 5 6 7 8 9 10 11 12

nots ebb ⊢ 1.7 knots flood → ⊢ 1.8 knots ebb → ⊢ 1.6 knots flood → ⊢ 1.9

WED OCT 2 dawn 5:55 sunrise 6:49 sunset 6:35 dark 7:29
moonrise 6:42 a.m. moonset 6:36 p.m.

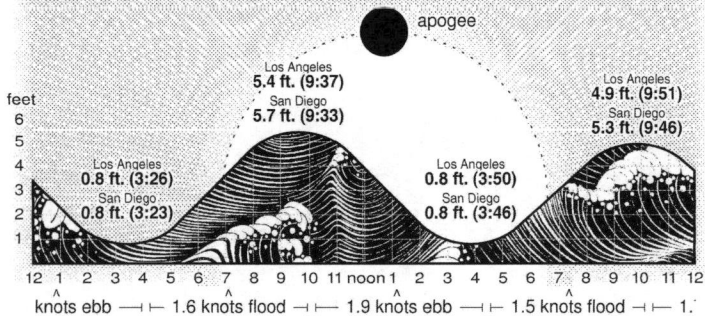

apogee

Los Angeles 5.4 ft. (9:37)
San Diego 5.7 ft. (9:33)

Los Angeles 4.9 ft. (9:51)
San Diego 5.3 ft. (9:46)

Los Angeles 0.8 ft. (3:50)
San Diego 0.8 ft. (3:46)

Los Angeles 0.8 ft. (3:26)
San Diego 0.8 ft. (3:23)

feet 6 5 4 3 2 1

12 1 2 3 4 5 6 7 8 9 10 11 noon 1 2 3 4 5 6 7 8 9 10 11 12

knots ebb ⊢ 1.6 knots flood → ⊢ 1.9 knots ebb → ⊢ 1.5 knots flood → ⊢ 1.

THU OCT 3 dawn 5:56 sunrise 6:49 sunset 6:34 dark 7:27
moonrise 7:38 a.m. moonset 7:00 p.m.

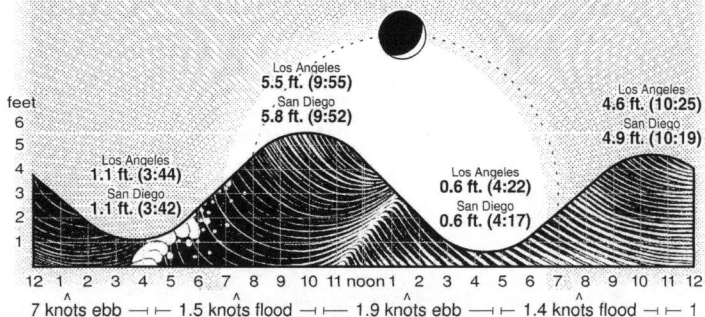

Los Angeles 5.5 ft. (9:55)
San Diego 5.8 ft. (9:52)

Los Angeles 4.6 ft. (10:25)
San Diego 4.9 ft. (10:19)

Los Angeles 0.6 ft. (4:22)
San Diego 0.6 ft. (4:17)

Los Angeles 1.1 ft. (3:44)
San Diego 1.1 ft. (3:42)

feet 6 5 4 3 2 1

12 1 2 3 4 5 6 7 8 9 10 11 noon 1 2 3 4 5 6 7 8 9 10 11 12

7 knots ebb ⊢ 1.5 knots flood → ⊢ 1.9 knots ebb → ⊢ 1.4 knots flood → ⊢ 1

FRI OCT 4

dawn 5:56 sunrise 6:50 sunset 6:32 dark 7:26
moonrise 8:34 a.m. moonset 7:27 p.m.

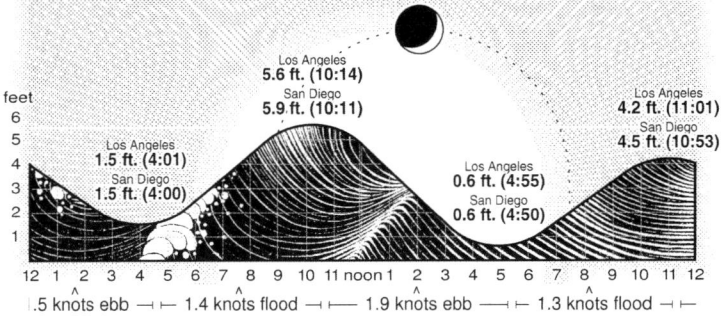

Los Angeles
5.6 ft. (10:14)
San Diego
5.9 ft. (10:11)

Los Angeles
1.5 ft. (4:01)
San Diego
1.5 ft. (4:00)

Los Angeles
0.6 ft. (4:55)
San Diego
0.6 ft. (4:50)

Los Angeles
4.2 ft. (11:01)
San Diego
4.5 ft. (10:53)

feet 6 5 4 3 2 1

12 1 2 3 4 5 6 7 8 9 10 11 noon 1 2 3 4 5 6 7 8 9 10 11 12

.5 knots ebb → ⊢ 1.4 knots flood → ⊢ 1.9 knots ebb —— ⊢ 1.3 knots flood → ⊢

SAT OCT 5

dawn 5:57 sunrise 6:51 sunset 6:31 dark 7:25
moonrise 9:32 a.m. moonset 7:57 p.m.

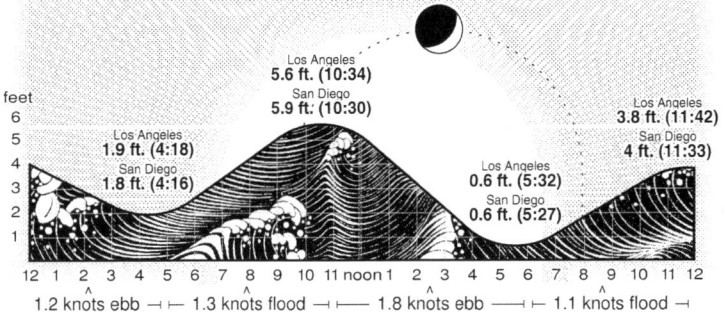

Los Angeles
5.6 ft. (10:34)
San Diego
5.9 ft. (10:30)

Los Angeles
1.9 ft. (4:18)
San Diego
1.8 ft. (4:16)

Los Angeles
0.6 ft. (5:32)
San Diego
0.6 ft. (5:27)

Los Angeles
3.8 ft. (11:42)
San Diego
4 ft. (11:33)

feet 6 5 4 3 2 1

12 1 2 3 4 5 6 7 8 9 10 11 noon 1 2 3 4 5 6 7 8 9 10 11 12

1.2 knots ebb → ⊢ 1.3 knots flood → ⊢ 1.8 knots ebb —— ⊢ 1.1 knots flood →

SUN OCT 6

dawn 5:58 sunrise 6:52 sunset 6:30 dark 7:24
moonrise 10:32 a.m. moonset 8:32 p.m.

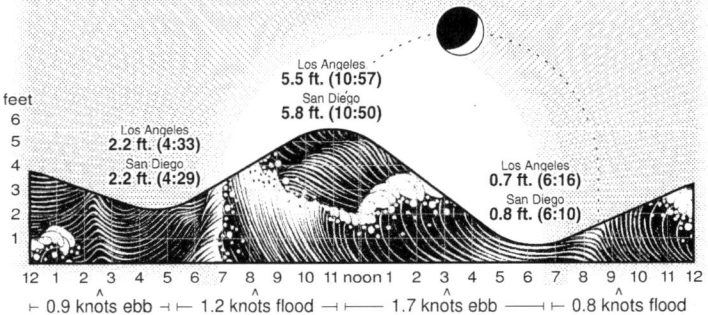

Los Angeles
5.5 ft. (10:57)
San Diego
5.8 ft. (10:50)

Los Angeles
2.2 ft. (4:33)
San Diego
2.2 ft. (4:29)

Los Angeles
0.7 ft. (6:16)
San Diego
0.8 ft. (6:10)

feet 6 5 4 3 2 1

12 1 2 3 4 5 6 7 8 9 10 11 noon 1 2 3 4 5 6 7 8 9 10 11 12

⊢ 0.9 knots ebb → ⊢ 1.2 knots flood → ⊢ 1.7 knots ebb —— ⊢ 0.8 knots flood

Annular Solar Eclipse The Oct 2nd annular solar eclipse will not
be visible from the United States. An annular eclipse occurs when the
new Moon partially covers the Sun's center leaving its outer edge visible
resulting in a "ring of fire" or annulus. This eclipse's shadow will run
from South America on a northwesterly track with only a partial eclipse
visible on the southern end of the Baja peninsula as its runs out to the
Pacific ocean.

MON OCT 7 dawn 5:58 sunrise 6:52 sunset 6:28 dark 7:22
moonrise 11:33 a.m. moonset 9:13 p.m.

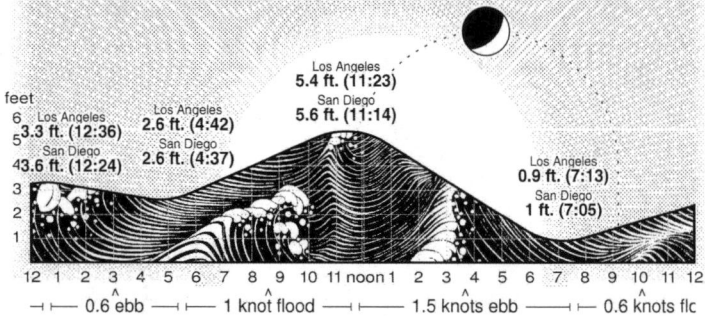

feet
6
5
4
3
2
1

Los Angeles **3.3 ft. (12:36)**
San Diego **3.6 ft. (12:24)**

Los Angeles **2.6 ft. (4:42)**
San Diego **2.6 ft. (4:37)**

Los Angeles **5.4 ft. (11:23)**
San Diego **5.6 ft. (11:14)**

Los Angeles **0.9 ft. (7:13)**
San Diego **1 ft. (7:05)**

12 1 2 3 4 5 6 7 8 9 10 11 noon 1 2 3 4 5 6 7 8 9 10 11 12

⊢— 0.6 ebb —⊣ ⊢— 1 knot flood —⊣ ⊢— 1.5 knots ebb —⊣ ⊢ 0.6 knots flc

TUE OCT 8 dawn 5:59 sunrise 6:53 sunset 6:27 dark 7:21
moonrise 12:33 p.m. moonset 10:03 p.m.

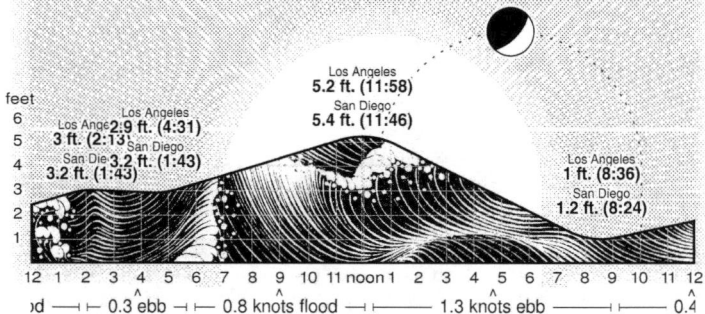

feet
6
5
4
3
2
1

Los Angeles **2.9 ft. (4:31)**
San Diego **3.2 ft. (1:43)**

Los Angeles **3 ft. (2:13)**
San Diego **3.2 ft. (1:43)**

Los Angeles **5.2 ft. (11:58)**
San Diego **5.4 ft. (11:46)**

Los Angeles **1 ft. (8:36)**
San Diego **1.2 ft. (8:24)**

12 1 2 3 4 5 6 7 8 9 10 11 noon 1 2 3 4 5 6 7 8 9 10 11 12

⊢od —⊣ ⊢— 0.3 ebb —⊣ ⊢— 0.8 knots flood —⊣ ⊢— 1.3 knots ebb —⊣ ⊢ 0.4

WED OCT 9 dawn 6:00 sunrise 6:54 sunset 6:26 dark 7:20
moonrise 1:30 p.m. moonset 11:00 p.m.

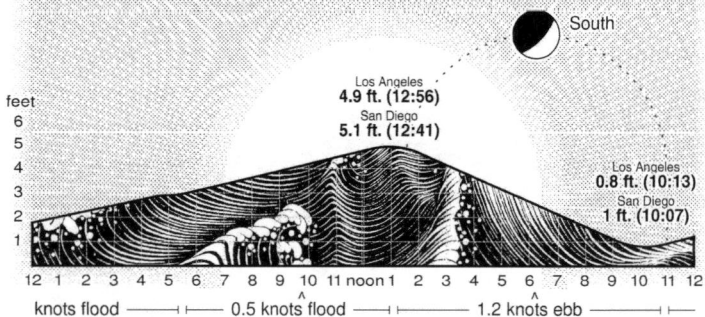

South

feet
6
5
4
3
2
1

Los Angeles **4.9 ft. (12:56)**
San Diego **5.1 ft. (12:41)**

Los Angeles **0.8 ft. (10:13)**
San Diego **1 ft. (10:07)**

12 1 2 3 4 5 6 7 8 9 10 11 noon 1 2 3 4 5 6 7 8 9 10 11 12

⊢ knots flood —⊣ ⊢— 0.5 knots flood —⊣ ⊢— 1.2 knots ebb —⊣

THU OCT 10 dawn 6:01 sunrise 6:55 sunset 6:25 dark 7:18
moonrise 2:21 p.m.

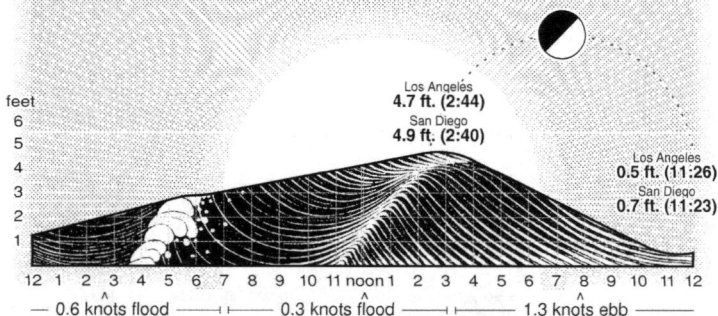

feet
6
5
4
3
2
1

Los Angeles **4.7 ft. (2:44)**
San Diego **4.9 ft. (2:40)**

Los Angeles **0.5 ft. (11:26)**
San Diego **0.7 ft. (11:23)**

12 1 2 3 4 5 6 7 8 9 10 11 noon 1 2 3 4 5 6 7 8 9 10 11 12

⊢— 0.6 knots flood —⊣ ⊢— 0.3 knots flood —⊣ ⊢— 1.3 knots ebb —⊣

FRI OCT 11

dawn 6:01 sunrise 6:55 sunset 6:23 dark 7:17
moonset 12:05 a.m. moonrise 3:06 p.m.

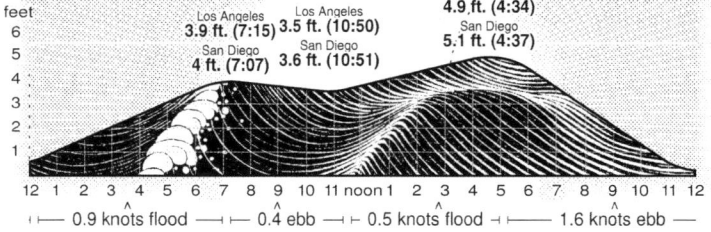

Los Angeles
3.9 ft. (7:15)
San Diego
4 ft. (7:07)

Los Angeles
3.5 ft. (10:50)
San Diego
3.6 ft. (10:51)

Los Angeles
4.9 ft. (4:34)
San Diego
5.1 ft. (4:37)

feet
6
5
4
3
2
1

12 1 2 3 4 5 6 7 8 9 10 11 noon 1 2 3 4 5 6 7 8 9 10 11 12

⊢ 0.9 knots flood ⟶ ⊢ 0.4 ebb ⟶ ⊢ 0.5 knots flood ⊣ ⊢ 1.6 knots ebb ⟶

SAT OCT 12

dawn 6:02 sunrise 6:56 sunset 6:22 dark 7:16
moonset 1:13 a.m. moonrise 3:45 p.m.

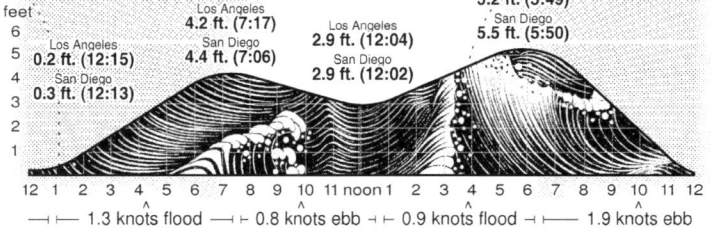

Los Angeles
0.2 ft. (12:15)
San Diego
0.3 ft. (12:13)

Los Angeles
4.2 ft. (7:17)
San Diego
4.4 ft. (7:06)

Los Angeles
2.9 ft. (12:04)
San Diego
2.9 ft. (12:02)

Los Angeles
5.2 ft. (5:49)
San Diego
5.5 ft. (5:50)

feet
6
5
4
3
2
1

12 1 2 3 4 5 6 7 8 9 10 11 noon 1 2 3 4 5 6 7 8 9 10 11 12

⟶ ⊢ 1.3 knots flood ⟶ ⊢ 0.8 ebb ⊣ ⊢ 0.9 knots flood ⊣ ⊢ 1.9 knots ebb

SUN OCT 13

dawn 6:03 sunrise 6:57 sunset 6:21 dark 7:15
moonset 2:24 a.m. moonrise 4:19 p.m.

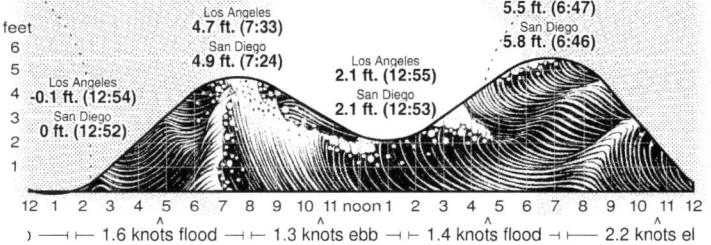

Los Angeles
-0.1 ft. (12:54)
San Diego
0 ft. (12:52)

Los Angeles
4.7 ft. (7:33)
San Diego
4.9 ft. (7:24)

Los Angeles
2.1 ft. (12:55)
San Diego
2.1 ft. (12:53)

Los Angeles
5.5 ft. (6:47)
San Diego
5.8 ft. (6:46)

feet
6
5
4
3
2
1

12 1 2 3 4 5 6 7 8 9 10 11 noon 1 2 3 4 5 6 7 8 9 10 11 12

) ⟶ ⊢ 1.6 knots flood ⟶ ⊢ 1.3 knots ebb ⟶ ⊢ 1.4 knots flood ⊣ ⊢ 2.2 knots el

ⓙ
Ⓜ
ⓥ
Ⓢ

Draconid Meteor Shower The Draconids are a minor shower active
annually between Oct 6th - 10th producing at peak up to 10 meteors per
hour. This year's peak falls on the evening of Oct 8th. This shower is
different from others in that it's best viewed in the early evening after
sunset. By sunset, the shower's radiant point, the constellation Draco,
will be high in the evening sky adjacent to the little dipper. The waxing
crescent Moon should not overwhelm the show as it sets before midnight.

MON OCT 14

dawn 6:04 sunrise 6:58 sunset 6:20 dark 7:14
moonset 3:36 a.m. moonrise 4:51 p.m.

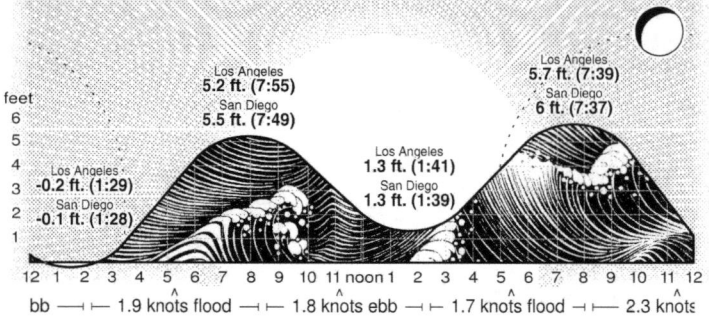

Los Angeles
5.2 ft. (7:55)
San Diego
5.5 ft. (7:49)

Los Angeles
5.7 ft. (7:39)
San Diego
6 ft. (7:37)

Los Angeles
1.3 ft. (1:41)
San Diego
1.3 ft. (1:39)

Los Angeles
-0.2 ft. (1:29)
San Diego
-0.1 ft. (1:28)

feet
6
5
4
3
2
1

12 1 2 3 4 5 6 7 8 9 10 11 noon 1 2 3 4 5 6 7 8 9 10 11 12

bb ⊢— 1.9 knots flood —⊢— 1.8 knots ebb —⊢— 1.7 knots flood —⊢— 2.3 knots

TUE OCT 15

dawn 6:04 sunrise 6:58 sunset 6:18 dark 7:12
moonset 4:47 a.m. moonrise 5:22 p.m.

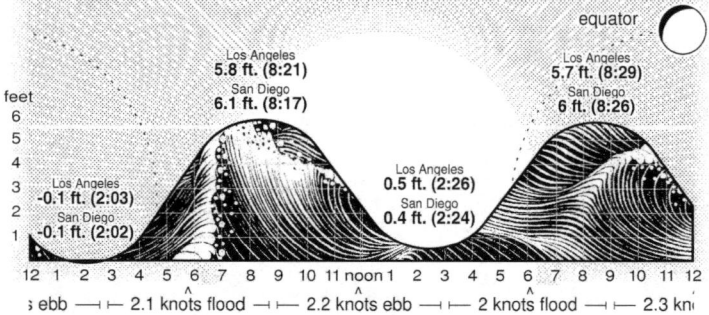

equator

Los Angeles
5.8 ft. (8:21)
San Diego
6.1 ft. (8:17)

Los Angeles
5.7 ft. (8:29)
San Diego
6 ft. (8:26)

Los Angeles
0.5 ft. (2:26)
San Diego
0.4 ft. (2:24)

Los Angeles
-0.1 ft. (2:03)
San Diego
-0.1 ft. (2:02)

feet
6
5
4
3
2
1

12 1 2 3 4 5 6 7 8 9 10 11 noon 1 2 3 4 5 6 7 8 9 10 11 12

s ebb ⊢— 2.1 knots flood —⊢— 2.2 knots ebb —⊢— 2 knots flood —⊢— 2.3 kn

WED OCT 16

dawn 6:05 sunrise 6:59 sunset 6:17 dark 7:11
moonset 5:59 a.m. moonrise 5:53 p.m.

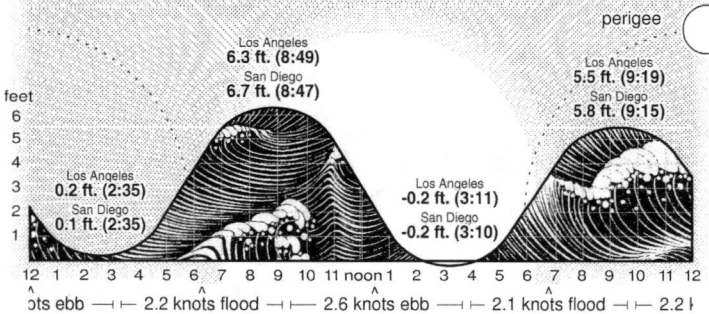

perigee

Los Angeles
6.3 ft. (8:49)
San Diego
6.7 ft. (8:47)

Los Angeles
5.5 ft. (9:19)
San Diego
5.8 ft. (9:15)

Los Angeles
-0.2 ft. (3:11)
San Diego
-0.2 ft. (3:10)

Los Angeles
0.2 ft. (2:35)
San Diego
0.1 ft. (2:35)

feet
6
5
4
3
2
1

12 1 2 3 4 5 6 7 8 9 10 11 noon 1 2 3 4 5 6 7 8 9 10 11 12

ots ebb ⊢— 2.2 knots flood —⊢— 2.6 knots ebb —⊢— 2.1 knots flood —⊢— 2.2 k

THU OCT 17

dawn 6:06 sunrise 7:00 sunset 6:16 dark 7:10
moonset 7:13 a.m. moonrise 6:27 p.m.

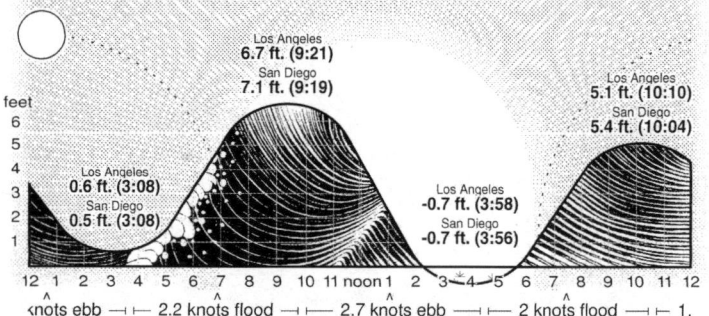

Los Angeles
6.7 ft. (9:21)
San Diego
7.1 ft. (9:19)

Los Angeles
5.1 ft. (10:10)
San Diego
5.4 ft. (10:04)

Los Angeles
0.6 ft. (3:08)
San Diego
0.5 ft. (3:08)

Los Angeles
-0.7 ft. (3:58)
San Diego
-0.7 ft. (3:56)

feet
6
5
4
3
2
1

12 1 2 3 4 5 6 7 8 9 10 11 noon 1 2 3 4 5 6 7 8 9 10 11 12

knots ebb ⊢— 2.2 knots flood —⊢— 2.7 knots ebb —⊢— 2 knots flood —⊢— 1.

FRI OCT 18

dawn 6:07 sunrise 7:01 sunset 6:15 dark 7:09
moonset 8:29 a.m. moonrise 7:05 p.m.

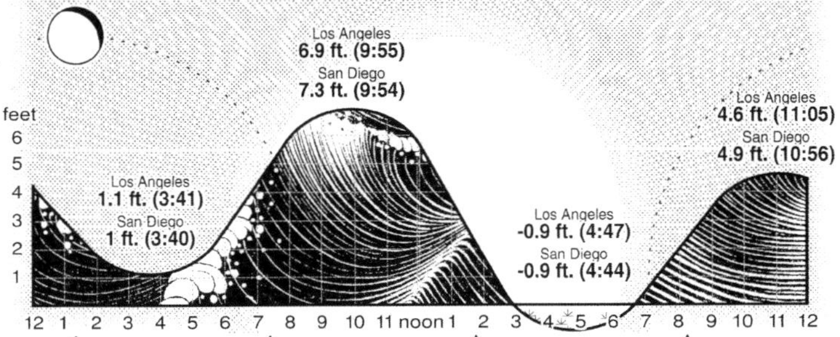
Los Angeles
6.9 ft. (9:55)
San Diego
7.3 ft. (9:54)
Los Angeles
4.6 ft. (11:05)
San Diego
4.9 ft. (10:56)
feet
6
5
4
3
2
1
Los Angeles
1.1 ft. (3:41)
San Diego
1 ft. (3:40)
Los Angeles
-0.9 ft. (4:47)
San Diego
-0.9 ft. (4:44)
12 1 2 3 4 5 6 7 8 9 10 11 noon 1 2 3 4 5 6 7 8 9 10 11 12

9 knots ebb ⊣ ⊢ 2.1 knots flood ⊣ ⊢ 2.8 knots ebb ⊣ ⊢ 1.9 knots flood ⊣ ⊢

SAT OCT 19

dawn 6:07 sunrise 7:02 sunset 6:14 dark 7:08
moonset 9:45 a.m. moonrise 7:49 p.m.

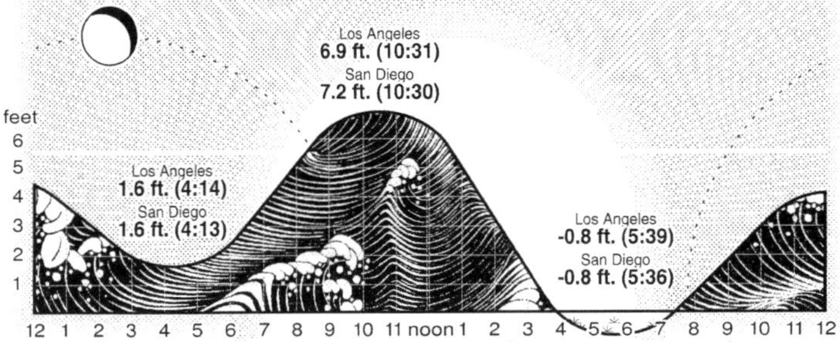
Los Angeles
6.9 ft. (10:31)
San Diego
7.2 ft. (10:30)
feet
6
5
4
3
2
1
Los Angeles
1.6 ft. (4:14)
San Diego
1.6 ft. (4:13)
Los Angeles
-0.8 ft. (5:39)
San Diego
-0.8 ft. (5:36)
12 1 2 3 4 5 6 7 8 9 10 11 noon 1 2 3 4 5 6 7 8 9 10 11 12

1.5 knots ebb ⊣ ⊢ 1.8 knots flood ⊣ ⊢ 2.6 knots ebb ⊣ ⊢ 1.6 knots flood –

SUN OCT 20

dawn 6:08 sunrise 7:02 sunset 6:12 dark 7:07
moonset 10:58 a.m. moonrise 8:40 p.m.

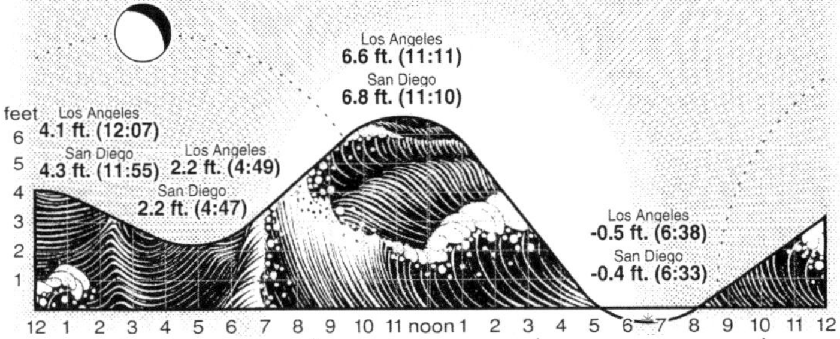
Los Angeles
6.6 ft. (11:11)
San Diego
6.8 ft. (11:10)
feet
6
5
4
3
2
1
Los Angeles
4.1 ft. (12:07)
San Diego
4.3 ft. (11:55)
Los Angeles
2.2 ft. (4:49)
San Diego
2.2 ft. (4:47)
Los Angeles
-0.5 ft. (6:38)
San Diego
-0.4 ft. (6:33)
12 1 2 3 4 5 6 7 8 9 10 11 noon 1 2 3 4 5 6 7 8 9 10 11 12

⊣ ⊢ 1.1 ebb ⊣ ⊢ 1.5 knots flood ⊣ ⊢ 2.3 knots ebb ⊣ ⊢ 1.2 knots floo

J
M
m
V
S

MON OCT 21
dawn 6:09 sunrise 7:03 sunset 6:11 dark 7:06
moonset 12:05 p.m. moonrise 9:38 p.m.

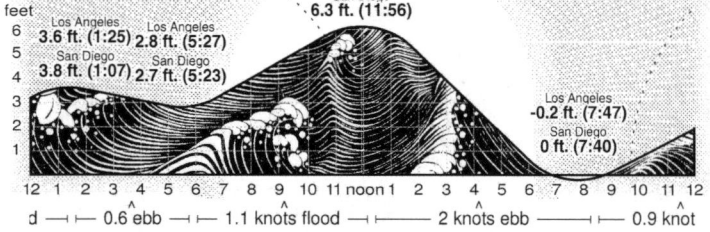

North

Los Angeles
6.1 ft. (11:56)
San Diego
6.3 ft. (11:56)

feet
Los Angeles
3.6 ft. (1:25)
San Diego
3.8 ft. (1:07)

Los Angeles
2.8 ft. (5:27)
San Diego
2.7 ft. (5:23)

Los Angeles
-0.2 ft. (7:47)
San Diego
0 ft. (7:40)

12 1 2 3 4 5 6 7 8 9 10 11 noon 1 2 3 4 5 6 7 8 9 10 11 12

d ⊢ 0.6 ebb ⊢ 1.1 knots flood ⊢ ⊢ 2 knots ebb ⊢ 0.9 knot

TUE OCT 22
dawn 6:10 sunrise 7:04 sunset 6:10 dark 7:05
moonset 1:02 p.m. moonrise 10:41 p.m.

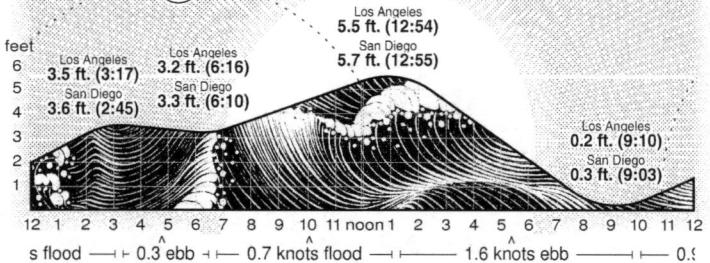

Los Angeles
5.5 ft. (12:54)
San Diego
5.7 ft. (12:55)

feet
Los Angeles
3.5 ft. (3:17)
San Diego
3.6 ft. (2:45)

Los Angeles
3.2 ft. (6:16)
San Diego
3.3 ft. (6:10)

Los Angeles
0.2 ft. (9:10)
San Diego
0.3 ft. (9:03)

12 1 2 3 4 5 6 7 8 9 10 11 noon 1 2 3 4 5 6 7 8 9 10 11 12

s flood ⊢ 0.3 ebb ⊣ ⊢ 0.7 knots flood ⊢ ⊢ 1.6 knots ebb ⊢ 0.9

WED OCT 23
dawn 6:10 sunrise 7:05 sunset 6:09 dark 7:04
moonset 1:50 p.m. moonrise 11:45 p.m.

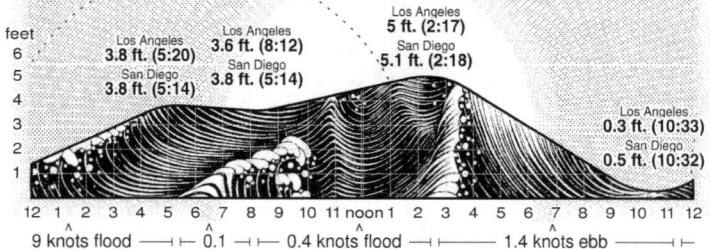

Los Angeles
5 ft. (2:17)
San Diego
5.1 ft. (2:18)

feet
Los Angeles
3.8 ft. (5:20)
San Diego
3.8 ft. (5:14)

Los Angeles
3.6 ft. (8:12)
San Diego
3.8 ft. (5:14)

Los Angeles
0.3 ft. (10:33)
San Diego
0.5 ft. (10:32)

12 1 2 3 4 5 6 7 8 9 10 11 noon 1 2 3 4 5 6 7 8 9 10 11 12

9 knots flood ⊢ 0.1 ⊣ ⊢ 0.4 knots flood ⊢ ⊢ 1.4 knots ebb ⊢ ⊢

THU OCT 24
dawn 6:11 sunrise 7:06 sunset 6:08 dark 7:03
moonset 2:29 p.m.

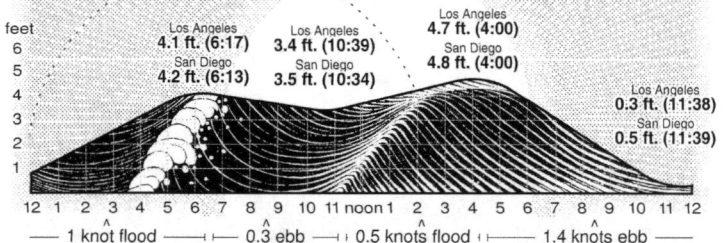

Los Angeles
4.7 ft. (4:00)
San Diego
4.8 ft. (4:00)

feet
Los Angeles
4.1 ft. (6:17)
San Diego
4.2 ft. (6:13)

Los Angeles
3.4 ft. (10:39)
San Diego
3.5 ft. (10:34)

Los Angeles
0.3 ft. (11:38)
San Diego
0.5 ft. (11:39)

12 1 2 3 4 5 6 7 8 9 10 11 noon 1 2 3 4 5 6 7 8 9 10 11 12

⊢ 1 knot flood ⊢ ⊢ 0.3 ebb ⊢ ⊣ 0.5 knots flood ⊢ ⊢ 1.4 knots ebb ⊢

FRI OCT 25
dawn 6:12 sunrise 7:07 sunset 6:07 dark 7:02
moonrise 12:48 a.m. moonset 3:02 p.m.

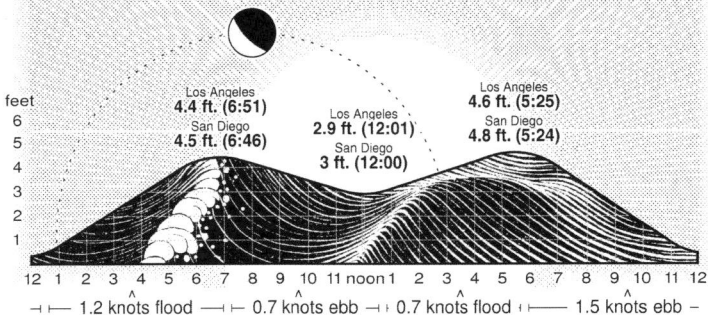

feet

Los Angeles
4.4 ft. (6:51)
San Diego
4.5 ft. (6:46)

Los Angeles
2.9 ft. (12:01)
San Diego
3 ft. (12:00)

Los Angeles
4.6 ft. (5:25)
San Diego
4.8 ft. (5:24)

12 1 2 3 4 5 6 7 8 9 10 11 noon 1 2 3 4 5 6 7 8 9 10 11 12

⊣ — 1.2 knots flood — ⊢ — 0.7 knots ebb — ⊣ ⊢ 0.7 knots flood ⊢ — 1.5 knots ebb –

SAT OCT 26
dawn 6:13 sunrise 7:08 sunset 6:06 dark 7:01
moonrise 1:48 a.m. moonset 3:30 p.m.

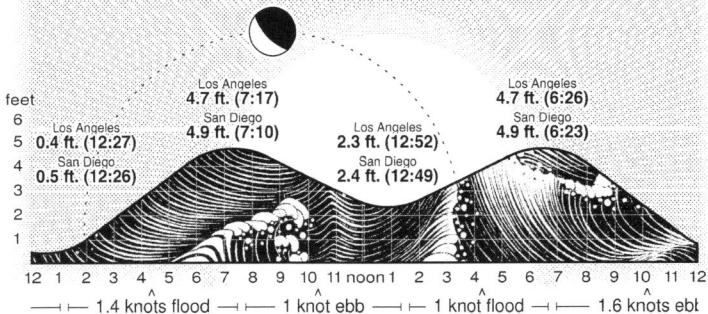

feet

Los Angeles
0.4 ft. (12:27)
San Diego
0.5 ft. (12:26)

Los Angeles
4.7 ft. (7:17)
San Diego
4.9 ft. (7:10)

Los Angeles
2.3 ft. (12:52)
San Diego
2.4 ft. (12:49)

Los Angeles
4.7 ft. (6:26)
San Diego
4.9 ft. (6:23)

12 1 2 3 4 5 6 7 8 9 10 11 noon 1 2 3 4 5 6 7 8 9 10 11 12

⊣ ⊢ 1.4 knots flood — ⊣ — 1 knot ebb — ⊣ ⊢ 1 knot flood — ⊣ ⊢ 1.6 knots ebb

SUN OCT 27
dawn 6:14 sunrise 7:08 sunset 6:05 dark 7:00
moonrise 2:46 a.m. moonset 3:55 p.m.

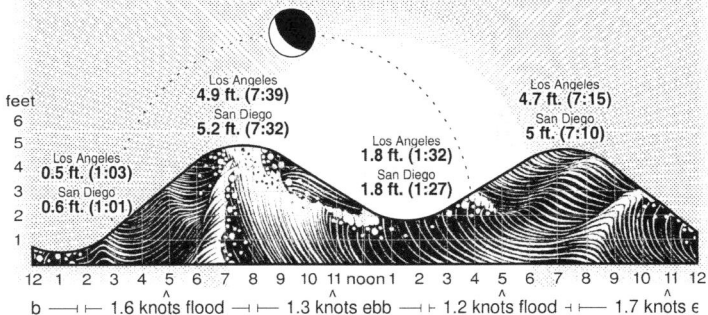

feet

Los Angeles
0.5 ft. (1:03)
San Diego
0.6 ft. (1:01)

Los Angeles
4.9 ft. (7:39)
San Diego
5.2 ft. (7:32)

Los Angeles
1.8 ft. (1:32)
San Diego
1.8 ft. (1:27)

Los Angeles
4.7 ft. (7:15)
San Diego
5 ft. (7:10)

12 1 2 3 4 5 6 7 8 9 10 11 noon 1 2 3 4 5 6 7 8 9 10 11 12

b — ⊣ ⊢ 1.6 knots flood — ⊣ ⊢ 1.3 knots ebb — ⊣ ⊢ 1.2 knots flood ⊣ ⊢ 1.7 knots ε

Orionids Meteor Shower The Orionids are prolific producing 50 - 70 per hour of fast meteors.   This shower is associated with comet Halley and its radiant point is the constellation Orion but meteors can be seen over a large area of the sky.   The shower is active annually between Oct 2nd - Nov 7th with this year's peak the night of Oct 21st and the following morning. This year the Moon, just 4 nights past full, may well overwhelm the shower as its radiant point, the constellation Orion, is just above the eastern horizon as the Moon rises.

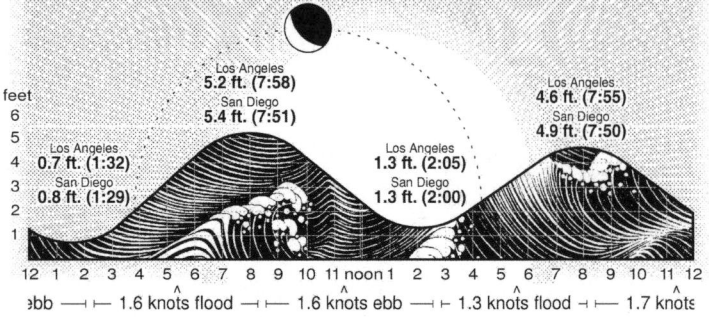

MON OCT 28
dawn 6:14 sunrise 7:09 sunset 6:04 dark 6:59
moonrise 3:42 a.m. moonset 4:18 p.m.

Los Angeles **5.2 ft. (7:58)**
San Diego **5.4 ft. (7:51)**

Los Angeles **4.6 ft. (7:55)**
San Diego **4.9 ft. (7:50)**

Los Angeles **0.7 ft. (1:32)**
San Diego **0.8 ft. (1:29)**

Los Angeles **1.3 ft. (2:05)**
San Diego **1.3 ft. (2:00)**

feet 6 5 4 3 2 1

12 1 2 3 4 5 6 7 8 9 10 11 noon 1 2 3 4 5 6 7 8 9 10 11 12

ebb ⟶ ⊢ 1.6 knots flood ⟶ ⊢ 1.6 knots ebb ⟶ ⊢ 1.3 knots flood ⊣ ⊢ 1.7 knots

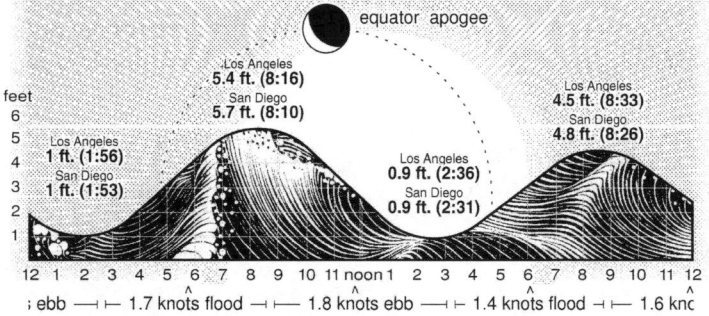

TUE OCT 29
dawn 6:15 sunrise 7:10 sunset 6:03 dark 6:58
moonrise 4:37 a.m. moonset 4:41 p.m.

equator apogee

Los Angeles **5.4 ft. (8:16)**
San Diego **5.7 ft. (8:10)**

Los Angeles **4.5 ft. (8:33)**
San Diego **4.8 ft. (8:26)**

Los Angeles **1 ft. (1:56)**
San Diego **1 ft. (1:53)**

Los Angeles **0.9 ft. (2:36)**
San Diego **0.9 ft. (2:31)**

feet 6 5 4 3 2 1

12 1 2 3 4 5 6 7 8 9 10 11 noon 1 2 3 4 5 6 7 8 9 10 11 12

; ebb ⟶ ⊢ 1.7 knots flood ⟶ ⊢ 1.8 knots ebb ⟶ ⊢ 1.4 knots flood ⊣ ⊢ 1.6 knc

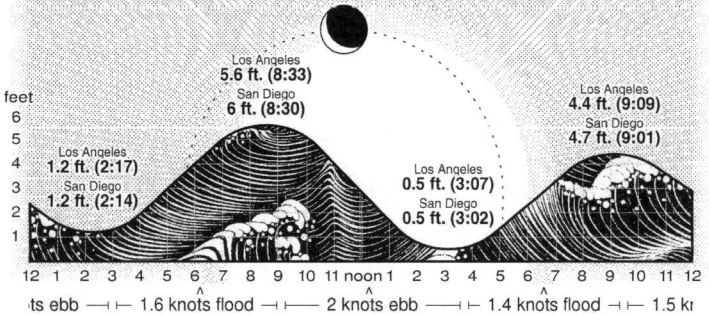

WED OCT 30
dawn 6:16 sunrise 7:11 sunset 6:02 dark 6:57
moonrise 5:32 a.m. moonset 5:05 p.m.

Los Angeles **5.6 ft. (8:33)**
San Diego **6 ft. (8:30)**

Los Angeles **4.4 ft. (9:09)**
San Diego **4.7 ft. (9:01)**

Los Angeles **1.2 ft. (2:17)**
San Diego **1.2 ft. (2:14)**

Los Angeles **0.5 ft. (3:07)**
San Diego **0.5 ft. (3:02)**

feet 6 5 4 3 2 1

12 1 2 3 4 5 6 7 8 9 10 11 noon 1 2 3 4 5 6 7 8 9 10 11 12

ts ebb ⟶ ⊢ 1.6 knots flood ⟶ ⊢ 2 knots ebb ⟶ ⊢ 1.4 knots flood ⊣ ⊢ 1.5 kr

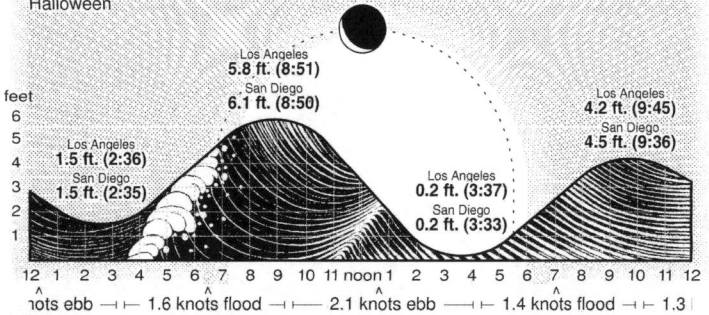

THU OCT 31
dawn 6:17 sunrise 7:12 sunset 6:01 dark 6:56
moonrise 6:28 a.m. moonset 5:30 p.m.

Halloween

Los Angeles **5.8 ft. (8:51)**
San Diego **6.1 ft. (8:50)**

Los Angeles **4.2 ft. (9:45)**
San Diego **4.5 ft. (9:36)**

Los Angeles **1.5 ft. (2:36)**
San Diego **1.5 ft. (2:35)**

Los Angeles **0.2 ft. (3:37)**
San Diego **0.2 ft. (3:33)**

feet 6 5 4 3 2 1

12 1 2 3 4 5 6 7 8 9 10 11 noon 1 2 3 4 5 6 7 8 9 10 11 12

knots ebb ⟶ ⊢ 1.6 knots flood ⟶ ⊢ 2.1 knots ebb ⟶ ⊢ 1.4 knots flood ⊣ ⊢ 1.3

FRI NOV 1

dawn 6:17 sunrise 7:13 sunset 6:00 dark 6:55
moonrise 7:26 a.m. moonset 5:59 p.m.

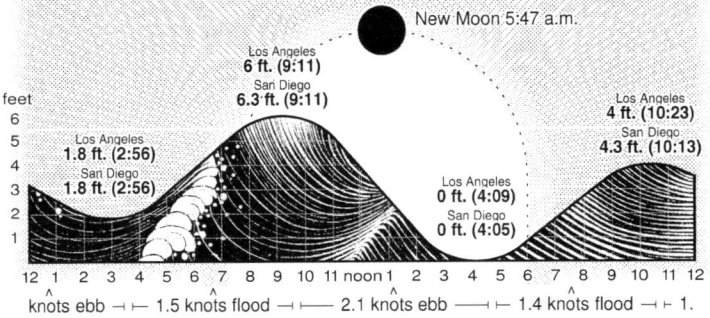

New Moon 5:47 a.m.

Los Angeles
6 ft. (9:11)
San Diego
6.3 ft. (9:11)

Los Angeles
4 ft. (10:23)
San Diego
4.3 ft. (10:13)

feet
6
5
4
3
2
1

Los Angeles
1.8 ft. (2:56)
San Diego
1.8 ft. (2:56)

Los Angeles
0 ft. (4:09)
San Diego
0 ft. (4:05)

12 1 2 3 4 5 6 7 8 9 10 11 noon 1 2 3 4 5 6 7 8 9 10 11 12

knots ebb → ← 1.5 knots flood → ← 2.1 knots ebb → ← 1.4 knots flood → ← 1.

SAT NOV 2

dawn 6:18 sunrise 7:14 sunset 5:59 dark 6:55
moonrise 8:26 a.m. moonset 6:33 p.m.

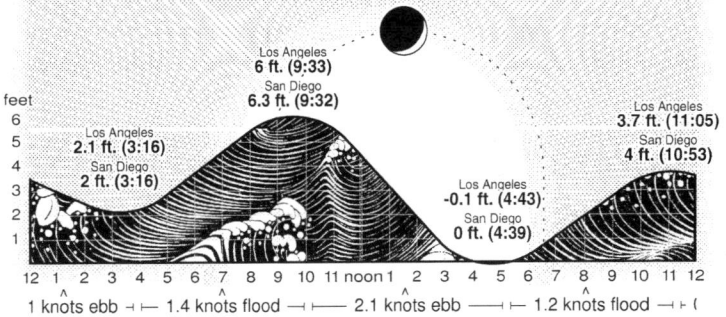

Los Angeles
6 ft. (9:33)
San Diego
6.3 ft. (9:32)

Los Angeles
3.7 ft. (11:05)
San Diego
4 ft. (10:53)

feet
6
5
4
3
2
1

Los Angeles
2.1 ft. (3:16)
San Diego
2 ft. (3:16)

Los Angeles
-0.1 ft. (4:43)
San Diego
0 ft. (4:39)

12 1 2 3 4 5 6 7 8 9 10 11 noon 1 2 3 4 5 6 7 8 9 10 11 12

1 knots ebb → ← 1.4 knots flood → ← 2.1 knots ebb → ← 1.2 knots flood → ← (

SUN NOV 3

dawn 5:19 sunrise 6:15 sunset 4:58 dark 5:54
moonrise 8:27 a.m. moonset 6:13 p.m.

Daylight Savings Time Ends

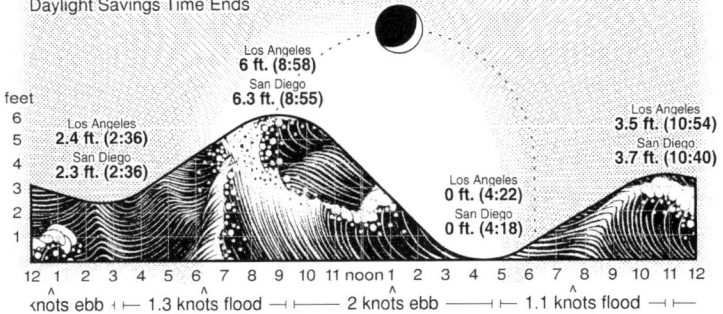

Los Angeles
6 ft. (8:58)
San Diego
6.3 ft. (8:55)

Los Angeles
3.5 ft. (10:54)
San Diego
3.7 ft. (10:40)

feet
6
5
4
3
2
1

Los Angeles
2.4 ft. (2:36)
San Diego
2.3 ft. (2:36)

Los Angeles
0 ft. (4:22)
San Diego
0 ft. (4:18)

12 1 2 3 4 5 6 7 8 9 10 11 noon 1 2 3 4 5 6 7 8 9 10 11 12

knots ebb → ← 1.3 knots flood → ← 2 knots ebb → ← 1.1 knots flood → ←

Ⓙ
Ⓜ
Ⓜ Ⓥ
Ⓢ

MON NOV 4

dawn 5:20 sunrise 6:15 sunset 4:57 dark 5:53
moonrise 9:27 a.m. moonset 7:00 p.m.

Taurids Meteor Peak

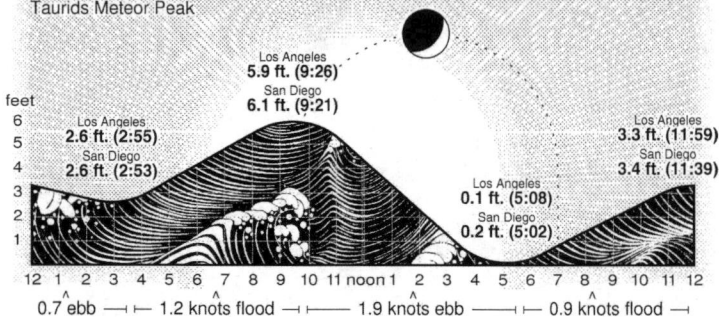

feet

Los Angeles
5.9 ft. (9:26)
San Diego
6.1 ft. (9:21)

Los Angeles
2.6 ft. (2:55)
San Diego
2.6 ft. (2:53)

Los Angeles
3.3 ft. (11:59)
San Diego
3.4 ft. (11:39)

Los Angeles
0.1 ft. (5:08)
San Diego
0.2 ft. (5:02)

6
5
4
3
2
1

12 1 2 3 4 5 6 7 8 9 10 11 noon 1 2 3 4 5 6 7 8 9 10 11 12

0.7 ebb ⟶ ⊢ 1.2 knots flood ⟶ ⊢ 1.9 knots ebb ⟶ ⊢ 0.9 knots flood ⊣

TUE NOV 5

dawn 5:21 sunrise 6:16 sunset 4:57 dark 5:52
moonrise 10:25 a.m. moonset 7:55 p.m.

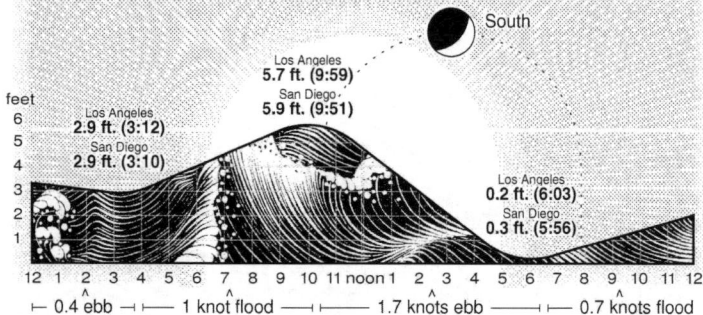

South

Los Angeles
5.7 ft. (9:59)
San Diego
5.9 ft. (9:51)

Los Angeles
2.9 ft. (3:12)
San Diego
2.9 ft. (3:10)

Los Angeles
0.2 ft. (6:03)
San Diego
0.3 ft. (5:56)

feet
6
5
4
3
2
1

12 1 2 3 4 5 6 7 8 9 10 11 noon 1 2 3 4 5 6 7 8 9 10 11 12

⊢ 0.4 ebb ⟶ ⊢ 1 knot flood ⟶ ⊢ 1.7 knots ebb ⟶ ⊢ 0.7 knots flood

WED NOV 6

dawn 5:22 sunrise 6:17 sunset 4:56 dark 5:52
moonrise 11:17 a.m. moonset 8:56 p.m.

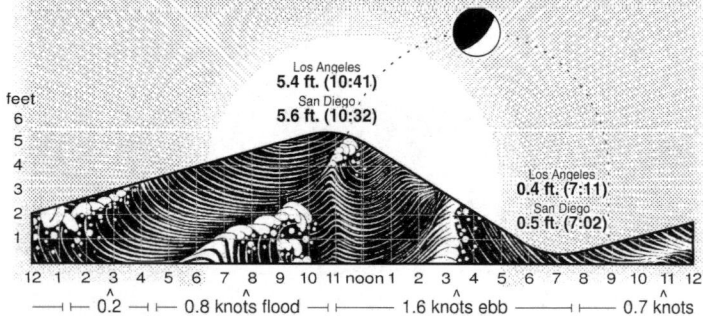

Los Angeles
5.4 ft. (10:41)
San Diego
5.6 ft. (10:32)

Los Angeles
0.4 ft. (7:11)
San Diego
0.5 ft. (7:02)

feet
6
5
4
3
2
1

12 1 2 3 4 5 6 7 8 9 10 11 noon 1 2 3 4 5 6 7 8 9 10 11 12

⊢ 0.2 ⊣ ⊢ 0.8 knots flood ⟶ ⊢ 1.6 knots ebb ⟶ ⊢ 0.7 knots

THU NOV 7

dawn 5:22 sunrise 6:18 sunset 4:55 dark 5:51
moonrise 12:03 p.m. moonset 10:02 p.m.

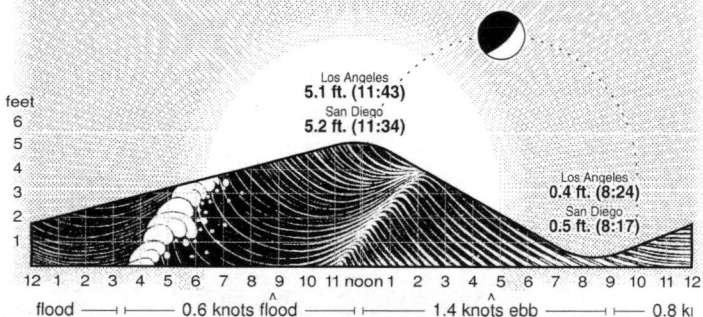

Los Angeles
5.1 ft. (11:43)
San Diego
5.2 ft. (11:34)

Los Angeles
0.4 ft. (8:24)
San Diego
0.5 ft. (8:17)

feet
6
5
4
3
2
1

12 1 2 3 4 5 6 7 8 9 10 11 noon 1 2 3 4 5 6 7 8 9 10 11 12

flood ⟶ ⊢ 0.6 knots flood ⟶ ⊢ 1.4 knots ebb ⟶ ⊢ 0.8 kₙ

FRI NOV 8
dawn 5:23 sunrise 6:19 sunset 4:54 dark 5:50
moonrise 12:43 p.m. moonset 11:10 p.m.

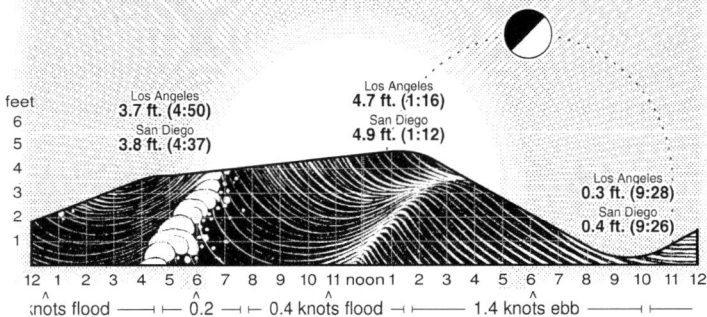

feet

Los Angeles
3.7 ft. (4:50)
San Diego
3.8 ft. (4:37)

Los Angeles
4.7 ft. (1:16)
San Diego
4.9 ft. (1:12)

Los Angeles
0.3 ft. (9:28)
San Diego
0.4 ft. (9:26)

6
5
4
3
2
1

12 1 2 3 4 5 6 7 8 9 10 11 noon 1 2 3 4 5 6 7 8 9 10 11 12

knots flood ⟶ ⊢ 0.2 ⟶ ⊢ 0.4 knots flood ⊣ ⊢ 1.4 knots ebb ⟶ ⊢

SAT NOV 9
dawn 5:24 sunrise 6:20 sunset 4:53 dark 5:50
moonrise 1:18 p.m.

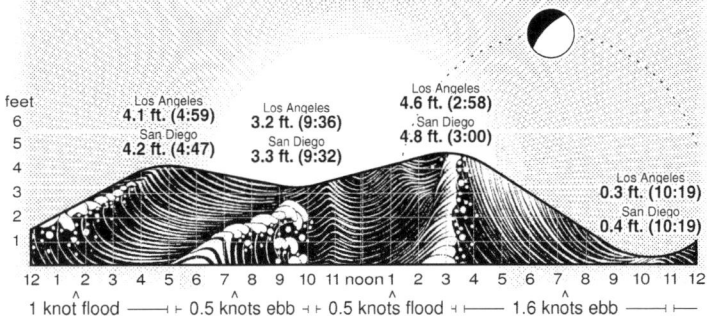

feet

Los Angeles
4.1 ft. (4:59)
San Diego
4.2 ft. (4:47)

Los Angeles
3.2 ft. (9:36)
San Diego
3.3 ft. (9:32)

Los Angeles
4.6 ft. (2:58)
San Diego
4.8 ft. (3:00)

Los Angeles
0.3 ft. (10:19)
San Diego
0.4 ft. (10:19)

6
5
4
3
2
1

12 1 2 3 4 5 6 7 8 9 10 11 noon 1 2 3 4 5 6 7 8 9 10 11 12

1 knot flood ⟶ ⊢ 0.5 knots ebb ⊣ ⊢ 0.5 knots flood ⊣ ⊢ 1.6 knots ebb ⟶ ⊢

SUN NOV 10
dawn 5:25 sunrise 6:21 sunset 4:53 dark 5:49
moonset 12:18 a.m. moonrise 1:49 p.m.

Saturn .9 degree S of Moon

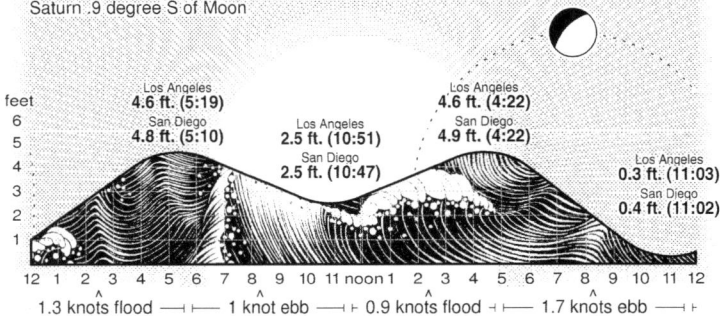

feet

Los Angeles
4.6 ft. (5:19)
San Diego
4.8 ft. (5:10)

Los Angeles
2.5 ft. (10:51)
San Diego
2.5 ft. (10:47)

Los Angeles
4.6 ft. (4:22)
San Diego
4.9 ft. (4:22)

Los Angeles
0.3 ft. (11:03)
San Diego
0.4 ft. (11:02)

6
5
4
3
2
1

12 1 2 3 4 5 6 7 8 9 10 11 noon 1 2 3 4 5 6 7 8 9 10 11 12

1.3 knots flood ⟶ ⊢ 1 knot ebb ⟶ ⊢ 0.9 knots flood ⊣ ⊢ 1.7 knots ebb ⟶ ⊢

Ⓙ Ⓜ Ⓥ Ⓢ ⓘ

Taurids Meteor Shower The northern Taurids are a minor shower, producing at zenith 5 - 10 meteors per hour. The shower runs annually from Sep 7th - Dec 10th with its peak on the night of Nov 4th. The radiant point is the constellation Taurus, the bull, that will rise above the eastern horizon by 7:00 p.m. and be high in the night sky as the first quarter Moon sets in the early evening leaving a dark sky for catching a Taurids meteor.

MON NOV 11
Veterans Day
dawn 5:26 sunrise 6:22 sunset 4:52 dark 5:48
moonset 1:27 a.m. moonrise 2:19 p.m.

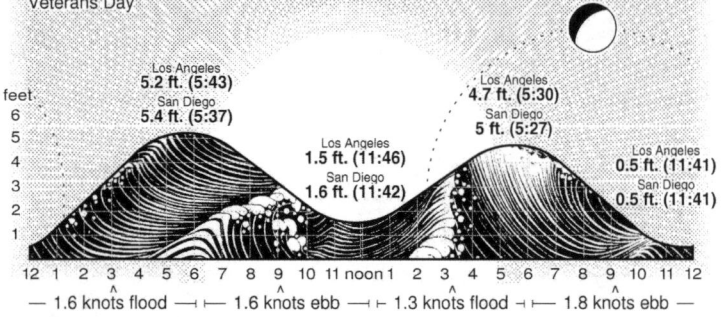

Los Angeles
5.2 ft. (5:43)
San Diego
5.4 ft. (5:37)

Los Angeles
4.7 ft. (5:30)
San Diego
5 ft. (5:27)

Los Angeles
1.5 ft. (11:46)
San Diego
1.6 ft. (11:42)

Los Angeles
0.5 ft. (11:41)
San Diego
0.5 ft. (11:41)

feet
6
5
4
3
2
1
12 1 2 3 4 5 6 7 8 9 10 11 noon 1 2 3 4 5 6 7 8 9 10 11 12

— 1.6 knots flood — ⊢ 1.6 knots ebb — ⊢ 1.3 knots flood ⊣ ⊢ 1.8 knots ebb —

TUE NOV 12
dawn 5:27 sunrise 6:23 sunset 4:51 dark 5:48
moonset 2:36 a.m. moonrise 2:49 p.m.

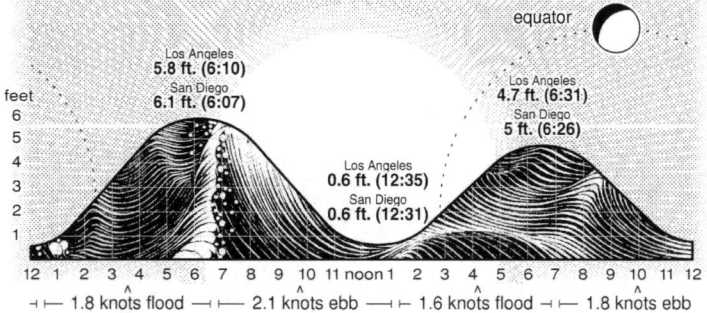

equator

Los Angeles
5.8 ft. (6:10)
San Diego
6.1 ft. (6:07)

Los Angeles
4.7 ft. (6:31)
San Diego
5 ft. (6:26)

Los Angeles
0.6 ft. (12:35)
San Diego
0.6 ft. (12:31)

feet
6
5
4
3
2
1
12 1 2 3 4 5 6 7 8 9 10 11 noon 1 2 3 4 5 6 7 8 9 10 11 12

⊣ ⊢ 1.8 knots flood — ⊢ 2.1 knots ebb — ⊢ 1.6 knots flood ⊣ ⊢ 1.8 knots ebb —

WED NOV 13
dawn 5:27 sunrise 6:24 sunset 4:51 dark 5:47
moonset 3:47 a.m. moonrise 3:20 p.m.

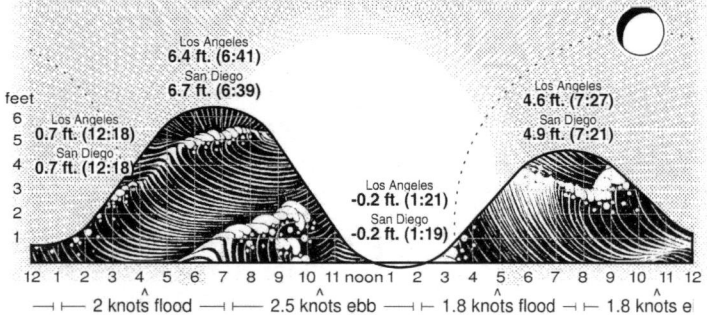

Los Angeles
6.4 ft. (6:41)
San Diego
6.7 ft. (6:39)

Los Angeles
0.7 ft. (12:18)
San Diego
0.7 ft. (12:18)

Los Angeles
4.6 ft. (7:27)
San Diego
4.9 ft. (7:21)

Los Angeles
-0.2 ft. (1:21)
San Diego
-0.2 ft. (1:19)

feet
6
5
4
3
2
1
12 1 2 3 4 5 6 7 8 9 10 11 noon 1 2 3 4 5 6 7 8 9 10 11 12

⊣ ⊢ 2 knots flood — ⊢ 2.5 knots ebb — ⊢ 1.8 knots flood ⊣ ⊢ 1.8 knots e

THU NOV 14
dawn 5:28 sunrise 6:25 sunset 4:50 dark 5:47
moonset 5:00 a.m. moonrise 3:55 p.m.

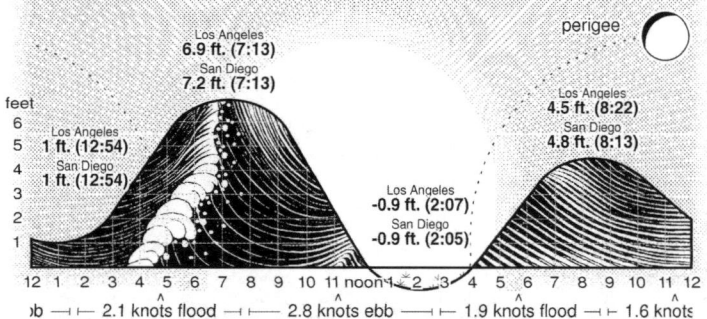

perigee

Los Angeles
6.9 ft. (7:13)
San Diego
7.2 ft. (7:13)

Los Angeles
1 ft. (12:54)
San Diego
1 ft. (12:54)

Los Angeles
4.5 ft. (8:22)
San Diego
4.8 ft. (8:13)

Los Angeles
-0.9 ft. (2:07)
San Diego
-0.9 ft. (2:05)

feet
6
5
4
3
2
1
12 1 2 3 4 5 6 7 8 9 10 11 noon 1 2 3 4 5 6 7 8 9 10 11 12

⊃b — ⊢ 2.1 knots flood — ⊢ 2.8 knots ebb — ⊢ 1.9 knots flood — ⊢ 1.6 knots

FRI NOV 15

dawn 5:29 sunrise 6:26 sunset 4:50 dark 5:46
moonset 6:15 a.m. moonrise 4:36 p.m.

Super Full Moon 1:28 p.m.

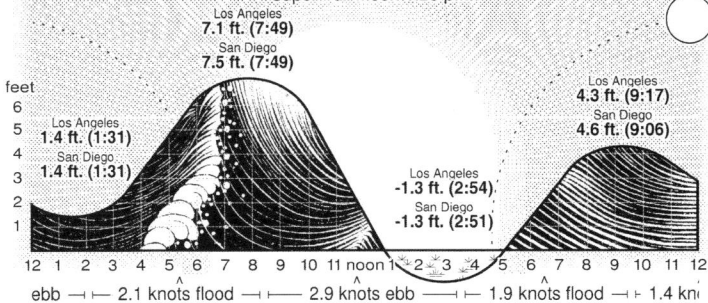

Los Angeles
7.1 ft. (7:49)
San Diego
7.5 ft. (7:49)

Los Angeles
1.4 ft. (1:31)
San Diego
1.4 ft. (1:31)

Los Angeles
4.3 ft. (9:17)
San Diego
4.6 ft. (9:06)

Los Angeles
-1.3 ft. (2:54)
San Diego
-1.3 ft. (2:51)

feet 6 5 4 3 2 1

12 1 2 3 4 5 6 7 8 9 10 11 noon 1 2 3 4 5 6 7 8 9 10 11 12

ebb ⊢— 2.1 knots flood —⊣ ⊢— 2.9 knots ebb —⊣ ⊢ 1.9 knots flood ⊣ ⊢ 1.4 kn

SAT NOV 16

dawn 5:30 sunrise 6:27 sunset 4:49 dark 5:46
moonset 7:31 a.m. moonrise 5:25 p.m.

Mercury eastern elongation

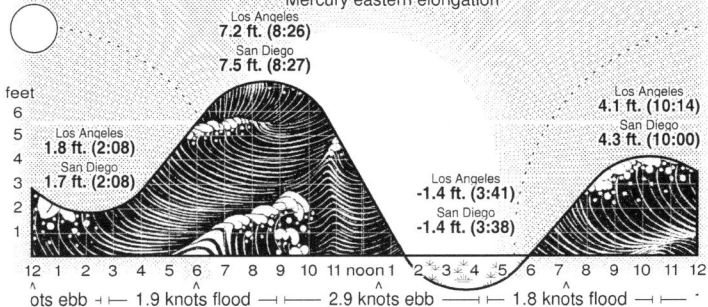

Los Angeles
7.2 ft. (8:26)
San Diego
7.5 ft. (8:27)

Los Angeles
1.8 ft. (2:08)
San Diego
1.7 ft. (2:08)

Los Angeles
4.1 ft. (10:14)
San Diego
4.3 ft. (10:00)

Los Angeles
-1.4 ft. (3:41)
San Diego
-1.4 ft. (3:38)

feet 6 5 4 3 2 1

12 1 2 3 4 5 6 7 8 9 10 11 noon 1 2 3 4 5 6 7 8 9 10 11 12

ots ebb ⊣ ⊢— 1.9 knots flood —⊣ ⊢— 2.9 knots ebb —⊣ ⊢ 1.8 knots flood —⊣ ⊢

SUN NOV 17

dawn 5:31 sunrise 6:28 sunset 4:49 dark 5:45
moonset 8:43 a.m. moonrise 6:21 p.m.

Leonids Meteor Peak

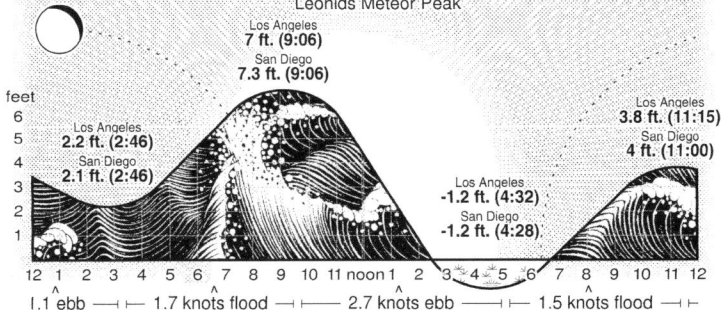

Los Angeles
7 ft. (9:06)
San Diego
7.3 ft. (9:06)

Los Angeles
2.2 ft. (2:46)
San Diego
2.1 ft. (2:46)

Los Angeles
3.8 ft. (11:15)
San Diego
4 ft. (11:00)

Los Angeles
-1.2 ft. (4:32)
San Diego
-1.2 ft. (4:28)

feet 6 5 4 3 2 1

12 1 2 3 4 5 6 7 8 9 10 11 noon 1 2 3 4 5 6 7 8 9 10 11 12

1.1 ebb ⊣ ⊢— 1.7 knots flood —⊣ ⊢— 2.7 knots ebb —⊣ ⊢ 1.5 knots flood —⊣ ⊢

Leonids Meteor Shower The Leonids run annually from Nov 6th - 30th
and have been known to produce 15 meteors per hour at peak. This
year's peak falls on the 17th and the following morning. The shower's
radiant point, the constellation Leo, will rise above the eastern
horizon by 1:00 a.m. The just past Full Moon will be high in the sky
all evening and likely reduce your chance to catch a bright Leonids Meteor.
Uranus at opposition At opposition on the 17th, Uranus will be at
its closest to Earth. Although the Sun will fully illuminate the planet due
to the great distance when viewed with a powerful telescope, Uranus
appears only as a tiny blue-green dot.

MON NOV 18
dawn 5:32 sunrise 6:28 sunset 4:48 dark 5:45
moonset 9:47 a.m. moonrise 7:24 p.m.

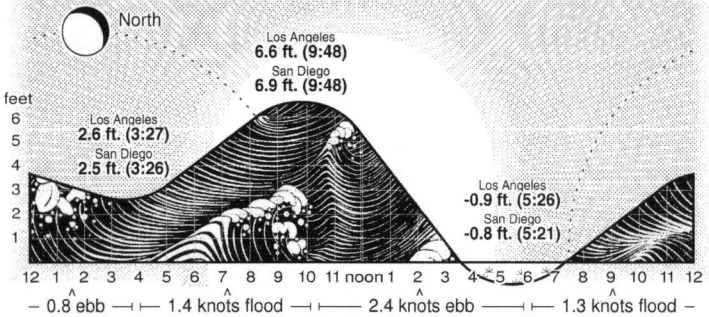

North

feet

Los Angeles
6.6 ft. (9:48)
San Diego
6.9 ft. (9:48)

Los Angeles
2.6 ft. (3:27)
San Diego
2.5 ft. (3:26)

Los Angeles
-0.9 ft. (5:26)
San Diego
-0.8 ft. (5:21)

6
5
4
3
2
1

12 1 2 3 4 5 6 7 8 9 10 11 noon 1 2 3 4 5 6 7 8 9 10 11 12

– 0.8 ebb ⊣ ⊢ 1.4 knots flood ⟶ ⊢ 2.4 knots ebb ⟶ ⊣ 1.3 knots flood –

TUE NOV 19
dawn 5:32 sunrise 6:29 sunset 4:48 dark 5:45
moonset 10:41 a.m. moonrise 8:30 p.m.

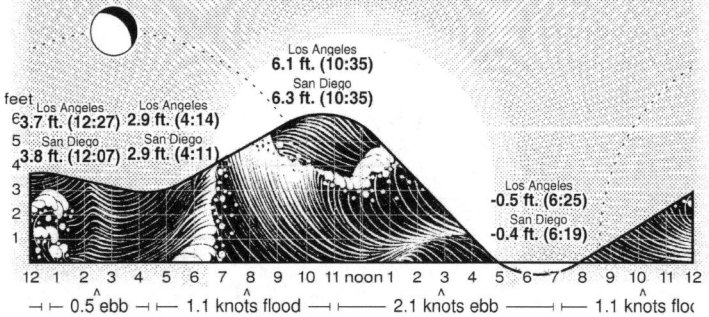

Los Angeles
6.1 ft. (10:35)
San Diego
6.3 ft. (10:35)

feet
Los Angeles
3.7 ft. (12:27)
San Diego
3.8 ft. (12:07)

Los Angeles
2.9 ft. (4:14)
San Diego
2.9 ft. (4:11)

Los Angeles
-0.5 ft. (6:25)
San Diego
-0.4 ft. (6:19)

6
5
4
3
2
1

12 1 2 3 4 5 6 7 8 9 10 11 noon 1 2 3 4 5 6 7 8 9 10 11 12

⊣ ⊢ 0.5 ebb ⊣ ⊢ 1.1 knots flood ⟶ ⊢ 2.1 knots ebb ⟶ ⊣ 1.1 knots floo

WED NOV 20
dawn 5:33 sunrise 6:30 sunset 4:47 dark 5:44
moonset 11:25 a.m. moonrise 9:35 p.m.

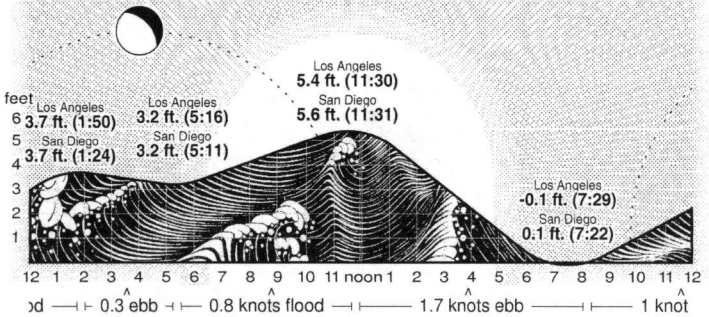

Los Angeles
5.4 ft. (11:30)
San Diego
5.6 ft. (11:31)

feet
Los Angeles
3.7 ft. (1:50)
San Diego
3.7 ft. (1:24)

Los Angeles
3.2 ft. (5:16)
San Diego
3.2 ft. (5:11)

Los Angeles
-0.1 ft. (7:29)
San Diego
0.1 ft. (7:22)

6
5
4
3
2
1

12 1 2 3 4 5 6 7 8 9 10 11 noon 1 2 3 4 5 6 7 8 9 10 11 12

od ⟶ ⊢ 0.3 ebb ⊣ ⊢ 0.8 knots flood ⟶ ⊢ 1.7 knots ebb ⟶ ⊢ 1 knot

THU NOV 21
dawn 5:34 sunrise 6:31 sunset 4:47 dark 5:44
moonset 12:01 p.m. moonrise 10:38 p.m.

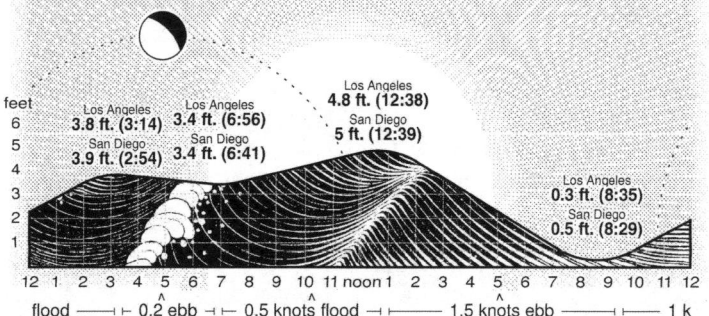

Los Angeles
4.8 ft. (12:38)
San Diego
5 ft. (12:39)

feet
Los Angeles
3.8 ft. (3:14)
San Diego
3.9 ft. (2:54)

Los Angeles
3.4 ft. (6:56)
San Diego
3.4 ft. (6:41)

Los Angeles
0.3 ft. (8:35)
San Diego
0.5 ft. (8:29)

6
5
4
3
2
1

12 1 2 3 4 5 6 7 8 9 10 11 noon 1 2 3 4 5 6 7 8 9 10 11 12

flood ⟶ ⊢ 0.2 ebb ⊣ ⊢ 0.5 knots flood ⟶ ⊢ 1.5 knots ebb ⟶ ⊢ 1 k

FRI NOV 22

dawn 5:35 sunrise 6:32 sunset 4:46 dark 5:44
moonset 12:31 p.m. moonrise 11:37 p.m.

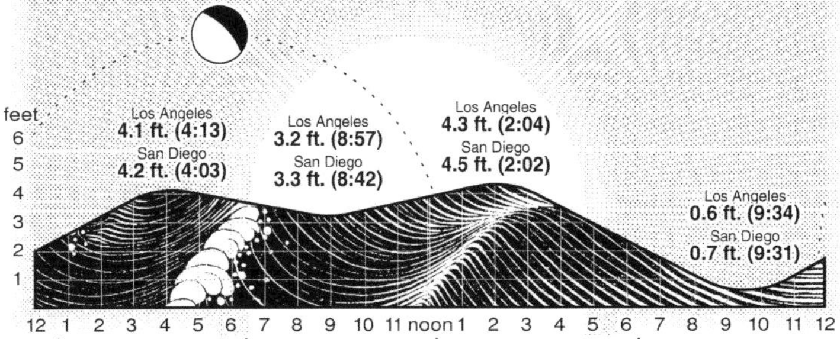

feet
6
5
4
3
2
1
Los Angeles
4.1 ft. (4:13)
San Diego
4.2 ft. (4:03)
Los Angeles
3.2 ft. (8:57)
San Diego
3.3 ft. (8:42)
Los Angeles
4.3 ft. (2:04)
San Diego
4.5 ft. (2:02)
Los Angeles
0.6 ft. (9:34)
San Diego
0.7 ft. (9:31)
12 1 2 3 4 5 6 7 8 9 10 11 noon 1 2 3 4 5 6 7 8 9 10 11 12

knot flood ——— 0.4 knots ebb 0.4 knots flood ——— 1.3 knots ebb ——— 1

SAT NOV 23

dawn 5:36 sunrise 6:33 sunset 4:46 dark 5:43
moonset 12:57 p.m.

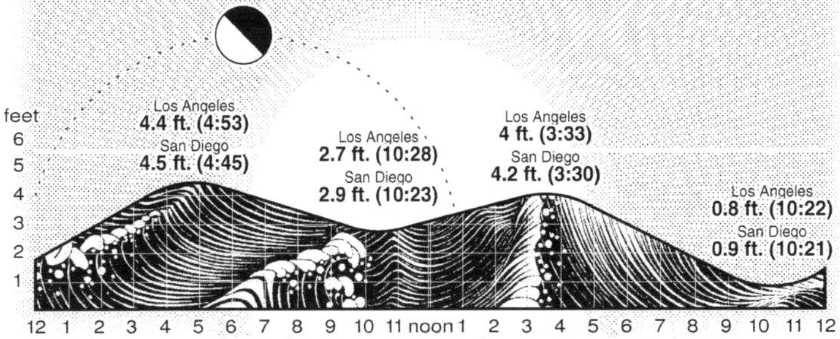

feet
6
5
4
3
2
1
Los Angeles
4.4 ft. (4:53)
San Diego
4.5 ft. (4:45)
Los Angeles
2.7 ft. (10:28)
San Diego
2.9 ft. (10:23)
Los Angeles
4 ft. (3:33)
San Diego
4.2 ft. (3:30)
Los Angeles
0.8 ft. (10:22)
San Diego
0.9 ft. (10:21)
12 1 2 3 4 5 6 7 8 9 10 11 noon 1 2 3 4 5 6 7 8 9 10 11 12

.1 knots flood ——— 0.7 knots ebb ——— 0.5 flood ——— 1.2 knots ebb ———

SUN NOV 24

dawn 5:36 sunrise 6:34 sunset 4:46 dark 5:43
moonrise 12:34 a.m. moonset 1:21 p.m.

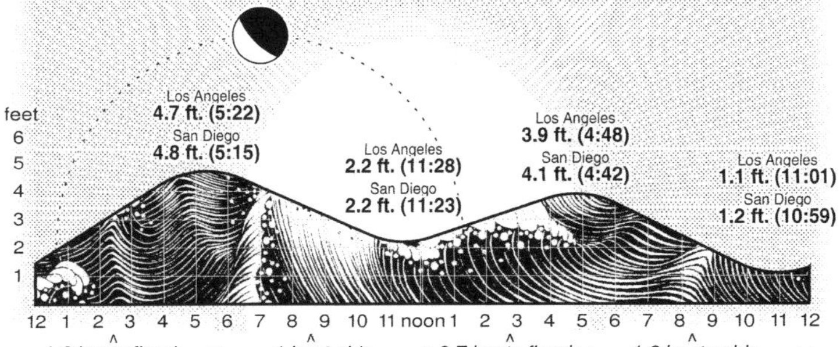

feet
6
5
4
3
2
1
Los Angeles
4.7 ft. (5:22)
San Diego
4.8 ft. (5:15)
Los Angeles
2.2 ft. (11:28)
San Diego
2.2 ft. (11:23)
Los Angeles
3.9 ft. (4:48)
San Diego
4.1 ft. (4:42)
Los Angeles
1.1 ft. (11:01)
San Diego
1.2 ft. (10:59)
12 1 2 3 4 5 6 7 8 9 10 11 noon 1 2 3 4 5 6 7 8 9 10 11 12

1.2 knots flood ——— 1 knot ebb ——— 0.7 knots flood ——— 1.2 knots ebb ———

J
M
m
V
S

MON NOV 25
dawn 5:37 sunrise 6:35 sunset 4:45 dark 5:43
moonrise 1:30 a.m. moonset 1:45 p.m.

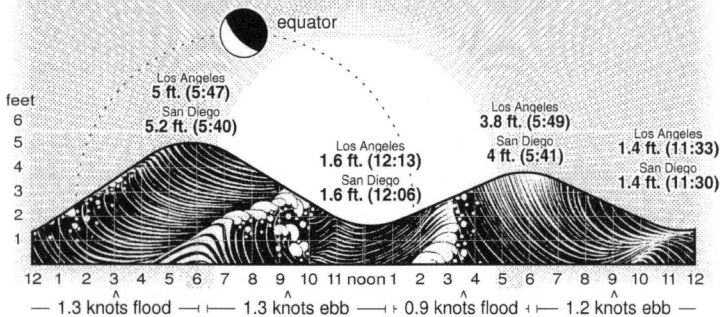

equator

Los Angeles
5 ft. (5:47)
San Diego
5.2 ft. (5:40)

Los Angeles
1.6 ft. (12:13)
San Diego
1.6 ft. (12:06)

Los Angeles
3.8 ft. (5:49)
San Diego
4 ft. (5:41)

Los Angeles
1.4 ft. (11:33)
San Diego
1.4 ft. (11:30)

feet
6 5 4 3 2 1

12 1 2 3 4 5 6 7 8 9 10 11 noon 1 2 3 4 5 6 7 8 9 10 11 12

— 1.3 knots flood — ⊢— 1.3 knots ebb —⊢ 0.9 knots flood ⊣ ⊢ 1.2 knots ebb —

TUE NOV 26
dawn 5:38 sunrise 6:36 sunset 4:45 dark 5:43
moonrise 2:24 a.m. moonset 2:08 p.m.

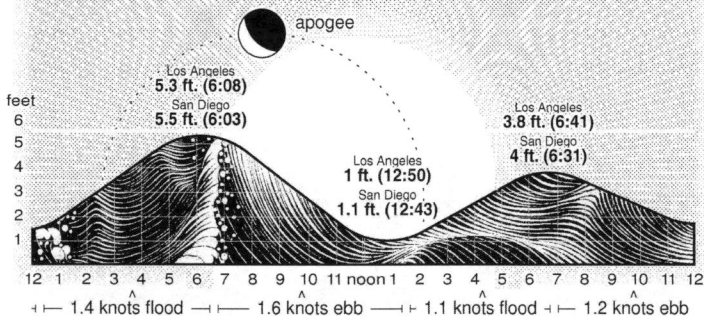

apogee

Los Angeles
5.3 ft. (6:08)
San Diego
5.5 ft. (6:03)

Los Angeles
1 ft. (12:50)
San Diego
1.1 ft. (12:43)

Los Angeles
3.8 ft. (6:41)
San Diego
4 ft. (6:31)

feet
6 5 4 3 2 1

12 1 2 3 4 5 6 7 8 9 10 11 noon 1 2 3 4 5 6 7 8 9 10 11 12

⊣ ⊢ 1.4 knots flood — ⊢— 1.6 knots ebb —— ⊢ 1.1 knots flood ⊣ ⊢ 1.2 knots ebb

WED NOV 27
dawn 5:39 sunrise 6:37 sunset 4:45 dark 5:43
moonrise 3:20 a.m. moonset 2:33 p.m.

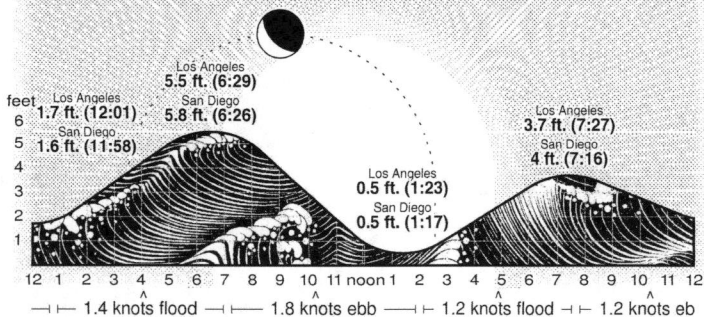

Los Angeles
1.7 ft. (12:01)
San Diego
1.6 ft. (11:58)

Los Angeles
5.5 ft. (6:29)
San Diego
5.8 ft. (6:26)

Los Angeles
0.5 ft. (1:23)
San Diego
0.5 ft. (1:17)

Los Angeles
3.7 ft. (7:27)
San Diego
4 ft. (7:16)

feet
6 5 4 3 2 1

12 1 2 3 4 5 6 7 8 9 10 11 noon 1 2 3 4 5 6 7 8 9 10 11 12

⊣ ⊢ 1.4 knots flood —⊣ ⊢— 1.8 knots ebb —— ⊢ 1.2 knots flood ⊣ ⊢ 1.2 knots eb

THU NOV 28
dawn 5:40 sunrise 6:38 sunset 4:45 dark 5:43
moonrise 4:17 a.m. moonset 3:01 p.m.

Thanksgiving Day

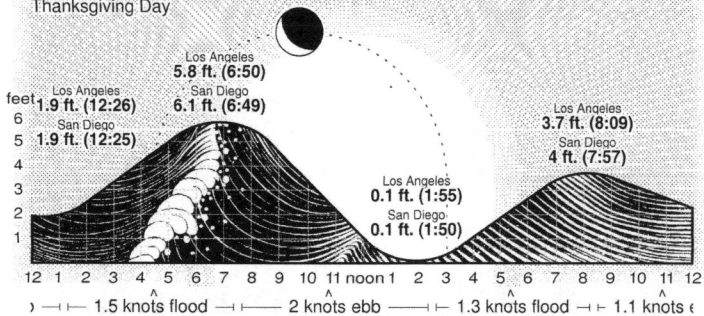

Los Angeles
1.9 ft. (12:26)
San Diego
1.9 ft. (12:25)

Los Angeles
5.8 ft. (6:50)
San Diego
6.1 ft. (6:49)

Los Angeles
0.1 ft. (1:55)
San Diego
0.1 ft. (1:50)

Los Angeles
3.7 ft. (8:09)
San Diego
4 ft. (7:57)

feet
6 5 4 3 2 1

12 1 2 3 4 5 6 7 8 9 10 11 noon 1 2 3 4 5 6 7 8 9 10 11 12

⟩ ⊣ ⊢ 1.5 knots flood ⊣ ⊢— 2 knots ebb —— ⊢ 1.3 knots flood ⊣ ⊢ 1.1 knots e

FRI NOV 29

dawn 5:41 sunrise 6:38 sunset 4:45 dark 5:43
moonrise 5:17 a.m. moonset 3:33 p.m.

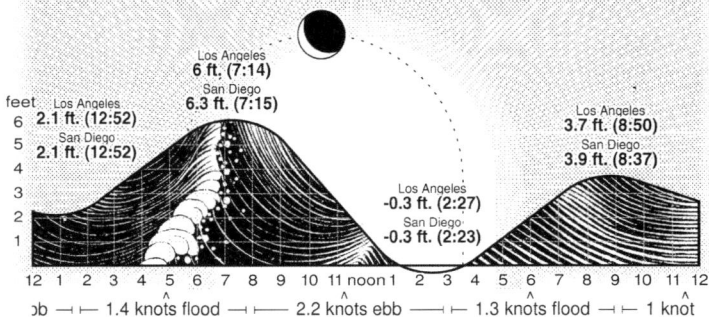

Los Angeles
6 ft. (7:14)
San Diego
6.3 ft. (7:15)

feet
6
5
4
3
2
1

Los Angeles
2.1 ft. (12:52)
San Diego
2.1 ft. (12:52)

Los Angeles
3.7 ft. (8:50)
San Diego
3.9 ft. (8:37)

Los Angeles
-0.3 ft. (2:27)
San Diego
-0.3 ft. (2:23)

12 1 2 3 4 5 6 7 8 9 10 11 noon 1 2 3 4 5 6 7 8 9 10 11 12

bb ⊢ 1.4 knots flood ⊣ ⊢ 2.2 knots ebb ⊣ 1.3 knots flood ⊢ 1 knot

SAT NOV 30

dawn 5:41 sunrise 6:39 sunset 4:44 dark 5:42
moonrise 6:18 a.m. moonset 4:11 p.m.

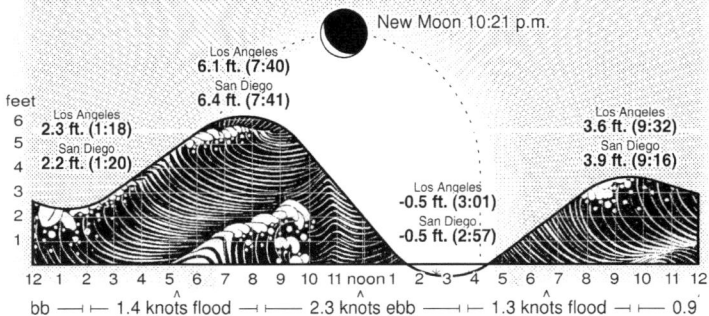

New Moon 10:21 p.m.

Los Angeles
6.1 ft. (7:40)
San Diego
6.4 ft. (7:41)

feet
6
5
4
3
2
1

Los Angeles
2.3 ft. (1:18)
San Diego
2.2 ft. (1:20)

Los Angeles
3.6 ft. (9:32)
San Diego
3.9 ft. (9:16)

Los Angeles
-0.5 ft. (3:01)
San Diego
-0.5 ft. (2:57)

12 1 2 3 4 5 6 7 8 9 10 11 noon 1 2 3 4 5 6 7 8 9 10 11 12

bb ⊢ 1.4 knots flood ⊣ ⊢ 2.3 knots ebb ⊣ 1.3 knots flood ⊣ 0.9

SUN DEC 1

dawn 5:42 sunrise 6:40 sunset 4:44 dark 5:42
moonrise 7:19 a.m. moonset 4:56 p.m.

Advent

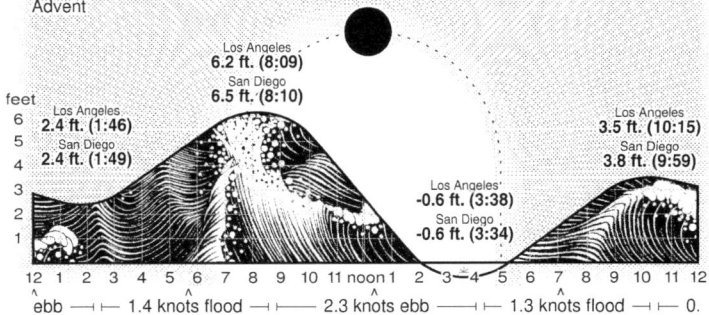

Los Angeles
6.2 ft. (8:09)
San Diego
6.5 ft. (8:10)

Los Angeles
2.4 ft. (1:46)
San Diego
2.4 ft. (1:49)

feet
6
5
4
3
2
1

Los Angeles
3.5 ft. (10:15)
San Diego
3.8 ft. (9:59)

Los Angeles
-0.6 ft. (3:38)
San Diego
-0.6 ft. (3:34)

12 1 2 3 4 5 6 7 8 9 10 11 noon 1 2 3 4 5 6 7 8 9 10 11 12

ebb ⊣ 1.4 knots flood ⊣ ⊢ 2.3 knots ebb ⊣ 1.3 knots flood ⊣ 0.

Ⓙ Ⓜ Ⓥ Ⓢ ⓜ

MON DEC 2
dawn 5:43 sunrise 6:41 sunset 4:44 dark 5:42
moonrise 8:19 a.m. moonset 5:49 p.m.

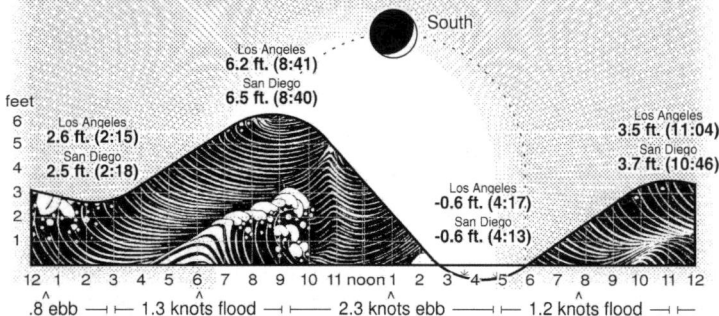

South

Los Angeles
6.2 ft. (8:41)
San Diego
6.5 ft. (8:40)

feet

Los Angeles
2.6 ft. (2:15)
San Diego
2.5 ft. (2:18)

Los Angeles
3.5 ft. (11:04)
San Diego
3.7 ft. (10:46)

Los Angeles
-0.6 ft. (4:17)
San Diego
-0.6 ft. (4:13)

12 1 2 3 4 5 6 7 8 9 10 11 noon 1 2 3 4 5 6 7 8 9 10 11 12

.8 ebb — 1.3 knots flood — 2.3 knots ebb — 1.2 knots flood —

TUE DEC 3
dawn 5:44 sunrise 6:42 sunset 4:44 dark 5:43
moonrise 9:13 a.m. moonset 6:50 p.m.

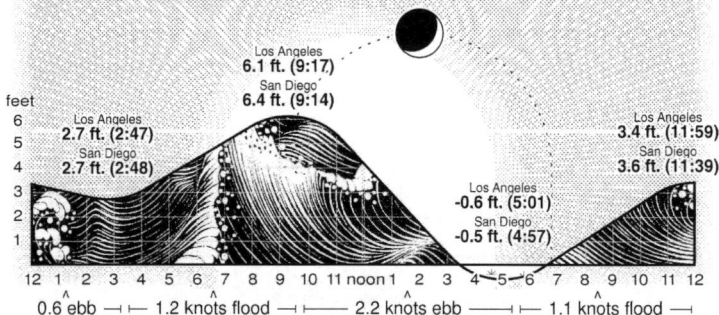

Los Angeles
6.1 ft. (9:17)
San Diego
6.4 ft. (9:14)

feet

Los Angeles
2.7 ft. (2:47)
San Diego
2.7 ft. (2:48)

Los Angeles
3.4 ft. (11:59)
San Diego
3.6 ft. (11:39)

Los Angeles
-0.6 ft. (5:01)
San Diego
-0.5 ft. (4:57)

12 1 2 3 4 5 6 7 8 9 10 11 noon 1 2 3 4 5 6 7 8 9 10 11 12

0.6 ebb — 1.2 knots flood — 2.2 knots ebb — 1.1 knots flood —

WED DEC 4
dawn 5:44 sunrise 6:43 sunset 4:44 dark 5:43
moonrise 10:02 a.m. moonset 7:55 p.m.

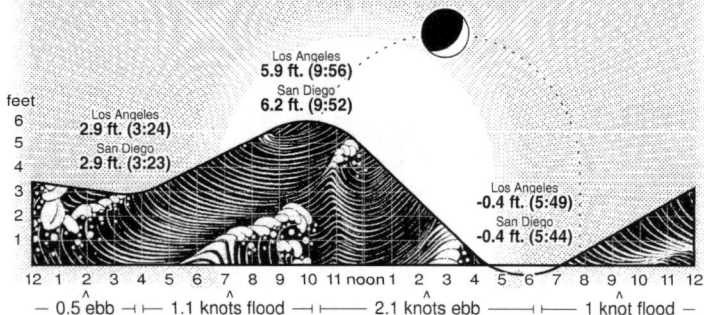

Los Angeles
5.9 ft. (9:56)
San Diego
6.2 ft. (9:52)

feet

Los Angeles
2.9 ft. (3:24)
San Diego
2.9 ft. (3:23)

Los Angeles
-0.4 ft. (5:49)
San Diego
-0.4 ft. (5:44)

12 1 2 3 4 5 6 7 8 9 10 11 noon 1 2 3 4 5 6 7 8 9 10 11 12

— 0.5 ebb — 1.1 knots flood — 2.1 knots ebb — 1 knot flood —

THU DEC 5
dawn 5:45 sunrise 6:44 sunset 4:44 dark 5:43
moonrise 10:43 a.m. moonset 9:02 p.m.

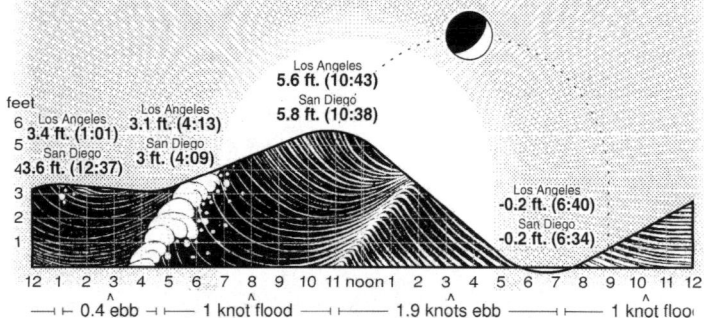

Los Angeles
5.6 ft. (10:43)
San Diego
5.8 ft. (10:38)

feet

Los Angeles
3.4 ft. (1:01)
San Diego
3.6 ft. (12:37)

Los Angeles
3.1 ft. (4:13)
San Diego
3 ft. (4:09)

Los Angeles
-0.2 ft. (6:40)
San Diego
-0.2 ft. (6:34)

12 1 2 3 4 5 6 7 8 9 10 11 noon 1 2 3 4 5 6 7 8 9 10 11 12

— 0.4 ebb — 1 knot flood — 1.9 knots ebb — 1 knot floo

FRI DEC 6

dawn 5:46 sunrise 6:44 sunset 4:44 dark 5:43
moonrise 11:19 a.m. moonset 10:09 p.m.

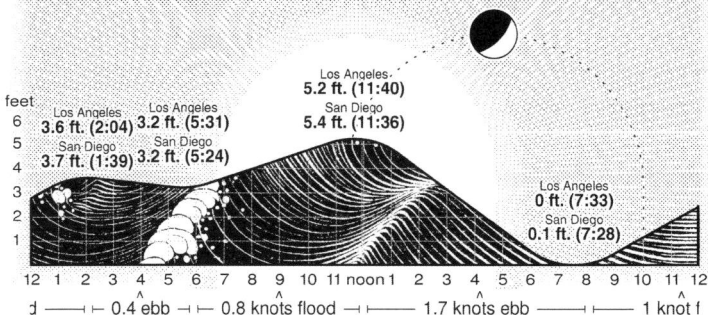

feet

Los Angeles
3.6 ft. (2:04)
San Diego
3.7 ft. (1:39)

Los Angeles
3.2 ft. (5:31)
San Diego
3.2 ft. (5:24)

Los Angeles
5.2 ft. (11:40)
San Diego
5.4 ft. (11:36)

Los Angeles
0 ft. (7:33)
San Diego
0.1 ft. (7:28)

12 1 2 3 4 5 6 7 8 9 10 11 noon 1 2 3 4 5 6 7 8 9 10 11 12

d ——⊢ 0.4 ˆebb ⊣⊢ 0.8 knots flood ⊣ ⊢—— 1.7 knots ebb —— ⊣ ⊢— 1 knot f

SAT DEC 7

dawn 5:47 sunrise 6:45 sunset 4:44 dark 5:43
moonrise 11:51 a.m. moonset 11:16 p.m.

Jupiter at opposition

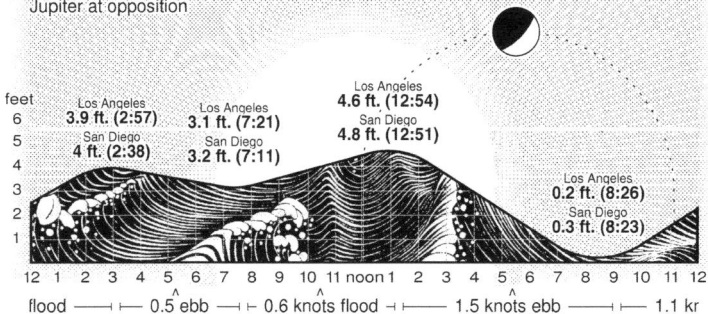

feet

Los Angeles
3.9 ft. (2:57)
San Diego
4 ft. (2:38)

Los Angeles
3.1 ft. (7:21)
San Diego
3.2 ft. (7:11)

Los Angeles
4.6 ft. (12:54)
San Diego
4.8 ft. (12:51)

Los Angeles
0.2 ft. (8:26)
San Diego
0.3 ft. (8:23)

12 1 2 3 4 5 6 7 8 9 10 11 noon 1 2 3 4 5 6 7 8 9 10 11 12

flood ——⊢ 0.5 ˆebb —⊣⊢ 0.6 knots flood ⊣ ⊢— 1.5 knots ebb —— ⊣ ⊢— 1.1 kr

SUN DEC 8

dawn 5:47 sunrise 6:46 sunset 4:45 dark 5:43
moonrise 12:20 p.m.

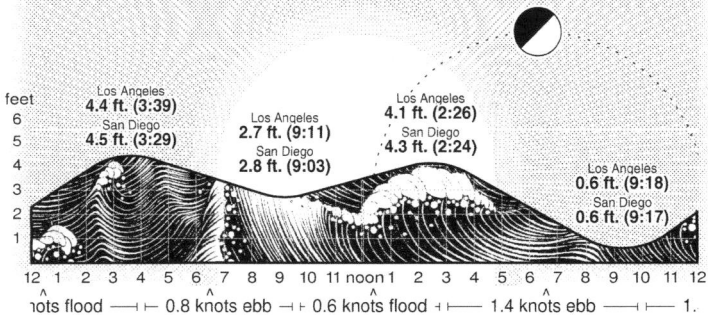

feet

Los Angeles
4.4 ft. (3:39)
San Diego
4.5 ft. (3:29)

Los Angeles
2.7 ft. (9:11)
San Diego
2.8 ft. (9:03)

Los Angeles
4.1 ft. (2:26)
San Diego
4.3 ft. (2:24)

Los Angeles
0.6 ft. (9:18)
San Diego
0.6 ft. (9:17)

12 1 2 3 4 5 6 7 8 9 10 11 noon 1 2 3 4 5 6 7 8 9 10 11 12

ıots flood ——⊢ 0.8 knots ebb ⊣⊢ 0.6 knots flood ⊣⊢ 1.4 knots ebb —— ⊣ ⊢— 1.

Ⓜ   Ⓥ   ⊘   Ⓙ

Jupiter at opposition On Dec 7th, the massive planet will be at it
closest approach to Earth and can be seen all night. If conditions are
favorable with a medium powered telescope you could make out some
details of Jupiter's cloud bands and 4 of its 79 moons. Even at its
closest approach to Earth, the four largest moons will appear only
as bright spots of light beside the planet.

MON DEC 9
dawn 5:48 sunrise 6:47 sunset 4:45 dark 5:43
moonset 12:23 a.m. moonrise 12:49 p.m.

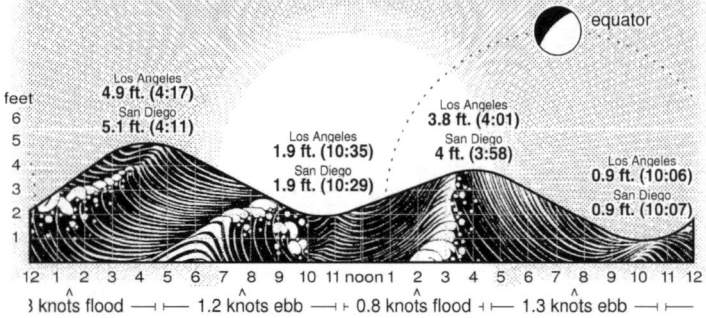

equator

feet

Los Angeles
4.9 ft. (4:17)
San Diego
5.1 ft. (4:11)

Los Angeles
1.9 ft. (10:35)
San Diego
1.9 ft. (10:29)

Los Angeles
3.8 ft. (4:01)
San Diego
4 ft. (3:58)

Los Angeles
0.9 ft. (10:06)
San Diego
0.9 ft. (10:07)

12 1 2 3 4 5 6 7 8 9 10 11 noon 1 2 3 4 5 6 7 8 9 10 11 12

3 knots flood ⟶ ⊢ 1.2 knots ebb ⟶ ⊢ 0.8 knots flood ⊣ ⊢ 1.3 knots ebb ⟶ ⊢

TUE DEC 10
dawn 5:49 sunrise 6:47 sunset 4:45 dark 5:44
moonset 1:30 a.m. moonrise 1:18 p.m.

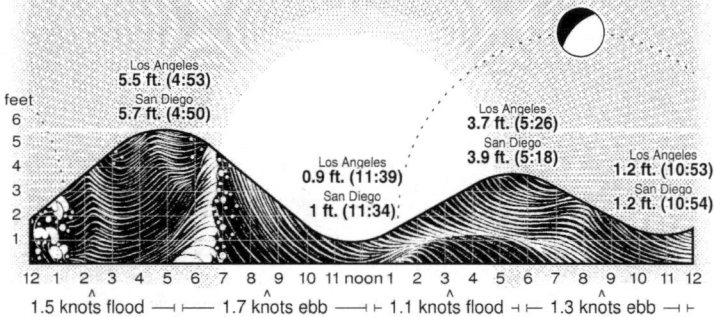

Los Angeles
5.5 ft. (4:53)
San Diego
5.7 ft. (4:50)

feet

Los Angeles
0.9 ft. (11:39)
San Diego
1 ft. (11:34)

Los Angeles
3.7 ft. (5:26)
San Diego
3.9 ft. (5:18)

Los Angeles
1.2 ft. (10:53)
San Diego
1.2 ft. (10:54)

12 1 2 3 4 5 6 7 8 9 10 11 noon 1 2 3 4 5 6 7 8 9 10 11 12

1.5 knots flood ⟶ ⊢ 1.7 knots ebb ⟶ ⊢ 1.1 knots flood ⊣ ⊢ 1.3 knots ebb ⊣ ⊢

WED DEC 11
dawn 5:49 sunrise 6:48 sunset 4:45 dark 5:44
moonset 2:40 a.m. moonrise 1:50 p.m.

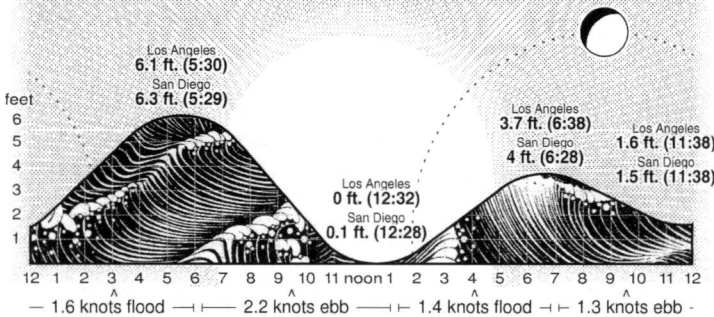

Los Angeles
6.1 ft. (5:30)
San Diego
6.3 ft. (5:29)

feet

Los Angeles
0 ft. (12:32)
San Diego
0.1 ft. (12:28)

Los Angeles
3.7 ft. (6:38)
San Diego
4 ft. (6:28)

Los Angeles
1.6 ft. (11:38)
San Diego
1.5 ft. (11:38)

12 1 2 3 4 5 6 7 8 9 10 11 noon 1 2 3 4 5 6 7 8 9 10 11 12

⟶ 1.6 knots flood ⟶ ⊢ 2.2 knots ebb ⟶ ⊢ 1.4 knots flood ⊣ ⊢ 1.3 knots ebb ⟶

THU DEC 12
dawn 5:50 sunrise 6:49 sunset 4:45 dark 5:44
moonset 3:52 a.m. moonrise 2:27 p.m.

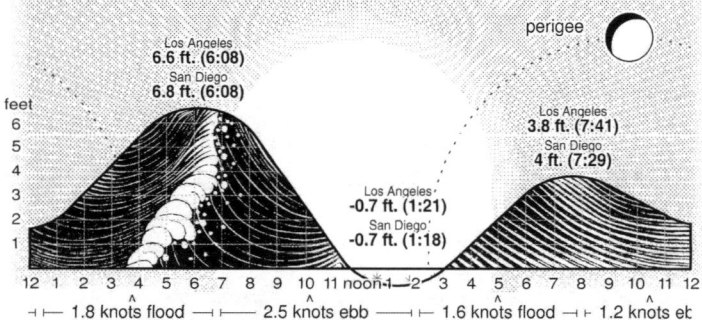

perigee

Los Angeles
6.6 ft. (6:08)
San Diego
6.8 ft. (6:08)

feet

Los Angeles
-0.7 ft. (1:21)
San Diego
-0.7 ft. (1:18)

Los Angeles
3.8 ft. (7:41)
San Diego
4 ft. (7:29)

12 1 2 3 4 5 6 7 8 9 10 11 noon 1 2 3 4 5 6 7 8 9 10 11 12

⊣ ⊢ 1.8 knots flood ⟶ ⊢ 2.5 knots ebb ⟶ ⊢ 1.6 knots flood ⟶ ⊢ 1.2 knots eb

FRI DEC 13

dawn 5:51 sunrise 6:49 sunset 4:46 dark 5:44
moonset 5:06 a.m. moonrise 3:11 p.m.

Geminids Meteor Peak

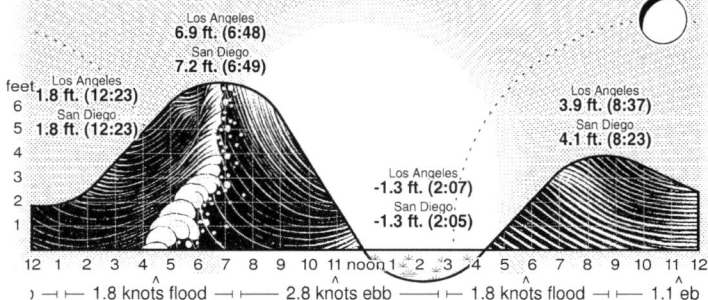

Los Angeles
6.9 ft. (6:48)
San Diego
7.2 ft. (6:49)

feet

Los Angeles
1.8 ft. (12:23)
San Diego
1.8 ft. (12:23)

Los Angeles
3.9 ft. (8:37)
San Diego
4.1 ft. (8:23)

Los Angeles
-1.3 ft. (2:07)
San Diego
-1.3 ft. (2:05)

12 1 2 3 4 5 6 7 8 9 10 11 noon 1 2 3 4 5 6 7 8 9 10 11 12

) ⊢ 1.8 knots flood ⟶ ⊢ 2.8 knots ebb ⟶ ⊢ 1.8 knots flood ⟶ ⊢ 1.1 eb

SAT DEC 14

dawn 5:51 sunrise 6:50 sunset 4:46 dark 5:45
moonset 6:19 a.m. moonrise 4:03 p.m.

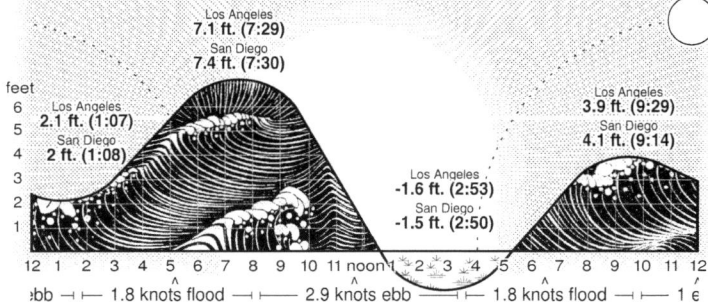

Los Angeles
7.1 ft. (7:29)
San Diego
7.4 ft. (7:30)

feet

Los Angeles
2.1 ft. (1:07)
San Diego
2 ft. (1:08)

Los Angeles
3.9 ft. (9:29)
San Diego
4.1 ft. (9:14)

Los Angeles
-1.6 ft. (2:53)
San Diego
-1.5 ft. (2:50)

12 1 2 3 4 5 6 7 8 9 10 11 noon 1 2 3 4 5 6 7 8 9 10 11 12

ebb ⊢ 1.8 knots flood ⟶ ⊢ 2.9 knots ebb ⟶ ⊢ 1.8 knots flood ⟶ ⊢ 1 ε

SUN DEC 15

dawn 5:52 sunrise 6:51 sunset 4:46 dark 5:45
moonset 7:27 a.m. moonrise 5:03 p.m.

Full Moon 1:02 a.m.

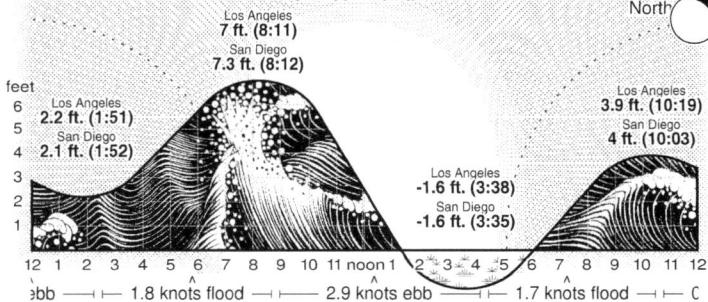

North

Los Angeles
7 ft. (8:11)
San Diego
7.3 ft. (8:12)

feet

Los Angeles
2.2 ft. (1:51)
San Diego
2.1 ft. (1:52)

Los Angeles
3.9 ft. (10:19)
San Diego
4 ft. (10:03)

Los Angeles
-1.6 ft. (3:38)
San Diego
-1.6 ft. (3:35)

12 1 2 3 4 5 6 7 8 9 10 11 noon 1 2 3 4 5 6 7 8 9 10 11 12

ebb ⟶ ⊢ 1.8 knots flood ⟶ ⊢ 2.9 knots ebb ⟶ ⊢ 1.7 knots flood ⟶ ⊢ C

Ⓜ ⓜ Ⓥ Ⓢ Ⓙ

Geminids Meteor Shower The Geminids can offer a spectacular show
with possible sighting of 120 meteors per hour at peak. The shower is
active Dec 4th - 17th and radiates from the constellation Gemini. However
on this year's peak, Dec 13th, the constellation Gemini will rise above
the eastern horizon after sunset and confront a nearly Full Moon high
in the sky all evening and overwhelming all but the brightest meteors.

MON DEC 16

dawn 5:53 sunrise 6:51 sunset 4:47 dark 5:46
moonset 8:27 a.m. moonrise 6:09 p.m.

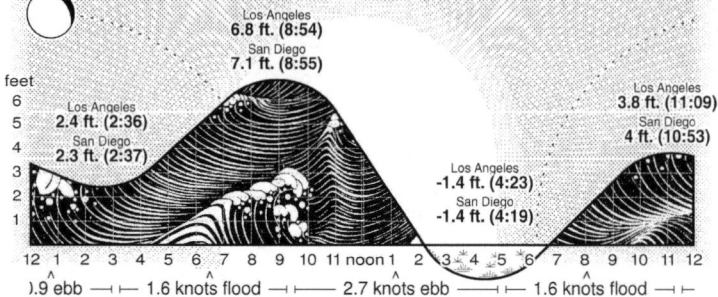

Los Angeles
6.8 ft. (8:54)
San Diego
7.1 ft. (8:55)

Los Angeles
2.4 ft. (2:36)
San Diego
2.3 ft. (2:37)

Los Angeles
3.8 ft. (11:09)
San Diego
4 ft. (10:53)

Los Angeles
-1.4 ft. (4:23)
San Diego
-1.4 ft. (4:19)

feet
6
5
4
3
2
1

12 1 2 3 4 5 6 7 8 9 10 11 noon 1 2 3 4 5 6 7 8 9 10 11 12

0.9 ebb ⊢—⊢ 1.6 knots flood —⊣ ⊢— 2.7 knots ebb ——⊣ ⊢— 1.6 knots flood —⊣ ⊢—

TUE DEC 17

dawn 5:53 sunrise 6:52 sunset 4:47 dark 5:46
moonset 9:16 a.m. moonrise 7:17 p.m.

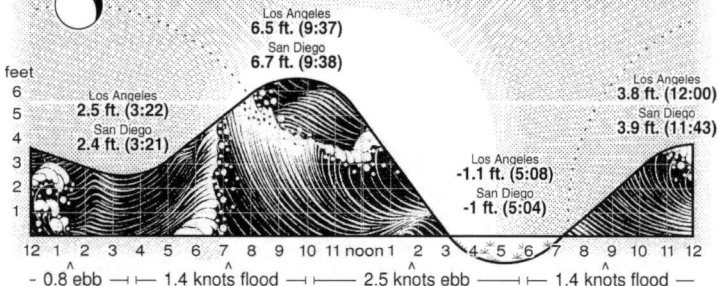

Los Angeles
6.5 ft. (9:37)
San Diego
6.7 ft. (9:38)

Los Angeles
2.5 ft. (3:22)
San Diego
2.4 ft. (3:21)

Los Angeles
3.8 ft. (12:00)
San Diego
3.9 ft. (11:43)

Los Angeles
-1.1 ft. (5:08)
San Diego
-1 ft. (5:04)

feet
6
5
4
3
2
1

12 1 2 3 4 5 6 7 8 9 10 11 noon 1 2 3 4 5 6 7 8 9 10 11 12

- 0.8 ebb —⊣ ⊢— 1.4 knots flood —⊣ ⊢— 2.5 knots ebb ——⊣ ⊢— 1.4 knots flood —

WED DEC 18

dawn 5:54 sunrise 6:53 sunset 4:48 dark 5:46
moonset 9:56 a.m. moonrise 8:22 p.m.

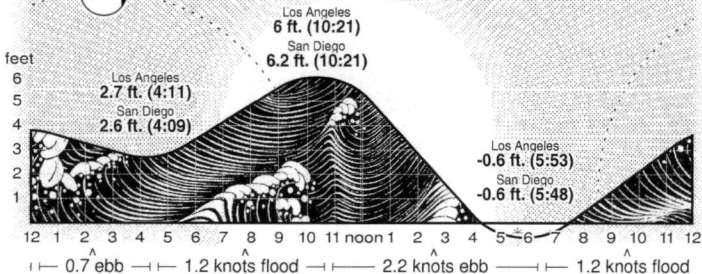

Los Angeles
6 ft. (10:21)
San Diego
6.2 ft. (10:21)

Los Angeles
2.7 ft. (4:11)
San Diego
2.6 ft. (4:09)

Los Angeles
-0.6 ft. (5:53)
San Diego
-0.6 ft. (5:48)

feet
6
5
4
3
2
1

12 1 2 3 4 5 6 7 8 9 10 11 noon 1 2 3 4 5 6 7 8 9 10 11 12

⊢— 0.7 ebb —⊣ ⊢— 1.2 knots flood —⊣ ⊢— 2.2 knots ebb ——⊣ ⊢— 1.2 knots flood

THU DEC 19

dawn 5:54 sunrise 6:53 sunset 4:48 dark 5:47
moonset 10:29 a.m. moonrise 9:24 p.m.

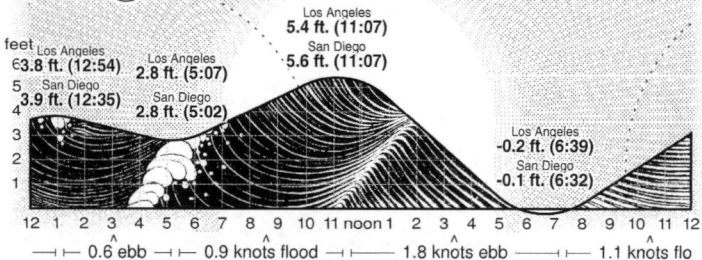

Los Angeles
5.4 ft. (11:07)
San Diego
5.6 ft. (11:07)

Los Angeles
3.8 ft. (12:54)
San Diego
3.9 ft. (12:35)

Los Angeles
2.8 ft. (5:07)
San Diego
2.8 ft. (5:02)

Los Angeles
-0.2 ft. (6:39)
San Diego
-0.1 ft. (6:32)

feet
6
5
4
3
2
1

12 1 2 3 4 5 6 7 8 9 10 11 noon 1 2 3 4 5 6 7 8 9 10 11 12

—⊣ ⊢— 0.6 ebb —⊣ ⊢— 0.9 knots flood —⊣ ⊢— 1.8 knots ebb ——⊣ ⊢— 1.1 knots flo

FRI DEC 20

dawn 5:55 sunrise 6:54 sunset 4:48 dark 5:47
moonset 10:58 a.m. moonrise 10:23 p.m.

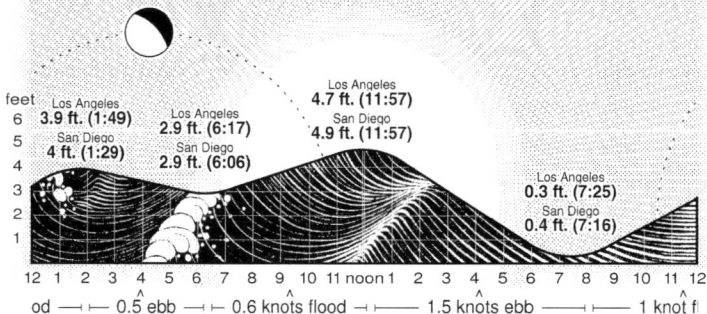

Los Angeles
4.7 ft. (11:57)
San Diego
4.9 ft. (11:57)

feet
Los Angeles
3.9 ft. (1:49)
San Diego
4 ft. (1:29)

Los Angeles
2.9 ft. (6:17)
San Diego
2.9 ft. (6:06)

Los Angeles
0.3 ft. (7:25)
San Diego
0.4 ft. (7:16)

6 5 4 3 2 1

12 1 2 3 4 5 6 7 8 9 10 11 noon 1 2 3 4 5 6 7 8 9 10 11 12

od — ⊢ 0.5 ebb — ⊢ 0.6 knots flood — ⊦ — 1.5 knots ebb — ⊢ 1 knot f

SAT DEC 21

dawn 5:55 sunrise 6:54 sunset 4:49 dark 5:48
moonset 11:23 a.m. moonrise 11:20 p.m.

Winter Solstice 1:21 a.m.

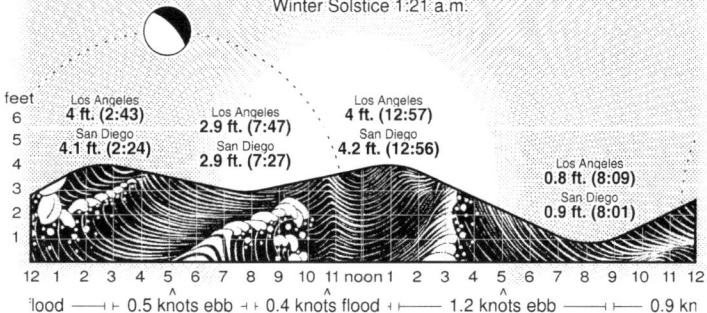

feet
Los Angeles
4 ft. (2:43)
San Diego
4.1 ft. (2:24)

Los Angeles
2.9 ft. (7:47)
San Diego
2.9 ft. (7:27)

Los Angeles
4 ft. (12:57)
San Diego
4.2 ft. (12:56)

Los Angeles
0.8 ft. (8:09)
San Diego
0.9 ft. (8:01)

6 5 4 3 2 1

12 1 2 3 4 5 6 7 8 9 10 11 noon 1 2 3 4 5 6 7 8 9 10 11 12

⎯lood — ⊢ 0.5 knots ebb — ⊦ 0.4 knots flood ⊣ ⊢ — 1.2 knots ebb — ⊣ — 0.9 kn

SUN DEC 22

dawn 5:56 sunrise 6:55 sunset 4:49 dark 5:48
moonset 11:47 a.m.

equator

Ursids Meteor Peak

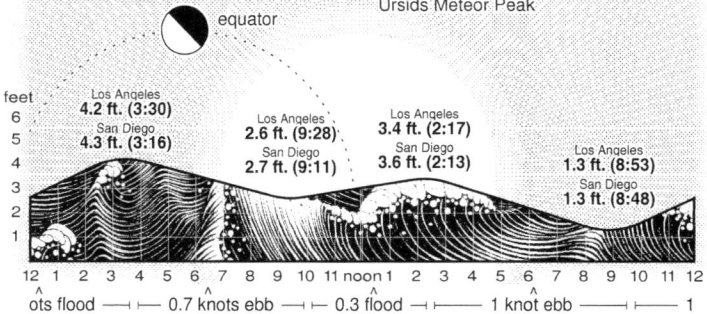

feet
Los Angeles
4.2 ft. (3:30)
San Diego
4.3 ft. (3:16)

Los Angeles
2.6 ft. (9:28)
San Diego
2.7 ft. (9:11)

Los Angeles
3.4 ft. (2:17)
San Diego
3.6 ft. (2:13)

Los Angeles
1.3 ft. (8:53)
San Diego
1.3 ft. (8:48)

6 5 4 3 2 1

12 1 2 3 4 5 6 7 8 9 10 11 noon 1 2 3 4 5 6 7 8 9 10 11 12

ots flood — ⊢ 0.7 knots ebb — ⊢ 0.3 flood — ⊣ ⊢ 1 knot ebb — ⊣ ⊢ 1

Ⓜ   ⓜ   Ⓥ ⊘   Ⓙ

Winter Solstice The solstice marks the start of winter with a day with the fewest hours of daylight for the year in the northern hemisphere. The solstice occurs at the instant when the North Pole is at its farthest tilt of 23.5 degrees away from the Sun plunging the North Pole into total darkness - the Polar Night. **Ursids Meteor Shower** The Ursids are a minor shower producing at peak 5 - 10 meteors per hour. This year's peak, Dec 22nd and the 23rd, will contend with a waning crescent moon setting close to midnight. The shower's radiant, the constellation Ursa Minor, is recognizable as the little dipper asterism with the north pole star, Polaris, at the end of the dipper's handle. After moonset look to Polaris and if condition are favorable this could be ideal for viewing.

MON DEC 23

dawn 5:56 sunrise 6:55 sunset 4:50 dark 5:49
moonrise 12:15 a.m. moonset 12:10 p.m.

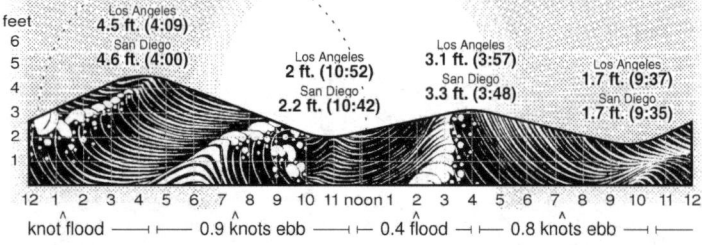

apogee

feet

Los Angeles
4.5 ft. (4:09)
San Diego
4.6 ft. (4:00)

Los Angeles
2 ft. (10:52)
San Diego
2.2 ft. (10:42)

Los Angeles
3.1 ft. (3:57)
San Diego
3.3 ft. (3:48)

Los Angeles
1.7 ft. (9:37)
San Diego
1.7 ft. (9:35)

6
5
4
3
2
1

12 1 2 3 4 5 6 7 8 9 10 11 noon 1 2 3 4 5 6 7 8 9 10 11 12

knot flood ⊢— 0.9 knots ebb —⊣ ⊢— 0.4 flood —⊣ ⊢— 0.8 knots ebb —⊣⊢

TUE DEC 24

dawn 5:57 sunrise 6:56 sunset 4:51 dark 5:49
moonrise 1:10 a.m. moonset 12:34 p.m.

Christmas Eve   Mercury western elongation

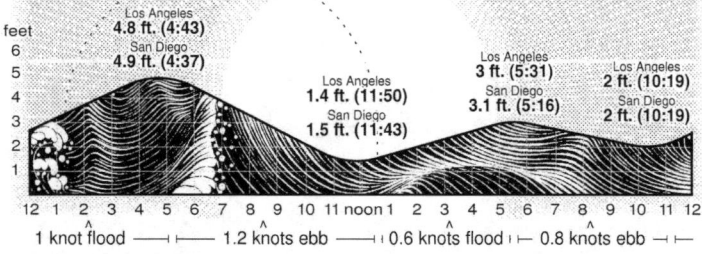

feet

Los Angeles
4.8 ft. (4:43)
San Diego
4.9 ft. (4:37)

Los Angeles
1.4 ft. (11:50)
San Diego
1.5 ft. (11:43)

Los Angeles
3 ft. (5:31)
San Diego
3.1 ft. (5:16)

Los Angeles
2 ft. (10:19)
San Diego
2 ft. (10:19)

6
5
4
3
2
1

12 1 2 3 4 5 6 7 8 9 10 11 noon 1 2 3 4 5 6 7 8 9 10 11 12

1 knot flood ——⊣ ⊢— 1.2 knots ebb ——⊣⊢ 0.6 knots flood ⊢⊢ 0.8 knots ebb —⊣⊢

WED DEC 25

dawn 5:57 sunrise 6:56 sunset 4:51 dark 5:50
moonrise 2:07 a.m. moonset 1:01 p.m.

Christmas Day   Hannukkah begins

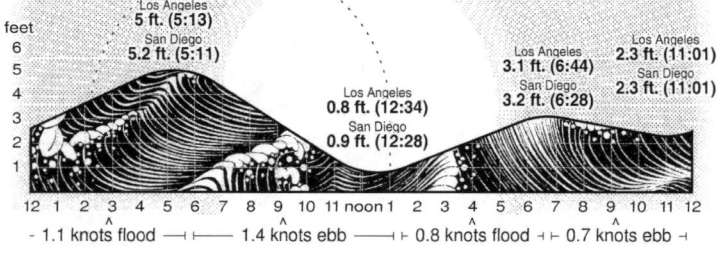

feet

Los Angeles
5 ft. (5:13)
San Diego
5.2 ft. (5:11)

Los Angeles
0.8 ft. (12:34)
San Diego
0.9 ft. (12:28)

Los Angeles
3.1 ft. (6:44)
San Diego
3.2 ft. (6:28)

Los Angeles
2.3 ft. (11:01)
San Diego
2.3 ft. (11:01)

6
5
4
3
2
1

12 1 2 3 4 5 6 7 8 9 10 11 noon 1 2 3 4 5 6 7 8 9 10 11 12

⊢ 1.1 knots flood —⊣ ⊢— 1.4 knots ebb ——⊢ ⊢ 0.8 knots flood ⊣⊢ 0.7 knots ebb ⊣

THU DEC 26

dawn 5:57 sunrise 6:56 sunset 4:52 dark 5:51
moonrise 3:05 a.m. moonset 1:31 p.m.

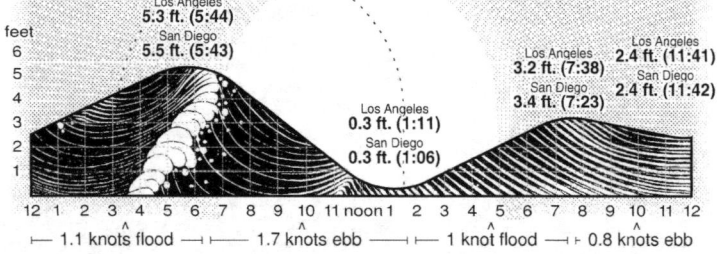

feet

Los Angeles
5.3 ft. (5:44)
San Diego
5.5 ft. (5:43)

Los Angeles
0.3 ft. (1:11)
San Diego
0.3 ft. (1:06)

Los Angeles
3.2 ft. (7:38)
San Diego
3.4 ft. (7:23)

Los Angeles
2.4 ft. (11:41)
San Diego
2.4 ft. (11:42)

6
5
4
3
2
1

12 1 2 3 4 5 6 7 8 9 10 11 noon 1 2 3 4 5 6 7 8 9 10 11 12

⊢— 1.1 knots flood —⊣ ⊢— 1.7 knots ebb ——⊣ ⊢— 1 knot flood —⊣ ⊢ 0.8 knots ebb ⊣

FRI DEC 27

dawn 5:58 sunrise 6:57 sunset 4:52 dark 5:51
moonrise 4:06 a.m. moonset 2:07 p.m.

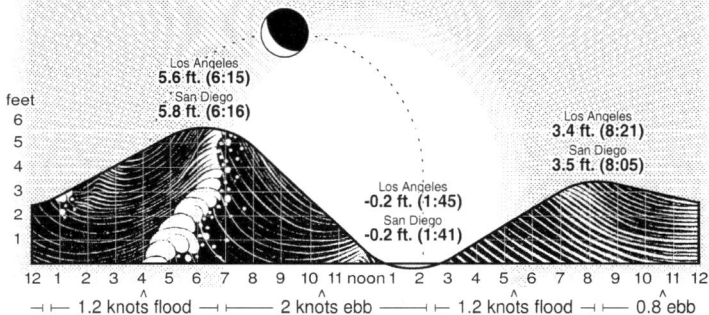

Los Angeles
5.6 ft. (6:15)
San Diego
5.8 ft. (6:16)

Los Angeles
3.4 ft. (8:21)
San Diego
3.5 ft. (8:05)

feet

6
5
4
3
2
1

Los Angeles
-0.2 ft. (1:45)
San Diego
-0.2 ft. (1:41)

12 1 2 3 4 5 6 7 8 9 10 11 noon 1 2 3 4 5 6 7 8 9 10 11 12

⊢ 1.2 knots flood ⟶ ⊢ 2 knots ebb ⟶ ⊢ 1.2 knots flood ⟶ ⊢ 0.8 ebb

SAT DEC 28

dawn 5:58 sunrise 6:57 sunset 4:53 dark 5:52
moonrise 5:07 a.m. moonset 2:49 p.m.

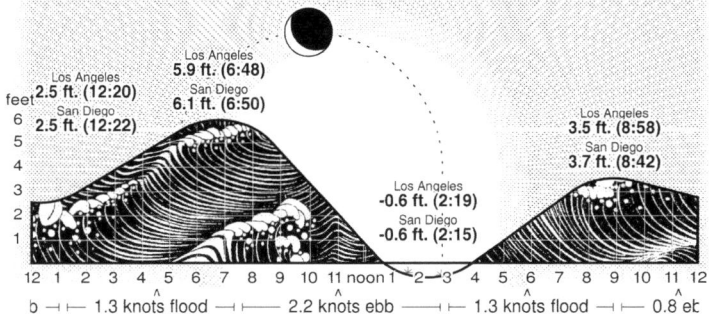

Los Angeles
5.9 ft. (6:48)
San Diego
6.1 ft. (6:50)

Los Angeles
2.5 ft. (12:20)
San Diego
2.5 ft. (12:22)

Los Angeles
3.5 ft. (8:58)
San Diego
3.7 ft. (8:42)

feet

6
5
4
3
2
1

Los Angeles
-0.6 ft. (2:19)
San Diego
-0.6 ft. (2:15)

12 1 2 3 4 5 6 7 8 9 10 11 noon 1 2 3 4 5 6 7 8 9 10 11 12

b ⊣ ⊢ 1.3 knots flood ⊣ ⊢ 2.2 knots ebb ⟶ ⊢ 1.3 knots flood ⟶ ⊢ 0.8 eb

SUN DEC 29

dawn 5:59 sunrise 6:57 sunset 4:54 dark 5:53
moonrise 6:08 a.m. moonset 3:40 p.m.

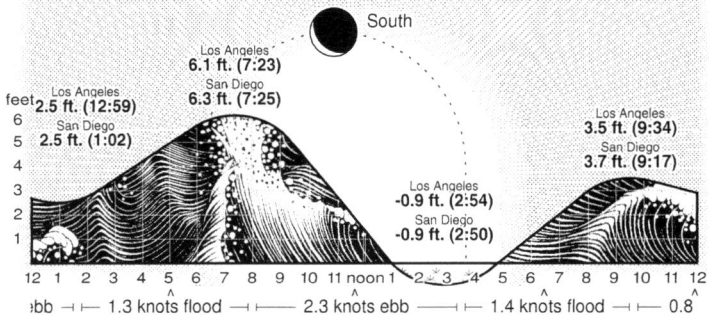

South

Los Angeles
6.1 ft. (7:23)
San Diego
6.3 ft. (7:25)

Los Angeles
2.5 ft. (12:59)
San Diego
2.5 ft. (1:02)

Los Angeles
3.5 ft. (9:34)
San Diego
3.7 ft. (9:17)

feet

6
5
4
3
2
1

Los Angeles
-0.9 ft. (2:54)
San Diego
-0.9 ft. (2:50)

12 1 2 3 4 5 6 7 8 9 10 11 noon 1 2 3 4 5 6 7 8 9 10 11 12

ebb ⊣ ⊢ 1.3 knots flood ⟶ ⊢ 2.3 knots ebb ⟶ ⊢ 1.4 knots flood ⟶ ⊢ 0.8

Ⓜ ⒣ Ⓥ ☿ Ⓙ

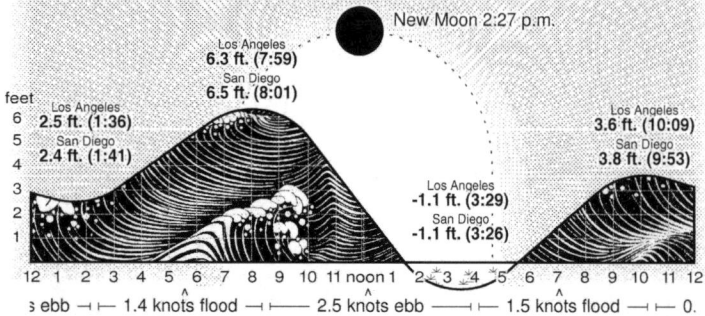

MON DEC 30

dawn 5:59 sunrise 6:57 sunset 4:55 dark 5:53
moonrise 7:06 a.m. moonset 4:39 p.m.

New Moon 2:27 p.m.

Los Angeles
6.3 ft. (7:59)
San Diego
6.5 ft. (8:01)

feet

Los Angeles
2.5 ft. (1:36)
San Diego
2.4 ft. (1:41)

Los Angeles
3.6 ft. (10:09)
San Diego
3.8 ft. (9:53)

Los Angeles
-1.1 ft. (3:29)
San Diego
-1.1 ft. (3:26)

6
5
4
3
2
1

12 1 2 3 4 5 6 7 8 9 10 11 noon 1 2 3 4 5 6 7 8 9 10 11 12

s ebb ⊢→ 1.4 knots flood ⊣→ ⊢— 2.5 knots ebb ——→ ⊢— 1.5 knots flood —→ ⊢— 0.

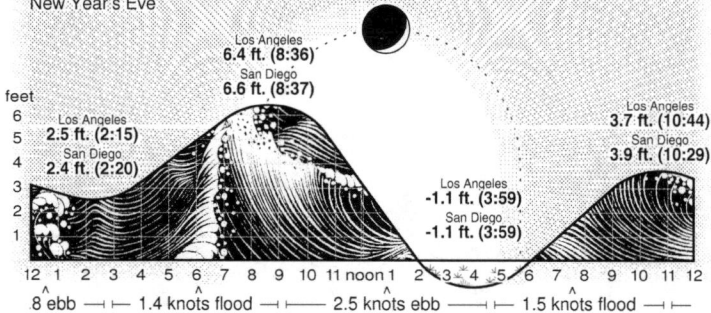

TUE DEC 31

dawn 5:59 sunrise 6:58 sunset 4:55 dark 5:54
moonrise 7:57 a.m. moonset 5:44 p.m.

New Year's Eve

Los Angeles
6.4 ft. (8:36)
San Diego
6.6 ft. (8:37)

feet

Los Angeles
2.5 ft. (2:15)
San Diego
2.4 ft. (2:20)

Los Angeles
3.7 ft. (10:44)
San Diego
3.9 ft. (10:29)

Los Angeles
-1.1 ft. (3:59)
San Diego
-1.1 ft. (3:59)

6
5
4
3
2
1

12 1 2 3 4 5 6 7 8 9 10 11 noon 1 2 3 4 5 6 7 8 9 10 11 12

8 ebb ⊢→ 1.4 knots flood ⊣→ ⊢— 2.5 knots ebb ——→ ⊢— 1.5 knots flood —→ ⊢—

Port San Luis Tides

(reference station for Point Arguello and San Simeon)

Day / Date	time	feet
Mon. 1/1	2:26a	3.9
	7:13a	2.9
	12:31p	4.2
	7:46p	0.6
Tue. 1/2	3:06a	4.1
	8:38a	2.7
	1:27p	3.6
	8:20p	1.0
Wed. 1/3	3:42a	4.3
	10:11a	2.3
	2:51p	3.1
	8:56p	1.5
Thu. 1/4	4:16a	4.6
	11:26a	1.8
	4:38p	2.8
	9:35p	1.9
Fri. 1/5	4:50a	4.9
	12:23p	1.1
	6:25p	2.8
	10:20p	2.3
Sat. 1/6	5:25a	5.2
	1:09p	0.5
	7:46p	3.0
	11:09p	2.6
Sun. 1/7	6:03a	5.5
	1:49p	-0.2
	8:38p	3.2
Mon. 1/8	12:02a	2.7
	6:44a	5.9
	2:28p	-0.7
	9:21p	3.4
Tue. 1/9	12:56a	2.8
	7:26a	6.2
	3:08p	-1.2
	9:59p	3.6
Wed. 1/10	1:46a	2.7
	8:10a	6.5
	3:49p	-1.5
	10:38p	3.7
Thu. 1/11	2:36a	2.6
	8:55a	6.6
	4:31p	-1.7
	11:16p	3.8
Fri. 1/12	3:28a	2.5
	9:41a	6.6
	5:12p	-1.7
	11:55p	4.0
Sat. 1/13	4:25a	2.4
	10:30a	6.3
	5:53p	-1.4
Sun. 1/14	12:35a	4.2
	5:27a	2.2
	11:22a	5.7
	6:34p	-1.0
Mon. 1/15	1:17a	4.4
	6:35a	2.1
	12:19p	5.0
	7:14p	-0.3
Tue. 1/16	2:02a	4.7
	7:54a	1.9
	1:26p	4.1
	7:56p	0.4
Wed. 1/17	2:49a	5.0
	9:27a	1.5
	2:54p	3.4
	8:42p	1.1
Thu. 1/18	3:39a	5.3
	10:56a	0.9
	4:45p	3.0
	9:35p	1.8
Fri. 1/19	4:30a	5.5
	12:10p	0.2
	6:39p	3.0
	10:35p	2.3
Sat. 1/20	5:22a	5.7
	1:11p	-0.3
	8:03p	3.2
	11:41p	2.6
Sun. 1/21	6:13a	5.8
	2:00p	-0.7
	8:56p	3.5
Mon. 1/22	12:45a	2.8
	7:02a	5.9
	2:43p	-1.0
	9:37p	3.6
Tue. 1/23	1:38a	2.7
	7:46a	5.9
	3:21p	-1.0
	10:11p	3.7

Day / Date	time	feet
Wed. 1/24	2:22a	2.6
	8:27a	5.9
	3:57p	-1.0
	10:42p	3.7
Thu. 1/25	3:02a	2.5
	9:04a	5.8
	4:30p	-0.9
	11:11p	3.7
Fri. 1/26	3:40a	2.4
	9:39a	5.6
	5:00p	-0.7
	11:39p	3.8
Sat. 1/27	4:19a	2.3
	10:14a	5.3
	5:28p	-0.4
Sun. 1/28	12:06a	3.8
	5:00a	2.2
	10:49a	5.0
	5:54p	-0.1
Mon. 1/29	12:33a	3.9
	5:45a	2.2
	11:26a	4.5
	6:18p	0.3
Tue. 1/30	1:01a	4.1
	6:36a	2.1
	12:06p	3.9
	6:40p	0.8
Wed. 1/31	1:31a	4.2
	7:38a	2.0
	12:55p	3.3
	7:01p	1.3
Thu. 2/1	2:05a	4.3
	9:01a	1.8
	2:11p	2.8
	7:22p	1.8
Fri. 2/2	2:45a	4.5
	10:31a	1.4
	4:23p	2.5
	7:44p	2.3
Sat. 2/3	3:33a	4.7
	11:44a	0.8
Sun. 2/4	4:28a	4.9
	12:40p	0.2
	8:12p	3.0
	10:20p	2.9
Mon. 2/5	5:24a	5.3
	1:27p	-0.4
	8:37p	3.2
	11:44p	2.9
Tue. 2/6	6:20a	5.7
	2:08p	-1.0
	9:03p	3.4
Wed. 2/7	12:51a	2.7
	7:12a	6.1
	2:47p	-1.4
	9:31p	3.6
Thu. 2/8	1:46a	2.4
	8:01a	6.4
	3:26p	-1.6
	10:01p	3.9
Fri. 2/9	2:38a	2.0
	8:49a	6.5
	4:05p	-1.7
	10:34p	4.1
Sat. 2/10	3:30a	1.7
	9:37a	6.3
	4:42p	-1.5
	11:08p	4.4
Sun. 2/11	4:25a	1.4
	10:27a	5.9
	5:19p	-1.0
	11:44p	4.7
Mon. 2/12	5:24a	1.1
	11:20a	5.2
	5:56p	-0.4
Tue. 2/13	12:22a	5.0
	6:26a	0.9
	12:18p	4.4
	6:31p	0.3
Wed. 2/14	1:03a	5.1
	7:37a	0.8
	1:27p	3.6
	7:08p	1.1
Thu. 2/15	1:49a	5.2
	9:02a	0.6
	3:05p	3.0
	7:50p	1.9

Day / Date	time	feet
Fri. 2/16	2:44a	5.2
	10:32a	0.3
	5:15p	2.8
	8:51p	2.5
Sat. 2/17	3:48a	5.2
	11:51a	-0.1
	7:13p	3.1
	10:24p	2.8
Sun. 2/18	4:55a	5.2
	12:55p	-0.4
	8:09p	3.4
	11:52p	2.8
Mon. 2/19	6:00a	5.2
	1:44p	-0.6
	8:44p	3.6
Tue. 2/20	12:58a	2.7
	6:55a	5.3
	2:25p	-0.8
	9:12p	3.7
Wed. 2/21	1:45a	2.4
	7:41a	5.4
	3:00p	-0.8
	9:37p	3.8
Thu. 2/22	2:23a	2.2
	8:20a	5.4
	3:30p	-0.7
	10:00p	3.8
Fri. 2/23	2:57a	1.9
	8:55a	5.3
	3:57p	-0.5
	10:22p	3.9
Sat. 2/24	3:31a	1.7
	9:28a	5.1
	4:21p	-0.3
	10:43p	4.0
Sun. 2/25	4:07a	1.5
	10:01a	4.9
	4:44p	0.0
	11:05p	4.2
Mon. 2/26	4:45a	1.4
	10:36a	4.5
	5:05p	0.4
	11:27p	4.3
Tue. 2/27	5:25a	1.3
	11:14a	4.1
	5:25p	0.8
	11:50p	4.4
Wed. 2/28	6:06a	1.2
	11:56a	3.6
	5:43p	1.3
Thu. 2/29	12:14a	4.5
	7:01a	1.2
	12:49p	3.1
	5:59p	1.8
Fri. 3/1	12:43a	4.6
	8:08a	1.1
	2:12p	2.6
	6:11p	2.2
Sat. 3/2	1:21a	4.6
	9:36a	0.9
Sun. 3/3	2:18a	4.6
	10:59a	0.5
Mon. 3/4	3:37a	4.7
	12:04p	-0.1
	8:01p	3.1
	10:15p	3.0
Tue. 3/5	4:54a	5.0
	12:55p	-0.6
	8:07p	3.4
	11:49p	2.8
Wed. 3/6	6:01a	5.4
	1:38p	-1.0
	8:26p	3.6
Thu. 3/7	12:53a	2.3
	6:59a	5.7
	2:17p	-1.2
	8:50p	3.9
Fri. 3/8	1:46a	1.8
	7:52a	5.9
	2:54p	-1.3
	9:17p	4.3
Sat. 3/9	2:37a	1.2
	8:42a	5.9
	3:30p	-1.1
	9:47p	4.7

Day / Date	time	feet
Sun. 3/10	4:28a	0.7
	10:32a	5.7
	5:05p	-0.7
	11:20p	5.1
Mon. 3/11	5:21a	0.3
	11:24a	5.2
	5:40p	-0.2
	11:54p	5.4
Tue. 3/12	6:16a	0.0
	12:20p	4.6
	6:15p	0.5
Wed. 3/13	12:31a	5.5
	7:14a	-0.1
	1:22p	3.9
	6:50p	1.2
Thu. 3/14	1:11a	5.5
	8:18a	-0.1
	2:39p	3.3
	7:26p	1.9
Fri. 3/15	1:56a	5.3
	9:35a	0.0
	4:28p	3.0
	8:09p	2.5
Sat. 3/16	2:52a	5.0
	11:01a	0.0
	6:38p	3.1
	9:33p	2.9
Sun. 3/17	4:07a	4.7
	12:20p	-0.1
	8:01p	3.4
	11:39p	3.0
Mon. 3/18	5:30a	4.6
	1:24p	-0.3
	8:40p	3.6
Tue. 3/19	1:04a	2.7
	6:43a	4.6
	2:13p	-0.4
	9:08p	3.8
Wed. 3/20	1:59a	2.4
	7:42a	4.7
	2:52p	-0.4
	9:31p	3.9
Thu. 3/21	2:40a	2.0
	8:28a	4.8
	3:24p	-0.3
	9:51p	4.0
Fri. 3/22	3:15a	1.6
	9:06a	4.8
	3:50p	-0.1
	10:10p	4.2
Sat. 3/23	3:47a	1.3
	9:42a	4.7
	4:13p	0.1
	10:29p	4.3
Sun. 3/24	4:20a	1.0
	10:16a	4.5
	4:34p	0.4
	10:47p	4.5
Mon. 3/25	4:54a	0.8
	10:52a	4.3
	4:54p	0.8
	11:07p	4.7
Tue. 3/26	5:30a	0.6
	11:31a	4.0
	5:14p	1.2
	11:28p	4.8
Wed. 3/27	6:09a	0.4
	12:13p	3.7
	5:34p	1.6
	11:50p	4.9
Thu. 3/28	6:51a	0.3
	1:03p	3.3
	5:53p	1.9
Fri. 3/29	12:15a	4.9
	7:39a	0.3
	2:06p	3.0
	6:09p	2.3
Sat. 3/30	12:46a	4.9
	8:38a	0.3
	3:51p	2.7
	6:19p	2.6
Sun. 3/31	1:27a	4.8
	9:56a	0.2
Mon. 4/1	2:29a	4.7
	11:16a	0.0

Port San Luis Tides
(reference station for Point Arguello and San Simeon)

Day/Date	time	feet
Tue. 4/2	4:00a	4.6
	12:21p	-0.3
	8:01p	3.4
	11:34p	3.0
Wed. 4/3	5:29a	4.7
	1:14p	-0.6
	8:17p	3.7
Thu. 4/4	12:53a	2.5
	6:42a	4.9
	1:58p	-0.7
	8:39p	4.1
Fri. 4/5	1:53a	1.8
	7:46a	5.1
	2:37p	-0.7
	9:04p	4.5
Sat. 4/6	2:45a	1.0
	8:43a	5.2
	3:14p	-0.5
	9:32p	5.0
Sun. 4/7	3:35a	0.3
	9:37a	5.1
	3:49p	-0.1
	10:02p	5.5
Mon. 4/8	4:25a	-0.3
	10:31a	4.8
	4:23p	0.4
	10:35p	5.8
Tue. 4/9	5:15a	-0.7
	11:27a	4.4
	4:59p	0.9
	11:10p	6.0
Wed. 4/10	6:08a	-0.9
	12:28p	4.0
	5:35p	1.5
	11:47p	5.9
Thu. 4/11	7:02a	-0.9
	1:35p	3.6
	6:13p	2.1
Fri. 4/12	12:28a	5.7
	8:00a	-0.7
	2:56p	3.3
	6:55p	2.6
Sat. 4/13	1:14a	5.3
	9:07a	-0.5
	4:40p	3.3
	7:51p	3.0
Sun. 4/14	2:10a	4.9
	10:23a	-0.2
	6:15p	3.4
	9:39p	3.2
Mon. 4/15	3:26a	4.4
	11:36a	-0.1
	7:14p	3.6
	11:37p	3.0
Tue. 4/16	4:55a	4.2
	12:36p	0.0
	7:51p	3.8
Wed. 4/17	12:52a	2.6
	6:12a	4.1
	1:24p	0.0
	8:18p	4.0
Thu. 4/18	1:44a	2.1
	7:14a	4.1
	2:02p	0.2
	8:41p	4.2
Fri. 4/19	2:25a	1.6
	8:05a	4.1
	2:32p	0.4
	9:00p	4.4
Sat. 4/20	3:00a	1.2
	8:48a	4.1
	2:58p	0.6
	9:18p	4.6
Sun. 4/21	3:34a	0.8
	9:29a	4.0
	3:20p	0.9
	9:36p	4.8
Mon. 4/22	4:07a	0.4
	10:08a	3.9
	3:41p	1.3
	9:55p	5.1
Tue. 4/23	4:41a	0.1
	10:50a	3.7
	4:03p	1.6
	10:16p	5.2
Wed. 4/24	5:18a	-0.2
	11:35a	3.6
	4:25p	1.9
	10:40p	5.3

Day/Date	time	feet
Thu. 4/25	5:57a	-0.3
	12:26p	3.4
	4:49p	2.3
	11:06p	5.4
Fri. 4/26	6:39a	-0.4
	1:23p	3.2
	5:13p	2.5
	11:37p	5.3
Sat. 4/27	7:27a	-0.4
	2:36p	3.1
	5:39p	2.8
Sun. 4/28	12:16a	5.2
	8:23a	-0.4
Mon. 4/29	1:04a	5.0
	9:28a	-0.4
Tue. 4/30	2:09a	4.8
	10:35a	-0.4
	6:25p	3.5
	9:52p	3.2
Wed. 5/1	3:37a	4.5
	11:34a	-0.4
	6:54p	3.8
	11:40p	2.7
Thu. 5/2	5:06a	4.4
	12:25p	-0.3
	7:21p	4.2
Fri. 5/3	12:52a	2.0
	6:25a	4.4
	1:10p	-0.2
	7:49p	4.7
Sat. 5/4	1:51a	1.2
	7:36a	4.3
	1:50p	0.1
	8:19p	5.2
Sun. 5/5	2:43a	0.4
	8:40a	4.3
	2:29p	0.5
	8:50p	5.7
Mon. 5/6	3:33a	-0.4
	9:39a	4.2
	3:06p	1.0
	9:23p	6.1
Tue. 5/7	4:21a	-0.9
	10:38a	4.0
	3:43p	1.5
	9:57p	6.3
Wed. 5/8	5:10a	-1.3
	11:38a	3.8
	4:21p	1.9
	10:34p	6.3
Thu. 5/9	5:59a	-1.4
	12:41p	3.7
	5:01p	2.3
	11:14p	6.1
Fri. 5/10	6:50a	-1.3
	1:46p	3.6
	5:46p	2.7
	11:57p	5.8
Sat. 5/11	7:43a	-1.0
	2:59p	3.5
	6:38p	2.9
Sun. 5/12	12:44a	5.3
	8:39a	-0.7
	4:17p	3.5
	7:44p	3.1
Mon. 5/13	1:37a	4.8
	9:40a	-0.3
	5:23p	3.7
	9:20p	3.2
Tue. 5/14	2:43a	4.3
	10:40a	0.0
	6:12p	3.8
	11:06p	2.9
Wed. 5/15	3:34a	3.9
	11:33a	0.2
	6:49p	4.0
Thu. 5/16	12:22a	2.5
	5:23a	3.7
	12:18p	0.5
	7:18p	4.2
Fri. 5/17	1:19a	2.0
	6:33a	3.5
	12:55p	0.8
	7:42p	4.5

Day/Date	time	feet
Sat. 5/18	2:04a	1.4
	7:36a	3.5
	1:27p	1.1
	8:03p	4.8
Sun. 5/19	2:42a	0.9
	8:32a	3.4
	1:55p	1.4
	8:24p	5.0
Mon. 5/20	3:18a	0.4
	9:21a	3.4
	2:21p	1.8
	8:46p	5.3
Tue. 5/21	3:52a	0.0
	10:09a	3.4
	2:48p	2.1
	9:10p	5.5
Wed. 5/22	4:28a	-0.4
	10:57a	3.4
	3:16p	2.3
	9:37p	5.7
Thu. 5/23	5:06a	-0.7
	11:48a	3.4
	3:45p	2.5
	10:07p	5.8
Fri. 5/24	5:47a	-0.9
	12:41p	3.4
	4:18p	2.7
	10:41p	5.8
Sat. 5/25	6:31a	-1.0
	1:37p	3.4
	4:55p	2.9
	11:20p	5.7
Sun. 5/26	7:17a	-1.0
	2:37p	3.4
	5:43p	3.0
Mon. 5/27	12:06a	5.6
	8:07a	-0.9
	3:39p	3.5
	6:48p	3.1
Tue. 5/28	12:59a	5.3
	8:59a	-0.7
	4:33p	3.7
	8:14p	3.1
Wed. 5/29	2:02a	4.9
	9:53a	-0.5
	5:15p	4.0
	10:02p	2.9
Thu. 5/30	3:21a	4.4
	10:45a	-0.2
	5:51p	4.4
	11:34p	2.3
Fri. 5/31	4:49a	4.0
	11:33a	0.2
	6:26p	4.9
Sat. 6/1	12:47a	1.5
	6:15a	3.7
	12:18p	0.6
	7:01p	5.4
Sun. 6/2	1:48a	0.6
	7:37a	3.6
	1:02p	1.1
	7:37p	5.9
Mon. 6/3	2:42a	-0.2
	8:49a	3.6
	1:45p	1.6
	8:14p	6.2
Tue. 6/4	3:31a	-0.8
	9:53a	3.6
	2:27p	2.0
	8:51p	6.5
Wed. 6/5	4:18a	-1.2
	10:53a	3.6
	3:10p	2.3
	9:30p	6.5
Thu. 6/6	5:04a	-1.4
	11:51a	3.7
	3:55p	2.6
	10:11p	6.4
Fri. 6/7	5:51a	-1.4
	12:47p	3.7
	4:41p	2.8
	10:53p	6.2
Sat. 6/8	6:37a	-1.2
	1:40p	3.7
	5:32p	2.9
	11:37p	5.8
Sun. 6/9	7:22a	-1.0
	2:33p	3.7
	6:27p	3.0

Day/Date	time	feet
Mon. 6/10	12:22a	5.4
	8:06a	-0.6
	3:27p	3.7
	7:27p	3.0
Tue. 6/11	1:10a	4.9
	8:52a	-0.2
	4:17p	3.8
	8:41p	3.0
Wed. 6/12	2:02a	4.3
	9:36a	0.2
	5:00p	4.0
	10:12p	2.8
Thu. 6/13	3:06a	3.8
	10:20a	0.6
	5:36p	4.2
	11:36p	2.4
Fri. 6/14	4:25a	3.4
	11:00a	1.0
	6:07p	4.4
Sat. 6/15	12:43a	1.9
	5:48a	3.1
	11:36a	1.4
	6:36p	4.7
Sun. 6/16	1:37a	1.3
	7:11a	3.0
	12:11p	1.8
	7:04p	5.0
Mon. 6/17	2:20a	0.8
	8:25a	3.0
	12:46p	2.2
	7:32p	5.3
Tue. 6/18	2:59a	0.2
	9:25a	3.1
	1:22p	2.4
	8:02p	5.6
Wed. 6/19	3:36a	-0.2
	10:16a	3.3
	2:01p	2.6
	8:35p	5.8
Thu. 6/20	4:14a	-0.6
	11:03a	3.4
	2:42p	2.8
	9:10p	6.0
Fri. 6/21	4:53a	-1.0
	11:49a	3.5
	3:23p	2.8
	9:49p	6.2
Sat. 6/22	5:35a	-1.2
	12:33p	3.5
	4:08p	2.9
	10:30p	6.2
Sun. 6/23	6:17a	-1.3
	1:16p	3.6
	4:59p	2.9
	11:15p	6.1
Mon. 6/24	6:59a	-1.3
	1:59p	3.7
	5:58p	2.9
Tue. 6/25	12:04a	5.9
	7:42a	-1.1
	2:43p	3.9
	7:05p	2.8
Wed. 6/26	12:57a	5.4
	8:25a	-0.7
	3:27p	4.2
	8:22p	2.6
Thu. 6/27	1:57a	4.8
	9:10a	-0.2
	4:11p	4.5
	9:54p	2.3
Fri. 6/28	3:12a	4.1
	9:56a	0.4
	4:54p	5.0
	11:23p	1.7
Sat. 6/29	4:44a	3.5
	10:42a	1.0
	5:36p	5.4
Sun. 6/30	12:40a	0.9
	6:22a	3.2
	11:30a	1.6
	6:19p	5.8
Mon. 7/1	1:44a	0.2
	7:57a	3.2
	12:20p	2.0
	7:03p	6.1
Tue. 7/2	2:39a	-0.5
	9:13a	3.3
	1:14p	2.4
	7:48p	6.3

Port San Luis Tides

(reference station for Point Arguello and San Simeon)

	time	feet
Wed. 7/3	3:28a	-0.9
	10:13a	3.5
	2:07p	2.6
	8:33p	6.4
Thu. 7/4	4:13a	-1.2
	11:03a	3.7
	2:59p	2.7
	9:17p	6.4
Fri. 7/5	4:56a	-1.2
	11:49a	3.7
	3:47p	2.8
	9:59p	6.3
Sat. 7/6	5:37a	-1.1
	12:30p	3.8
	4:34p	2.8
	10:41p	6.1
Sun. 7/7	6:17a	-1.0
	1:08p	3.8
	5:22p	2.7
	11:22p	5.8
Mon. 7/8	6:53a	-0.7
	1:45p	3.9
	6:11p	2.7
Tue. 7/9	12:03a	5.4
	7:28a	-0.3
	2:22p	3.9
	7:02p	2.7
Wed. 7/10	12:44a	4.9
	8:00a	0.1
	2:59p	4.0
	8:00p	2.7
Thu. 7/11	1:28a	4.3
	8:31a	0.6
	3:36p	4.2
	9:11p	2.5
Fri. 7/12	2:20a	3.8
	9:01a	1.1
	4:13p	4.4
	10:37p	2.3
Sat. 7/13	3:32a	3.2
	9:33a	1.6
	4:49p	4.6
	11:56p	1.8
Sun. 7/14	5:12a	2.9
	10:08a	2.0
	5:25p	4.8
Mon. 7/15	1:01a	1.3
	7:05a	2.8
	10:51a	2.4
	6:04p	5.1
Tue. 7/16	1:53a	0.7
	8:38a	3.0
	11:42a	2.7
	6:44p	5.4
Wed. 7/17	2:37a	0.2
	9:33a	3.2
	12:39p	2.9
	7:27p	5.7
Thu. 7/18	3:16a	-0.3
	10:13a	3.4
	1:36p	2.9
	8:11p	6.0
Fri. 7/19	3:55a	-0.7
	10:48a	3.6
	2:29p	2.9
	8:55p	6.3
Sat. 7/20	4:34a	-1.1
	11:22a	3.7
	3:19p	2.7
	9:38p	6.5
Sun. 7/21	5:13a	-1.3
	11:57a	3.8
	4:09p	2.6
	10:23p	6.5
Mon. 7/22	5:52a	-1.3
	12:32p	4.0
	5:03p	2.4
	11:10p	6.3
Tue. 7/23	6:31a	-1.1
	1:08p	4.2
	6:01p	2.2
	12:00p	5.9
Wed. 7/24	7:09a	-0.7
	1:46p	4.5
	7:05p	2.0
Thu. 7/25	12:54a	5.3
	7:47a	-0.2
	2:26p	4.8
	8:15p	1.8

	time	feet
Fri. 7/26	1:56a	4.5
	8:25a	0.5
	3:10p	5.1
	9:39p	1.5
Sat. 7/27	3:14a	3.8
	9:07a	1.2
	3:58p	5.4
	11:08p	1.1
Sun. 7/28	4:57a	3.2
	9:55a	1.9
	4:50p	5.7
Mon. 7/29	12:28a	0.5
	6:51a	3.1
	10:55a	2.4
	5:45p	5.8
Tue. 7/30	1:36a	0.0
	8:28a	3.3
	12:04p	2.8
	6:42p	6.0
Wed. 7/31	2:32a	-0.5
	9:29a	3.6
	1:14p	2.9
	7:36p	6.1
Thu. 8/1	3:19a	-0.7
	10:12a	3.8
	2:14p	2.9
	8:27p	6.2
Fri. 8/2	4:01a	-0.8
	10:47a	3.9
	3:04p	2.7
	9:11p	6.1
Sat. 8/3	4:39a	-0.8
	11:20a	4.0
	3:48p	2.6
	9:52p	6.1
Sun. 8/4	5:14a	-0.7
	11:50a	4.0
	4:28p	2.4
	10:30p	5.9
Mon. 8/5	5:46a	-0.4
	12:18p	4.1
	5:09p	2.3
	11:07p	5.6
Tue. 8/6	6:15a	-0.1
	12:46p	4.2
	5:51p	2.2
	11:44p	5.2
Wed. 8/7	6:41a	0.2
	1:13p	4.3
	6:36p	2.2
Thu. 8/8	12:22a	4.7
	7:05a	0.7
	1:40p	4.4
	7:24p	2.1
Fri. 8/9	1:04a	4.2
	7:28a	1.2
	2:08p	4.5
	8:21p	2.0
Sat. 8/10	1:53a	3.7
	7:49a	1.7
	2:40p	4.6
	9:34p	1.9
Sun. 8/11	3:05a	3.2
	8:10a	2.2
	3:19p	4.7
	11:01p	1.6
Mon. 8/12	5:05a	2.9
	8:31a	2.6
	4:09p	4.8
Tue. 8/13	12:18a	1.2
	5:06p	5.0
Wed. 8/14	1:19a	0.7
	8:59a	3.3
	11:03a	3.2
	6:05p	5.3
Thu. 8/15	2:08a	0.2
	9:22a	3.5
	12:28p	3.2
	7:01p	5.6
Fri. 8/16	2:49a	-0.3
	9:45a	3.7
	1:33p	3.0
	7:54p	6.0
Sat. 8/17	3:28a	-0.7
	10:10a	3.9
	2:27p	2.7
	8:42p	6.3

	time	feet
Sun. 8/18	4:05a	-0.9
	10:37a	4.1
	3:17p	2.3
	9:29p	6.5
Mon. 8/19	4:41a	-1.0
	11:07a	4.3
	4:07p	1.9
	10:16p	6.4
Tue. 8/20	5:18a	-0.8
	11:39a	4.7
	5:00p	1.6
	11:05p	6.1
Wed. 8/21	5:54a	-0.5
	12:14p	5.0
	5:57p	1.3
	11:57p	5.6
Thu. 8/22	6:29a	0.1
	12:50p	5.3
	6:57p	1.1
Fri. 8/23	12:55a	4.9
	7:05a	0.8
	1:29p	5.5
	8:03p	0.9
Sat. 8/24	2:02a	4.2
	7:41a	1.5
	2:13p	5.6
	9:20p	0.8
Sun. 8/25	3:31a	3.5
	8:23a	2.2
	3:06p	5.6
	10:48p	0.6
Mon. 8/26	5:29a	3.3
	9:20a	2.8
	4:10p	5.6
Tue. 8/27	12:09a	0.3
	7:24a	3.5
	10:51a	3.1
	5:21p	5.6
Wed. 8/28	1:18a	0.0
	8:33a	3.8
	12:22p	3.2
	6:30p	5.6
Thu. 8/29	2:14a	-0.3
	9:13a	4.0
	1:33p	3.0
	7:31p	5.7
Fri. 8/30	2:59a	-0.4
	9:44a	4.1
	2:25p	2.7
	8:22p	5.7
Sat. 8/31	3:37a	-0.3
	10:11a	4.2
	3:07p	2.4
	9:05p	5.7
Sun. 9/1	4:09a	-0.2
	10:36a	4.3
	3:44p	2.1
	9:42p	5.7
Mon. 9/2	4:38a	0.0
	10:58a	4.4
	4:19p	1.9
	10:17p	5.5
Tue. 9/3	5:03a	0.3
	11:21a	4.5
	4:55p	1.7
	10:52p	5.2
Wed. 9/4	5:27a	0.6
	11:42a	4.6
	5:33p	1.6
	11:29p	4.8
Thu. 9/5	5:48a	1.0
	12:04p	4.7
	6:13p	1.5
Fri. 9/6	12:08a	4.4
	6:09a	1.5
	12:27p	4.8
	6:56p	1.4
Sat. 9/7	12:53a	4.0
	6:28a	1.9
	12:51p	4.9
	7:44p	1.4
Sun. 9/8	1:47a	3.5
	6:45a	2.4
	1:19p	4.9
	8:46p	1.4
Mon. 9/9	3:10a	3.2
	6:59a	2.8
	1:55p	4.9
	10:08p	1.3

	time	feet
Tue. 9/10	2:50p	4.8
	11:32p	1.0
Wed. 9/11	4:11p	4.9
Thu. 9/12	12:38a	0.6
	8:36a	3.6
	11:10a	3.5
	5:32p	5.1
Fri. 9/13	1:30a	0.2
	8:44a	3.8
	12:35p	3.2
	6:39p	5.4
Sat. 9/14	2:13a	-0.2
	9:02a	4.1
	1:34p	2.7
	7:37p	5.8
Sun. 9/15	2:51a	-0.5
	9:24a	4.4
	2:25p	2.2
	8:29p	6.0
Mon. 9/16	3:27a	-0.5
	9:49a	4.7
	3:14p	1.6
	9:19p	6.1
Tue. 9/17	4:02a	-0.4
	10:17a	5.1
	4:04p	1.0
	10:09p	5.9
Wed. 9/18	4:36a	0.0
	10:48a	5.5
	4:55p	0.6
	11:01p	5.5
Thu. 9/19	5:11a	0.5
	11:22a	5.9
	5:49p	0.2
	11:58p	5.0
Fri. 9/20	5:46a	1.1
	11:59a	6.1
	6:47p	0.0
Sat. 9/21	1:01a	4.4
	6:23a	1.8
	12:39p	6.1
	7:49p	0.0
Sun. 9/22	2:16a	3.9
	7:02a	2.4
	1:25p	5.9
	9:00p	0.1
Mon. 9/23	3:57a	3.6
	7:50a	3.0
	2:20p	5.6
	10:23p	0.2
Tue. 9/24	5:53a	3.7
	9:11a	3.4
	3:34p	5.3
	11:42p	0.1
Wed. 9/25	7:16a	3.9
	11:12a	3.4
	5:00p	5.1
Thu. 9/26	12:49a	0.1
	8:04a	4.2
	12:39p	3.1
	6:17p	5.1
Fri. 9/27	1:43a	0.0
	8:37a	4.4
	1:39p	2.7
	7:20p	5.2
Sat. 9/28	2:25a	0.1
	9:04a	4.5
	2:23p	2.3
	8:10p	5.2
Sun. 9/29	3:00a	0.2
	9:26a	4.6
	3:01p	1.9
	8:52p	5.1
Mon. 9/30	3:28a	0.5
	9:47a	4.8
	3:35p	1.6
	9:30p	5.0
Tue. 10/1	3:52a	0.8
	10:06a	4.9
	4:08p	1.3
	10:06p	4.8
Wed. 10/2	3:28a	1.1
	10:24a	5.1
	4:41p	1.0
	10:43p	4.6

Port San Luis Tides
(reference station for Point Arguello and San Simeon)

Date	time	feet
Thu. 10/3	4:33a	1.5
	10:43a	5.2
	5:17p	0.8
	11:23p	4.3
Fri. 10/4	4:53a	1.9
	11:04a	5.3
	5:54p	0.7
Sat. 10/5	12:07a	4.0
	5:13a	2.3
	11:26a	5.3
	6:35p	0.7
Sun. 10/6	12:58a	3.7
	5:32a	2.6
	11:51a	5.3
	7:21p	0.7
Mon. 10/7	2:02a	3.5
	5:49a	3.0
	12:20p	5.2
	8:17p	0.7
Tue. 10/8	3:50a	3.3
	5:56a	3.2
	12:59p	5.1
	9:28p	0.7
Wed. 10/9		
	1:56p	4.9
	10:47p	0.6
Thu. 10/10		
	3:26p	4.8
	11:52p	0.4
Fri. 10/11	7:37a	3.9
	11:22a	3.5
	5:00p	4.9
Sat. 10/12	12:44a	0.1
	7:52a	4.2
	12:36p	3.0
	6:15p	5.1
Sun. 10/13	1:28a	0.0
	8:12a	4.5
	1:32p	2.3
	7:19p	5.3
Mon. 10/14	2:07a	0.0
	8:36a	5.0
	2:22p	1.5
	8:18p	5.3
Tue. 10/15	2:43a	0.2
	9:02a	5.5
	3:11p	0.8
	9:12p	5.3
Wed. 10/16	3:18a	0.5
	9:32a	6.0
	3:59p	0.1
	10:07p	5.1
Thu. 10/17	3:52a	1.0
	10:04a	6.4
	4:49p	-0.4
	11:04p	4.8
Fri. 10/18	4:28a	1.5
	10:39a	6.6
	5:42p	-0.7
Sat. 10/19	12:05a	4.4
	5:05a	2.1
	11:17a	6.6
	6:36p	-0.8
Sun. 10/20	1:13a	4.1
	5:46a	2.6
	11:59a	6.4
	7:34p	-0.6
Mon. 10/21	2:32a	3.9
	6:32a	3.1
	12:47p	6.0
	8:38p	-0.4
Tue. 10/22	4:09a	3.8
	7:34a	3.4
	1:44p	5.5
	9:51p	-0.1
Wed. 10/23	5:37a	4.0
	9:16a	3.6
	2:59p	5.0
	11:04p	0.1
Thu. 10/24	6:37a	4.2
	11:14a	3.4
	4:29p	4.7
Fri. 10/25	12:06a	0.3
	7:19a	4.4
	12:32p	2.9
	5:49p	4.5

Date	time	feet
Sat. 10/26	12:56a	0.4
	7:51a	4.6
	1:28p	2.4
	6:55p	4.5
Sun. 10/27	1:37a	0.6
	8:16a	4.8
	2:12p	1.9
	7:50p	4.4
Mon. 10/28	2:10a	0.9
	8:38a	5.0
	2:49p	1.4
	8:37p	4.4
Tue. 10/29	2:36a	1.2
	8:57a	5.2
	3:23p	1.0
	9:20p	4.3
Wed. 10/30	2:59a	1.5
	9:16a	5.4
	3:56p	0.7
	10:00p	4.2
Thu. 10/31	3:21a	1.9
	9:35a	5.6
	4:29p	0.4
	10:42p	4.0
Fri. 11/1	3:42a	2.2
	9:55a	5.7
	5:04p	0.1
	11:28p	3.9
Sat. 11/2	4:04a	2.5
	10:18a	5.8
	5:41p	0.0
Sun. 11/3	12:17a	3.7
	3:26a	2.8
	9:44a	5.7
	5:22p	0.0
Mon. 11/4	12:14a	3.6
	3:49a	3.1
	10:13a	5.7
	6:07p	0.0
Tue. 11/5	1:24a	3.5
	4:14a	3.3
	10:49a	5.5
	6:58p	0.0
Wed. 11/6		
	11:33a	5.3
	7:58p	0.1
Thu. 11/7		
	12:32p	5.0
	9:02p	0.1
Fri. 11/8	5:04a	3.9
	8:20a	3.7
	1:55p	4.7
	10:01p	0.1
Sat. 11/9	5:29a	4.2
	10:17a	3.2
	3:30p	4.5
	10:52p	0.2
Sun. 11/10	5:54a	4.6
	11:30a	2.5
	4:53p	4.5
	11:36p	0.4
Mon. 11/11	6:20a	5.1
	12:28p	1.7
	6:07p	4.4
Tue. 11/12	12:17a	0.7
	6:49a	5.6
	1:20p	0.8
	7:14p	4.4
Wed. 11/13	12:56a	1.0
	7:20a	6.2
	2:08p	-0.1
	8:16p	4.4
Thu. 11/14	1:34a	1.5
	7:53a	6.6
	2:56p	-0.7
	9:15p	4.3
Fri. 11/15	2:12a	1.9
	8:29a	6.9
	3:45p	-1.1
	10:15p	4.2
Sat. 11/16	2:52a	2.3
	9:07a	6.9
	4:35p	-1.3
	11:17p	4.1
Sun. 11/17	3:34a	2.7
	9:48a	6.8
	5:26p	-1.2

Date	time	feet
Mon. 11/18	12:22a	4.0
	4:21a	3.0
	10:33a	6.4
	6:18p	-1.0
Tue. 11/19	1:30a	3.9
	5:17a	3.2
	11:22a	5.9
	7:14p	-0.7
Wed. 11/20	2:43a	3.9
	6:25a	3.4
	12:17p	5.4
	8:12p	-0.3
Thu. 11/21	3:50a	4.1
	7:56a	3.4
	1:21p	4.8
	9:12p	0.1
Fri. 11/22	4:42a	4.3
	9:44a	3.2
	2:40p	4.3
	10:07p	0.5
Sat. 11/23	5:23a	4.5
	11:06a	2.7
	4:04p	3.9
	10:54p	0.8
Sun. 11/24	5:55a	4.7
	12:07p	2.2
	5:20p	3.7
	11:34p	1.2
Mon. 11/25	6:22a	4.9
	12:55p	1.6
	6:28p	3.6
Tue. 11/26	12:08a	1.5
	6:46a	5.2
	1:34p	1.0
	7:27p	3.6
Wed. 11/27	12:37a	1.9
	7:08a	5.4
	2:09p	0.6
	8:18p	3.6
Thu. 11/28	1:04a	2.2
	7:30a	5.6
	2:43p	0.2
	9:05p	3.6
Fri. 11/29	1:31a	2.5
	7:54a	5.8
	3:17p	-0.2
	9:51p	3.6
Sat. 11/30	1:59a	2.7
	8:21a	5.9
	3:53p	-0.4
	10:38p	3.6
Sun. 12/1	2:29a	2.9
	8:50a	6.0
	4:31p	-0.6
	11:27p	3.6
Mon. 12/2	3:00a	3.0
	9:22a	6.0
	5:12p	-0.7
Tue. 12/3	12:18a	3.6
	3:36a	3.2
	9:58a	5.9
	5:54p	-0.7
Wed. 12/4	1:12a	3.6
	4:19a	3.3
	10:40a	5.7
	6:39p	-0.6
Thu. 12/5	2:08a	3.7
	5:18a	3.3
	11:27a	5.4
	7:27p	-0.4
Fri. 12/6	3:01a	3.8
	6:37a	3.4
	12:24p	5.0
	8:17p	-0.2
Sat. 12/7	3:44a	4.1
	8:20a	3.2
	1:36p	4.5
	9:07p	0.1
Sun. 12/8	4:21a	4.5
	10:02a	2.7
	3:06p	4.0
	9:56p	0.5
Mon. 12/9	4:55a	5.0
	11:20a	1.8
	4:40p	3.7
	10:42p	1.0
Tue. 12/10	5:30a	5.5
	12:23p	0.9
	6:08p	3.6
	11:27p	1.4

Date	time	feet
Wed. 12/11	6:07a	6.0
	1:18p	0.1
	7:26p	3.6
Thu. 12/12	12:13a	1.8
	6:45a	6.5
	2:07p	-0.7
	8:32p	3.7
Fri. 12/13	12:59a	2.2
	7:25a	6.8
	2:54p	-1.2
	9:31p	3.8
Sat. 12/14	1:45a	2.5
	8:07a	6.9
	3:41p	-1.5
	10:27p	3.9
Sun. 12/15	2:32a	2.7
	8:49a	6.8
	4:27p	-1.5
	11:20p	3.9
Mon. 12/16	3:21a	2.8
	9:33a	6.6
	5:13p	-1.4
Tue. 12/17	12:11a	3.9
	4:12a	2.9
	10:18a	6.2
	5:59p	-1.1
Wed. 12/18	1:01a	3.9
	5:08a	3.0
	11:05a	5.8
	6:43p	-0.8
Thu. 12/19	1:52a	3.9
	6:08a	3.0
	11:52a	5.2
	7:26p	-0.3
Fri. 12/20	2:43a	4.0
	7:18a	3.0
	12:43p	4.6
	8:10p	0.2
Sat. 12/21	3:30a	4.2
	8:47a	2.8
	1:44p	3.9
	8:53p	0.7
Sun. 12/22	4:11a	4.4
	10:19a	2.5
	3:06p	3.4
	9:35p	1.2
Mon. 12/23	4:46a	4.6
	11:33a	1.9
	4:39p	3.0
	10:15p	1.7
Tue. 12/24	5:18a	4.8
	12:31p	1.4
	6:13p	3.0
	10:54p	2.1
Wed. 12/25	5:49a	5.1
	1:15p	0.8
	7:32p	3.1
	11:32p	2.4
Thu. 12/26	6:20a	5.3
	1:53p	0.3
	8:30p	3.2
Fri. 12/27	12:13a	2.7
	6:51a	5.8
	2:29p	-0.2
	9:16p	3.4
Sat. 12/28	12:54a	2.8
	7:25a	5.8
	3:04p	-0.6
	9:56p	3.5
Sun. 12/29	1:35a	2.9
	7:59a	6.0
	3:40p	-0.8
	10:35p	3.6
Mon. 12/30	2:15a	2.9
	8:35a	6.1
	4:17p	-1.0
	11:13p	3.6
Tue. 12/31	2:56a	2.9
	9:13a	6.1
	4:17p	-1.0
	11:48p	3.7

Historical Tide Corrections

Times with a minus sign occur *before* predictions; those with a plus sign occur *after*.
*Heights preceded by an asterisk are ratios; multiply by predicted tidal height.

| | POSITION | | DIFFERENCES | | | |
| | | | Time | | Height | |
	Latitude	Longitude	High Water	Low Water	High Water	Low Water
	North	**West**	h m	h m	ft	ft
MEXICO		*(corrections apply to San Diego tides)*				
Manzanillo	19° 03'	104° 20'	+0 37	+0 45	-2.9	-0.5
Puerto Vallarta	20° 37'	105° 15'	+0 22	+0 31	*0.62	*0.56
TIME MERIDIAN, 105° W						
Isla Socorro	18° 44'	111° 01'	-0 38	-0 29	-1.9	-0.5
Mazatlan	23° 12'	106° 25'	-0 38	-0 29	*0.70	*0.56
GULF OF CALIFORNIA						
Topolobampo	25° 36'	109° 03'	+0 49	+0 57	*0.68	*0.78
Puerto Penasco	31° 18'	113° 33'	+4 59	+5 08	*2.58	*1.33
BAJA CALIFORNIA						
San Carlos	24° 47'	112° 07'	-0 09	+0 00	0.0	-0.2
TIME MERIDIAN, 120° W						
Isla Guadalupe	28° 53'	116° 18'	-0 30	-0 21	*0.78	*0.78
Ensenada, Todos Santos Bay	31° 51'	116° 38'	-0 19	-0 11	*0.92	*0.89
CALIFORNIA						
Imperial Beach	32° 34.7'	117° 08.1'	+0 00	-0 03	*0.93	*0.96
Point Loma	32° 40'	117° 14'	-0 09	-0 02	*0.92	*0.92
Ballast Point, San Diego Bay	32° 41.2'	117° 14.0'	-0 03	-0 04	*0.96	*0.91
San Diego, Quarantine Station	32° 42'	117° 14'	-0 04	+0 02	*0.96	*0.96
San Diego (Broadway)	32° 42.8'	117° 10.4'	daily predictions			
National City, San Diego Bay	32° 40'	117° 07'	+0 04	+0 10	+0.2	0.0
Sweetwater Channel, San Diego Bay	32° 38.9'	117° 06.7'	+0 00	-0 01	*1.02	*0.93
Quivira Basin, Mission Bay	32° 46'	117° 14'	+0 05	+0 04	*0.95	*0.95
Crown Point, Mission Bay	32° 46.8'	117° 14.1'	-0 03	+0 16	*0.96	*0.96
La Jolla (Scripps Institution Wharf)	32° 52.0'	117° 15.5'	+0 00	-0 04	*0.92	*0.97
San Clemente	33° 25'	117° 37'	-0 15	-0 11	*0.92	*0.92
SAN PEDRO CHANNEL		*(corrections apply to Los Angeles tides)*				
Newport Bay Entrance, Corona del Mar	33° 36.2'	117° 53.0'	-0 03	-0 04	*0.98	*0.98
Balboa Pier, Newport Beach	33° 35.9'	117° 54.0'	-0 09	+0 00	*0.96	*0.96
Santa Ana River entrance (inside)	33° 38'	117° 57'	+0 23	+1 47	*0.54	*0.20
Los Patos (highway bridge)	33° 43'	118° 03'	+1 00	+1 12	*0.83	*0.60
Long Beach, Terminal Island	33° 45.1'	118° 13.7'	-0 01	+0 00	*1.01	*1.01
Long Beach, Inner Harbor	33° 46.3'	118° 12.6'	+0 04	+0 05	*0.96	*0.96
Cabrillo Beach	33° 42.4'	118° 16.4'	+0 00	+0 00	*1.00	*1.00
Los Angeles (Outer Harbor)	33° 43.2'	118° 16.3'	daily predictions			
Los Angeles Harbor, Mormon Island	33° 45'	118° 16'	+0 04	+0 02	-0.1	0.0
King Harbor, Santa Monica Bay	33° 50.8'	118° 23.9'	+0 08	+0 07	*0.96	*1.00
El Segundo, Santa Monica Bay	33° 55'	118° 26'	+0 13	+0 13	*0.96	*0.96
Santa Monica, Municipal Pier	34° 00.5'	118° 30.0'	+0 03	+0 03	*0.99	*0.99
SANTA BARBARA CHANNEL						
Mugu Lagoon (ocean pier)	34° 06'	119° 06'	+0 03	+0 11	*0.96	*0.96
Port Hueneme	34° 09'	119° 12'	+0 10	+0 13	-0.1	0.0
Ventura	34° 16'	119° 17'	+0 09	+0 16	-0.1	0.0
Rincon Island, Mussel Shoals	34° 20.9'	119° 26.6'	+0 20	+0 18	*0.99	*1.05
Santa Barbara	34° 24.5'	119° 41.1'	+0 23	+0 21	*0.98	*1.04
Gaviota State Park	34° 28.1'	120° 13.7'	+0 27	+0 25	*0.96	*1.04
Oil Platform Harvet	34° 28.1'	120° 40.4'	+0 37	+0 35	*0.95	*1.06
CHANNEL ISLANDS		*(corrections apply to Los Angeles tides)*				
Wilson Cove, San Clemente Island	33° 00.3'	118° 33.4'	-0 01	-0 03	*0.95	*0.95
Catalina Harbor, Santa Catalina Island	33° 26'	118° 30'	+0 11	+0 17	*0.94	*0.94
Avalon, Santa Catalina Island	33° 21'	118° 19'	+0 06	+0 09	*0.96	*0.96
Santa Barbara Island	33° 29'	119° 02'	-0 02	+0 04	*0.92	*0.92

Historical Tide Corrections

Times with a minus sign occur *before* predictions; those with a plus sign occur *after*.
*Heights preceded by an asterisk are ratios; multiply by predicted tidal height.

	POSITION		DIFFERENCES			
			Time		Height	
	Latitude	Longitude	High Water	Low Water	High Water	Low Water
	North	**West**	h m	h m	ft	ft
CHANNEL ISLANDS, cont.		*(corrections apply to Los Angeles tides)*				
San Nicolas Island	33° 16'	119° 30'	+0 10	+0 21	*0.88	*0.88
Prisoners Harbor, Santa Cruz Island	34° 01.2'	119° 41.0'	+0 19	+0 18	*0.94	*1.01
Bechers Bay, Santa Rosa Island	34° 00.5'	120° 02.8'	+0 27	+0 27	*0.93	*1.03
Cuyler Harbor, San Miguel Island	34° 03'	120° 21'	+0 33	+0 34	*0.94	*0.94
OUTER COAST		*(corrections apply to Port San Luis tides)*				
Point Arguello	34° 35'	120° 39'	-0 03	-0 08	*0.96	*0.96
Port San Luis	35° 10.1'	120° 45.1'	daily predictions			
San Simeon	35° 38'	121° 11'	+0 08	+0 07	*0.99	*1.00
Mansfield Cone	35° 57.0'	121° 28.9'	+0 16	+0 16	*0.98	*0.99

Historical Current Corrections

Times with a minus sign occur *before* predictions; those with a plus sign occur *after*.
Maximum current speed = predicted current multiplied by speed ratio.

	POSITION		FLOOD			EBB		
	Latitude	Longitude	Slack before	Max flood	Speed ratio	Slack before	Max ebb	Speed ratio
	North	**West**	h. m.	h. m.		h. m.	h. m.	
SAN CLEMENTE ISLAND		*(corrections apply to San Diego Bay Entrance currents)*						
China Point Light, 20 miles SSW of	32° 29'	118° 32'	- - -	- - -	- -	- - -	- - -	- -
SAN DIEGO BAY								
Point Loma Light, 0.8 nm E of	32° 39.95'	117° 13.57'	-0 18	-0 43	0.5	-0 05	+0 45	0.4
San Diego Bay Entrance	32° 40.90'	117° 13.80'	daily predictions					
Ballast Point, S of	32° 41.07'	117° 13.93'	-1 04	-1 02	0.4	-1 01	-2 03	0.2
Ballast Point, 100 yards N of	32° 41'	117° 14'	-0 27	-0 24	1.0	-0 23	-0 02	0.9
Ballast Point, 0.55 nm N of	32° 41.75'	117° 13.95'	-0 05	-0 39	0.5	-0 34	+0 24	0.4
Quarantine Station, La Playa	32° 42'	117° 14'	-0 03	+0 15	0.8	+0 10	+0 20	0.8
North Island	32° 42.78'	117° 12.77'	-0 26	-0 56	0.5	-0 54	-0 03	0.4
Harbor Island (east end), SSW of	32° 43.15'	117° 11.50'	+0 29	+0 09	0.3	-0 24	+0 23	0.3
San Diego, 0.5 mile W of	32° 43'	117° 11'	-0 16	-0 08	0.6	-0 12	-0 12	0.5
Airport CGS, 0.3 nm SE of	32° 43.32'	117° 10.67'	*current weak and variable*					
B St. Pier (San Diego)[1]	32° 43.02'	117° 10.58'	*current weak and variable*					
G St. Pier (San Diego), 0.22 nm SW of	32° 42.50'	117° 10.65'	+0 10	+0 20	0.3	-0 03	+0 41	0.3
Fifth Avenue Marina Entrance	32° 42.33'	117° 09.92'	-0 12	+0 09	0.1	+1 46	+1 07	- -
Coronado, off NE end	32° 41.88'	117° 09.83'	-0 24	-0 58	0.7	-0 51	+0 09	0.5
28th St. Pier (San Diego), 0.92 nm SW	32° 40.48'	117° 08.97'	-0 44	-1 17	0.2	-1 10	-0 05	0.1
28th St. Pier (San Diego), 0.35 nm SW	32° 40.97'	117° 08.57'	-0 14	+0 15	0.3	+0 15	+0 13	0.2
National City	32° 39'	117° 07'	+0 23	+0 00	0.4	-0 02	+0 50	0.4
National City, WSW of Pier 12	32° 39.73'	117° 07.53'	+0 22	+0 34	0.2	+0 34	+0 58	0.2
Sweetwater Channel, SW of	32° 38.70'	117° 07.37'	+0 29	-0 33	0.1	-0 05	+0 46	0.2

END NOTES

1. It is reported that an eddy is usually encountered along the ends of the municipal piers which makes docking difficult.

HISTORIC NOAA TIDE & CURRENT CORRECTIONS

As of 2020 NOAA stopped supporting the correction tables on the previous pages. The tables included in your Tidelog are historic and can provide only a reasonable approximation of the tide/current at the locations listed. NOAA does provide daily predictions for both harmonic and subordinate stations at:

tidesandcurrents.noaa.gov

The prudent mariner should always check the site above for the most accurate data and be aware of the other factors, including the weather, which may affect the tides and currents.

NAUTICAL CHARTS

YOUR SOURCE FOR NOAA NAUTICAL CHARTS!

We offer beautiful nautical charts printed on either

Heavy Duty Paper or Synthetic Material

We also offer "Chart Art" - charts in non navigational sizes which can be displayed in your home or business.

Visit us at www.tidelog.com to find out more or to place your order!

ANGLER'S LOG

Our Angler's Log is the perfect way to keep all your fishing adventures at your finger tips. Track weather conditions, favorite locations and details of all the fish you've caught.

CAPTAIN'S LOG

A handy little book with plenty of space for you to keep all your vessel information in one handy place along with maintenance records and notes from your trips. Useful for anything from weekend outings to circumnavigations.

JOURNALS

Are you looking for an attractive place to store your thoughts, sketches and grocery lists? We have two great options for you.

Blank Journals are just what you need if you don't want to have to worry about staying in the lines.

Lined Journals give you a little more structure to your to-do list or great novel.

Your choice of twelve different cover designs:

Seahorses

Shell Trio

Kayak

Scatter of Shells

Turtles

Octopus

Sailboats

Sea Star

Compass

Dolphin

Fish on a Line

Reindeer

TIDELOG WEST COAST REGIONS COVERED

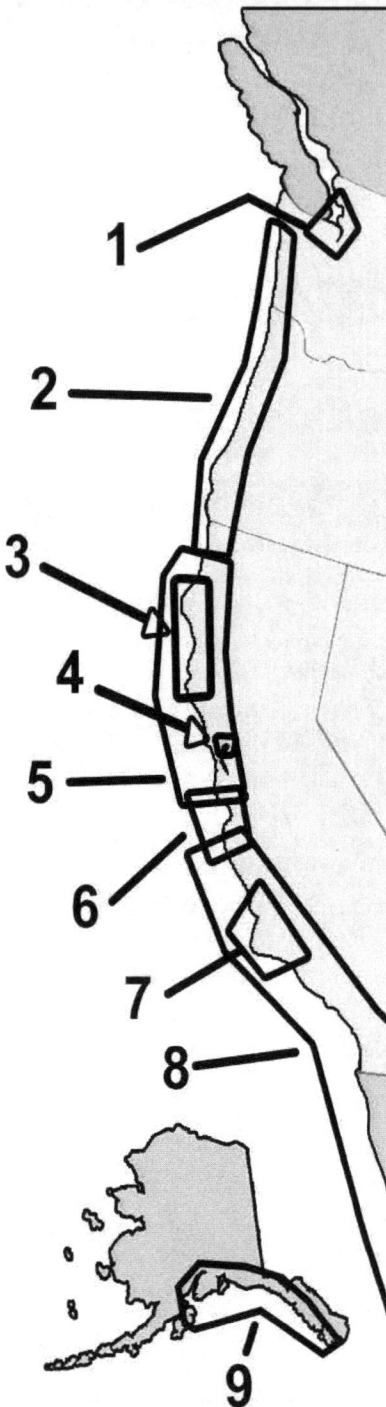

1. **PUGET SOUND:** including Seattle, Port Townsend, south to Tacoma and Olympia, and north to the San Juan Islands

2. **PACIFIC NORTHWEST:** including the Pacific Coast of Washington and Oregon, and south to Humboldt Bay, CA

3. **COAST OF NC:** including Arena Cove north to Humboldt Bay

4. **SUISUN BAY & DELTA:** including Suisun Bay and surrounding areas

5. **NORTHERN CALIFORNIA (SF BAY):** including San Francisco Bay and Delta, south to Monterey Bay and north to Shelter Cove

6. **MONTEREY BAY:** including Monterey Bay and Carmel

7. **MORRO BAY:** for the coast of Southern California near Morro Bay

8. **SOUTHERN CALIFORNIA:** including Los Angeles, San Diego, and the Gulf of California

9. **GULF OF ALASKA:** including tides for Ketchikan and Sika with Wrangell Narrows currents

TIDELOG ORDER FORM

West Coast Editions: *please specify below*

☐ **PUGET SOUND**	☐ **NORTHERN CALIFORNIA**
☐ **Pacific Northwest**	☐ **Monterey Bay**
	☐ **Morro Bay**
☐ **Coast of Northern CA**	☐ **SOUTHERN CALIFORNIA**
☐ **Suisun Bay & Delta**	☐ **Gulf of Alaska**

			QUANTITY	AMOUNT
Tidelogs:	$17.95*		( )	$
Quantity discounts: 5 to 9 copies, subtract $2 each; 10 to 19 copies, subtract $3 each; 20 to 29 copies, subtract $4 each. Please call for quotes on larger quantities.				
2 Year Subscription:	$32.00*		( )	$
3 Year Subscription:	$43.00*		( )	$

START MY SUBSCRIPTION WITH THE 20___ TIDELOG.

Angler's Log:	$14.00*		( )	$
Captain's Log:	$14.00*		( )	$
Lined Journal:	$12.00*		( )	$
Blank Journal:	$10.00*		( )	$

Lined & Blank Journals, please specify: ☐ Seahorse ☐ Shell Trio ☐ Starfish ☐ Compass ☐ Scatter ☐ Kayak ☐ Reindeer ☐ Fish on Line ☐ Turtles ☐ Sailboats ☐ Dolphin ☐ Octopus

⋆ *Plus Shipping, Please See Below* ⋆

Shipping:

Order value	$10 - $25	$26 - $40	$51 - $80	$81+	
Ground	$5.00	$8.00	$11.00	$14.00	$
Air	$10.00	$13.00	$16.00	$19.00	

GEORGIA Sales Tax: *GA residents only*, add 7% tax ☐ $

☐ My check, payable to **Pacific Publishers**, is enclosed
☐ Charge my credit card

Total: $

NAME _____

ADDRESS _____

CITY, STATE, ZIP _____

EMAIL _____

CARD # _____

EXP DATE _____ CVC _____

Mail To: **Pacific Publishers LLC, P.O. Box 2813, Tybee Island, GA 31328**
Phone Orders: (912) 472-4373 *Fax:* (912) 786-7921
Order Online: www.tidelog.com

TIDELOG EAST COAST REGIONS COVERED

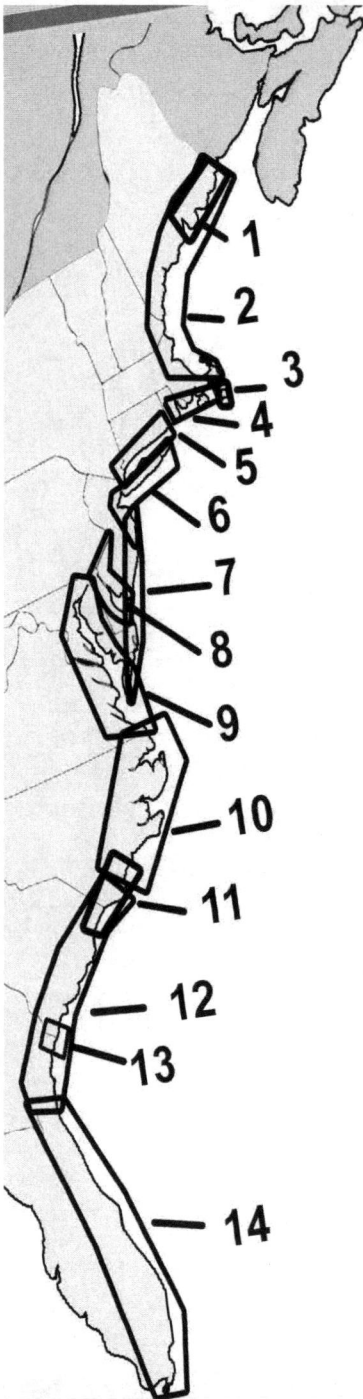

1. **EASTPORT & BAR HARBOR:** including Eastport south to Bar Harbor

2. **NORTHERN NEW ENGLAND:** including the coasts of ME, NH and MA

3. **NANTUCKET & MARTHA'S VINEYARD**

4. **SOUTHERN NEW ENGLAND:** including Rhode Island's Narragansett Bay, Buzzards Bay, Block Island Sound and Long Island's Peconic Bay

5. **LONG ISLAND SOUND:** including the north shore of Long Island from Willets Point to Orient, NY; the NY/CT shore from Throgs Neck to Old Saybrook

6. **NEW YORK/NEW JERSEY:** including New York Harbor

7. **MIDATLANTIC:** including coastal New Jersey, Delaware and Maryland

8. **DELAWARE BAY:** including Delaware Bay and River

9. **CHESAPEAKE TIDEWATER:** including Chesapeake Bay, Baltimore, Washington, DC and the Tidewater area of Virginia and south to Virginia Beach

10. **OUTER BANKS:** including the entire coast of North Carolina, including Cape Hatteras and south to Myrtle Beach, SC

11. **MYRTLE BEACH**

12. **SOUTHEASTERN:** including the entire coasts of South Carolina and Georgia

13. **SAVANNAH & TYBEE ISLAND**

14. **FLORIDA ATLANTIC:** including the entire Atlantic Coast of Florida, Miami and the Keys

TIDELOG ORDER FORM

East Coast Editions: *please specify below*

- [ ] **Eastport & Bar Harbor**
- [ ] **Northern New England**
- [ ] **Nantucket & Martha's Vineyard**
- [ ] **Southern New England**
- [ ] **Long Island Sound**
- [ ] **New York/New Jersey**
- [ ] **MidAtlantic**
- [ ] **Delaware Bay**
- [ ] **Chesapeake Tidewater**
- [ ] **Outer Banks**
- [ ] **Myrtle Beach**
- [ ] **Southeastern**
- [ ] **Savannah & Tybee Island**
- [ ] **Florida Atlantic**

		QUANTITY	AMOUNT
Tidelogs: $17.95*		( )	$

Quantity discounts: 5 to 9 copies, subtract $2 each; 10 to 19 copies, subtract $3 each; 20 to 29 copies, subtract $4 each. Please call for quotes on larger quantities.

		QUANTITY	AMOUNT
2 Year Subscription:	$32.00*	( )	$
3 Year Subscription:	$43.00*	( )	$

START MY SUBSCRIPTION WITH THE 20___ TIDELOG.

Angler's Log:	$14.00*	( )	$
Captain's Log:	$14.00*	( )	$
Lined Journal:	$12.00*	( )	$
Blank Journal:	$10.00*	( )	$

Lined & Blank Journals, please specify:
- [ ] Seahorse
- [ ] Shell Trio
- [ ] Starfish
- [ ] Compass
- [ ] Scatter
- [ ] Kayak
- [ ] Reindeer
- [ ] Fish on Line
- [ ] Turtles
- [ ] Sailboats
- [ ] Dolphin
- [ ] Octopus

⋆ *Plus Shipping, Please See Below* ⋆

Shipping:

Order value	$10 - $25	$26 - $40	$51 - $80	$81+	
Ground	$5.00	$8.00	$11.00	$14.00	$
Air	$10.00	$13.00	$16.00	$19.00	

GEORGIA Sales Tax: *GA residents only*, add 7% tax $

- [ ] My check, payable to **Pacific Publishers**, is enclosed
- [ ] Charge my credit card

Total: $

NAME _____

ADDRESS _____

CITY, STATE, ZIP _____

EMAIL _____

CARD # _____

EXP DATE _____ CVC _____

Mail To: **Pacific Publishers LLC, P.O. Box 2813, Tybee Island, GA 31328**
Phone Orders: (912) 472-4373 *Fax:* (912) 786-7921
Order Online: www.tidelog.com

PERSONALIZATION

Imprinting is available should you wish to personalize your Tidelog. We can imprint one line of up to 22 characters (including spaces) on the cover. Imprinting is $10.00 per copy, per year (for subscriptions).

Please print clearly to ensure accurate imprinting.

#1:																						
#2:																						
#3:																						
#4:																						
#5:																						

Add up the total of your imprinting and include it on the reverse when totaling your order.

$10.00 per copy

QUANTITY

AMOUNT $

Tidelogs make great gifts! We can design custom dies should you wish to imprint Tidelogs with your company logo or a phrase. Please call or email us for details and quantity pricing information.

U.S. SHIPPING

Ground shipping is by USPS "Media Mail" (Special 4th Class). On average, media mail packages are received in 7 to 10 business days.

Air shipping is by USPS Priority or First Class Mail. It's more consistent than ground shipping, and is most advantageous to the West Coast, where it often cuts shipping time down to 3 or 4 days.

Order value:	$10 - $25	$26 - $40	$51 - $80	$81+
Ground	$5.00	$8.00	$11.00	$14.00
Air	10.00	$13.00	$16.00	$19.00

In a real hurry? Our Premium Shipping option is by FedEx or UPS Overnight, which starts at $41 but is not always "overnight" from our location. 2nd Day Air, at $20 to $26, is usually a better deal. Mark your choice on the order blank, or tell our order person.

Order value:	$10 - $25	$26 - $40	$51 - $80	$81+
2nd Day Air	$20.00	$22.00	$24.00	$26.00
Overnight	$41.00	$45.00	$49.00	$53.00

PRIVACY POLICY

We consider your name, address, e-mail address and telephone number to be confidential. Your phone number is only used if there's a problem with your order. All that's mailed to your address is a reminder if we haven't received your renewal by a certain date. None of your information is ever shared with any third party.

We also safeguard your credit card information. Your card number is available only to our order personnel, whether your order is placed by phone, mail, fax or left on our voicemail. After processing, the number is not retained in our computer database.

WWW.TIDELOG.COM

TIDAL FACTORS

Earth's tides are primarily produced by the gravitational forces of the moon and sun. Even though the moon is millions of times smaller than the sun, its proximity to the Earth gives it a tidal influence more than twice that of the sun's. Although the moon's gravitational pull is only one-ten millionith of the Earth's, when it is combined with the centrifugal force produced as the Earth spins on its axis, tractive force is created. Tractive force is responsible for creating a tidal bulge on the side of the Earth facing away from the moon twice a day, resulting in two high and low tides per day for most locations.

Twice a month, when the moon is full and when it is new, the moon, sun, and Earth are aligned. The resulting spring tides often have a greater range, with higher highs and lower lows than ordinarily. Conversely, when the moon is in quarter phase, the moon and sun's gravitational forces tend to counteract each other resulting neap tides, which are in turn much weaker.

Since the moon's orbit around the Earth is elliptical, its distance varies by about 11% during a month. At perigee, the moon is closest and its tidal influence is increased. The opposite is true at apogee, the farthest point of its monthly orbit. The sun's influence is increased in January when the Earth is at perihelion and decreased in July when the Earth is at aphelion. When a new or full moon coincides with perigee (augmented in winter by perihelion), the result is dramatically increased tidal ranges, called perigean spring tides.

The moon's declination also affects the tides. Since its orbit is inclined relative to the earth's equator, the moon appears to cross over the equator twice a month, reaching maximum North declination and maximum South declination about two weeks apart. Either point of maximum declination tends to encourage inequality between day's two high (or low) tides. Note the difference in Tidelog's tide curves when the moon is at maximum declination compared with those when the moon is over the equator. (This effect is more pronounced on the Pacific coast than on the Atlantic.)

Planetary tidal influence is mostly negligible. Since a planet's tidal attraction varies directly with mass and inversely with distance squared, the planet having the greatest influence on Earth's tides (Venus, the closest) exerts a force only a few thousandths of one percent of that of the moon. Tidelog's indications of planetary positions are intended as a guide to observation, not as a clue to tidal behavior.

Some geologists theorize that the same forces which cause the highest tides may also trigger earthquakes, with most major quakes occurring near times when a new or full moon closely coincides with perigee. In earthquake prone coastal areas, some suggest this theory has some basis, while others claim the relationship is hit or miss. Those who like to see for themselves will be able to identify several such periods in the year to come and form their own conclusions.

"Second Day of Creation"
~ M.C. Escher
Woodcut

Pacific Publishers, LLC
P.O. Box 2813
Tybee Island, GA 31328
(912) 472-4373
www.tidelog.com